Hanging C

Thanks to: the webmaster of *SacredDM.net*, Angelinda and everyone at *dmtvarchives*, Alan Wilder and the Shunt staff, Gareth Jones, Steve Lyon, Benjamin, Pete Fisher, Fran, Sky, Carole, Sean, Chris, Laura, Ingo, Jörg, Holger, Mary, Silke and all my "homies", Daniel, Felix and Aesculap, Tim (Paranoid World - Design.Layout.Graphic) as well as everyone who helped with the website and the service print edition, all photographers who allowed me to show their pictures on the website, all critics, supporters, followers and readers.

Hanging on your Words

A Depeche Mode biography

- English edition -

Service Print Edition of *depechemodebiographie.de*

© 2013 Lilian R. Franke, 2nd edition 2018
Youndercover Autorenservice
Weetzener Str. 64, 30974 Wennigsen, Germany
dmbiographie@hotmail.de

Editors: Pete Fisher, Lilian R. Franke, Sky, Fran, Benjamin Schulz
Layout block: Lilian R. Franke
Photography block: © 2013, 2018 Ingo Bittrich, © 2013, 2018 Lilian R. Franke
Layout cover: Paranoid World (Design - Layout - Graphic www.paranoid-world.de)
Photography cover: © 2013 Ingo Bittrich
(http://www.fotocommunity.de/fotograf/ingo-b/554253)
Webmaster of *depechemodebiographie.de*: Lilian R. Franke
© 2007-2018
Find us on Facebook:
 https://www.facebook.com/Depeche-Mode-Biographie-Depeche-Mode-Biography-143724062333458/

Published and printed by:
independently published
E-Book by KDP

All rights reserved.

TABLE OF CONTENTS

Preface	p. 7
Vince Clarke	p. 13
Andrew John Fletcher	p. 15
Martin Lee Gore	p. 19
David Gahan	p. 22
Alan Charles Wilder	p. 28
Foundation	p. 33
1981	p. 42
1982	p. 57
1983	p. 73
1984	p. 85
1985	p. 100
By the Way	p. 117
1986	p. 118
1987	p. 138
1988	p. 151
1989	p. 159
1990	p. 168
1991	p. 180
1992	p. 187
1993	p. 203
1994	p. 219
1995	p. 231
By the Way	p. 245
1996	p. 247
1997	p. 255
1998 & 1999	p. 268
2000	p. 272
2001 & 2002	p. 279
2003	p. 287
2004	p. 293
2005	p. 296
2006	p. 302
2007	p. 306
2008	p. 312
2009	p. 315
2010	p. 323
2011	p. 330
2012	p. 333
2013 & 2014	p. 339
2015, 2016 & 2017	p. 349
Sources	p. 357

PREFACE

Dear Reader,

Even though you might tend not to read prefaces, in this case you should consider doing so, because I'm going to tell you some things you really ought to know, before you read this biography.
It is based on my personal view and interest. I'm not a journalist who woke up one day and decided: 'Why don't I write a biography about *Depeche Mode,* and make some money with it?' Actually, I used to be a fan in the **1980's**, and lost interest in them when Alan left the band in **1995**. I "came back" to them when they released the song *Lilian* on their album *Playing the Angel* in **2005**. Not that I liked the song that much, (the opposite is the case), but I had got curious about what had happened to this band I used to like, who had now released a song with my name as the title.
I discovered the now no longer functional website *sacred-DM.net* that offered a large collection of articles about the band through the years. I started to read them and tried to find answers to questions like, "Why did Alan really leave the band?", "Why is this band popular with a large group of people, but is nevertheless misinterpreted, misunderstood or even ignored by large sections of the general music business?", and "How and why did the band change from a certain point onwards, without being bothered by the fact that some of their more critical fans don't like everything they are doing and releasing today?"
What I had noted down for my own interest soon developed into a very long, detailed biography. I decided to publish it on a website, so that other fans could read it too. It started with a small publication on the website of a friend in **2007**, moved on to a ready-made homepage done with a website creator, and in **2009**, I finally created *depechemodebiographie.de*, having learnt html from scratch.

People sent in a lot of feedback right from the start. I received (and still receive) many emails with questions, ideas, criticisms, requests - concerning the biography itself and regarding the layout of the website. So this biography is based on a fans' view, and is influenced by the suggestions, opinions and questions of fans and readers. I looked into some topics that people were concerned about. However, if there were topics I'm not personally interested in at all, or I thought that an idea was unsuitable, (e.g. personal matters of the band members), I didn't go into it.

It was a fans' desire to have an international version in English, parallel to the original German version. This was completed in **2009**. For a long time, it remained just a (rather bad) translation, because I was too lazy to find all the sources again. In **2011** I finally re-did the English version, replaced all the translated quotations by the originals. I had to note that some of the sources were gone. The latest chapters were affected especially, so some parts had to be rewritten, which in turn had its effect on the German version. Furthermore, all quotations were given footnotes, so now it is easier to see from which sources the quotations come, and how the statements were put together.

I also collected fans' opinions from national and international message-boards and other commentaries in the internet, and tried to combine them, to portray different groups and opinions on special topics.

In **2010** I asked some fans about their own backgrounds, and their opinions on some of the special events in the band's career. Some of the studies from this survey found their way into the biography.

I also tried to answer questions which people sent me. Some answers are based on facts, some are interpretations (e.g., when I was asked about the meaning of lyrics), some are based on my personal opinion. All interpretations, opinions and theories that appear in this biography are what they are: interpretations and opinions! It's up to you whether you accept them as possible explanations, or come to different conclusions. On no account should you take them as facts, unless they are declared as such, or proved by a quotation.

It was also suggested I should bring in quotations from people surrounding the band as well. I decided against it – for the following reasons:

Not being a journalist as such, I'm not able to travel around the world and interview a lot of people surrounding the band, or the band members themselves. So I could only work with existing stuff. And that's a lot of stuff! It took several years to get through it, and at some point you have to decide what you want. My interest was in the band members and not so much in the people surrounding them. So I collected quotations from the (former) band members, in an attempt to let them tell their story in their own words.

This meant leaving out interviews with (co-)producers, managers, photographers etc., unless I was able to talk to someone myself.

In **2011** I interviewed some musicians about general topics, to be able to give some theories a background and to show up some parallels. (These interviews were anonymous.)

In **2012** I had the opportunity to talk to Gareth Jones. It was an interview in general about his work as a producer for the webzine *truetrash.de*, but he was nice enough to answer some questions about *Depeche Mode* as well.

And in **2013** – right in the middle of preparing the service print edition – I had the opportunity to talk to Steve Lyon.

Another reason for leaving out all the people working with the band was that most of the other existing biographies are based on interviews with those people. I didn't want to write yet another biography based on the views of managers, producers etc. ON the band, but of course it was interesting to chat with Gareth Jones and Steve Lyon.

So this biography is mainly based on statements from the (former) band members, in a variety of interviews with different magazines and other media, from **1981 to 2017**.

Full interviews are not quoted, but small quotations have been taken from them. The individual quotations are seldom represented in the original context. The quotations have been edited, and then reassembled in a new, independent context. I have taken care, however, not to distort any statements, and to ensure there are no false interpretations, or anything that makes fun of the band members.

For the quotations based on newspaper articles and other media, it's important to note that the original quotations themselves may not be correct! The band members did not write the articles themselves, (except quotations taken from Alan's website or from interviews I made myself, or transcriptions of radio/video-interviews), and they had to rely solely on the journalists to reproduce everything accurately.

There may be assertions in articles that were not actually comments of any of the band members, and therefore appear as "rumour." Some rumours may now have been dispelled, thanks to Alan, who kindly granted me a short interview in **2008**.

I showed the biography to Alan and to *Mute* because I wanted the (former) band members to know what I'm doing, so they would be able to make criticisms, or object to anything they didn't like. I have never received any answer from anyone from the band or from their management - only Alan was kind enough to answer. (This doesn't mean he authorized anything! This biography is as unauthorized as any that is on the market.)

Who is this biography meant to reach in general? It may be of special interest to those who have only just discovered *Depeche Mode* recently. It's also for people who may not wish to read, listen to, or watch separately about 2,000 interviews or more, which I had read, listened to, or watched.

It doesn't offer anything new to the fan who has already read at least one biography. Or as Martin would say: *I'm not trying to tell you anything you didn't know when you woke up today.* (From *Nothing, Music for the Masses.*)

Nevertheless, I tried to move away from the "dark" picture full of pain and suffering a lot of articles and biographies used to show. This band has a lot more to offer than just debauchery and suffering. So I also collected anecdotes, nonsense, the professional side – but mostly left out the technical details. This may disappoint some people, but this, for example, is a topic I'm not interested in personally. And – as I've mentioned before – I tried to find answers (or at least theories) to the questions above.

In **2012** I decided to fulfil a readers' desire, and to publish a print edition of the biography. I had refused to do so for a long time. To run a non-commercial website is one thing, to have it in print and sell it is something completely different. I didn't want to be one of those people who make money with the name "*Depeche Mode.*" Another reason for being against it was that the concept had always been to run a website you could update every day if necessary. On the other hand, many people asked about a print edition, because they didn't want to read the biography on a screen, but rather as a real book, in their garden or on the sofa.

Copyright law and licence law concerning photos is difficult. While it was a lot of work, but nevertheless quite easy to obtain permission to SHOW pictures of the band as well as "fan-art" on the website, it is something completely different to have pictures printed in a commercial book.

It would have been awfully difficult to get permission and licences in this case, as it requires the permission of the band as well as each photographer, for band photos and "fan-art." To make it worse these photographers and artists come from all over the world, and in every country there are different laws applying to photos. As I do not have a publishing company supporting me, and as I'm not married to a lawyer, and as this is only a service print edition parallel to the website, I decided to create the first band biography that doesn't contain a single band photo! Take it as something special! ;)

But, of course, a book needs a cover photo, and on the whole a book about art in the broadest sense is boring without any art, but just words inside. Of all the "fan-art" I have collected over the years, there were two photos for which I had a title in mind, because a book also needs a title. You can't write "this is a *Depeche Mode* biography" on a black cover and that's it. I talked to the photographer who took the photo I preferred, and wheedled him into the project, so that there is only one person to consult about licences and stuff like that.

Both of us have a preference for a kind of "industrial romance" style, and think it suits *DM* well. (Think about "technically orientated" pictures and videos like the one for *People Are People,* or using a "throwaway" angle for videos for *Stripped* for example, or later the cover art of *SubHuman* (*Recoil*). There are also a lot of cars, buildings, machines and stuff like that used in the art work and in the videos. The industrial angle also symbolizes energy, and in a way the personal background of the actual band members who came from a working class background.)

Most pictures were made in and around Berlin. This is another angle that suits *DM* well, because many people still connect them with this city. We tried to find some places that have a connection with *DM,* without using the well-known and all too often shown places like the Berlin Wall, or *Hansa Studios.*

The print edition was a lot of work, and sometimes unforeseeable difficulties arise. English editors disappeared, and it took a long time to find a good one. People at a message-board for writers from the UK and U.S. were confused by my many questions about grammar and other stuff. Friends were wheedled in to favours or had to listen to "I'm so f*** tired", or "Why is this sh** not working?" stuff after long days of editing or working on the layout. (Thanks to everyone who was involved.)

The photographer also probably thought it would be easy enough, but then he found himself outside in the dark photographing bulbs (and meeting a marten), or driving around with a rose on the roof of his car. And he had to spend many hours trying to think of something when I came up with stuff like, "At this point it would be great to have a picture with ..." (Thank you, Ingo.)

Although the text was edited a few times, please note that I'm not a native speaker. Be gentle with me and understand me. ;)

Lilian R. Franke.
depechemodebiographie.de

VINCE CLARKE

Vince Clarke was born as Vincent John Martin on **3 July 1960** in South Woodford, Essex, and was raised in nearby Basildon. It was rumoured that he named himself "Vince Clarke," so he could go on claiming unemployment benefits, around the time of starting DM.

Nothing relevant has been mentioned in the media about his parents, Dennis and Rose Martin. Various sources merely say that Vince's mother complained about the "noise," which came from the keyboards while the band was practising (some sources say: in the garage.) Vince has two brothers, Rodney and Michael, and a sister, Carol.

I have to admit that I wasn't very interested in Vince. His part in DM's history is a small (but nevertheless essential) one, and when I started to write this biography I decided to leave Vince's story with *Yazoo* and *Erasure* (and the many other projects he did) aside, because it would have taken up too much space, and would have wandered too far away from the thread of DM's story. But this chapter about him was so short that I finally did some research, and found some interviews in which Vince talked about his youth, and how he ended up in DM.

"There really wasn't that much music in our family when I was a child," **Vince** said. "When I was about 13 or 14 my mom bought a second-hand radiogram – like a big record player with a radio on it. She had this big collection of 78s, of classical music and singles of songs like *Ruby Tuesday* by *The Rolling Stones*."

It was the first time he was exposed to music. In his teens he used to listen to the radio mostly. "My father had a reel-to-reel tape recorder and he had a Frank Sinatra *At the Sands* [tape] and we used to tape the radio, and he only had one tape. Gradually his recording of Frank Sinatra got smaller and smaller and smaller ... When I first started working in my teens I bought my first stereo record player. It was life changing. I just couldn't believe stereo – it was so magical.[1] As far as electronic music is

---

[1] Taken from: Interview: Erasure's Vince Clarke. Thewigfitsallheads.com, 15 July 2007. Words: Dagmar Patterson.

concerned, the first band that really made an impression on me was *The Human League*. Their first two early albums. Bands like *Orchestral Manoeuvres in the Dark*, they were one of the first bands that I felt made emotional electronic music."[2]

Vince left school at the age of 15 because he wanted to earn money for a music career. He had all kinds of jobs – in a yoghurt factory, at a cosmetics company, for the post office, for a supermarket and in a plastics factory. "The best job that I had in my teens – I worked at a small airport near my town. It was my job to empty the buckets of the toilets and also prepare the food for the flight, and also – it was only small airplanes - but when they landed it was my job to get up a ladder and clean the window. I didn't really want to be a banker or a civil servant or anything. I just wanted to earn the money to buy the next best guitar or synthesizer."[3]

Vince left *DM* at the **end of 1981**, and started the band *Yazoo* together with Alison Moyet in **1982**. The band dissolved soon after. From **1983 to 1985** Vince released several singles on his own label *Reset Records*, in addition to an album with Robert Marlow.

Since 1985 Vince has been together with Andy Bell in *Erasure*, and they have sold more than 25 million records. He carried out several other projects as well, some of them in his studio in Maine, *The Cabin*. Vince has been living in Maine, USA, since **2003**. He married his wife Tracy in **2004**. Their son Oscar was born in **2005**. He also owns a house in New York City.

In **2008**, *Yazoo* made a comeback and toured. Alison Moyet got in touch with **Vince** a year and a half before, asking him if he was interested in doing something to celebrate the 30th anniversary of *Yazoo*. "I said, 'No.' I couldn't, I was very busy doing an *Erasure* tour. At the end of that Andy [Bell] mentioned to me he would like to take a couple of years off to make a solo record so *Yazoo* fitted in and we got together and did it."

In **2010, Vince** started to work on a "dancy" record together with Martin. "It's nothing to do with *Depeche Mode*.

---

[2] Taken from: Personality Clash: Vince Clarke vs Andy Butler, clashmusic.com, 1 February 2010. Words: Robin Murray.
[3] Taken from: Interview: Erasure's Vince Clarke. Thewigfitsallheads.com, 15 July 2007. Words: Dagmar Patterson.

It's a little project that we have got going. We've been collaborating online. It's one of those things where I will send an idea to Martin and it goes back and forth."[4]

They released the EPs/singles *Spock, Blip* and *Aftermath* as well as the album *Ssss* in **2011/12** and chose the name *VCMG* for the project.[5]

ANDREW JOHN FLETCHER

Andrew John Fletcher, called "Fletch", "Andy" or "An" - as Martin calls him sometimes - (I will use "Fletch" to avoid confusion between him and Alan because of the same first letter), was born on **6 July 1961** in Nottingham.

Fletch's father, John (who passed away in **2009**), worked as an engineer, and his mother, Joy, was a housewife. His sisters Karen and Susan were born in **1964** and **1966** respectively, and his brother Simon in **1976**. (I was unable to find exact birth dates, only articles that mention their ages.)

Some sources mention that Karen died of stomach cancer in **1986**, but there aren't any quotations from Fletch about it, only some speculations and rumours about Fletch's depression, linked to the manic-depressive psychosis of his father and the early death of his sister. Official confirmation can't be found, so no further speculation will be made.

In the early days of the band British journalists were so fixated by the connection between *DM* and Basildon – as if it was some kind of wonder that a band could be founded in this city – that they also doggedly assumed that every band member had been born there. In fact, none of them was born in Basildon. In Fletch's case, the birth place was Nottingham.

---

[4] Taken from: Music Interview: Vince Clarke, Yazoo. Yorkshire Evening Post, 29 September 2010. Words: uncredited.
[5] Dates and information were taken from: Collect-a-Page: VINCE, Look-In, 21 November 1981. Words: Uncredited; Modish Musings, Sounds, 7 November 1981. Words: Uncredited; SacredDM.net; erasure.de; depechemode.com; vinceclarkemusic.com.

"We moved down to Basildon in Essex when I was two years old,"[6] **Fletch** said in one of many "who is who and where are you from?"-articles of the early days. "It was a job for a house. If you could get a job, you could get a house.[7] My parents were among the first to move to Basildon when it was still a very new town in the **early 1960s**.[8] But in the **1970s** it started to go wrong - the town expanded quickly, there were no jobs left. When I was growing up we had fields, football, cricket, countryside - but then it all went wrong economically.[9] As the factories closed down and unemployment grew in the **1970s** it became a violent town."[10]

So Basildon went the way many British cities did in the **1970s**. These were the grass-roots of the punk movement that would fundamentally change the social, fashion and musical landscape. Maybe *DM* would have never got so popular if they hadn't been born on the punk movement. After punk you could get away with almost everything. It sprouted the strange musical flowers of *New Wave, Post Punk* and *New Romantic*.

But back to **Fletch**. Although he was critical about his hometown, he felt completely connected to Basildon, and it took a long time before he left it. Being a member of the Methodist church, he was strongly involved in the social life of the town. He became involved in church when he was about eight years old and his father suggested he should join the *Boys' Brigade* so he could play football.

He was a member of the *Boys' Brigade* until he was 17 or 18 years old and went to church almost every day. Later he got more critical about it and was no longer a practising Christian. He did, however, take religion seriously for a long time. "Me and Vince Clarke were into the preaching side – trying to convert non-believers. Vince was

---

[6] Taken from: A Broken Frame Tour Programme, 1982. Words: Andrew Fletcher.
[7] Taken from: Just Can't Get Enough, Uncut, May 2001. Words: Stephen Dalton.
[8] Taken from: Andy Fletcher: The Brigade Boy, No. 1, 18 May 1985. Words: Andrew Fletcher.
[9] Taken from: Just Can't Get Enough, Uncut, May 2001. Words: Stephen Dalton.
[10] Taken from: Songs of Innocence and Experience, Mojo, November 2005. Words: Danny Eccleston.

number three in the local hierarchy, although he's a total atheist now."[11]

Fletch went to *Nicholas Comprehensive School* and was in the same form class as Alison Moyet and Martin. He got to know Martin when he made him come to the *Boys' Brigade* too. He thought he might have converted Martin, but he had to realise that Martin was just interested in the singing and the atmosphere, albeit Martin must have been influenced strongly by this experience. Many of his lyrics have a religious background.

Church also was the "driving force" to bring **Fletch** to music. There were many musical activities, and he was about 14 years old when he picked up a guitar for the first time. Later from this the pre-*Depeche Mode*-bands were formed. "Vince and I had a group when we were 16 called *No Romance in China* which tried to be like *The Cure*. We were into their *Imaginary Boys* LP. Vince used to attempt to sing like Robert Smith. At that time we were going to a club called *Van Gogh* where Martin was playing in a guitar duo called *Norman and the Worms*. Alison's group *The Vandals* were also regulars. It was a good scene. Martin, Vince and I teamed together and started rehearsing in *Woodlands Youth Club*. The earliest *Depeche* songs like *Photographic* were written there."

Blasphemous Rumours wasn't written at the time, but Martin found the inspiration for this song at the local church. "There was a prayer list of people who were sick in some way and you'd pray for the person on top of that list until they died," **Fletch** said. "When Martin first played me *Blasphemous Rumours* I was quite offended. I can see why people would dislike it."

In **1979 Fletch** did A-levels at politics and wanted to study but instead, he began job training at the *Sun Life* insurance company. He never disclosed why he decided against university. "People at work didn't take my group seriously until *Dreaming of Me* got into the charts followed by *New Life*. I was doing *Top of the Pops* or playing in, say, Leeds, and then working the next day. It got very awkward."[12]

---

[11] Taken from: Hanging in the Balance, NME, 26 March 1983. Words: Matt Snow.
[12] Taken from: Andy Fletcher: The Brigade Boy, No. 1, 18 May 1985. Words: Andrew Fletcher.

In fact, 30 years later he would still feel like some kind of pension quotations clerk. "My whole life is dealing with numbers," he said in **1993**. "I don't find it very stimulating making music. I'm a useless musician. When I played bass, I never had any ambitions to be a great bass player, and when I took up keyboards, I never had any ambitions to be a great keyboard player. With the band, I still find the whole job challenging and rewarding, the fact of creating something and releasing it, the marketing, the promotion side of things."[13]

His role led to some tensions within the band – especially around *SOFAD*, and it divides fans into three groups. One group can't imagine *DM* without him and also sees him as a musician, the second group can't imagine *DM* without him, but does not see him as a musician as such, and the third group asks what the man is good for since the band has had a professional management.

Despite all the debauchery of the band in the last 30 years **Fletch** remained down to earth. "My private life away from music is simple and ordinary. If I go out I do things like play snooker or football or hang out with friends. I go to see *Chelsea* when I can. I'm very patriotic, very pro-British. I know some people think that's wrong, but I can't help it."[14]

This quotation dates from **1985**, but I think Fletch hasn't changed much basically. He still likes football, politics and getting up early in the morning to watch the sunrise.

Today Fletch is married to Grainne and lives in London. Daughter Megan was born in **1991**, son Joseph in **1994**.

Note: Although the band members sometimes tell something about their families and children and although some family members have their own *Twitter* accounts and public *Facebook* sites I won't go into the private lives of the band members as long as it doesn't have any relation to the history of the band itself.

---

[13] Taken from: Mope Now, Party Later, Musician, October 1993. Words: Jon Pareles.
[14] Taken from: Andy Fletcher: The Brigade Boy, No. 1, 18 May 1985. Words: Andrew Fletcher.

MARTIN LEE GORE

Martin Lee Gore was born in London, **23 July 1961**. While there are differing stories regarding his place of birth, he mentioned that he was born in London in two different articles. I do hope he knows for sure! ;)

"I was born in London, but raised as a kid in Dagenham where Dad was a *Ford*'s worker and Mum was a telephonist at the car factory.[15] Then we moved to Hornchurch in Essex. After a brief stay of one year we moved again, this time to the centre of the Universe - Basildon!"[16]

Martin's biological father is Afro-American, a fact that Martin learned shortly before the birth of his daughter Viva-Lee. However, his mother Pamela told him at the age of 13 that David, the father with whom he was growing up, was his stepfather.

Martin has two younger half sisters, Karen, born in **1967**, and Jacqueline, born in **1968**. There are different articles with different age details. According to one of them Jacqueline is older than Karen and the birth dates were **1968** and **1969**. Their actual birth dates have never been mentioned.

Martin described his childhood as normal and family life as stable. "I remember I was a very good boy until the age of five when I went through a phase of beating up other children. One day my mother caught me putting a brick over another child's head. My father was furious. He told me never to hit anyone else again. I'm glad I got such a talking to, it made me very passive and harmless."[17]

He was a strange child and quite introverted according to his own words. He did not have many friends. "I spent most of the time alone in my room reading fairy-tales. I lost myself in fairy-tale books and lived in another world.

---

[15] Taken from: Martin Gore: The Decadent Boy, No. 1, 11 May 1985. Words: Martin Lee Gore.
[16] Taken from: A Broken Frame Tour Programme, 1982. Words: Martin Lee Gore.
[17] Taken from: Martin Gore: The Decadent Boy, No. 1, 11 May 1985. Words: Martin Lee Gore.

In school as well I had a big shortage of self-confidence. The teachers only seldom heard my voice."[18]

Martin and Fletch first met at primary school, but got to know each other at *Nicholas Comprehensive School* when Fletch made Martin come to the *Boys' Brigade* with him.

But in opposite to Fletch **Martin's** interest in music didn't start with church. When he was about ten years old he discovered his mother's old rock 'n' roll singles. "Stuff like Elvis, Chuck Berry, Del Shannon, and I played those records over and over again, and I realised then that that was the only thing I was really interested in, and it went on from there.[19] I was heavily into the teen mag *Disco 45*. I had hundreds of them and used to read all the song words. I can still remember all those lyrics though I haven't got a good memory for anything else. When I was about 12 my mum and dad bought me a guitar for my birthday and together with a few friends *Norman and the Worms* was born. This group continued in one form or another until **1979**.[20] About that time, 13, I had a crush on *Donna* by *10cc*. A friend taught me a few guitar chords and we started to write songs. Obviously, looking back they were awful, but I was proud of them then."

Martin learned French and German at school. He found German a boring subject, although he liked to go to school very much and enjoyed staying on a farm during a school exchange to Erfde in Schleswig-Holstein, Germany.

He stayed on at school until he was 18 because he liked it so much and had no idea of what to do in the future. He was also suffering from a "suburban outlook" as he said. "I only used to go to London for work. I never used to go out there as getting back took ages: 60 km when you don't drive and the trains stop running at midnight, it's like the other end of the world!"[21]

He got French and German A-Levels and then didn't know what to do next. "I didn't want to leave school, I felt secure there. If all this fell through I could see myself

---

[18] Taken from: Depeche Mode prive (Part 3: Martin Gore), unknown author, media and date.
[19] Taken from: The Life and Loves of Depeche Mode, I-D, October 1993. Words: Michael Fuchs-Gambock.
[20] Taken from: A Broken Frame Tour Programme, 1982. Words: Martin Lee Gore.
[21] Taken from: 80's, Mode d'Emploi, Best, October 1987. Words: Gerard Bar-David.

studying, I certainly wouldn't go back to bank work. Aah, the bank. My first job. I worked at the *NatWest* clearing house in the city for a year and a half on grade one. [22] Because I was so young, my colleagues treated me a little in a step-motherly fashion.[23] It was mind-crushingly dull, but my lack of imagination and confidence meant I couldn't see an alternative. Languages were what I wanted to work with, but translation jobs were hard to find."[24]

In opposite to Fletch **Martin's** relationship with his home town wasn't the best. He didn't feel well there. "I really hated Basildon. I wanted to get out as quickly as I could. I think being in a band was an escape. There was very little to do. It's one of those places where you go drinking because that's your only option. When I was about 17 or 18, me and my friend were walking back from a party in Laindon, which is close to Basildon, and we heard this running behind us. We didn't think anything of it, but suddenly we were surrounded by six guys saying, 'Which one of you called my mate a f*** wanker?' One of those, you know? So then they started punching and kicking us ..."[25]

Martin got married to Suzanne with whom he has three children: Viva-Lee, born in **1991**, Ava-Lee, born in **1995**, and Calo Leon, born in **2002**. He divorced Suzanne and got married to Kerrilee in **2014**, who gave birth to Johnnie Lee, a baby girl, in **2016**.

In addition to his work with *DM*, he released some solo works: a single song (a tribute to Leonard Cohen) *Coming Back to You* in **1995**, the *Counterfeit e.p.* in **1989** and the album *Counterfeit 2* in **2003**. In **2011/12** he was the vocalist of the song *Man Made Machine* of the band *Motor*, and he released the EPs/singles *Spock, Blip* and *Aftermath* as well as the album *Ssss* together with Vince Clarke (project name: *VCMG*).[26] In **2015** he released an instrumental record titled *MG*.

---

[22] Taken from: Martin Gore: The Decadent Boy, No. 1, 11 May 1985. Words: Martin Lee Gore.
[23] Taken from: Depeche Mode prive (Part 3: Martin Gore), unknown author, media and date.
[24] Taken from: Martin Gore: The Decadent Boy, No. 1, 11 May 1985. Words: Martin Lee Gore.
[25] Taken from: Just Can't Get Enough, Uncut, May 2001. Words: Stephen Dalton.
[26] Additional dates and information were taken from: Collect-a-Page: MAR-

DAVID GAHAN

David Gahan (who more than likely has a second name since all his brothers and sisters do but has left it out) was born on **9 May 1962** in Chigwell. Similar to Fletch and Martin's story, there are different places (Basildon, of course, and quite often: Epping) mentioned regarding where Dave was born, but **Dave** himself said "Chigwell" in two or three different articles.

"I was born at 5:00 am on **May 9th 1962** weighing in at 8 1/2 lbs. We lived in Romford Road, Chigwell in Essex in a semi which is also where I was born."

Dave's biological father left the family when Dave and his elder sister Susan Christine (born in **1960**) were very young. Some sources say that the name of his biological father was Leonard William F Callcott, a man who is listed in the British register of deaths and whose life data would fit.

Dave's Mother, Sylvia Ruth, remarried and "we moved to another semi in sunny Basildon,[27] for this new town, the new world, where it's greener and there are better schools. But it was miserable."[28]

He always thought his stepfather, whose surname he got, was his biological father. "But my biological father has Malaysian ancestors.[29] My stepdad died when I was nine."[30] (Other sources quote he was seven.) Dave's two younger half-brothers, Peter Eric, born in **1966**, and Philip Michael, born in **1967**, come from his mother's second marriage.

"When I was young I was rather tubby all round and a bit of a moaner, always crying in fact," **Dave** said about himself, "my earliest memory of my childhood is being

---

TIN, Look-In, 12 December 1981. Words: Uncredited; Hero's Welcome for Four Boys in the Band, Basildon Evening Echo, 12 November 1981. Words: Don Stewart.
[27] Taken from: A Broken Frame Tour Programme, 1982. Words: Dave Gahan.
[28] Taken from: Interview with Dave Gahan, Mojo, 22 March 2013. Words: Martin Aston.
[29] Taken from: Ask Dave, Bong 7, October 1989. Words: Dave Gahan.
[30] Taken from: Facing my Monsters, Daily Mirror, 27 June 2003. Words: Gavin Martin.

made to drink hot milk with the skin on at nursery school, but I can't remember if I liked it or not."[31]

In the course of time he revealed a lot of little things about himself, for example that he was scared of many things when he was a child and that he still battles fear, consequently he's not always doing what he would like to do. He also admitted that he had always been a person trying to attract other people's attention. When he was young he liked to do an impression of Mick Jagger or Gary Glitter, just to get a reaction. He even described himself as a people-pleaser who wanted the whole world to love him.

The first time he was mentioned in a newspaper was for winning a prize for a home-baked cake with the *Boy Scouts*. **Dave** had his first appearances as a singer of Christmas carols with the *Salvation Army* to which his mother belonged. "I've never been religious although she stuck to her beliefs. I used to go down to Sunday School with my sister on our bikes and instead of going in we'd just ride around for a couple of hours, and when we got back we'd say it was great."[32]

Problems started when his stepfather died and his biological father appeared. "Then I came home one day - I was about 11," (other sources say he was 10), "and found this bloke at home who turned out to be my father. I was very upset and we all had a huge argument because I thought I should have been told."[33]

Some sources say that this was the first and the last time he saw his father while a Belgian teenage-magazine quoted him with: "From that day on, Len often visited the house until one year later, he disappeared again, forever this time. Since then he gave no sign of life anymore. By growing older I thought about him more and more. The only thing my mother wanted to say, was that he moved out to Jersey to open a hotel."[34]

---

[31] Taken from: A Broken Frame Tour Programme, 1982. Words: Dave Gahan.
[32] Taken from: Blasphemy Rewarded, Melody Maker, 22 September 1984. Words: Mark Jenkins.
[33] Taken from: Dave Gahan: The Wild Boy, No. 1, 4 May 1985. Words: Dave Gahan.
[34] Taken from: Depeche Mode begs for a vacation, Joepie, 1984. Words: uncredited.

Dave was angry about this article, so maybe he was quoted wrong here. On the other hand, it suits the life data of Leonard William F Callcott again.

However, it wasn't a positive experience. He said that after that there had always been distrust for people you were meant to feel safe with. In fact, he got totally out of control and in a lot of trouble. His drug career had actually begun at the age of 12 when he stole barbiturates from his mother who was suffering from epilepsy. Then the alcohol came, later all possible pills, speed and even heroin.

"I first took heroin when I was probably 17, when I was living in a squat in *King's Cross*. But I didn't like it, 'cos speed was the thing at that time. I realise now I've had a very addictive nature when it comes to getting off my head and escaping from myself."[35]

The story with "living in a squat" sounds a bit strange, and many years later he told the same story differently, "I was around 18 or 19 years old. I remember it was at a gig in London and I thought the heroin was amphetamines, so I took a bunch and then I got violently ill. I missed the whole gig and came to in the corner of the club."[36]

As a pupil **Dave** wasn't very successful. "I hated school. It's really funny because I can remember everything over the last seven years or so really vividly, but I can't remember a thing about me school life."[37]

He just remembered that he had been bored most of the time and that he was more interested in looking out of the window than paying attention in class. He was often sent to the headmaster.

"I refused school because I was being dictated a way of behaving so as to bury me in a boring, stupid, repetitive job. I left everything and fled to London."[38]

He described himself as a very destructive teenager, and instead of studying for school, he preferred to hang around. "First I was a soulboy, I've done it all, I've been

---

[35] Taken from: Dead Man Talking, NME, 18 January 1997. Words: Keith Cameron.
[36] Taken from: Through That Darkness You'll Find the Light, EB Magazine, 12 March 2013, Words: A.J. Samuels.
[37] Taken from: Intimate Details, No. 1, 12 September 1987. Words: Dave Gahan.
[38] Taken from: 80's, Mode d'Emploi, Best, October 1987. Words: Gerard Bar-David.

everything. I used to like soul and jazz-funk like *The Crusaders*. I used to go to soul weekends and hang around with the crew from *Global Village* and I went to, like, *The Lyceum* on a Friday night.[39] I tried to fit in with lots of different groups of friends but I was just different; an odd kid. In a way, you could say I was a bit nerdy even though I was hanging out with street kids who were getting in trouble and all that.[40] But, really, I was drowning. My mother says that I was very stubborn and hard-headed. I liked to think I wasn't following the norm. I liked the reaction of doing bad things, teenage stuff. It was a good way to get a reaction."[41]

Music was something he could find a hold in. He once said that he had to share a small bedroom with his two little brothers and only had a mattress and a sleeping bag. Obviously, he couldn't sleep in this environment because he used to listen to music late at night, music that wasn't played on the radio regularly.

Then punk came along. "I, much to my mum's dismay, became involved in it, dyeing my hair various colours and sporting clothes from *Seditionaries*.[42] But I ended up being bored by punk because everybody looked the same: same clothes, same haircuts, it had become the norm, it was a pain."[43]

And he got into conflict with law over and over again. "From the age of about 12 I was getting into trouble. I was a proper tearaway. I was nicking cars, joy-riding, writing graffiti. I wasn't such a bright graffiti artist either. Used my surname as my graffiti tag. There weren't too many Gahans in the whole of England never mind Basildon.[44] I got into trouble with the police and mixed with a lot of people who got into trouble.[45] I just wanted attention. I

---

[39] Taken from: Three Modes in a Boat, NME, 22 August 1981. Words: Paul Morley.
[40] Taken from: Through That Darkness You'll Find the Light, EB Magazine, 12 March 2013. Words: A.J. Samuels.
[41] Taken from: Interview with Dave Gahan, Mojo, 22 March 2013. Words: Martin Aston.
[42] Taken from: A Broken Frame Tour Programme, 1982. Words: Dave Gahan.
[43] Taken from: 80's, Mode d'Emploi, Best, October 1987. Words: Gerard Bar-David.
[44] Taken from: The Basildon Bond, The Times Magazine, 14 April 2001. Words: Paul Connolly.
[45] Taken from: Coming up Smiling, The Face, February 1985. Words: Sheryl Garratt.

put my mum through a rough time, in and out of juvenile court."[46]

He ended up in weekend custody at a sub-Borstal attendance centre. It's not quite clear how many weekends he had to go there, but he was told very clearly that his next stop was detention centre.

And there was another disappointment that could be described as a crucial experience: "The one girl I did end up falling for as a teenager, my best mate Mark ended up s***. I was at this party and I couldn't find my girlfriend anywhere. Everyone was looking at me. They knew. I pushed open the bedroom door and there's Mark's white a*** bouncing up and down. That was my first reality check. It set me on this idea that I'm not good enough. I've been battling it ever since."[47]

Dave left school at the age of 16 because he was so bored with it and didn't like being pushed around. "My qualifications in art and technical drawing didn't seem much use. I went through loads of jobs. In eight months I had 20 occupations from *Yardley's* perfume factory to labouring to *Sainsbury's* soft drink man.[48] I never held out very long and my bosses hated my rebellious attitude.[49] Finally, I realised I had no career so I went for a job as apprentice fitter with *North Thames Gas*. My probation officer told me to be honest at the interview, say I had a criminal record, but I was a reformed character blah blah. Course I didn't get the job because of that. It cost me a lot of confidence, having been through so many IQ tests and been shortlisted. I went back and trashed the probation office."

I couldn't find out if he had really done this. Only one thing is sure: Sometimes Dave tends to embellish stories a bit.

Finally, he went to "art college". Here, I would like to clarify that the words "college" and "study" refer to studies at a higher level than they actually were in this case. My

---

[46] Taken from: Just Can't Get Enough, Uncut, May 2001. Words: Stephen Dalton.
[47] Taken from: The Ten Commandments: Dave Gahan, Q, November 2005. Words: Dave Gahan / Johnny Davis.
[48] Taken from: Dave Gahan: The Wild Boy, No. 1, 4 May 1985. Words: Dave Gahan.
[49] Taken from: Depeche Mode prive (Part 2: Dave Gahan), unknown author, media and date.

understanding is that Dave's qualifications would have never been good enough to attend university. He told the story a little different from time to time and embellished it a bit, so in the end it sounds as if he had studied fashion design or art.

Actually, it was probably more geared towards a manual/technical education with the aim of learning the profession of a window dresser. But as such, the subjects of fashion design and art are applicable. Some sources say he had finished this degree. Another source says he "was asked politely to leave the school" because he was absent too often. The last one is correct.

However, he liked art school, at least for a while. Nevertheless, he often went off to see *Gen X* and *The Damned*. He also met Joanne, his later first wife, at a *Damned* concert. He even wanted to become a punk front man actually and sometimes practised with a band named *The Vermin*.

When he was no longer interested in punk he went to the clubs in London and listened to music like David Bowie, *Roxy Music*, *Kraftwerk* and Gary Numan. "A gang of us hung out together all living for the weekend, saving up for a bag of blues (pills), going without dinner all week. We'd go to London all night, end up at some party then catch the milk train from Liverpool Street to Billericay. It was a bloody long walk home! I got bored with that, but for a while it was exciting. I had a double life, mixing with the art school mob then going home to Bas. I'd go to the pub wearing makeup, but cos I knew the local beer boys, the spanners, I was OK."[50]

Finally, his ways crossed those of Vince, Fletch and Martin, and he took the chance to become a member of a band that played the music he liked.

Today Dave is the father of son Jack, born in **1987**, from his first marriage with Joanne. Dave's second wife was Theresa with whom he did not have any children. **Since 1999**, he has been married to Jennifer and officially adopted her son Jimmy in **2010**. Together they have a daughter, Stella Rose, born in **1999**.

In addition to *DM*, Dave also did some solo work. He contributed a single song *A Song for Europe* (originally by

---

[50] Taken from: Dave Gahan: The Wild Boy, No. 1, 4 May 1985. Words: Dave Gahan.

Roxy Music) to the *Dream Home Heartache Sampler* (**1997**) and gave his voice to some songs of other bands. Solo albums are: *Paper Monsters* (**2003**) and *Hourglass* (**2007**). In **2012** he released the album *The Light the Dead See* together with the band *Soulsavers*, which was followed by a second album called *Angels & Ghosts* in **2015**.

ALAN CHARLES WILDER

Alan Charles Wilder was born on **1 June 1959** in London at the *Hammersmith Hospital*. He is the third child of Albert and Kathleen Wilder and the younger brother to Stephen, born in **1952**, and Andrew, born in **1954**. No exact dates were mentioned, but **Alan** said, "My brothers are five and seven years older respectively so they teased me a bit when they were bored, but I think I was too young to be really bothered with."[51]

His place of birth has also been mixed up many times which tempted him to begin almost all of those "who are you actually and where are you from"-articles of the early days with: "I don't come from Basildon in Essex."[52]

"I'm happy to say that my knowledge about Basildon is rather limited, particularly I was there only about three times. All my visits there were with *DM* and at a time within the early days when I was very interested in photography and always carried a shoulder bag with camera equipment around with me. My most insistent memory of Basildon is to sit in a disgusting pub and to get told I better shouldn't cross my legs and should hide the shoulder bag because otherwise I could be beaten up because someone might think I was a poof."[53]

So, no "Basildon boy." Instead, **Alan** grew up in Acton, West-London, in a normal, and presumably conservative, middle class environment. "The youth isn't so rebellion there like in Basildon, where the others come from. My parents weren't rich nor poor."[54] They "wanted their chil-

---

[51] Taken from: recoil.co.uk. Words: Alan Wilder.
[52] Taken from: A Broken Frame Tour Programme, 1982. Words: Alan Wilder.
[53] Taken from: recoil.co.uk. Words: Alan Wilder.
[54] Taken from: Depeche Mode Prive (part 1: Alan Wilder), unknown author, media and date.

dren to have a musical education. Classical music was played at our house the whole time mainly due to my brothers practising the piano.[55] One of my brothers is a pianist today and accompanies different singers. The other one teaches music in Norway."[56]

He himself was forced to have piano lessons and do grades, when he was about eight years old. "I didn't like practising but my parents wouldn't let me stop. My interest has always been with modern music starting from being four, five years old when I spent some time at our neighbour's house - for babysitting, y'know? - who heard a lot of music like Manfred Man etc."[57]

Nevertheless, he was a leading member of the school orchestra and the brass band. As a second instrument, he learned the flute. And he did well in his piano lessons. "I got up to grade 8 and now I'm really pleased that I did have them."[58]

Alan wasn't really enthusiastic about the boys' grammar school which he attended. "I mostly stayed in the background. I was doing quite well, but I wasn't interested in most of the subject-matter. I only found music and languages to be absorbing.[59] I simply hadn't the desire of listening to the teachers. Maybe because it wasn't interesting enough what they had to tell. I couldn't take schooling seriously (although I'd love to go back and really learn now) - it wasn't what I needed at the time. My mind would wander."

He summed his teenage years up with, "I was rude, scruffy, obnoxious, arrogant and blushed in front of girls." He didn't keep in touch with anyone from school, had to learn to discern friends from friends. "It's a well known English trait to resent success in others and I found most of my 'friends' didn't want to know when things took off for me. True friends are not like that of course."

He only got three O-levels, because he was too lazy as he said and left school during the sixth form and went on

---

[55] Taken from: HotNewsTV.ro, 2 April 2010. Interviewer: Unknown.
[56] Taken from: recoil.co.uk. Words: Alan Wilder.
[57] Taken from: HotNewsTV.ro, 2 April, 2010. Interviewer: Unknown.
[58] Taken from: Chatting with Alan Wilder, September 1997. Words: Henrik Wittgren.
[59] Taken from: Depeche Mode Prive (part 1: Alan Wilder), unknown author, media and date.

the dole. "There wasn't an idea of what I wanted to do but a lot of things I wouldn't want to do. Then I went back to school once again and tried to study for the A-levels but it didn't work really.[60] My parents pushed me into writing off to recording studios, the only thing I'd expressed an interest in. After being turned down 40 times I got a job at *DJM Studios* in New Oxford Street. I was a tea boy, really, an over-worked gofer. The only good thing about *DJM* was that when bands finished studio sessions they'd often leave their instruments behind so I could muck about on a keyboard or bash some drums."[61]

It became a strong ambition for him to be a musician. There wasn't anything else he was interested in. "And, as arrogant as it sounds, I always had absolute conviction that I'd be able to forge a career for myself in music. I had to pay my dues by making tea for other people (for no money), living in a floorless building once, in Hammersmith (much to my mother's dismay, didn't bother me though), and slumming around the toilets of England in various unknown bands for a few years but I still enjoyed it and, more importantly, it made me appreciate success much more when it came."[62]

The first band **Alan** joined was *The Dragons*. He moved to Bristol to work with them. The first song he played on was *Misbehavin* (sort of **1970s** soft rock stuff) which was released as a single on *DJM records* around **1977**.

"After two years in Bristol, life got too lethargic so I was glad when a friend dragged me home to join a band called *Daphne and the Tenderspots*."[63] [Some sources use the spelling *Dafne*.] "They were playing five nights a week at *Obelix* – a specialist restaurant. They were playing a mixture of jazz, R&B (in the traditional sense) and blues etc. I was roped on keyboards for a few quid in my pocket and a free cheese, ham and tomato pancake at the end of the night. We were also starting to write our own songs and jumped onto the *New Wave* bandwagon. After many weeks rehearsing on Graham and Daf's houseboat in Datchet, we

---

[60] Taken from: recoil.co.uk. Words: Alan Wilder.
[61] Taken from: Alan Wilder: The Band Boy, No. 1, 25 May 1985. Words: Alan Wilder.
[62] Taken from: recoil.co.uk. Words: Alan Wilder.
[63] Taken from: Alan Wilder: The Band Boy, No. 1, 25 May 1985. Words: Alan Wilder.

managed to get a rep from *MAM records* along.[64] We had all these terrible clothes made and worse skinny ties. We were awful but again we had a deal and made a single, *Disco Hell*."[65]

Apparently his parents weren't enthusiastic about his way of life and wouldn't give him any financial support. There was also a possibility that he had been too proud to accept money from his parents. It seems as if this led to a longer break of relationships. Many years later, Alan would say that one of the things he regretted was that he hadn't been in touch (or seldom in touch) with his parents for a while because of "some sort of teenage angst".[66]

Life as a musician (in **1977** *The Dragons*, in **1978** *Daphne and the Tenderspots*, in **1979** *Real to Real* with white man reggae and in **1980** *The Hitmen* with **1980s** Bowiesque rock) definitely had its dark sides. There often wasn't any money left for quite simple, essential things. Before **Alan** joined *DM* at the **end of 1981**, he was once arrested for shoplifting. "I stole a chicken and got caught. I was a struggling musician at the time, destitute and hungry ..."[67]

Today Alan is the father of a daughter, Paris, born in **September 1995**, and a son, Stanley, born in **January 2001**. They date from his second, meanwhile divorced, marriage with Hepzibah Sessa. His first marriage was with Jeri Young. With his third partner, Britt Rinde Hvål, he has another daughter, Clara Lake, born in **November 2011**.

Alan now works solo as *Recoil* and has released the following: *1+2* (**1986**), *Hydrology* (**1988**), *Bloodline* (**1992**), *Unsound Methods* (**1997**), *Liquid* (**2000**) and *SubHuman* (**2007**). *Selected,* which was released in **2010**, was a kind of Best of. He released some remixes (even for *DM*), was the musical and production supervisor for *Spirit of Talk Talk*, a double tribute album, released *Collected* **(2012)** about his memorial auction with *DM* items in **2011**, and

---

[64] Taken from: The Palace and the Punks, Northern Lights Ltd., 2011. Words: Tony Hill.
[65] Taken from: Alan Wilder: The Band Boy, No. 1, 25 May 1985. Words: Alan Wilder.
[66] Source can't be found anymore
[67] depechemodebiographie.de

finally released *A Strange Hour in Budapest*, a concert film about performing *Selected*, in **2012**.

Other than in Vince's case I decided not to leave out Alan after he had left the band. His story is too fused with the history of the band (I was especially glad about this decision in **2010**), and his reasons for leaving the band were a kind of leitmotif for this biography. He (and his website) is an important source as well. In fact, Alan is prominently mentioned in this biography because there are many more quotations from him than from any other band member, and as most of them were written by himself, it is certain that they are correct.

FOUNDATION

The details on the formation of the group(s) are a bit contradictory and confusing. This is due to three problems: firstly, there aren't any articles from **1980**, and all information about that period is based on the memories of the band members in later articles. It is understandable that the further back in time it got, the hazier the memories became.

Secondly, in the early days, there were often no clear questions put forward, but rather suggestions, which the band members tended to "jump on." Journalists also often tended to refer to earlier articles instead of asking their own questions.

Thirdly, *DM* weren't taken seriously at all when they started. They were seen as little boys who had nothing important to say, so they generally weren't asked anything of importance.

However, in **1977**, Vince and Fletch founded *No Romance in China*, with Vince on vocals and guitar, and Fletch on bass. Another source says that *No Romance in China* was founded in **1979**. I tend to go for **1977**, because Fletch once said they had this band when he was 16, and he was definitely 16 in **1977**.

There are two different sources that mention a band named *The Plan* with Robert Marlow on vocals and Vince on guitar in **1978**. Until **1979** Martin played guitar in an acoustic duo called *Norman and the Worms* with Philip Burdett on vocals. Simultaneously, in **1979**, Martin and Vince were in another band.

"Vince had a band," **Dave** said, "*The French Look* with Martin, Rob Marlow, and Rob Allen who I mixed sound for. Then Vince started *Composition of Sound* with Andy and Martin. The two groups fell out because both wanted Martin. Typically, he couldn't make up his mind, being nice to everyone."[68]

Other sources say that *The French Look* had the following members: Martin, Robert Marlow and Paul Redmond, and some say that Robert Allan is the real name of Robert Marlow. These sources are probably correct, especially as

---

[68] Taken from: Dave Gahan: The Wild Boy, No. 1, 4 May 1985. Words: Dave Gahan.

Dave was a friend of Paul Redmond and got known to these bands through him.

It's not quite clear how much Vince, Martin and Fletch were in touch with Dave at that time. On one occasion the impression is given that they only knew him by sight. Another time **Martin** said, "It wasn't as if he was a total stranger. In fact we've all known each other since schooldays."[69] Of course, this could also mean that they only knew him by sight, especially because they didn't go to the same school.

There is another source quoting **Dave** as saying, "Vince Clarke I met one day outside a pub in the city centre."[70] So he might have known Vince better than Martin and Fletch. On the other hand, he must have known Martin – at least by sight - because of mixing the sound for *The French Look*, as he said.

However, in **1980**, Vince, Fletch and Martin started *Composition of Sound* with two guitars, bass (played by Fletch), and a drum machine. Although Martin wrote some songs too, Vince was the leader of the band, wrote the songs and took care of the lead vocals.

While Fletch and Vince were friends, just like Fletch and Martin were, Martin didn't know Vince well. This became clear from later sources.

They had two gigs as a trio – one at *Scamps* in Southend and another at Deb Danahay's party (the latter wasn't a real gig; Deb Danahay was Vince's girlfriend.)

"When we first started, we did concerts around people's houses in Basildon, that's before Dave joined, and it was quite good. One of the gigs we'd played, we played in front of seven people and ten teddybears," **Fletch** laughed. "And we dressed up in eh ..."

"Pyjamas," **Dave** chipped in and giggled.

"Pyjamas," **Fletch** confirmed. "It was just a good laugh. We still got the tape of that concert."[71] (I bet many people would like to hear this tape.)

---

[69] Taken from: Angels with shining Faces, Record Mirror, 1 August 1981. Words: Mike Nicholls.
[70] Taken from: Dave Gahan: The Wild Boy, No. 1, 4 May 1985. Words: Dave Gahan.
[71] Taken from: Interview with Dave and Fletch, Radio 1 (UK), 19 February 1982. Interviewer: Unknown.

Unfortunately, no one seems to be sure about the exact dates. Maybe no one can remember because these gigs weren't even minor successes. There were a lot of young people who had never seen a synthesizer before, so they asked a lot of questions about it, instead of listening to the music.

Something was still missing in order to be successful.

"So although we desperately wanted a singer we were prepared to take our time and be patient," **Martin** said, "and wait for the right person to come along."[72]

This right person ran into them short time later.

"We needed a front man, a singer," **Fletch** remarked, "and we got a front man. What happened was, we got him just on the strength of him singing *Heroes* [of David Bowie] in a jamming session. We weren't even sure if it was him singing it, there was so many people singing!"[73]

This was apparently the first time the other ones really got aware of Dave, regardless of whether they had known him before. Vince thought they should have him in the band because "he thought," **Dave** said, "I looked so pretty in my *Marks & Spencer* jumper and my corduroy trousers."[74]

Probably that wasn't the main reason. In fact, Dave was part of the so-called in crowd in London and in Essex at the time. He knew a lot of people, so **Vince** saw that they had an in to some cool clubs. "Dave Gahan was the local fashion accessory of Basildon. He was the *New Romantic*. He was rumoured to have attended the club *Blitz* in London, so it was all very glamorous. So, we decided to get him in as a front man because he was flamboyant and extrovert and very, very confident."[75]

"He did have a sense of style, and I think that was one of the reasons why we recruited him as a band member. I think we recruited him because he was hanging out with a core crowd of people. He seemed to have a lot of friends, which gave us an instant audience," **Martin** laughed.

---

[72] Taken from: Depeche Mode, Bobcat Books, London 1986. Words: Dave Thomas.
[73] Taken from: Depeche Mode: Hurried Fashion, The Face, June 1981. Words: Ian Cranna.
[74] Taken from: Depeche Mode, Published by HMV / Melody Maker, 22 September 1990. Words: Uncredited.
[75] Taken from: The Story Of Depeche Mode, BBC Radio London Live94.9, 7 May 2001, Producer: Tony Wood.

And **Fletch** added, "During the *New Romantic* time, he looked amazing as a *New Romantic*. Us generally, when we tried to become *New Romantics*, we weren't so successful, especially me."[76]

About a week after the rehearsal in which Dave had sung *Heroes* he got a phone call from Vince who asked him to sing at a rehearsal. The new band was complete now.

It's not quite clear when the first common gig took place. Some people say it was **31 May 1980**, other people say it was **14 June**. Probably it was **31 May**, because at both dates *Composition of Sound* played at Fletch's and Martin's old school in Basildon as an opening act for *The French Look*. At that time, Martin was still playing with both groups. He first played with *Composition of Sound*, then changed his shirt and got back on stage – this time with *The French Look*.

Dave was rather nervous and needed - according to Fletch – "ten cans of *Lager*" to calm down.[77] This is a nice story when you know that he is one of the most self-confident front men nowadays.

To ease his nervous tendency he invited a lot of friends - most of them so-called *New Romantics* - which was some kind of start-up for the project and made it go. It seems that Dave really was very useful at this early stage of their career.

They started at the *Bridge House* in London where the promoter gave them a chance to play. These gigs were very valuable as well as the ones at *Crocs* in nearby Rayleigh. There was also someone who helped them along. "The resident DJ, Rusty Egan," **Dave** said, "liked us and so we then got a spot on one of the Thursday nights he was running at the venue."[78]

"We must have played at *Crocs* fifteen times," **Fletch** added, "and that gave us a lot of encouragement.[79] Every Saturday we'd go along and play in front of 300 people,

---

[76] Taken from: My interview with Depeche Mode, 29 January 2010, words: oyvindholen.
[77] Taken from: Going U.P.!, Smash Hits, 9-22 July 1981. Words: Steve Taylor.
[78] Taken from: Angels with shining Faces, Record Mirror, 1 August 1981. Words: Mike Nicholls.
[79] Taken from: Going U.P.!, Smash Hits, 9-22 July 1981. Words: Steve Taylor.

280 of whom we knew."[80] The number of people is different in each source – 30, 50, 100, 200, 300. Probably sometimes 30 friends came along and sometimes 100.

While the other three band members were quite satisfied with just playing some gigs in front of some friends, **Vince**, in contrast, had ambitions to become big and to develop musically. "When we started we wanted to sound very clear. You go and see a band, and the drums and guitars and saxophone, it's like a wall of sound. I'd rather have a sound where you can pick out each instrument, each melody line. And also, we wanted the rhythm to be at the forefront, so you can dance to it."[81]

But it wasn't Vince then who gave the start for becoming a synthesizer band during **summer 1980**. Martin was the first who bought a synthesizer. He admitted that he had had it for one month before he found out that he could change the sound. But finally he managed it, and it didn't take long for the others to follow suit because they thought that synthesizers were a lot easier to learn to play from scratch than most other instruments.

"To us, the synth was a punk instrument because it was still fairly new," **Martin** said, "its potential seemed limitless. It gave us a chance to explore."[82]

It had been quite easy for them to turn into a synth band. "Vince'd spent about six months trying to save up to get a guitar," **Fletch** recalled, "and he was a bit annoyed when Martin bought his synth and it seemed pretty good so then he saved up another six months and got a synth, so we had two, and then I was playing bass. And then Vince turned round one day and said, 'I think it might be good if you get a synth as well - make it all electronic.'"[83]

There had been some other (known) gigs before they changed their name from *Composition of Sound* to *Depeche Mode*.

---

[80] Taken from: Mode Ahead, Muzik, July 2001. Words: Ralph Moore.
[81] Taken from: Play for Tomorrow, New Sounds, New Styles, August 1981. Words: Pete Silverton.
[82] Taken from: Depeche Mode, HMV / Melody Maker, 22 September 1990. Words: Uncredited.
[83] Taken from: Depeche Mode: The Interview, Talking Music SPEEK013, 1988.

From the start they weren't good with names and titles. So they thought of many names for the band – most of them quite strange (no examples were mentioned), but nothing really occurred to them. "Dave was doing fashion design and window display and used the magazine *Mode Dépêche* as a reference,"[84] **Martin** said. It means "fashion news dispatch" or "fashion update;" but they didn't care much about the meaning. "It's always a tough job trying to get something that you like and appeals to other people too. We saw the name on the magazine cover and it clicked. We've never bothered to find out what it stands for!"[85] (Hard to believe when you know that Martin had an A-level in French.)

On **16 October 1980** they appeared as *"Depeche Mode"* for the first time, playing a gig at the *Bridge House*.

From that point things moved on step by step. At *Crocs* DJ Rusty Egan introduced them to Stevo Pearce, another DJ, who asked them whether they wanted to contribute a song to the *Some Bizarre Album*. The album consisted of tracks by unsigned *New Wave* groups. Stevo believed in the music that was included on the album, as opposed to the fashion or style aspects.

"At the time we had no record company contract and we were kind of interested in this sort of thing so we did it," **Vince** said. "We kind of regret it now because of the *Futurist* connotations."[86]

In fact, it took them years to get rid of this *"Futurist* thing" and also to get rid of the *New Romantics* image.

During that period they, (or at least Martin, Fletch and Dave), still didn't have ambitions to become a big successful band. Nevertheless, they wanted to make a record. So they recorded a demo tape and approached all kinds of record companies. (Many years later some of these tapes appeared on *eBay,* which caused a small sensation among the fans.) But it took some time until someone took an interest in them, although they went to many record companies, sometimes even 12 companies a day. They got turned down or got strange offers like the one of a Rasta-

---

[84] Taken from: Martin Gore: The Decadent Boy, No. 1, 11 May 1985. Words: Martin Lee Gore.
[85] Taken from: The Name's the Game! Zig Zag, November 1982. Words: John Kercher.
[86] Taken from: Basildon a La Mode, NME, 21 March 1981. Words: Chris Bohn.

farian who wanted to turn them into an electronic reggae group. Even Daniel [Miller of *Mute Records*] wasn't interested at first.

"We were at *Rough Trade* with our tape,"[87] **Dave** said. "They were our last hope, we thought at least we've got them, surely they'll like it, after all they've got some pretty bad bands, but even they turned us down! They were all tapping their feet and that and we thought – this is the one! – then they went, 'Hey, that's pretty good, it's just not *Rough Trade.*' Then they said, 'How about this man?', pointing at Daniel who'd just walked into the room. He took one look at us, went 'Yeech!', walked out and slammed the door!"[88]

But on **11 November**, when *DM* played the opening for *Fad Gadget* (later *Fad Gadget* would play the opening for *DM*) at the *Bridge House*, Daniel Miller approached them and invited them to do a one-off single.

"We've got a better chance on *Mute*," **Vince** guessed, "Daniel's been good to us and we like the way he operates. He had a big success with the *Silicon Teens*, and we've got that same sort of lightweight feeling to us.[89] *Mute* are one of the most honest companies going. We like the one to one way of working. We spoke to all the majors and found they weren't nearly as pleasant as they first appeared, we were a bit dubious about them. I suppose we were just lucky to meet the right person at the right time ..."[90]

"Daniel was the first one we could trust," **Dave** added, "he said that if either party didn't like the other, we'd call it a day."[91]

The contract was sealed on a mere handshake (an inside source says, however, that there was a signed agreement from the beginning, but I'm not sure about, see **1987**) - and *DM* became, after *Fad Gadget* and *Non*, the third band on *Mute* that didn't even have their own office at that time.

---

[87] Taken from: Play for Tomorrow, New Sounds, New Styles, August 1981. Words: Pete Silverton.
[88] Taken from: The Bright Side of the Moon, Sounds, 4 September 1982. Words: Karen Swayne.
[89] Taken from: This Year's Model(I), Sounds, 31 January 1981. Words: Betty Page.
[90] Taken from: Mute Speak, NME, 2 May 1981. Words: Vivien Goldman.
[91] Taken from: Going U.P.!, Smash Hits, 9-22 July 1981. Words: Steve Taylor.

The right light, dark room (Photographic)
(© Ingo Bittrich)

Daniel Miller started his career as the founder and head of *Mute Records* in **1977**, when he released the single *TVOD / Warm Leatherette* on his own. He never thought of approaching a major label. In fact, he didn't like them at all. The idea of being an independent appealed to him, and he started with 500 copies of *TVOD / Warm Leatherette*. Due to the success he started a co-operation with *Rough Trade*. When he met *Fad Gadget*, Miller decided to work with other people's music.

He became a kind of "musical father" for *DM*, and for a long time he was something like the "secret fifth member" of the band. These days he is still involved in everything the band is doing. The band appreciated this very much and stayed with *Mute*, although some bigger companies had approached them after their initial success, and tried to sign them.

"All of a sudden, everyone was interested and the majors were queuing to sign us," **Dave** said. "Suddenly that style of music came in, and they were all after us.[92] They'd come to the gigs, buy us meals and generally fatten us up.

---

[92] Taken from: Modish Musings, Sounds, 7 November 1981. Words: Uncredited.

They offered us loads of money, it was quite tempting really, but we trusted Daniel, didn't want to let him down."

"I think we lose out a bit because there's things we can't do as we haven't got hundreds of thousands of pounds behind us," **Fletch** added, "we've got a partnership deal, so anything we do we pay for ourselves."[93]

On the other hand, they could release whatever they wanted to, and were in control of everything concerning them. They were allowed to (as Alan would say many years later) develop and make their own mistakes - something many other artists aren't able to do, because most of them are more like victims of their record companies than their partners. There are enough examples of young bands that are just the puppets of their record companies, instead of being real artists. Some have to release one album after another, others aren't able to make a record at all because they are blocked. It's a dirty business. *DM* were to learn this, but they would always be in a very fortunate position. On the other hand, they have always had the status of outsiders in the music business. Maybe this is part of the mystery of why they are big, without being really famous.

"With *Mute* it was always step by step, as it still is," **Martin** said. "Originally it was just a one off single deal where everyone else was trying to get us to sign up to make nine albums. That seemed too much."[94]

There was still the *Some Bizarre*-project, but as Miller also had some connections to Stevo, both projects were fulfilled in the end. At the **end of 1980** *DM* recorded *Photographic* for the *Some Bizarre Album* - with Daniel Miller as producer. The band set up their equipment in the studio, and ran through some of their live tracks, finally selecting *Photographic*. It was recorded and mixed in a day.

---

[93] Taken from: The Bright Side of the Moon, Sounds, 4 September 1982. Words: Karen Swayne.
[94] Taken from: Everything Counts (in Large Amounts), Number One, 19 October 1985. Words: Paul Bursche.

1981

- Complicating, circulating, new life -

On **31 January 1981** *Photographic* was released on the *Some Bizarre Album*, which was released by *Some Bizarre Records*. This was founded in **1981** as an independent label and owned by Stevo Pearce. The acts that appeared on the *Some Bizarre Album* weren't signed to the label.

On the release day the first longer article about *DM* appeared in the magazine *Sounds*. The journalist Betty Page described *DM* as "very young, tender and fresh-as-a-mountain-stream"[95] etc. Maybe she actually found them cute, but she stamped the image of *DM* in England with that for the next ten years.

A couple of years later **Dave** remarked on that period, "You know what England's like - the first thing you ever do, that's it. It's written on your gravestone."[96]

Later they not only regretted their early naivety, according to the media, but they also regretted their appearance on the *Some Bizarre Album,* because from that time onwards they had to ward off prejudice against being part of the *Futurist* scene or being one of the *New Romantics*.

"I don't like that scene at all," **Dave** said, "all the bands involved with it are in one bunch together and they'll never escape from it. We write pop music, electric pop, so we couldn't get tagged by appearing on that album. Once people hear the single [*Dreaming of Me*], they'll change their minds!"[97]

Well, they didn't. Not really. There are statements of this type until about **1985**, when they were asked about the *Futurist* scene and *New Romantics* over and over again. And it also took them a long time not to be seen as cute anymore.

---

[95] Taken from: This Year's Model(I), Sounds, 31 January 1981. Words: Betty Page.
[96] Taken from: Just Can't Get Enough, Uncut, May 2001. Words: Stephen Dalton.
[97] Taken from: This Year's Model(I), Sounds, 31 January 1981. Words: Betty Page.

As well as in **1980**, *DM* also played a lot of gigs in small clubs in **1981**, but at that time they were still a long way from something you might call a tour. They simply travelled by train or car, the synthesizers tucked under their arms, strange to imagine when you know that they were to travel with a big crew and lots of equipment only a few years later. Maybe this is one of the reasons why their fans like them so much. They weren't a casted band, with tons of money behind them from the word go. They came "from the street," and learned the business from scratch.

On **20 February** *Dreaming of Me / Ice Machine* was released as *DM*'s first own single. It had been recorded at *Blackwing Studios*. Due to the poor chart placement, *Dreaming of Me* did not originally appear on *Speak & Spell*. In the U.S., it wasn't commercially released as a single, but it was on the original pressing of the album, replacing *I Sometimes Wish I Was Dead*.

Nevertheless, it was a special moment for the band when the single got on No. 57 of the charts and was played on the radio for the first time. They all came to *Mute*'s small office and sat around the radio.

"By comparison doing things like *Top of the Pops* later in the year for *New Life* wasn't the great thing I expected it to be - no excitement at all," **Fletch** said.

"Hovering around the Top 40 with *Dreaming* was a great feeling – unrepeatable,"[98] **Dave** added.

On the 30th "birthday" of the song fans brought *Dreaming of Me* back into the charts. The action failed in most countries except in Germany, where the track entered the singles charts at No. 45.

At that time all of them were still doing day-jobs or job-training. Fletch worked as a pension clerk for the *Sun Life* insurance company, Martin worked for the *National Westminster Bank*, Dave was training to become a window-dresser, Vince was out of work or doing casual jobs, like at a yoghurt factory.

And although they played a lot of gigs, and had other commitments, they didn't dare give up their jobs. Martin and Fletch hesitated especially. This was understandable, considering the high unemployment rate in England at the

---

[98] Taken from: A Year in the Life of Depeche Mode, The Face, January 1982. Words: Paul Tickell.

time. If the band were to fail, it would have been very difficult to get back into a "straight" job. With their increasing success, however, it became more and more difficult to keep their day-jobs. But when *New Life* charted and Daniel Miller told them they should give up their jobs, they were still unsure.

For **Dave** it seemed to be much easier. "I used to be a window dresser on Oxford Street, *John Lewis*. We'd started playing the clubs and someone tapped on the window: 'Are you in *Depeche Mode*?' I left that afternoon."[99]

This is actually not completely correct. He might have given up this job but he was rather gone from college than having given it up himself.

"When the band first started, I was at college studying fashion," **Dave** said, "I loved it – the lecturers, the people there – but[100] I wasn't that happy with what I was doing at college, because I didn't go that much, and college makes you very lazy, and the band really came along at the right time."[101]

However, he was forever missing days and disappearing off to rehearse with the rest of the band. "So in the end, there was only one thing the principal could do – expel me. I was pretty upset at first as I enjoyed the course, but I know it wasn't totally right for me. But I've been forgiven, thank goodness. When we got to the charts with our first single, the principal sent me a note congratulating us on our success – I was really pleased. I didn't think he'd ever speak to me again."[102]

According to rumours it was made clear that the college was the last stop before borstal. So it wasn't "harmless" that he had to leave school. Therefore, he was apparently only "forgiven" because of the visible success.

After *Dreaming of Me* a licence-contract with *Sire* for the U.S.-market was sealed. Besides, European deals were made for the next single *New Life / Shout* which was released on **13 June**. The single became the band's break-

---

[99] Taken from: The Ten Commandments: Dave Gahan, Q, November 2005. Words: Dave Gahan / Johnny Davis
[100] Taken from: We're in the Mode!, Oh Boy!, 24 October 1981. Words: Uncredited.
[101] Taken from an interview with Radio 1 (UK), 19 February 1982. Interviewer: Unknown.
[102] Taken from: We're in the Mode!, Oh Boy!, 24 October 1981. Words: Uncredited.

through hit in the UK, peaking at No. 11. The B-side *Shout* was the first song to get a 12" extended remix, called the *Rio Remix*.

New Life (© Ingo Bittrich)

Right after releasing *New Life* the band began to record *Speak & Spell*. The first song to be recorded was the third single *Just Can't Get Enough*. It was recorded in the *Blackwing Studios*, as well as *Dreaming of Me* and *New Life*.

"*Just Can't Get Enough* took an age to record because we still had *New Life* on the boil and a lot of our time was taken up with interviews," **Dave** said. "We just couldn't concentrate on recording and the first time we did *Just Can't Get Enough* it was terrible. It was a relief when it came out."[103]

On **16 July** DM had their debut at *TOTP*, (another source says it was on **25 June**), then they travelled "to Europe" for the first time - to The Hague where they played a gig at *Zuiderspark* on **25 July**.

With *Just Can't Get Enough* an all-time classic was released on **7 September**, and *DM* travelled to the continent again. On **25 September** they had their first gig in Germany - in the *Markthalle* in Hamburg - a country that

---

[103] Taken from: Modish Musings, Sounds, 7 November 1981. Words: Uncredited.

would become important for them. Besides, they played in Amsterdam, Brussels and Paris.

Just Can't Get Enough was the first single to be released in the U.S. The single version was the same that appeared on the UK version of *Speak & Spell*. The 12" single featured the *Schizo Mix*, which appeared on the U.S. version of *Speak & Spell*.

In addition, the single's B-side *Any Second Now* was the first commercially available instrumental track. A version including vocals - sung by Martin - appeared on the album as *Any Second Now (Voices)*. The single reached No. 8 on the UK Singles Charts. Besides, *Just Can't Get Enough* was the first song to get a music video, directed by Clive Richardson.

"The *Just Can't Get Enough* video was a funny one," **Fletch** recalled. "Made in London – it was a real cheapo as we had to pay for it. We are in this club (in the video) and there's all these girl dancers and we're drinking cocktails, we chat them up and Martin gets left without a bird – really funny."[104]

Success was mainly credit of Vince. Not at least because he had written the first hit singles.

"He was pushing and pushing," **Fletch** said. You've got to give him credit – he was very ambitious.[105] It was his aim to make money and drive a Rolls-Royce through the centre of Basildon. He used to work in a yoghurt factory and earn £30 a week, of which he'd save £29.50. Without Vince's drive *Depeche Mode* wouldn't have happened."[106]

At that time, the rest of the band still hadn't such ambitious endeavours. The events appeared as if in a dream. Sometimes the band members were quite realistic, but sometimes they could hardly believe what was happening.

"We've managed to avoid making the mistakes that so many young bands make," **Dave** remarked. "We had lots of offers from big record companies and it was very tempt-

---

[104] Taken from: Bop Eye, Issue 3, Undated, 1982. Words: Jane-Nina Buchanan.
[105] Taken from: Hanging in the Balance, NME, 26 March 1983. Words: Matt Snow.
[106] Taken from: Songs of Innocence and Experience, Mojo, November 2005. Words: Danny Eccleston.

ing 'cos they offer you a big advance, but what's the point, you only have to pay it back!"[107]

Maybe they could have managed to avoid making mistakes like these. Instead, they made another one. Dealing with the media was very difficult for them in those early days. A lot of journalists wrote articles in which they introduced the band to the public. Unfortunately, most of them found the band "cute," and ridiculed them. Sometimes you got the feeling that the journalists didn't know what to ask them. It seems as if the boys were simply too nice, and somehow not interesting enough as people. On the one hand, this is not a nice situation. On the other hand, it shows that they could let their music speak for them, and that they had a strong live performance from the beginning. Otherwise, people wouldn't have bought their records or turned up at their gigs.

Typical British working class towns were quite desolate and boring in the 1970s and 1980s. (The picture shows Leeds, not Basildon, though) (© Lilian R. Franke)

---

[107] Taken from: Basildon Band!, My Guy, 5 September 1981. Words: Uncredited.

Because the band itself didn't seem interesting enough, many journalists picked on Basildon as the main topic. There are many descriptions of the town, but Basildon was and is such a boring place, that I don't know why they even tried to find out how on earth a band could be founded in a town like that. A band can be founded in any town on the planet, so there was no need to make such a fuss about it. Nevertheless, journalists managed to force the band members into making statements like those that follow:

"We're from Basildon, Essex," **Dave** said. "It's a new town. A lot of people think it's just a country town but it's quite built up. Housing estates ... and there's an industrial estate there ..."[108]

"In fact it has a population of 180,000," **Fletch** remarked.

"Oh, Andy knows everything, even the population," **Martin** said.

But **Fletch** was serious. "Believe me, it's got an electoral roll of 107,000 and that's not including kids. That's the biggest in the country, and next time it has got to be split up into Basildon East and West."[109]

"When Simon Bates introduces us on *Top of the Pops*, he makes a special point about us coming from Basildon – why?" **Dave** asked.

"Because nothing good ever comes out of here?"[110] **Martin** suggested.

When they were asked about the music they were mostly cliché questions to which the band members felt forced to explain over and over again that they weren't a *Futurist* band but just wrote pop songs.

"I think the word *pop* is really good because it's light and happy," **Vince** explained. "I think it's a nice word. I like words. I like the sound of words, and the way words fit together and rhyme - things like that. Or the way they sound coming from my mouth. The sound of words rather than the meaning of words. I don't really write about any-

---

[108] Taken from: Play for Tomorrow, New Sounds, New Styles, August 1981. Words: Pete Silverton.
[109] Taken from: Three Modes in a Boat, NME, 22 August 1981. Words: Paul Morley.
[110] Taken from: Going U.P.!, Smash Hits, 9-22 July 1981. Words: Steve Taylor.

thing. I think in the sort of stuff we're doing, it's good to use certain words. I think words are very fashionable. I'll give you an example, right? Words to use in a good electronic song - *fade, switch, light* - anything like that. *Room, door* - words like that. It's quite nice. *Fade* - that's an excellent word. It's a word for **1981** - it's got to be! I think the word *pop*, it's not just the words, right? It's the whole feel of the song. And it's just light, y'know?"[111]

Or in a short form: "It's just the pop sound of the **1980s**, that's what I would describe *Depeche Mode* as," **Dave** said.

"A lot of people still don't realise that the whole of our set is pop," **Fletch** remarked. "Virtually all our songs are pop songs. I think people think it might not be like that."

"They think we're jokes!" **Martin** chipped in.

"Naah ... a lot of people have still got this thing – synthesiser, he must be moody," **Fletch** said. "You get a lot of *Numanoids* [fans of Gary Numan] coming to our gigs."

"There was this bloke come to see us the other day," **Dave** recalled, "and he said to me after the show, 'I think it's really bad the way you have all your friends in the audience talking to you and that, and then we're all over here and you don't react to us.' I said, 'Well what do you mean?' He said, 'I think it's really bad that you have like all your friends in the changing room.' I said, 'Well what do you want me to say c'mon all the audience into the changing room?' He said, 'Well have you got lots of friends?' I said, 'Well I've got a few.' He said, 'Well I haven't got any.' 'Well pity you mate! Isn't that a friend?' a guy who was with him. He said, 'Yeah he's a friend, but not a friend like that.' It was really weird! I couldn't be bothered talking to him. He thought that we should be like Gary Numan and have the distant lonely look and image. Because we play synthesisers and we're supposed to look strange at people, and not smile. The bloke didn't like the way I smiled at people!"[112]

Unfortunately, most of the questions they were asked were simply ridiculous. Like the one what they would do as soon as the innocence was gone ...

---

[111] Taken from: Depeche Mode: Hurried Fashion, The Face, June 1981. Words: Ian Cranna.
[112] Taken from: Three Modes in a Boat, NME, 22 August 1981. Words: Paul Morley.

"Grow into something else I suppose," **Vince** replied, "I dunno. We haven't contrived any particular image for ourselves. If people draw any conclusion from the lyrics it's up to them. We don't set out to portray any particular image of innocence, we don't pretend or anything."[113] ...

or which tooth paste they used ...

Dave: "Well, round me girlfriend's house, I use *Colgate*." (And at home none? :D)

Fletch: "*Ultrabrite* I use."

Dave: "There's one really horrible one."

Martin: "*Crest*."

Dave: "Bloody horrible, that."

Martin: "It ain't that bad."

Dave: "It is. S'horrible."

Fletch: "It's alright on toast ... a ham and *Crest* sandwich."

Dave: "This is a joke ... ho, ho, ho."[114]

... and they found out that Martin liked to strip. (A topic that would become "interesting" in later years.)

Dave: "When we play Basildon again it'll be crazy. Martin's just going to have a loincloth. Mart likes to show his top off ... you like your body, don't you, Mart?"

Fletch: "He loves it ..."

Dave: "Yeah, that's how he ended up on *Top of the Pops*, he took his shirt off in the dressing room and said, 'shall I go on like this'."

Fletch: "He's even been known to kiss his own body."

Martin: "You're making this up ... At least I don't wear Y-fronts. Andy used to wear Y-fronts until a week ago, but we converted him to a briefs man ..."

Fletch: "What!? ... I don't wear them – you do!"

Martin: "Yeah, he said, 'what shall I do if I get a girl on this tour' ... this bit's going to be embarrassing."[115]

In the course of time it became clear to them that they couldn't handle the media at all.

"We made a lot of mistakes in terms of the way we put ourselves across and put ourselves about," **Dave** said

---

[113] Taken from: Basildon a La Mode, NME, 1 March 1981. Words: Chris Bohn.
[114] Taken from: Play for Tomorrow, New Sounds, New Styles, August 1981. Words: Pete Silverton.
[115] Taken from: Learning the Highway Mode, Melody Maker, 14 November 1981. Words: Paul Colbert.

many years later. "We were prepared to do anything. Not necessarily to sell ourselves. We were just completely naive. We thought it would be good to be in *Smash Hits* answering questions about our socks, appearing on Saturday morning television, making prats of ourselves. We didn't realise at the time that we were degrading ourselves. Then it reached a point where we realised it wasn't helping us anymore. In fact, it was becoming very negative."[116]

But there was already some self-criticism in **1981**, when they noticed that there was nothing people could say about them. They didn't stand for anything united, and they didn't have an extrovert, domineering member with strong political views. They thought it was good, but "on the other hand, that's why our interviews are very empty," **Fletch** realised, "'cause usually the loudmouth of a band goes on about what the *Labour party* are doing or something."

They have always been proud of being a democracy. On the other hand, that's the reason for all their internal problems. Not the democratic principle itself, but the lack of communication between equal partners.

Sometimes they tried to be more serious. Some of these quotations show the starting conflict with **Vince**, however. "We want to change our sound, get some new stuff together, get a good live show. We don't want to get like *Kraftwerk*, we don't want to use tapes anymore."[117]

The reel-to-reel tape machine was a standard feature in the early years. It was visible on the stage because they didn't want to seem to pretend to be doing something they weren't doing. While Vince obviously had other plans the rest of the band felt quite comfortable with the tape machine.

"The tapes we've got now sound like real drums anyway," **Dave** said, "we don't need a drummer anyway – it's just another person to pay!"[118] As we know today, it took a long time before they would actually use live drums on stage and even more time before they would employ a full paid drummer for live shows.

---

[116] Taken from: Depeche Mode Hip it up and Start Again, Melody Maker, 10 March 1990. Words: Jon Wilde.
[117] Taken from: Depeche Guevara, Sounds, 27 June 1981. Words: Betty Page.
[118] Taken from: This Year's Model(l), Sounds, 31 January 1981. Words: Betty Page.

Vince didn't feel well in the band and the whole project from a certain point. Probably it was a growing dissatisfaction, although a special event was blamed for it. In an interview, Vince said that it was an advantage in life to be good looking. The journalist made it out that Vince had said, "Ugly bands never make it, if you're good looking then you're number one." Allegedly Vince was so upset about it that he suffered from a bad depression.

From this point onwards, Vince hardly took part in any group interviews. In a biography, it was alleged that Vince consumed a lot of speed at that time. There's also another source mentioning this, but it has never been confirmed officially. Maybe this was a reason for Vince's depressions. Another rumour is that he didn't like Martin and Dave letting their girlfriends take part in everything. He preferred not to mix business with private, but I doubt that these two things were the main reasons for Vince's strange behaviour.

Vince finished work at *Speak & Spell* (a title the band wasn't able to explain, while another source says that the album title alludes to an electronic toy that was popular at that time) - and was ready to go on tour with the band in order not to spoil the just sealed contracts.

But before the tour-start, **Vince** told the other members that he was going to leave the band. "Breaking the news was terrible. They were expecting it in some ways. I'd been going through a gloomy phase, but I had to go round to their houses and tell them."[119]

"I was the one person Vince didn't tell," **Martin** disagreed. "He went round and knocked on Andy's door, knocked on Dave's door. He said he would continue with the tour he'd committed to with us, but basically after that he'd be leaving. But he never had that conversation with me. Andy phoned me."

"I definitely felt betrayed," **Dave** added, "but in retrospect I see why he left. What Vince saw was that being in a band, you kind of have to listen to each other. You all have ideas, but Vince didn't want that."[120]

None of the other three thought about giving up the band. Martin could replace Vince as a songwriter, and at

---

[119] Taken from: Depeche Mode, Bobcat Books, London 1986. Words: Dave Thomas.
[120] Taken from: Songs of Innocence and Experience, Mojo, November 2005. Words: Danny Eccleston.

that time - after they had given up their jobs - there was no return.

"I think we should have been slightly more worried than we were," **Martin** said some years later. "When your chief songwriter leaves the band, you should worry a bit. I suppose that's one of the good things about being young. If we had panicked, we probably wouldn't be here today."[121]

On **5 October** *Speak & Spell* was released. The album peaked at No. 10 in the UK Albums Chart. It's interesting that *Tora! Tora! Tora!*, the first song written by Martin, is one of the favourite songs (from the *Speak-&-Spell* era) of many fans although *Just Can't Get Enough* is the best known track.

At the same time *DM* started their first real tour. It took place in the UK, started on **31 October** in Newcastle, comprised 14 gigs and ended on **16 November** in London.

They did the tour with a mini-bus, together with the two musicians of the opening band, *Blancmange*, the tour manager and the fiancées of Dave and Martin – Jo[anne] and Anne. The girls worked on the promotional side of the tour, dealing with requests from fans and selling t-shirts.

The atmosphere between the remaining band members and Vince was quite cold. Vince hardly spoke to the other ones. And although they tried not to let their internal problem show to the surface during the tour you could guess where the band was heading to when reading between the lines.

Sources are not sure about the correct date of Vince's official leaving. Some say that the last gig with him was the one on **16 November**; others count the *TVS TV Show* in Chichester on **3 December** as the last common concert. Some say that **20 November** was the day when Vince's leaving was announced officially, another says it was in the **beginning of December** and yet another still says it was on **12 December**. However, his leaving the band was one of the catalytic forces that marked the band's change of direction.

"I never expected the band to be this successful," **Vince** explained, "I didn't feel happy. Or contented. Or fulfilled. And that's why I left. All the things that come with success

---

[121] Taken from: Violator, Alligator, NME, 7 July 1990. Words: Jeff Giles.

had suddenly become more important than the music. We used to get letters from fans saying: 'I really like your songs;' then we got letters saying: 'Where do you buy your trousers from?' There was never enough time to do anything. Not with all the interviews and photo sessions.[122] Everything happened for us very, very quickly. We had these massive egos by that time and you know sitting inside the van was intolerable for all of us. We were all intolerable to each other. We were all pretty young, it just went to our heads."[123]

But I almost can't imagine that this was true. Most sources say the band members were pretty naive and shy at this time. "Massive egos" and "intolerable" therefore sounds strange. So it's difficult to understand why Vince really left. It seems that the other three band members didn't understand it either.

In **1982 Dave** commented it with, "He didn't like what was happening to *Depeche Mode*, didn't like being famous, didn't like touring. Now he's had a couple of hit singles with *Yazoo*, they've got an album out and they go on tour in **September** – it's a bit hypocritical really."[124]

And in **1990** simply with, "That's what he said, but I think that's a lot of bulls***, to be quite honest."[125]

Well, I can't help but agree. In the fan survey that was done for *depechemodebiographie.de*, 20% of the participants also say that everything he said seems to be illogical.

Vince's main argument that he didn't like being a star and couldn't handle the fuss seems absurd, because he founded a new band right after leaving *DM*. There must also have been interviews - *Yazoo* had a number-one-hit! – photo-shootings, letters from fans, touring ... - all these things that had been going on before, and hadn't made him happy.

Speculation from fans like "he felt that they weren't at the same level," or "he wanted to have control over the music, and the others weren't the right partners for his

---

[122] Taken from: A Clean Break, Smash Hits, 21 January – 3 February 1982. Words: Mark Ellen.
[123] Taken from: The Story Of Depeche Mode, BBC Radio London Live94.9, 7 May 2001, Producer: Tony Wood.
[124] Taken from: The Bright Side of the Moon, Sounds, 4 September 1982. Words: Karen Swayne
[125] Taken from: Violator, Alligator, NME, 7 July 1990. Words: Jeff Giles.

plans," probably hit the spot much better. Maybe he felt that "the band was moving into another direction (although they were too shy to tell him directly.)"

He once said that "Martin is a genius but he doesn't know it." Maybe he was anxious that Martin was the better songwriter, and would replace him silently in the course of time.

Many years later Dave told a story about that there was someone who promised a golden future for Vince while he disqualified the rest of the band. To Dave it seemed as if a little light went on in Vince's head, that he could do it all himself, without compromising. All he needed was a singer and someone to perform on-stage with him. It's just another theory, but one that would suit.

It's interesting that only 32% of the fans see Vince's role as "crucial because there would be no *DM* without him" while 21% are "very glad that he's gone because otherwise *DM* would never have become what they are today."

So maybe it was a good thing that they refused when Vince offered to write songs for *DM* later on. (Something that is also strange: Why did he still want to write songs for them, but didn't want to be in the band anymore?) He offered two new songs to them, one of them was *Only You*, the later number-one-hit of *Yazoo*, but the band thought they were terrible.

In **December** *DM* were looking for a stage-musician to replace Vince at gigs. "After various other bands like *The Hitmen*," **Alan** said, "I was in my customary state – broke, bored and leafing through the classifieds in the *Melody Maker*, I saw an ad which said, 'Known Band seek synth player. Must be under 21'."[126] He didn't like the music of *DM* at all, as he said later, and it was clear to him that it could be only *DM* because he had heard about Vince's leaving. Nevertheless, he went to the rehearsal and lied about his age (he was 22 at this time) – "because I needed the money."[127]

Daniel Miller met the applicants first and reduced them to about five people, some of them real *DM* fans. Then the band had an audition at the *Blackwing Studios*.

---

[126] Taken from: Alan Wilder: The Band Boy, No. 1, 25 May 1985. Words: Alan Wilder.
[127] Taken from: recoil.co.uk. Words: Alan Wilder.

"Alan is a really great classically trained musician", **Fletch** said, "and we went, 'what you have to do, you play this little one ... *de de de* but the hardest thing, you have to sing this as well.' We were going, 'what, that's amazing, in two seconds he's done that!' It was really funny."[128]

Daniel Miller wasn't that enthusiastic about **Alan** at first. "I think Daniel felt I was overqualified with my classical background ... that I could play, y'know, complicated pieces on the piano, and *Depeche Mode* was born on the punk move really."[129]

Instead, Miller had a liking for another guy, but the band preferred Alan. There were some discussions and a second rehearsal although time was tight. There were already plans for a tour.

"I went to two auditions before landing the job.[130] It was quite a shock, because at the time they were using three of the smallest synths you could find. At my audition, Martin had a little *Yamaha CS5*, Fletch was on a *Moog Source*, and I was given a *Moog Prodigy*. We all played one-note riffs," **Alan** laughed, "and I have to admit I felt a little bit naked without more keyboards around me.[131] I thought they were a bit wimpy – understandable at the time. On the other hand they were charming and friendly and the music was simple. I could appreciate that.[132] Therefore I decided to stay with them a couple of months."[133] It's well-known that these months turned into years and probably *DM* wrote a couple of songs Alan liked within this time. ;)

In addition, *See You* was recorded in **December 1981** - just with the remaining three band members, without Alan, but with Daniel Miller as producer.

Up to this point the band's story is not that spectacular. You find this in almost every band biography: Some lads get together, make music, start a band, are lucky enough to get a record contract, one of the founding mem-

---

[128] Taken from: The Story Of Depeche Mode, BBC Radio London Live94.9, 7 May 2001, Producer: Tony Wood.
[129] Taken from: Videointerview (DLCTrading) 2010
[130] Taken from: Alan Wilder: The Band Boy, No. 1, 25 May 1985. Words: Alan Wilder.
[131] Taken from: Unsound Recordings, Sound On Sound, January 1998. Words: Bill Bruce.
[132] Taken from: Alan Wilder: The Band Boy, No. 1, 25 May 1985. Words: Alan Wilder.
[133] Taken from: recoil.co.uk. Words: Alan Wilder.

bers leaves, and someone else joins. Having once worked for a music magazine for a while, I've read the same story a hundred times. And of course later in the story there are also many analogies with other bands - but you seldom find a truly independent band becoming that successful, and there are also some other unique points in the history of *DM* that will feature in this biography.

1982

- My secret garden is not so secret anymore -

In the **middle of January** (unfortunately, no one seems to remember the exact date) Alan had his first gig with *DM* at *Crocs* in Raleigh. The band commented on Alan that "he's a good musician, though they're not certain that's what they needed. He was somewhat shaken by the mayhem surrounding *Depeche* as crushed kids in the front row were plucked out of their very shoes to save them from severe damage."[134]

Remember that this happened just about one year after they'd started! They were really a hip boy-band, especially loved by young girls, whereas people who used to come before didn't come anymore.

Fletch was a bit worried about this trend. "When you go for the teenage market, in a couple of years the teenagers will be grown up and they'll forget you."[135]

Sometimes they had to play special early gigs because most of these girls were too young to go to a gig later in the evening, and because they were playing places that were mostly over 18. The band felt it was only fair to let the people that were buying their records to see them.

On **22 and 23 January**, the band played at the club *Ritz* in New York. It was the first time they played a gig in the U.S., and it wasn't one of their best experiences.

---

[134] Taken from: No Time to Even Think, New Sounds New Styles, March 1982. Words: Mike Stand.
[135] Taken from: Andy Fletcher interview, Electric Sleeve Notes, May 1982. Words: David Martin.

"Alan came to New York – I remember, it was so funny," **Fletch** said. "He had a little jacket on and a woolly scarf and I think New York was minus 40 degrees."[136]

Dave appeared with an arm in the loop. He had had a tattoo removed and the scars swelled up. The rest of this mini-tour wasn't much better. They had done *TOTP* the night before, and then were sent over on *Concorde*. So it was quite exhausting. Besides, none of their equipment worked, and they got on stage very late. These weren't the only difficulties they had when they tried to find their way on the American market and it would take some time until they became really big there.

When Alan was engaged as a stage musician, the media wasn't interested in him at first. It was Vince who had the attention - although he wasn't there anymore.

"He presents you with riddles, things you can't explain," **Martin** said, and **Fletch** remarked: "The impression he likes to give is that no-one knows him."

"We thought we knew him, but we discovered we didn't," **Dave** said.

"Vince always wanted to do a lot in the studio and the rest of us would feel restricted," **Fletch** explained. "If we had an idea we'd be frightened to say anything."

Dave disagreed, "No, not frightened. We were uncomfortable."[137]

Now Martin was writing the songs, and they tried to produce songs with more substance and more difficult chords. Sometimes it was difficult for them to ignore the fact that they had lost their main songwriter. On the other hand, they had to admit that they didn't understand Vince's lyrics at all.

Dave remembered, "Walking through town in Basildon one night and I saw these two girls following along behind me. I knew they'd recognised me. And they start singing, y'know," (high-pitched squeak), "*I stand still stepping on a shady street.* And I start walking a bit faster," he laughed, "turns me collar up like this! And then ...," he wailed, " *And I watch that man to a stranger.* And I'm thinking: 'oh no, this is embarrassing! Do they understand these lyr-

---

[136] Taken from: The Story Of Depeche Mode, BBC Radio London Live94.9, 7 May 2001, Producer: Tony Wood.
[137] Taken from: No Time to Even Think, New Sounds New Styles, March 1982. Words: Mike Stand.

ics?! Perhaps they do and we don't!'"[138] (The lyrics belong to *New Life*.)

The media wouldn't make it easy for **Martin**. "We have problems with the rock press: they don't like us, it's too nice, too cute. It was not aggressive enough for their taste and it is true: *Depeche Mode* is not a malicious group. I bet that if you swung a glass of beer at the head of our interviewers, they would write twice about us."[139]

Today we know him as a genius writer, but he was thrown in at the deep end in the early days when *See You / Now, This is Fun* was released on **29 January**. Most people in the media and among their fans expected something like *Speak & Spell*. Most other bands would have gone swiftly downhill after losing the main songwriter. It was difficult for *DM*, but they were lucky that people didn't lose interest in them. I think it was also part of the zeitgeist. In the **early 1980s**, Europeans were really up for minimalist electronic music and were open for musical experiments.

By the way, the music video for *See You* was directed by Julian Temple. The first part of the video was filmed at *Hounslow* railway station in London.

We'd sit on a bench for a while (See You) (© Ingo Bittrich)

---

[138] Taken from: A Clean Break, Smash Hits, 21 January – 3 February 1982. Words: Mark Ellen.
[139] Taken from: Chronique Just Can't Get Enough et See You, January 1982, Best N°174. Words: Gerard Bar-David.

"After *New Life* a lot of people thought *Depeche Mode* were 'sweet' and 'cute' and everything," **Fletch** said, "and we wanted to show them we could be a lot of other things as well. On the new B-side, *Now, This is Fun* we tried to ...," he paused while they all bursted out laughing, "we tried to sound ... really ... mean! Didn't work though."[140]

The understanding of the new lyrics didn't work that properly either. So **Martin** was asked about the meaning of the line *Well, I know that five years is a long time and that times change but I think you'll find people are basically the same* from *See You*. "It's good. Serious. But funny. I like it because those words aren't used much in songs. It's just the things people say. I can't tell the story behind it. It's private. I wrote it when I was 18."[141] The age detail is different in each source, 15, 17 etc.

"My style of writing has changed since I started writing more seriously. Sometimes I write the words first, sometimes the music, sometimes both together. I have to lock myself away. The thing is a lot of ideas I come up with are embarrassing so you have to be on your own when you come up with them!"[142] *See You* isn't as instant as the earlier singles, so we thought a lot of our old fans wouldn't buy it. It's also full of musical references to people like the *Ronettes* and the *Beach Boys*. I know they're not very fashionable at the moment, but everybody knows their earlier songs, and we used to do *And Then I Kissed Her* as a live cover version."

"Two years ago *See You* probably wouldn't have been a hit," **Dave** added, "but the radio has been getting more adventurous. I think punk made all that possible. After punk, you could do anything."[143]

Some of their early appearances on TV, performing the new songs, were also quite adventurous. "We arrived on time, at 12 o'clock," **Dave** told about a French TV show, "but there were no cameras or crew. We went to have a bite to eat then returned at three o'clock. They told us

---

[140] Taken from: A Clean Break, Smash Hits, 21 January – 3 February 1982. Words: Mark Ellen.
[141] Taken from: No Time to Even Think, New Sounds New Styles, March 1982. Words: Mike Stand.
[142] Taken from: Some people think you're cute, but other people think you're slightly vile ..., Look In, 22 May 1982, Words: Phil Parsons.
[143] Taken from: A La Mode, Kicks, 6 April 1982. Words: Johnny Black.

they wanted us to record six songs. They took about three hours to do the first song. The second song took slightly less and the third song took about an hour. By the time we came to the fifth song it was 11.30 pm and since the studio lights were due to be turned off at midnight they had to film it in next to no time. The camera man was jumping about all over the place trying to get us into shot. We didn't have time to do the sixth song because the caretaker turned the lights off."[144]

And **Alan** on his first appearance at *TOTP*, performing *See You*, "It was an all-day affair, mainly spent hanging around in our dressing room while the union-led *BBC* staff took their various tea, lunch and back-strain breaks. The audience consisted of about 15 people being goaded with cattle-prods to move them swiftly around the studio from stage to stage. We had the dubious honour of appearing on the same show as one-hit-wonder Adrian Gurwitz. The lyrics of his unforgettable tunes were as follows *gonna write a classic, gonna write it in an attic ...*"

It's not surprising that he didn't like the video for *See You* (nor any of the other videos which were made in **1982**.) "You can pretty much lump all the Julian Temple videos (*See You, Meaning of Love, Leave in Silence*) into one collective disaster. But you should not forget that video was a very new and experimental genre at that time so we weren't the only ones to suffer at the hands of spotty students fresh out of film school."[145]

The *See You*-Tour started in Cardiff on **12 February** - with Alan as a stage musician. The European leg, which comprised 27 gigs, ended on **12 April** in St. Peter Port. Among other cities, *DM* played in Madrid, Stockholm, Hamburg, Berlin - and in Oberkorn in Luxembourg. Thus it happened that on **26 April** the single *The Meaning of Love / Oberkorn (It's a Small Town)* was released.

"Oberkorn was a curious kind of village with a population that would hardly fill the first few rows of any ordinary theatre so it was quite a fascination for us to find out what was going to happen," **Martin** said. "Instead of our gig being a handful of people, the place was packed as the audience came from all around and even from across the

---

[144] Taken from: Welcome to the Working Week - 7 Days In The Life of Dave 'Have A Banana' Gahan of Depeche Mode, Flexipop, June 1986. Words: Dave Gahan.
[145] Taken from: recoil.co.uk. Words: Alan Wilder.

borders. When we got back to our hotel our record company told us that whilst the A-side of our single was all set, they need a title rapidly for the B-side. Like I said we're never all that good on names and the first thing that sprang to mind was the name of this village. Oberkorn."[146]

The video for *The Meaning of Love* was directed by Julian Temple again, and again, the band didn't like it at all. It's really an embarrassing video with the band acting like some kind of magicians. It's only bested by the video for *Leave in Silence*, when the band members smashed vegetables and other things on a treadmill and jumped around on big balls, their faces painted in different colours; and of course, by the backdrop and setting of a German TV show in which the band members were forced to hold live hens in their arms while performing *See You*.

The American leg, comprising 8 concerts, took place from **7 to 18 May**. Even at this stage, *DM* played in Pasadena - but not at the *Rosebowl*.

On his first tour with the band, **Alan** had the opportunity to get used to *DM*'s early live set and wasn't fond of it. "I have had the dubious pleasure of actually performing *Television Set*. I'm also familiar with *Tomorrow's Dance* although I've never played or heard an actual performance of the song. Dave's rendition / impersonation of the embryonic *DM* performances were enough to have left an indelible imprint on my musical memory."

Strange but true, there were really some songs **Alan** liked. "*Tora, Tora, Tora* is my favourite from *Speak & Spell*, *The Sun and the Rainfall* from *A Broken Frame*."

Alan, of course, also had the opportunity to get to know his new band mates a bit better. "Fletch and Martin have a quite strange relationship. The main role of Fletch seems to be Martin's voice because Martin is very shy - unless he's drunk. If he has a problem you can't ask him directly but you have to talk with Fletch." So two groups quickly formed within the band – Martin and Fletch on the one hand, and Alan and Dave on the other – because Dave also had little place in the friendship between Fletch and Martin, and because "Dave's a very friendly and open per-

---

[146] Taken from: The Name's the Game! Zig Zag, November 1982. Words: John Kercher.

son, and easy to get along with. He has a very sharp and wicked sense of humour."

In this context **Alan** once said that it was fun to see those female fans who think "he's sort of this poor little fluffy bunny-wunny who needs to be protected all the time. If these girls ever met Dave for more than two minutes after a show, or if they came on with this attitude, he'd eat them alive with a few chosen words."[147]

Allegedly, Alan had huge problems adapting himself to the band. This is stressed particularly in one biography, and the different social backgrounds - working class and middle class – are emphasised. Of course, this makes a difference in British society, especially in the generation the four lads belong to. But in my opinion, it is wrong to say that THIS was the problem. The real problems seemed to be a) that English men of this generation aren't able to talk about their feelings and thoughts in general, and this group had communication problems in particular and b) that the others, especially Martin and Fletch, had known each other for a long time before Alan became a member.

It is also definitely wrong to say that Alan was not adaptable. He was self-confident enough, and had the knack of being able to adapt himself to every situation, wherever and whenever, giving the impression that he was part of the given picture and master of the situation, anytime, anywhere. Have a look at the promotion shots of the bands Alan had been a member of before joining *DM*, and then have a look at pictures of *DM* taken in **1982**. You will find Alan looking serious, grown up, cool and even acceptably dressed on shots with *Real To Real* and *The Hitmen*, but looking as shy and as "cute" as his new band members in **1982** - and dressed in the ugliest clothes you could find on the planet. ;) And there are enough videos from the early days showing him joking around with the others. It's also known that he was very fond of Dave's parodies.

Maybe there had been some teething troubles in the first year - as happens to everyone who is new at a company / school / group - and he probably had (as he said himself) some problems "integrating" himself "fully into what was (and still is) a very tight unit" (which is probably

---

[147] Taken from: recoil.co.uk. Words: Alan Wilder.

referring to the close friendship between Martin and Fletch) but I think it's exaggerated to suggest he was never a real part of this band, something some people still believe today.

At this point I would like to explain that my main personal ambition in writing this biography was to find an answer to the question why Alan finally left the band in **1995**, and why it seems to be impossible to reintegrate him in the band today.

Every reader will probably have one answer in mind and will say, "hey, he left because ...," but you will see that it isn't that easy. When I asked this question in the survey at *depechemodebiographie.de* I got **26 (!)** different answers! And reading through message-boards you will find a lot of theories as well, some of them put forward as irrevocable truth, e.g. like the one above, "Alan left because he had never been a real part of the band and felt like an outsider." Well, if he had felt unwelcome from the beginning, he would have left the band after the *Broken Frame*-Tour, and would have refused to become a full member.

I have a theory that has evolved over the course of time, based on all the available information, that can sometimes be quite contradictory – probably the reason why almost every fan has a different view about why Alan left the band.

My theory is simply that it came to a point when the team didn't work anymore. Teamwork is always difficult, no matter if it concerns a company, a project or a band. Each member of the team needs a specific task, has to fit into the whole picture, and "deliver" his part regularly, exactly and punctually. Everyone has to rely on everybody else. These tasks needn't necessarily have anything to do with the creative process itself. It can also mean organising something, or being responsible for a good equilibrium, or a good team-spirit. As long as each member works in the way he or she is supposed to, the team will work, no matter whether the members like each other personally. But as soon as something no longer fits, the whole thing is inevitably going to crumble.

I think the friendship between the band members is overstated. You don't need to be friends to play in a band together or work on a project generally. Martin and Fletch definitely were and are friends, but they weren't and aren't good friends with Dave. They don't see each other much outside the band, simply because they have different interests. Also Dave and Alan are quite different - they were buddies, but probably no real friends.

When a project is as interesting and as successful as *DM*, you don't need to be good friends at all to work on it together. But of course, when there are personal differences, it is "easier" to spoil the whole thing at a certain point – mostly when additional problems arise: musical differences, or different working methods. I'll come back to this later, because at that point, in **summer 1982**, the team hadn't started working together.

Even though Alan, a trained musician, became part of the band, Martin, Fletch and Dave decided to record the next album on their own and went into the studio (*Blackwing Studios* in London) in **July** together with Daniel Miller and the engineers John Fryer and Eric Radcliffe. On the one hand, **Alan** was a bit frustrated, "I had been on tour with them and they expected from me to promote the new album with them", on the other hand, he understood, "They were very carefully because of me. They blamed Vince that he had left and had the feeling they must prove him that they could go on without him. I think it was a question of pride and they didn't want someone to think they just get someone new at the 'transfer market'. They were very self-critical and little self-confident. I had never met such a band before and I wondered how they had come so far in such a short time. Then it got clear to me which great influence Daniel Miller had on them. He and Vince were it who had taken them there."[148]

He probably was quite right here. Some journalists also suspected Daniel Miller of manipulating the band in some way.

"Daniel's like a friend really," **Dave** tried to explain. "It's not like a business relationship. He comes everywhere with us. In the studio he doesn't actually take part in the recording apart from the producing."

"He advises us what to do, but we find it hard to say no, so in a way he manipulates us,"[149] **Fletch** admitted.

---

[148] Taken from: recoil.co.uk. Words: Alan Wilder.
[149] Taken from: Sound of the Suburbs, NME, 20 March 1982. Words: Lynn Hanna.

"In a way, Daniel acts as our manager, because we don't actually have one," **Dave** said. "He's also the head of our record company though, so he can't do everything that a manager would. We have group meetings to discuss tours, money and things like merchandising."[150]

The band claimed it had been their decision to go into the studio without Alan. According to rumours, there had been some trouble between the band members and Alan because of this decision, but **Alan** said, "I would have liked to have been involved in the studio for that album but was told by Daniel Miller (the band have never spoken to me about it) that I wouldn't be needed."[151]

On **16 August** the single *Leave in Silence* was released, followed by the album *A Broken Frame* on **27 September**. *Leave in Silence* was the band's first single in the UK with the *Bong* label on it (*Bong* No. 1).

In those days they found that *A Broken Frame* was more mature concerning the music and the lyrics. They put a lot of time and effort into every single song and tried to explore new ways of recording. They used a lot of percussion, walking and marching sounds and sampled different instruments like a saxophone which was recorded backwards.

"The new album has the same sort of weight really," **Dave** said. "Rather than doing more of the light weight pop we decided to experiment in the studio. Martin can write poppy things as well, there's a couple of poppy tracks on the album like *The Meaning of Love* and there's one called *A Photograph of You* but we also wanted to do something really different to see if we could do it and I think it has turned out well."[152]

Later they wouldn't be so satisfied with this album anymore. (The same with *Speak & Spell*.) But considering their age, their background and their story so far, they probably had to record this album exactly as it is.

The *Broken Frame*-Tour started on **4 October** in Chippenham.

---

[150] Taken from: A La Mode, Kicks, 6 April 1982. Words: Johnny Black.
[151] Taken from: recoil.co.uk. Words: Alan Wilder.
[152] Taken from: Modey Old Dough, unknown magazine, 1982. Words: Bill Prince.

Despite all success, it was a tough time for the band. They still weren't taken seriously by the media and general public, and they still didn't manage to get rid of the image of the *New Romantics* and *Futurists*.

"Obviously the sort of people who buy *Duran Duran* or *Spandau Ballet* records might buy ours as well," **Dave** said, "but I think we're in a slightly different market. There's not so many *New Romantics* in our audience as their used to be. I mean we've done about thirty interviews – mostly in Europe –[153] and we are still asked about *New Romanticism* and *Futurism*. We tell them that we have nothing to do with this.[154] And then they go and print this right next to these awful photos of us in frilly shirts! That was from the first photo session we ever had done and they were so bad! They keep turning up all over the place."

"That is why we'll never be like *Duran Duran*," **Martin** chipped in. "'Cos our photos are so awful!"[155]

Next to the known problems some new ones arrived. They had the impression that the audience didn't listen to them anymore or didn't seem to care whether they made mistakes or not. They had become an event. Time seemed to run shorter and shorter. They had to plan six months ahead, and they began to wonder what good it actually did.

"What's happened is we've become more and more busy and less and less involved with all the small decisions which affect us", **Fletch** said. "When you've got enough money you end up giving it to someone else and saying 'Do this for us'."[156]

Another problem they had to face now was the fame.

"There was a thing in the *Sun* reviewing our single and it said, 'another record by a faceless group'," **Fletch** said. "I think people who read music papers might know about us, but the general public couldn't put a face to the name. People say, 'what's it like to be famous?' But there's no difference. When I walk along in Basildon they might rec-

---

[153] Taken from: A Clean Break, Smash Hits, 21 January – 3 February 1982. Words: Mark Ellen.
[154] Source can't be found anymore
[155] Taken from: A Clean Break, Smash Hits, 21 January – 3 February 1982. Words: Mark Ellen.
[156] Taken from: No Time to Even Think, New Sounds New Styles, March 1982. Words: Mike Stand.

ognise me, but if I go up to London and walk along the *King's Road*, I wouldn't be recognised."

"I think it's better not to be hip, it's definitely safer," **Dave** guessed. "We don't go clubbing it in London or anything. I don't know how bands can do that. They're touring the world and they've got records out every week. They must be so tired.[157] There was this time when I did a personal appearance at the *Camden Palace* and I was practically pulled apart. It was really scary, when I got inside I was trapped and there were people clawing at me, ripping my clothes, pulling my hair – I was so frightened I ran and hid myself in the loo, I just didn't want to come out. I think that was one of my worst experiences, those kids could kill you."[158]

They tried to keep both feet on the ground and tried not to become a liggers band. But they lost touch with many old friends and had to learn to differentiate between real friends and false friends.

"You know when you talk to them and when you're out with them, they don't see you as a different person," **Dave** explained. "But then you get some of them who weren't really your proper friends when you began and then they become your real big friends when you're successful."

"I think there were about 10,000 people who used to go to school with you," **Fletch** said.

"Yeah, the class must have about 1,000 people in it according to some people," **Dave** confirmed. "There were only 40. You think you're going mad when people say they were at school with you and you can't remember them."[159]

It got increasingly difficult to have a private life. Dave's girlfriend Jo[anne] gave up her job as a nurse, and ran the fan club, together with Martin's girlfriend Anne, who had just finished school. They also accompanied the band on every tour.

The band called this "luxury." I personally think that it offers a basis for an "excellent" conflict potential.

---

[157] Taken from: Sound of the Suburbs, NME, 20 March 1982. Words: Lynn Hanna.
[158] Taken from: The Bright Side of the Moon, Sounds, 4 September 1982. Words: Karen Swayne.
[159] Taken from: Essex Appeal, Record Mirror, 21 August 1982. Words: Simon Tebbutt.

"Although I reckon it's fair to say that when we first took the girls they took a while to adjust to the fan reaction," **Dave** admitted. "That was funny really, because our girls also run our fan information service so you'd figure on them knowing what to expect. But the reality of hundreds of girls trying to rush us and kiss us was a bit too much! It seems to be Alan the girls are attracted to. We don't mind him shouldering that responsibility!"[160]

While the others had given up asking for the name of everyone who wanted their autographs, Alan, who was still a "part-time Mode" at that time, still did it. This, and the fact that he was pretty handsome, was the reason why most of the girls were screaming for him.

And they still tried to find an image for themselves – or to have no image at all.

"The band with the best image of all is *Pink Floyd*, they're a really faceless group," **Fletch** said. "I mean I don't really like their music, but although they're one of the world's biggest bands if you saw Brian Waters ..."

Dave interrupted him, "Roger Waters you idiot."

"Oh yeah, well that's what I mean, they're really anonymous," **Fletch** said.

Dave thought that, "it's much better to have some kind of design. The new LP sleeve is really good, much better than the last one, that was awful! The guy who did it, Brian Griffin, when he was explaining it he was going, 'I imagine a swan floating in the air', and we're going, 'yeah, right', then he's talking about it floating on this sea of glass and it sounded really great. It turned out to be a stuffed swan in a plastic bag! It was meant to be all nice and romantic, but it was just comical!"[161]

Nevertheless, Brian Griffin took several other photos for album- and singles-covers, so the *Speak & Spell*-cover couldn't have been that bad – or they were too shy to tell him that they didn't like it. However, according to polls, most fans think that the *Speak & Spell*-cover isn't the worst one *DM* has ever had.

So there was a lot they had to learn. And they had to learn it quickly. "We realise **1982**'s the most important

---

[160] Taken from: The Name's the Game! Zig Zag, November 1982. Words: John Kercher.
[161] Taken from: The Bright Side of the Moon, Sounds, 4 September 1982. Words: Karen Swayne.

year for us," **Fletch** summed it up. "We either establish ourselves or go to pot."¹⁶²

I can't stand this emotional violence, leave in silence.
(© Ingo Bittrich)

Here are two bits with hindsight to the future:

Fletch showed the first symptoms of his depressive vein which was to have serious consequences later: "I get depressed, on tour especially, because I've got quite a lot of friends at home, and I miss keeping up on the gossip and all that. I've lost a lot of friends because I can't talk to them; we've always told each other what we're doing, but now it's a case of well, we flew to Spain and did a TV thing, we're going on tour ... I feel really guilty, and I can't talk about what I'm doing 'cos all I'm doing is the band.

---

¹⁶² Taken from: A Clean Break, Smash Hits, 21 January – 3 February 1982. Words: Mark Ellen.

But I think more than them, really. Well, I worry. I'm more depressing."
Laughter all round. Don't you mean depressed?
Alan: "Both, probably."[163]

The next one isn't that serious, but it is one of those things that show how people change over a period of time, also due to the circumstances of their lifestyle.

"We're not the kind who enjoy partying it up every other night or travelling to clubs," **Martin** said. "Most of the time when we're not working we tend to stay at our parents' places in our home town. We all feel that it's essential to have this firm home base, because otherwise you tend to find yourselves leading a very insular existence, only mixing with people in the music business, and that isn't really good for your mind or your lifestyle. I can't see us changing. We've no desire to move up to the bright lights of London."[164]

According to Martin (especially when you look at the lyrics of *See You*) people basically stay the same. This applies to the (former) band members quite nicely. All of them still have "this firm home base," and in essence they are still just normal people. Today all of them are family men, and they have never really mixed with people from the music business. But the fans, of course, know that the part with the "enjoying partying it up every other night or travelling to clubs" would change drastically in the following years.

At the end of the year, Alan was declared as a full member and future plans were made. **Martin** explained that they had decided to record *A Broken Frame* without Alan because they wanted to make certain that any change in direction in their music wasn't attributable to Alan joining. "We needed to show we were capable of musical alteration by ourselves. So we recorded *A Broken Frame* with that in mind, although Alan will be playing on our tours when we perform songs from the album. Now we feel free for him to be a full time recording member of the

---

[163] Taken from: On The Mode, Record Mirror, 20 March 1982. Words: Sunie.
[164] Taken from: The Name's the Game! Zig Zag, November 1982. Words: John Kercher.

group now that the change in pattern has been established!"[165]

Well, the real development began with *Construction Time Again*, and Martin would reconsider the "established change."

"I don't blame the others for being cautious about me, after what happened with Vince,"[166] **Alan** said. "Somebody in their position doesn't get somebody new in the first week who might turn out to be a complete a***h***. So I was touring and doing TV but wasn't actually recording with them."[167]

In **1987** he said, "They were a very tight-knit bunch, and it took me quite a while to become one of them. Between **1982 and '83** I was never sure if I was in or out until one day Fletch just told me I was a full-time member."[168] (In a different source he is quoted that Daniel Miller told him.)

---

[165] Taken from: The Name's the Game! Zig Zag, November 1982. Words: John Kercher.
[166] Taken from: A La Mode, Kicks, 6 April 1982. Words: Johnny Black.
[167] Taken from: Hanging in the Balance, NME, 26 March 1983. Words: Matt Snow.
[168] Taken from: Depeche Mode Magazine, Circuit Communications, 1987. Words: Mike Martin.

1983

- Lots of surprised in store (More Than a Party) -

In **January**, DM went into the studio together with Alan for the first time. They worked with the sound engineers Eric Radcliffe and John Fryer at *Blackwing Studios* in London. The result was released on **31 January** - the single *Get the Balance Right / The Great Outdoors! Get the Balance Right* was not included on the following album *Construction Time Again*, but does appear on the American compilation *People Are People* and the compilation *The Singles 81-85*.

The single's B-side *The Great Outdoors!*, an instrumental track written by Martin and Alan, featured on the *Broken Frame*-Tour as the introduction theme on selected shows. The single reached No. 13 in the UK charts. The 12" of *Get the Balance Right* was geared towards the clubs and marked some kind of new era in this field.

First the band, of course, tried to say something positive about their new single.

"I think *Get the Balance Right* is a lot harder, more powerful and more direct," **Martin** said. "It's quite moody, too. I think our new material's going to be more to the point, about more general topics that everyone can relate to rather than having more personal lyrics."[169]

"*Get the Balance Right* is about telling people to go their own way," **Dave** explained. "It also takes a dig at people who like to be different just for the sake of it. You've just got to reach the right balance between normality and insanity."[170]

Later it became clear that they weren't happy about *Get the Balance Right*. Especially **Alan** was very self-critical. "I don't think I made a great deal of difference. I probably made it worse."

"Well, that is actually our least favourite single," **Martin** said. "It was hell to record.[171] Things have been going

---

[169] Taken from: Modes to Freedom, Record Mirror, 22 January 1983. Words: Betty Page.
[170] Taken from: Depeche Mode - Nearly There, Smash Hits, 3-16 March 1983. Words: Peter Martin.
[171] Taken from: Everything Counts (in Large Amounts), Number One, 19 October 1985. Words: Paul Bursche.

pretty badly for us press-wise recently – it had to come. It's no surprise, just a bit annoying, especially when there's a lot of people who used to like you and for some reason they suddenly don't. Before, you couldn't do anything wrong, now you can't do one thing right."[172]

The video for *Get the Balance Right* was one of their strange ones. Not at least because **Alan** appeared singing at the beginning of the video. "This was because the director didn't actually know who the singer of the band was and for some reason made the assumption that it was me. As an indication of our naivety, we were too embarrassed to point out his mistake."[173]

After a trip to the musicfair in Frankfurt, Germany, on **7 February**, the band went on the last leg of the *Broken Frame*-Tour from **24 March** to **10 April**, comprising 11 concerts in North America and later in Asia - in Tokyo, Hong Kong and Bangkok.

"The Japan trip has really come out of the blue," **Dave** said. "We've never been before but we sell loads of records over there so we thought it would be best to go over there and do some gigs."[174]

In Asia they were considered very hip and were welcomed by many excited fans at the International airports. Asia also had a big influence on the songs that Martin wrote at that time.

"When you see things that are poorer than you've ever seen," **Dave** explained, "when we saw people begging and little kids coming up to us with disgusting, dirty clothes hanging off them, showing themselves or holding their hands out for food ... When you experience that, you begin to understand what a lucky position all of us here are in. We were in this really expensive hotel full of businessmen, but as soon as you went outside the gates, it was a totally different world."[175]

Later that year the media was busily assigning *DM* a "working class background" because of their lyrics, and

---

[172] Taken from: Modes to Freedom, Record Mirror, 22 January 1983. Words: Betty Page.
[173] Taken from: recoil.co.uk. Words: Alan Wilder. / depechemode-biographie.de.
[174] Taken from: Poppix, 1982. Words: Uncredited.
[175] Taken from: Coming up Smiling, The Face, February 1985. Words: Sheryl Garratt.

writing about the band's "socialist ambitions" and their "world improvement thinking," For years, the band tried to ditch that image – albeit rather unsuccessfully, and tried to explain that Construction Time Again wasn't a "political album," and that the lyrics were only written because of these new impressions.

"I think the politically conscious aspects of *DM*'s early songs were more to do with age than any great desire to make a statement," **Alan** said. "We were hardly Billy Bragg. We never had a collective political view. We all had different ideas on most things (despite our backgrounds) and apart from the tracks on Construction Time Again, I think you'd be hard pressed to find anything else that was directly politically motivated."

In **May**, recording of Construction Time Again began in John Foxx's Garden Studios in London, together with Daniel Miller and Gareth Jones. As a result of the new band constellation, Fletch was now more involved with the organisation, while Alan took over most of the musical tasks. It was the beginning of the team-work. Everyone was trying to find their place in the team and fulfil a particular role.

Contrary to some opinions that there were difficulties due to Alan's role in the studio from the very beginning, **Alan** maintained, "I had no problem getting involved - the others weren't particularly precious about the studio. The most protective person was actually Daniel Miller who very much controlled the studio direction at that time." Sampling technology was also new, at which they were supported by sound engineer Gareth Jones, who encouraged them to create an industrial-sound.

"*Construction Time Again* also marked the introduction of *Emulator* and *Synclavier*," **Alan** said, "and I think it marked a turning point in *DM*'s musical history. It was a very creative time.[176] There's a track called *Pipeline* on the album. It's got a lot of strange percussion in it. What we did was to just go out and start banging on anything we could find."[177]

"We were like smashing corrugated iron and old cars," **Fletch** added. "The vocals were recorded in a railway arch

---

[176] Taken from: recoil.co.uk. Words: Alan Wilder.
[177] Taken from: New Life, No.1, 13 August 1983. Words: Paul Bursche.

in Shoreditch - you've got the train three-quarters of the way through and the aeroplane up above. It's really interesting doing that."[178]

It has hinted that at this first collective recording session, it became clear that their characters were very different. While Alan was more a part of the serious side - Miller and Jones - and tried to learn as much as possible about the technology, it is said that Fletch and Martin joked around a lot and played the fool, while Fletch and Dave were arguing the whole time.

Admittedly I have to say that this description seems exaggerated to me. There is a quote from Alan about it, but it seems to me as if it was taken from a different or a greater context. It gives the impression of three serious hard-working grown-ups, who felt disturbed by three children playing very loudly around them. I don't think that this really reflects what actually happened. Videos from that time depict a relaxed atmosphere, but don't give the impression that Fletch, Martin and Dave NEVER did a thing in the studio.

Gareth Jones also gave a slightly different impression, with regard to the relationships and working methods, "Daniel [Miller] did a lot of hands-on crafting of those sounds, as did Martin and Alan, who was also a major production figure within the band. Alan was extremely involved in the crafting of the studio product; a full-on, very musical guy, very interested in beats programming, and very interested in every aspect of the studio. So, there was a trio of us all the time in the studio, with Alan representing the band, Daniel overseeing everything, and me taking care of the engineering side. After Martin had written a song, I think he considered it tedious to be endlessly playing around with synthesizers and making different versions. Maybe we were just too slow for him. Dave was very committed and hard-working and absolutely wanted to get it right. He wouldn't take part in the vocal comp'ing, because like many singers he found it a bit soul destroying. For him, as for most vocalists, it was like ripping his performance apart.[179]

---

[178] Taken from: Crushing The Wheels Of Industry, Meldody Maker, 7 January 1984, Words. Lynden Barber.
[179] Taken from: Article in Sound on Sound, February 2007. Words: Richard Buskin.

"When I worked with the band in the **80's**, everyone had a really good relationship. Alan was the new boy in the band obviously at *Construction Time Again*, but it was a wonderful creative time we all had. So, everyone was getting on really well. Of course, sometimes there would be an argument or something, but this is something normal in any relationship. There were some arguments between any of the group sometimes, me and Fletch had an argument at some stage, whatever, it wasn't a big deal. What I saw was a very creative and positive working relationship."[180]

Construction Time Again was the first album that was mixed at *Hansa Studios* in Berlin. With this, a period began which was to bring about a lot of change, and would connect *DM*'s history with Berlin pretty much up to now. There are still sometimes articles nowadays that mention the Berlin connection. It was also the kind of "birth" of the "real *DM*". At this point it might be good to give you some background information about the world the band grew up in – for readers from other cultures, and for those who are simply too young to know much about the **1970s** and **1980s**.

The band members themselves grew up in the England of the **1970s**. It was a harsh and very difficult decade in the UK. It was a decade of strikes - postal workers, coalminers and dustmen - many of the state industries were in trouble, and there was an ongoing struggle on the part of trade unions for better working and living conditions. Many factories, shipyards and coal mines were shut down, leaving lots of people without jobs. Northern England was especially hard-hit, but typical working class towns like Basildon were affected too.

Of course the bleak political backdrop was also a platform for strange fashion, strong musical attitudes and new sounds like *Glam Rock*, the punk movement and, finally, *New Wave* in the **beginning of the 1980s**. A lot of things changed around that time, but as well as a bringing a lot of problems, it also meant there were new experiences and even new opportunities for young people.

I think it's wrong to see the **1970s** as gloomily as some people do, or to see them too positively, like some other

---

[180] depechemodebiographie.de

people do. For the working class, it definitely was a difficult decade, and many towns – like Basildon – weren't able to offer much because of the economic depression. I've never been to Basildon myself, but I spent some time in British cities that had been hit hard by the crisis in the **1970s**, and still hadn't recovered from it in the **late 1980s**. They really were desolate, broke and boring, with nothing to do for young people, and without any perspectives for them. That's also how the band members described Basildon.

Apart from Alan, who had grown up in a middle class environment in London, the band members hadn't seen and didn't know about much of the world, until they left Basildon to play concerts abroad.

So West-Berlin must have been a kind of culture shock for them. In the **early 1980s**, West-Berlin was a kind of strange island, surrounded by the "No-Go Zone" of East Germany. The world still was in the middle of the so-called "Cold War," and was divided into the "Western world" and the "Eastern Bloc." The border between these two worlds was right in the middle of Germany – right in the middle of Berlin. West-Berlin was a magnet for artists of all kinds as well as for hippies, eco-fanatics, punks, activists and freaks. It was a kind of big village (with about 2 million inhabitants), on the other hand, it was a wild city with lots of places to go out.

It also had a lot to offer for the band, so it is probably not surprising that the Berlin connection was forged, although its beginnings were unspectacular.

Gareth Jones had worked at the *Hansa Studios* before and suggested to work there because the computer desk had 56 channels, something that was necessary for their work. Besides, they wanted to get a different atmosphere, wanted to work on a different place. So they went over and had a look at it.

In connection with this the question of the year was put forward: Did you visit the Berlin Wall?

"Well, we were recording right next to it," **Alan** replied. "You look out of the studio window and there it is. If you went out on the balcony you could actually see right over it."[181]

---

[181] Taken from: Enter the Countdown Mode, Record Mirror, 17 September 1983. Words: Sharon Machola.

When you know the background, it comes as no surprise that Berlin also represented a change in the personal lives of the band members. **Martin** especially, who speaks and understands German, felt very comfortable there. He left girlfriend Anne – "she was a devout Christian who really had me on reins. She was ridiculous - anything was perverted. If I watched something on TV and there was somebody naked, I was a pervert" – met his German girlfriend, Christina, and "discovered all this freedom."[182]

This "freedom" was to cause quite a sensation in the coming years. Some journalists at that time wondered about Martin's "sudden change." In **1982** he still looked like a well-behaved schoolboy, but by **1983** he had become "wild," and seemed to have changed completely. But I don't think it was a real surprise. He felt really bored in Basildon, and now a different world had opened up to him, that allowed him to act out all the feelings and tendencies he had had before, but hadn't been able to show in a place like Basildon.

The bridge belongs to "Berlin Hochbahn" that is seen in the video for Everything Counts *(© Ingo Bittrich)*

---

[182] Taken from: Just Can't Get Enough, Uncut, May 2001. Words: Stephen Dalton.

With *Everything Counts / Work Hard* the first hit single of the new quartet was released on **11 July**. It reached No. 6 of the UK charts. There was only one remix of *Everything Counts* available, the 12" version called *Everything Counts (In Larger Amounts)*. The single's B-side *Work Hard* was the first and only "real" song (except of some instrumental tracks and remixes) that was co-written by Martin and Alan. There was a remix of it available called *East End Remix*.

Everything Counts did not only mark a new musical era, the band also tried to create a new visual image (although it would take another three years before they wouldn't look "some kind of strange" anymore.) It was felt that after the Julian Temple years that they needed to harden up not only their sound but also their image. Clive Richardson who filmed the video for *Everything Counts* in and around West-Berlin had lots of new ideas which didn't involve storyboards, something the band appreciated.

Martin explained that *Everything Counts* is about companies that are getting so big and important that single persons have no meaning anymore and everyone can push them around. But usually he didn't like talking about his songs. "It's up to people to make of them what they want. A lot of people try and make me explain what every line means, but it takes away any sort of mystique."[183]

The album *Construction Time Again* was released on **22 August**. The title refers to the line *get out of the crane, construction time again* in the track *Pipeline*.

The cover photography was done by Brian Griffin featuring the Matterhorn and a friend of someone of the crew who was acting as the model. The overall design was done by Martyn Atkins.

The band was very proud of *Construction Time Again* and tried to explain that they had combined serious and alarming lyrics like the possibility of a nuclear war (*Two Minute Warning*), with a nice tune and simple melodies. They liked the idea of most people humming along to the melody without thinking about the meaning of the lyrics.

They claimed to have a unique sound now - which they truly had, which is nevertheless rather funny when you

---

[183] Taken from: Modes to Freedom, Record Mirror, 22 January 1983. Words: Betty Page.

know that they had talked about an "established change" before, if you listen to *A Broken Frame*. However, they felt much more self-confident about this new album than ever before, and had a lot of fun. It seems as if making this record also made them feel jettisoned.

"When I hear tracks from the first album, I get embarrassed," **Dave** said. "Though at the time we thought it was great. Then on the second album, it was very hard in the studio, people were letting us drift, there was a lack of enthusiasm ... but then with *Construction Time* it was very UP in the studio, everyone was really working to make it happen.[184] I think we're becoming tighter as a unit. I think it's a bond really, we just get on very well together and we enjoy what we're doing at the moment. As long as we keep enjoying it we'll keep doing it. As soon as we stop enjoying it, we won't stay together. I mean, sometimes I argue with Fletch, but it's not anything to do with the music we're making or the songs."[185]

On **7 September** the *Construction Time Again*-Tour began. It consisted of three legs. In between, on **19 September**, the single *Love, in Itself / Fools* was released.

About *Love, in Itself* **Dave** said, "This is the s-s-s-s's track. It had a very soft vocal with lots of s's, it sounded awful. I was a bit disappointed with this, it could have been brilliant."[186]

"Actually, it was a weird track all round," **Alan** said, "not least because from the moment we first heard it, a standing joke was born that the verses sounded just like a particular nursery rhyme - I can't quite put my finger on which one but I'm pretty sure it's *Ugly Duckling*. When pushed, Martin admitted that he had in fact based the tune around the rhyme and I'm afraid I could never quite listen to the song seriously again."

And about *Fools* he said, "It sounds like me when trying to write a pop song. This is something what doesn't come out of me normally. This is the reason why I then stopped writing songs for *DM*. I forced myself to try but it isn't easy

---

[184] Taken from: Red Rockers over the Emerald Isle, NME, 17 September 1983. Words: X. Moore.
[185] Taken from: Enter the Countdown Mode, Record Mirror, 17 September 1983. Words: Sharon Machola.
[186] Taken from: Everything Counts (in Large Amounts), Number One, 19 October 1985. Words: Paul Bursche.

for me to write lyrics for a pop song. I don't like this. Once I tried to make Martin to write songs together but he said he couldn't work that way. I think he suddenly has an idea for a song and then it's almost ready."[187]

I was asked several times if there are any songs Alan is singing. He sang some backing vocals (you can hear him well on *Everything Counts* e.g.), but he never took care of the leading vocals. He was asked once why he never considered it, whether he was too shy.

"Partly, and partly I just don't think I've got the kind of voice required to carry off a lead vocal," **Alan** replied. "I can sort of handle backing vocals, but no, I never really considered that."[188]

The graph on the wall tells the story of it all (Everything Counts) (© Ingo Bittrich)

The second leg of the tour started on **1 December** in Stockholm. Eighteen gigs were played in Europe, most of them in Germany where *DM* had great success. The leg ended on **23 December** in the *Musikhalle* in Hamburg. The third leg took place in **1984**.

---

[187] Taken from: recoil.co.uk. Words: Alan Wilder.
[188] Taken from: Interview on K-ROQ, 17 April 1992. Interviewer: Richard Blade.

"I get a big kick from the gig if the audience are really into what I'm doing," **Dave** said, "then I can really feel it.[189] In Sweden we were spoilt really, the audiences were so very, very warm. And Berlin yesterday was very very good: usually Berlin's very cold and people just stand, but everyone was joining in and it was good fun."[190]

No wonder that they decided not to be so focussed on America. It didn't work for them there. It was probably simply the zeitgeist. A little later, there came a time when British bands became quite hip in the U.S., but generally the interest in English music was low. Most Americans were into rock music. So *DM* decided to focus on Germany instead, where things went very well for them.

"To be honest though, America isn't the end, isn't our aim at all," **Fletch** said. "Germany for us is definitely more important at the moment. Germany is the market to break."

"It's an exciting market as well," **Dave** added. "You can see something's happening, that we're building. We can see ourselves getting bigger every time we come over here and play.[191] It's very odd. When we play German cities the word gets around that we're in town as if we're some big hip band. I'm pleased. It shows that our music does have a wider appeal."[192]

To say that they weren't interested in breaking the American market is, of course, not quite honest. They couldn't make it there at that time, and they knew it. But instead of getting all desperate, they enjoyed becoming "big in Germany." This is a kind of inside-joke of the band, because despite all their success they would never become a real mainstream band.

This is part of the *DM* "mystery" of being big without being really mainstream. I know some people will say that they are mainstream meanwhile, but I don't think you can put *DM* in the same category as Madonna, or typical chart-music. Most people know them, and at least one song springs to their mind, (mostly *Enjoy the Silence*), and

---

[189] Taken from: Enter the Countdown Mode, Record Mirror, 17 September 1983. Words: Sharon Machola.
[190] Taken from: Interview 83, Mode7CD, label unknown. Interviewer: unknown.
[191] Taken from: Hanging in the Balance, NME, 26 March 1983. Words: Matt Snow.
[192] Taken from: New Life, No.1, 13 August 1983. Words: Paul Bursche.

the band is able to sell out stadium-tours. Nevertheless they never appealed to the general public. Public opinion about them is very strange, and it's obvious that not much is known about them outside their fanbase.

Despite the success, they still had a lot of problems with the media. Typical topics like their image were brought up over and over again, and they were rarely taken seriously. Some reporters couldn't remember the names of the band members. Some sneered at Dave's "gimpy dancing" and still asked for Vince in all seriousness.

Fletch on the question whether he still liked Vince and what he thought about his music: "Oh yeah, I really like him as a person. I mean he was my best friend for years and years, so I can't dislike someone, he's never done any harm to me, I still get on well with him now. I'm not so sure about the music."

Could Vince try to return to *DM*?

"No, no," **Fletch** answered. "We wouldn't have him, never. There's no chance, you know, because we wouldn't have him back. Because Alan's too ... we're so friendly with Alan, you know. Alan's rooted now, and we don't need Vince."[193]

All this led to a sense of frustration concerning the media. "Also it's only the journalist's view of us," **Alan** said, "so whatever we say always gets distorted, so what people are reading about us is often incorrect. In a way, being misinterpreted is worse than being misquoted because misinterpretation can destroy your whole point of view!"

I'm afraid it's still like this, even today, which perhaps is the reason for the strange general opinion about them.

And here is a little tit-bit at the end of this chapter: "We still haven't got a record contract at all," **Fletch** said. "We're really proud that our deal with *Mute* is based on trust, we're proud of the fact that we could go out tomorrow and sign to *EMI*!"[194]

This sentence is amusing because one day *DM* would be a part of *EMI* when *Mute Records* was sold to it.

---

[193] Taken from: Interview 83, Mode7CD, label unknown. Interviewer: unknown.
[194] Taken from: Up For Grabs, Sounds, 20 August 1983. Words: Johnny Waller.

1984

*- There's a new game we like to play
(Master and Servant) -*

In **January and February 1984**, the band was mainly in Berlin. Martin wrote the songs for *Some Great Reward* there, some of them obviously about his relationship with his new girlfriend Christina.

So **Fletch** was joking about the songs on the new album, "One's not just a love song. It's a real moon-in-June, lovey-dovey ... Martin's in love again, see?"

"The point is to see something that's important and to write about it honestly, even if it's only important to yourself," **Martin** said. "A love song can be completely throwaway or it can ring true, y'know. Some people tend to think that love songs shouldn't be treated seriously, that it's only if you're writing about social problems that a song becomes serious."[195]

It's almost the opposite of what he said the year before, talking about *Construction Time Again,* but of course, times change ...

Dave and his girlfriend Jo moved to a house of their own in Basildon, and Dave filled his leisure time with nice hobbies like hinges, although he wasn't able to explain why he bothered.

"Berlin was an absolutely important phase," **Alan** remarked, "in which some of us got a little more familiar with the world. It came to some changes there. I think at least with Dave. There wasn't any dramatic radical change at him but I noticed that he lost weight, that he got wirier and more aggressive in his appearance. Perhaps he felt a certain pressure in his private life with Jo."[196] The complete opposite was Martin: "We certainly saw Martin come out of his shell during this time. It seemed as though he had some catching up to do, having been a quiet and reserved teenager by all accounts. Frequenting clubs and bars became more routine and we all saw a very different side to Martin when he was let loose, so to speak - heavy

---

[195] Taken from: The Basildon Bond, Melody Maker, 10 March 1984. Words: Micky Senate.
[196] Taken from: recoil.co.uk. Words: Alan Wilder.

drinking followed by apparel- removal being top of his list of favourite activities."[197]

"We'd grown up in Essex, hardly one of us had ever been out of Essex or London for a long time," **Fletch** said, "so going to all these new places was so interesting for us, especially Berlin in those days. Living and recording in Berlin did have a big impression because there were so many weird and interesting people there."[198]

The experiences mustn't have been too fulfilling for Fletch because he moved to his girlfriend Grainne and her mother in Basildon, instead of living in Berlin or in London. He often emphasised that he never wanted to leave Basildon.

Alan also seemed rather well-behaved, lived together with his girlfriend Jeri and her child in Kilburn, London. The child, Jason, was mentioned very seldom, mostly in doubtful sources. For a long time it wasn't quite clear whether it was only Jeri's son or also Alan's.

Alan was quoted saying, "Jeri is not only the mother of my child, but also a great hairdresser."[199] Something that of course one can understand as that he regarded the child as his without being his biological father. If I'm not mistaken Alan was at least ten, or even more, years younger than Jeri and the child was 12 years old in **1984** (just half as old as Alan). When I had the opportunity to ask **Alan** about it, he explained, "It is correct that she was a good deal older than me, and that I lived with her and her son, who wasn't mine. We had no children together."[200]

In addition, the single *People Are People / In Your Memory* was recorded at the **beginning of the year**. It was released on **12 March**. *People Are People* was the first track to benefit from a period of pre-programming to save studio time, so it was done in a rehearsal room in Dollis Hill, North London.

"We would have finished it sooner," **Alan** said, "except that some of the work had to be redone after the infamous

---

[197] Taken from: Just Can't Get Enough, Uncut, May 2001. Words: Stephen Dalton.
[198] Taken from: The Story Of Depeche Mode, BBC Radio London Live94.9, 7 May 2001. Producer: Tony Wood.
[199] Source can't be found anymore
[200] depechemodebiographie.de.

incident when a particular member of the band turned up, only to trip over the main power cable and pull the plug."[201] (Guess to whom he is referring ...)

Although the lyrics of *People Are People* were quite obvious they had to be explained.

"Although it's a song about racism that's just one example of people not getting on," **Martin** said. "It's about all sorts of differences between people."

"You could interpret it as being anti-war as well,"[202] **Alan** added.

"Martin's lyrics have really come on and he feels really concerned about things, like he's not into violence," **Dave** explained. "But he's also a very private person and he doesn't like to talk about it. With *People Are People* we had the same excitement in the studio as we had with *Everything Counts* because we knew it was such a good song. And the sleeve is also important as it's a strong symbol showing a soldier and a priest and that those two people could meet together despite the fact that they are opposites."[203]

This somehow reinforced the image of the "political band," and it was suggested they had become more serious now.

"I don't think so," **Martin** disagreed. "When people say you're a serious band they think you don't have a good time anymore - you walk around all the time with your cheeks sucked in, things like that. But we don't. We're still exactly the same. It's just the things we're writing about and the way we want to come across in interviews that has changed."[204]

Didn't help really. Instead, the "red worker image" of *Construction Time Again* still adhered to them. At a performance on Belgian television it was brought up once again. They wanted the band to play with gigantic red flags in the background blown out by a wind machine. And as an extra, hammers and sickles should be swung by some men. But the band refused.

---

[201] Taken from: recoil.co.uk. Words: Alan Wilder.
[202] Taken from: Clunk Clunk Every Trip, Record Mirror, 10 March 1984. Words: Jim Reid.
[203] Taken from: Yeah, yeah, he's a Mode - interview with Dave Gahan, Rip It Up, July 1984. Words: George Kay.
[204] Taken from: Clunk Clunk Every Trip, Record Mirror, 10 March 1984. Words: Jim Reid.

"People don't seem to see Martin's wit," **Dave** said. "A lot of journalists seem to see something ... see Martin's got a very weird sense of humour, and that sense of humour comes across in his lyrics. For instance, the lyric in *People Are People*: *people get along so awfully*. The word *awfully* is a funny word. You don't really say that in conversation: *I get on with you so awfully* ... There wasn't really anybody who picked up on that."[205]

They always tried to explain that there is a lot of humour in their music and that they used many phrases people from Basildon use, e.g. *The world we live in and life in general* (from *Somebody*). They used those phrases to be seen as not really serious. But there are still a lot of people who see *DM* as "moody and dark." Mostly the opposite was the case, as you can see by the following example.

A couple of years later Alan was asked by a fan, "*People ARE People*. What excellent lyrics. I'm sure this is a song you are very proud of. What does it mean?"

Alan replied, "It means exactly this: people are people, no bears or wallabies. I think this says a lot."[206]

They weren't happy with the video for *People Are People* - one of the most often shown videos of theirs, however. Clive Richardson directed it, and it was released in two versions. The original video was made for the single version, but an alternate video was made using the *Different Mix*. The video featured footage of various war scenes and scenes from Moscow, mixed with footage of the band aboard *HMS Belfast*.

They weren't happy with the song itself anymore some years later as well.

"Basically it's our least favourite song," **Fletch** said. "It's Martin's least favourite song, I don't know if there was a story behind it", (I think with *People Are People* Martin might regard the story he told about Basildon – see the chapter "Martin Lee Gore" – when he and a friend were attacked by some people without any reasons, kicking and shouting at them), "it's just that he brought it to us one day, we liked it and went in the studio, recording it, and it was a big hit."[207]

---

[205] Taken from: Aces High, Zig Zag, August 1985. Words: William Shaw.
[206] Taken from: recoil.co.uk. Words: Alan Wilder.
[207] Taken from: Depeche Mode: The Interview, Talking Music SPEEK013, 1988.

It really was a big success, especially in Germany where it was a Number-One-hit. German TV even used the song for their coverage of the *Olympic Summer Games* in **1984**. In the UK it reached No. 4. Even in the U.S. it was a success, where it reached No. 13 in the charts. The song has become an anthem for the gay community there, and is regularly played at gay establishments and gay pride festivals. Some people even think that *DM* changed American society with this song.

A compilation album with the title *People Are People* was released in North America on **2 July** to capitalise on the successful radio play of the song.

"It was around that time that things started changing for us in America", **Martin** remarked. "On the tour for that album, we were totally shocked by the way fans were turning up in droves at the concerts. Suddenly, we were playing to 10,000 people. Although the concerts were selling really well, though, we still found it a struggle to actually sell records."[208]

They weren't able to explain this discrepancy. "I don't know the reasons," **Alan** said. "Sometimes you hear of artists selling records and not doing well in concerts. We're doing it the other way around. Nobody does it that way."[209]

However, *People Are People* was indeed a kind of breakthrough. Even today some people, who are not really familiar with the band, at least remember this song.

The success of that single surprised the band at the time, and years later they were still wondering about it.

"Not bad for a song whose rhyming hook - *People are people so why should it be, you and I should get along so awfully* - is a candidate for 'worst lyric ever written',"[210] **Alan** remarked.

In **March**, *DM* played five gigs in Italy and Spain as a kind of last leg of the *Construction Time Again*-Tour.

In **May**, they began to record *Some Great Reward* in the *Hansa Studios* in Berlin, a time that everyone who was involved, described as "happy and creative." There was a

---

[208] Taken from: Violator, Alligator, NME, 7 July 1990. Words: Jeff Giles.
[209] Taken from: Depeche Mode gains fans despite its critics, Times Staff Writer, 29 March 1985. Words: Dennis Hunt.
[210] Taken from: recoil.co.uk. Words: Alan Wilder.

dynamic atmosphere in the studio, and the band had a lot of fun.

They took more care on the vocals this time, and **Dave** even took a couple of lessons with the vocal coach Tona De Brett because he wanted to do more for the breathing control. He was enthusiastic about in **1984**, but **two years later** he said, "A few years back I thought I ought to have proper singing lessons and went to Tona De Brett. All she did was try to make me sing like Barbra Streisand, which was not much use to me. I try to get a feeling when I sing. I might not get every note right, but I don't think that's important."[211]

They supposed they had matured a bit, thought that the songs were more serious now. They were very into sample stuff, created a lot of their own sounds.

"For *Master and Servant* we've used quite a lot of toy instruments," **Martin** explained. "Me and Andy went to *Hamley's* and bought nearly everything in the musical department – xylophones, toy pianos, toy saxophones.[212] One we used a lot was a Marina. It sounded pretty terrible as a toy but when we took it down a couple of octaves it sounded really good."

"People tend to think that if you're using toy instruments then they have to sound whacky," **Alan** added, "but we put some to very good use because as soon as you sample them they take on a whole new quality and when you transpose them it puts them in a completely new context."[213]

Some of the sounds on *Master and Servant* – such as the whip effect – are based on Daniel Miller standing in the studio hissing and spitting ("we tried to sample a real whip but it was hopeless."[214])

They had a break during recording to have a gig with Elton John on **2 June** in Ludwigshafen. But this wasn't the reason that they couldn't meet the deadline.

---

[211] Taken from: Basildon Bond, Blitz, April 1986. Words: Bruce Dessau.
[212] Taken from: Construction Time Again, Smash Hits, 16 August 1984. Words: Tim de Lisle.
[213] Taken from: Sampling Mode, International Musician And Recording World, November 1984. Words: Adrian Deevoy.
[214] Taken from: Blasphemy Rewarded, Melody Maker, 22 September 1984. Words: Mark Jenkins.

They returned from *Music Works* in London, where they had recorded first, to *Hansa Studios* to mix the album but ended up getting horribly behind schedule.

"As a result, myself, Dan and Gareth completed the album alone because the other three band members had all booked their summer holidays and didn't want to cancel them," **Alan** said. "I foresaw the fact that we were going to go over deadline and held off arranging one myself because I didn't want to miss out on the whole mixing process."

When reading lines like these you start to get an idea why things became so difficult later. The rest of the band felt fine about going on holiday, to leave Alan behind in the studio, knowing he and the other two would do a good job. Alan didn't mind at the time, but it was to get to a point at which he would notice an imbalance in the workload.

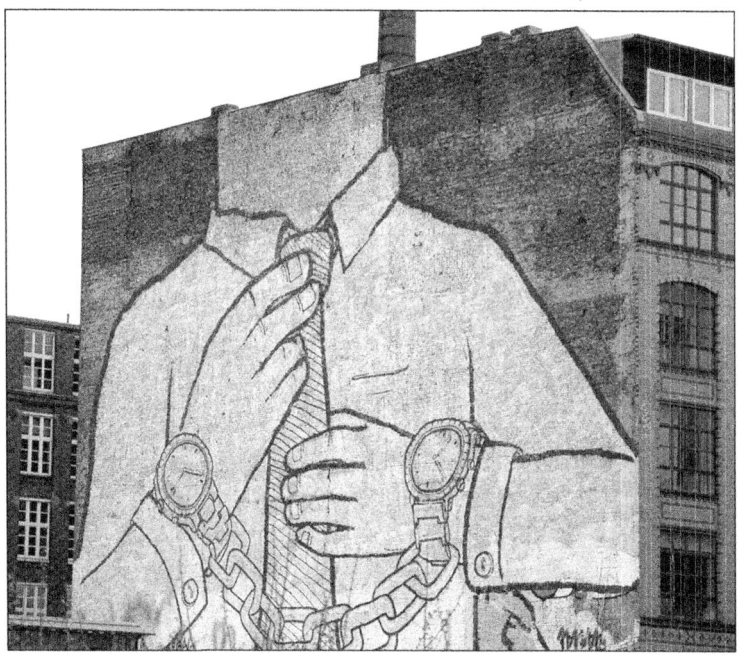

Master and Servant (© Ingo Bittrich)

Released at the same time as *Frankie Goes To Hollywood's* massive hit *Relax* the aim was to emulate the same "fat, round bass sound" for *Master and Servant*.

"We went completely up our a*** and ended up with exactly the opposite, topping it all off at the end of a seven day mix by leaving out a small detail - the snare drum," **Alan** remembered. "The cost of this crucial omission was realised when Gareth and Dan hot-footed it down to a local Berlin club one night, armed with a test pressing and fully expecting to blow the local's minds. By the law of sod, the track came on straight after the pounding bass of *Relax*. Not surprisingly, it cleared the dance floor, leaving both of them standing, red-faced in their raincoats, clutching their briefcases."[215]

On **20 August** the single *Master and Servant / (Set Me Free) Remotivate Me* was released.

The promo for *Master and Servant* was filmed in Berlin. "Clive [Richardson] hired a French choreographer who put together the hilarious 'Eetsa lot, eetsa lot' dance routine," **Alan** recalled. "One of the most embarrassing video moment ever - and believe me, there were many."

Furthermore he described, "The cancellation of a day filming after 'fisticuffs' ensued between two band members. Brought about when one party berated the other for excessive drinking, the *Depeche Mode* camp was decidedly uncomfortable for an entire week thereafter until the status quo was eventually restored, a peace agreement reached and the happy couple reconciled over *Hansa Studio*'s 'Space Invader' machine."

I'm not quite sure, but it's possible that he's referring to the same incident with this anecdote: "There was one particular video shoot where a fight between two band members did occur. Not that I'm mentioning any names of course except to say that when Dave tried to attract my attention to witness this amusing spectacle, I was preoccupied with something else and missed it."[216]

"With the video to *Master and Servant* we steered clear of the sexual side a bit," **Martin** said. "It's very easy to make a video like that ... *Relax II*. There's a bit of rolling around with chains and hanging up with chains ... but nothing too blatant."

Dave pointed to the fact that "obviously you have to think about it getting banned. It might mean hundreds or

---

[215] Taken from: recoil.co.uk. Words: Alan Wilder.
[216] Taken from: recoil.co.uk. Words: Alan Wilder.

thousands of people not actually seeing the thing because of one thing in the video."[217]

They had some problems with the song, indeed. The *BBC* called for a copy of the lyrics and checked them out. But finally they believed in Martin's explanation that the song was about domination and exploitation and was just using a sexual angle to get that point across. His band mates didn't really believe in his words.

"Yeah, but on the record it's sexual, isn't it?" **Dave** asked.

"No, it's not, it's not just about sex," **Alan** disagreed. "Martin?"

Dave insisted on his opinion. "On the record it is, I think that's pretty obvious from the lyric."

"Alright then,"[218] **Martin** gave in.

On **24 September** the album *Some Great Reward* was released. The title refers to the line *make me think that at the end of the day some great reward will coming my way* from the song *Lie To Me*.

Martin sang *Somebody* naked, according to his own statement and confirmed by Alan - a story that was brought up over and over again - at least it was at Alan's appearance in *Hansa Studios,* at one of his *Selected* events (with *Recoil*) in **2010**. But the story was told differently every time. One time it was said that Martin and Alan hadn't been in the same room - Alan was at the piano in the *Meistersaal* and Martin in a room next door or in the cellar. Another time it was said that they had been in the same room, and Alan had the piano turned around because Martin got undressed.

"*Somebody* is pretty much a straightforward 'I love you' song if you like, certainly not an anti-love song,"[219] **Martin** said, but added, "A pleasant song to me is unfinished, it isn't telling the full story. Which is why I introduced the twist at the end of *Somebody* because the song was just too nice. You say I'm cynical about love in my songs and perhaps I am but I think that's an interesting angle. Oth-

---

[217] Taken from: Master of the Game, Record Mirror, 29 September 1984. Words: Eleanor Levy.
[218] Taken from: Everything Counts (in Large Amounts), Number One, 19 October 1985. Words: Paul Bursche.
[219] Taken from: Blasphemy Rewarded, Melody Maker, 22 September 1984. Words: Mark Jenkins.

erwise you just become mundane like most chart music. Relationships do have their darker side and I like to write about it."[220]

Nevertheless, *Somebody* is chosen whenever it comes to a wedding between *DM*-fans. People seem not to be bothered by the twist at the end of the song, that almost spoils everything.

Grey sky over black town (Something to Do)
(© Ingo Bittrich)

Martin wrote *Something to Do* as an expression of the boredom he felt for Basildon: "You can become what we call a total spam, which is like a real beer boy, out every night drinking, Cockney accent develops, all that. Or basically you start wearing women's clothing - it's all you can turn to."[221]

And he began to wear women's clothing! A topic the media were to deal with over the next two, three years - very intensively. It started when he bought a leather skirt, and wore it over leather trousers. This caused huge waves of enthusiasm in the media, who rushed at the skirt in the true sense of the word. This attention increased when Martin intensified his outfit, and wore the skirt without trousers, then dresses, silk stockings, (every woman would turn pale with envy at the sight of his legs :D) and pearl necklaces.

---

[220] Taken from: Sin Machine, NME, 17 February 1990. Words: Stuart Maconie.
[221] Taken from: Coming up Smiling, The Face, February 1985. Words: Sheryl Garratt.

The rest of the band took this - depending on temperament - in good humour, or with: "You've got to take that off!" Apparently Martin took the latter literally when he made a name for himself as a "club stripper."

Most journalists and biographers tended to take the thing with the skirt much too seriously. I think it was exactly what Martin said about it – fun, and "discovering freedom," because he would never have been able to wear something like that in Basildon. He wasn't "strange" or "perverted" or "effeminate." It was simply the fun of "wearing strange dresses and being a bit different," and it was part of Martin's special sense of humour that - as some fans in the survey of *depechemodebiographie.de* said - some people simply didn't get. *I'd put your pretty dress on* (*Something to Do*) was a joke - and dressing up like this was a joke, too.

Speaking of jokes - sometimes they delivered the proof of not being serious and grown up at all.

Martin: "Fletch, apart from being in a quite successful band, has also got the smallest nipples in the world."

Dave: "They're like two freckles."

Fletch: "They've just never grown. But they're not that bad."

Martin: "They are, Fletch."

Dave: "You're a weird guy, Fletch."

Fletch: "I just haven't got very big what-do-you-call-its. The round bit... the dark bit around it."

Dave: "That IS your nipple, Andy."

Fletch: "No, it isn't."

Dave: "I'll talk to you later Fletch. Man talk. I'll give you a few books on the subject."[222]

Alan described how he styled his hair: "Hot HAIR (about 1983/84)

You will need:

1 STUPID PRATT (preferably aged - about 22 should do it) 1 LARGE MIRROR (doctored to look as flattering as possible) 1 HEAD OF STRAGGLY, UNKEMPT HAIR (do NOT wash thoroughly) FULL HOLD HAIR GEL (2 tubes)

1 COMB

---

[222] Taken from: Master of the Game, Record Mirror, 29 September 1984. Words: Eleanor Levy.

HOVIS BREAD (1 loaf)
ELNETTE TURBO-NUTTER-BASTARD STRENGTH HAIRSPRAY (3 cans)
1 BLINKERED ATTITUDE
1 POOFY EIGHTIES POP BAND GAGGLE OF TEENAGE GIRLS
1 PACKET CONDOMS

Take stupid pratt and stand for half an hour in front of the large mirror. Start by coating straggly hair thoroughly with both tubes of full hold hair gel, being careful to ensure sideburns are not missed. Using comb, scoop upwards to resemble loaf of bread and immediately cover LIBER-ALLY with hair spray (remembering to save some for the garnish). DO NOT MOVE UNTIL SET.

Next, ignore the fact that everyone's saying "Look at that stupid pratt who looks like he's got a loaf of bread on his head" and place firmly in an equally badly dressed and follically-disastrous **80's** pop band. Finally, add one more spray of *Elnette* and serve immediately to gaggle of teenage girls who'll tell him he looks great ..."[223]

No fun for the band in those days, but in review the stories teenage- magazines wrote were quite funny.

The British journalist Don Watson and *DM* entered a hotel and spotted a reporter team of a German teen-magazine with cameras.

"It's no good refusing to talk to them," **Fletch** said. "They'll just go ahead and make it up anyway. The last time we refused an interview with them, they made up a story about Dave having to be carried off-stage at the end of every performance, taken to a separate dressing room and kept supplied with constant fluids. The time before that they said we hated everyone under 20, which made us very popular with their readership."

As they made their way through the swing doors, **Dave** made a theatrical fall on the hotel courtyard. "Help! I need a cup of coffee!"

"Oh God!" **Alan** shamed, "This happens all the time."[224]

The first story to which Fletch alluded was actually rather revealing. It was dramatically reported how Dave had been carried into the dressing room. Unfortunately, it

---

[223] Taken from: recoil.co.uk. Words: Alan Wilder.
[224] Taken from: Deconstruction Time Again, NME, 22 December 1984. Words: Don Watson.

was said that helpers made sure that nobody could enter the room, not even band members. However, two lines further on, it was reported that Dave was still lying on the bench. If nobody was allowed to enter the room, how did the reporters know about this?

A Belgian teenage-magazine jumped on this bandwagon, too, and quoted **Dave** with, "I never did any sports when I was young. When *Depeche Mode* started to become a little more popular, I collapsed immediately after the first few gigs. Now I can handle it, lucky for me. Whenever I have a day off, you can find me in the gymnasium. There I train myself to exhaustion. Shadowboxing, weightlifting ..."[225]

I can't tell you if he really said this. There are some more professional sources saying that he would go to the gym before starting a tour. But they are referring to later tours.

The reaction to the second story – that they hated everyone under 20 - actually turned out dramatically. Quite a number of fans were indignant by the "arrogance" of the band, and wrote angry letters to the magazine.

There were a lot of faults in the stories that were published in these teen-magazines, all kinds of things got mixed up continuously, or wild assertions were made. According to these, Martin and Vince had been schoolmates [it was Fletch and Martin] and the sole founders of *DM*. A whole album, *Construction Time Again,* was demoted to a song, and Alan lost his songwriting credits to Martin, because *Two Minute Warning* was ascribed to him. "He thinks the end of the world has come."

Stripped was so misinterpreted, that German teenagers thought for a long time *DM* wanted all girls they met to undress in front of them. (Which some certainly did ...)

Shake the Disease was connected with AIDS. And Dave stole cars because his family had nothing to eat. And he removed several tattoos with extremely painful etching chemicals. [He only had one removed - with a laser].[226]

---

[225] Taken from: Depeche Mode begs for a vacation, Joepie, 1984. Words: Uncredited.
[226] Basing on several articles in the Bravo and other German teenage-magazines.

The next tour kicked off on **27 September**. The tours got longer and became more exhausting. And although **Dave** developed as front man, liked moving about the stage now and felt a great deal of power to make the audience do what he wanted, he also had to notice the dark sides of touring. "There are a few days off, but the gigs are mostly back to back – when we get a day off it's always a Sunday in Hanley. Have you ever been in Hanley on a Sunday? You look at a couple of antique shops, you wander about thinking 'what the hell can I do?', you go back to the hotel and watch a couple of videos. It's awful."[227]

"It's pretty much the same every night, so it can get a bit boring," **Alan** admitted. "The worst thing is finding something to fill in three hours in a hotel bedroom in the afternoon. I take photographs to relieve the boredom. I can't write songs or anything, neither can Martin. There's something about touring that stops you doing that."[228]

Just a while later this boredom would lead to massive partying during the tours, but already at that time they weren't exactly "well-behaved boys" anymore. There are some personal reports from people who met them at parties in West-Berlin and London, saying they drank quite a lot. There were stories about "pouring everything into a bucket and downing it."

In the meantime, on **29 October**, the single *Blasphemous Rumours / Somebody* was released. It was the first double A-side single in *DM*'s history.

Just like *Master and Servant,* they had some problems with *Blasphemous Rumours*. The *BBC* refused to play it, and other people also re-acted negatively to this song.

"If we can say God so loved the world that He sent His only son, if He did that He cannot have a sick sense of humour,"[229] a priest from Basil-don said in a local newspaper as a comment on *Blasphemous Rumours.*

The band tried to explain the song, but it was difficult. "Religion is a more sensitive subject than sex," **Alan** said. "You've got to be careful with it. In that song it's handled tastefully. Talking about something dealing with religion

---

[227] Taken from: Blasphemy Rewarded, Melody Maker, 22 September 1984. Words: Mark Jenkins.
[228] Taken from: Strange but True, Smash Hits, 22 November – 5 December 1984. Words: Neil Tennant.
[229] Source can't be found anymore

that's offensive, I've watched American religious TV programs. If anything is sick, they're sick. Anything we sing about is tame compared to those shows. Americans who complain about us should be complaining about those shows."[230]

They didn't see *Blasphemous Rumours* as an anti-religious song. "It's a personal statement on Martin's part," **Dave** explained, "but at the same time it's a statement of how everybody must feel at one time or another."

"People get too much preaching – even around the town in Basildon, you know?" **Martin** said. "People cling to religion through fear of death. It's not a bad thing to be religious, in fact I think I'd be happier if I did believe."[231]

Fletch turned away from religion at the time, because it didn't suit the lifestyle of the band anymore. Though simultaneously he felt it was a shame that Christianity was perverted and hyped so much because in his opinion it did have something to offer.

The second leg of the tour took place from **15 November** to **18 December**, comprising 16 concerts in Europe. But of course, *Blasphemous Rumours* was also performed on some TV shows. While the metal-like sound had been produced with a hammer on a concrete floor originally, the band decided to "play" a bicycle wheel and a breeze block combination for TV performances.

"But the only real recollections [about TV performances] are that we always took the opportunity to get very drunk backstage - particularly the year when *Frankie Goes To Hollywood* were also on the show,"[232] **Alan** admitted.

There had even been a drinking competition that was won by *DM* - probably something that must be seen as "consolation for the boredom" (one of Martin's favourite topics by the way) at those TV performances.

---

[230] Taken from: Depeche Mode gains fans despite its critics, Times Staff Writer, 29 March 1985. Words: Dennis Hunt.
[231] Taken from: Blasphemy Rewarded, Melody Maker, 22 September 1984. Words: Mark Jenkins.
[232] Taken from: recoil.co.uk. Words: Alan Wilder.

1985

- Understand me (Shake the Disease) -

At the **beginning of 1985,** *DM* took a break, which they obviously used to record *Shake the Disease* and *Flexible* because this single was released shortly after the end of the third leg of the *Some Great Reward-* Tour. From **14 March** to **12 April** *DM* played 12 gigs in the U.S. and Japan.

On **29 April** the live-video *The World We Live In and Live In Hamburg* was released. The concert had been recorded in the *Alsterdorfer Sporthalle* in Hamburg on **9 December 1984**. On the same day, *Shake the Disease / Flexible* was released.

"*Shake the Disease* is a good song which is something that's been lacking in the charts lately – they've been in a real state," **Dave** said. "There's a lot of American music there and nothing to really grab hold of, no new thing. Some of the things that have been successful recently have just been rhythm tracks, basically what we did on the new B-Side as a bit of fun in the studio."

"*Flexible* is a kind of a joke," **Martin** explained, "cos I'm sure for instance if my mum looked at me now, she'd think 'what has it done to you?'[233] A lot of the tracks were written when I was very young. So I think that from *Construction Time Again* there is some kind of link between the songs. Sometimes it's very obvious, there are things like references 'cos I really like references to other songs. In *Shake the Disease* there's a reference to another song. You know it says, *Now I've got things to do and I've said it before I know you have too*. And in another song it said, *Now I've got things to do and you have too*."[234] For those who don't get it at once: the other song is *Stories of Old* (*Some Great Reward*.)

I'd been asked by a reader once if there is a further connection between these two songs than just these two lines. Many lyrics of Martin's have a connection because

---

[233] Taken from: The Last of the Futurists, Record Mirror, 25 May 1985. Words: Betty Page.
[234] Taken from: Boys on Film, Melody Maker, 15 April 1989. Words: Francesco Adinolfi.

he has a penchant for certain special topics. *Stories of Old* is about liking the girl, he feels great when he's with her (*I'm really in heaven whenever we kiss*) and enjoys being with her sometimes, but he *wouldn't sacrifice anything at all to love*. He doesn't like compromising, being tied to someone. Both of them should be able to live a life of their own.

The same topic appears in *Shake the Disease*, when he says that *some people have to be permanently together*. He also asks here for independence, but while he sounds quite self-confident in *Stories of Old* (*You won't change me!*), in *Shake the Disease* it has become much more difficult to explain why this is so important to him. This is mainly because of this *disease that takes hold of* his *tongue in situations like these*.

You could understand *Shake the Disease* as some kind of continuation of *Stories of Old,* but the relationship in question has changed meanwhile. It seems as if the girl doesn't accept his need for independence any longer, and is trying to draw the reins tighter, trying to tighten the relationship.

"*Shake the Disease* is still one of my favourite Martin songs but I don't think we really got the best out of it," **Alan** recalled. "I suspect everybody was trying too hard to make it sound extra special, not least Daniel who thought it would be worthwhile to spend days and days recording every sound he could get from his *Synclavier* onto 24 individual tracks, and then bounce them down to just 2. And the result? Something that sounded like a sine wave."[235]

The video for *Shake the Disease* was directed by Peter Care who used an "upside down machine." The promo used 'free fall' sequences that make for a fairly simple optical illusion. The subject is strapped to a motorized pole that runs through the back of his jacket. As the pole rotates taking the subject with it, the camera follows at the same angle giving the impression that the subject is remaining still and everything in the background is actually moving.

Another similar trick was used where the camera is attached to the subject on a kind of stiff harness. As the subject moves around with the camera, the subject again appears still while the background moves around.

---

[235] Taken from: recoil.co.uk. Words: Alan Wilder.

They had two months off, before they played the last leg of the *Some Great Reward*-Tour from **6 to 30 July**, comprising 8 concerts, mainly festivals.

Since there weren't many musical activities the journalists could ask them about, you will find a lot of "reviews", and people trying to find out more about the personalities of the band members in the media in this year. Martin had changed his outfit and lifestyle drastically, so he stepped out of line a bit. Many journalists tried now to "understand him" (by way of *Shake the Disease* maybe), and learn more about him. But it wasn't that easy. Sometimes it was because Martin wasn't ready to open up, sometimes it was because he was being too witty, and sometimes it was because the journalists simply didn't understand his humour.

However, one of the two main topics of this year was **Martin**, because of his style of clothing, his striptease tendencies and his "theories." A couple of these "theories":

"I've got a theory that if you don't over-expose yourself you stick around longer. When we started we got a lot of flak because we had such a terrible image, very sickly. Even I thought we were wimps. Gradually we've changed that around. It's been a challenge."

"After a few nice little pop singles you're allowed a bit of perversion. In fact the working title of *Some Great Reward* was *Perversions* but we didn't think that mums would buy it for their daughters."

"I am quite a pessimist and happy to be one. Sometimes I paint things too black but even when we're doing well I tend to notice bad things."

"Conventional humour bores me. Still, I wish a few people could see some of the humour in what we do."[236]

"I see life as quite boring. So I kind of see our stuff as ... *Love and Sex and Drink against the Boredom of Life*. When I write love songs people think they're really soppy, but I see love as ... a consolation for the boredom of life. And drink and sex ... Personally speaking I think we're quite decadent. When we're on tour, which is generally very boring, we, or some of us, tend to go out every night, have a lot to drink and generally have a good time. Consolation, see? I know it's all expected of rock bands, but go-

---

[236] Taken from: Boys Keep Swinging, No. 1, 19 January 1985. Words: Max Bell.

ing out is enjoyable, drinking is enjoyable and collapsing is enjoyable."

Martin dashed down another Whiskey whereupon the reporter dared to ask whether he never had the urge to do something really wild.

"I want to represent life's boredom ..."

Sorry I asked.

"... and if you take things to absurd extremes you're not really reflecting life," **Martin** remarked. "Real life is not extreme, so we're not, and nor is our music. But if I make boring records and people identify with them, then I've achieved my aim."[237]

Well, maybe not "boring records," but music that many people - with very different musical backgrounds and from different cultures - can identify with in a very individual way. This is the bottom line of what fans answered in the survey of *depechemodebiographie.de* when they were asked what is so special for them about *DM*'s music.

"How can Mart know what goes on in my head?" is probably the sentence that hits the mark. So people don't identify with the "boring records" but with their own personality that they "find through the music." The music of *DM* is "somehow different and individual" but nevertheless "absolutely normal," because everyone "feels exactly the same in a situation like this" and is able to "tell a story to every song, every album" because it is connected to one's personal life.

Martin is absolutely right there, that real life usually isn't extreme. So his songs reflect the life most people know or wish to lead.

"Martin is most definitely an underrated songwriter," **Alan** said. "His songs have managed to touch people in a way that very few songwriters have been able to do. And it's quite clear that his songwriting capabilities have been the major part of *Depeche Mode*'s longevity."[238]

And there were many articles about the gear ...

"I hardly have to buy any clothes these days," **Martin** said. "When the fans realise what sort of style you're after,

---

[237] Taken from: Fake the Disease, NME, 5 October 1985. Words: Danny Kelly.
[238] Taken from: Depeche Mode: A Short Film, EPKMUTEL5, included with The Singles 86>98 promotional box set, PBXMUTEL5. Director: Sven Harding.

they throw things onstage – I've got tons of necklaces. My mother accepts it now, I'm quite surprised really. When I went home this time I was wearing stockings and things. I went to me mum and said, 'what do you do with stockings mum, do you just put them in the washing machine?' And she went, 'just put them in with the blacks, dear'."[239]

The whole band had a preference for black leather at that time which caused some speculations that the entire band might be gay. Especially in England they got stick for their style.

In **1989 Martin** said, "Looking back I'm not very happy about some of the clothes I've worn. Every interview we do the skirt is mentioned. I actually think it's quite funny, though I didn't look at it deeply. I regret that so much attention was paid to it and that even now there are still people who think I go round dressed like a tranny."[240]

Dave thought that they had got away with it if it had been T. Rex or Gary Glitter in the **1970s**. But I wouldn't be so sure about it. Not everyone was cool in the **1970s**.

For Martin it was just fun. All band members had a good laugh about it. Then they realised that it wasn't good for their image at all. But the more they tried to persuade Martin to dress up in a different way, the more he carried on doing it.

"The funny thing was that we just about got away with it," **Dave** said. "See, pop music isn't something which should be taken too seriously. We're very serious about our music. At the same time, we have to laugh at ourselves and laugh at the whole music business. It gets so nauseating when you get these bands going on and on about charity records. If we want to do something for charity, then we'll do it in private, as quietly as possible. We don't ever want to be seen to be using any kind of charity to help boost our career. No matter what the intentions of these bands are, that's how it comes across to me. It's become very trendy. We'll always avoid things like that like the bloody plague. I think the reason Martin wore dresses was just for fun. Nothing deeper than that. People read other things into it, like he was some sort of trans-

---

[239] Taken from: The Last of the Futurists, Record Mirror, 25 May 1985. Words: Betty Page.
[240] Taken from: The Unlikely Lads, Q, April 1989. Words: Mat Snow.

vestite or something.[241] Martin said to me once, 'I like to look into the mirror before I go out, and laugh and think, 'Look what I'm getting away with tonight'. He'd wear leather trousers and then wear a skirt over the top. And then he sort of extended to just wearing a skirt. We used to sit backstage saying, 'Martin, you can't f*** wear that, man! You've got to take that off!'."[242]

"I never was comfortable with Martin dressing up in girls' clothing," **Alan** admitted, "and the rest of the group would often comment and try to dissuade him but I think the more we might do that the more belligerent he would become about it.[243] Ironically, he now gets irritated when people bring up the 'dress' period - what did he expect? Unfortunately, people will always base their opinions of people on how they look and much of the style of the **early 1980s** was quite effeminate. Martin wearing a skirt didn't help. But you must also say that from the very early days, the band attracted a very large gay following (long before Martin ever considered wearing a dress) which has been very supportive. The interesting point however, is that Martin is not gay and it annoys him when people make the assumption that he is. Strangely, he seems oblivious to the fact that many people still associate transvestism with homosexuality."[244]

Alan is wrong here – I couldn't find any quotation of Martin being annoyed about the assumption he might be gay. He just reacted irritated when this question was put forward too often. If he was annoyed, it wasn't taken to public.

They didn't care about the "gear-thing" and its consequences in **1985**. "I bought my first leather jacket when I was 18," **Martin** said. "I've developed a love for black leather which is hypocritical because, like Alan, I'm a vegetarian – for moral and health reasons." (I don't know about Martin but Alan is not longer a vegetarian. It seems he was just for a while because he had been influenced by his former girlfriend and first wife Jeri.) "Black leather is

---

[241] Taken from: Depeche Mode Hip it up and Start Again, Melody Maker, 10 March 1990. Words: Jon Wilde.
[242] Taken from: Violator, Alligator, NME, 7 July 1990. Words: Jeff Giles.
[243] Taken from: The Story Of Depeche Mode, BBC Radio London Live94.9, 7 May 2001. Producer: Tony Wood.
[244] Taken from: recoil.co.uk. Words: Alan Wilder.

striking and simple. People imagine I've got kinky habits but my worst vice is video games. Well, I have got a few others but you'd be far too interested in them ... An average day for me might start by getting up at midday and composing on my guitar, sampling sounds until eight. I'm not a great musician. None of us is except Alan. My interest is in melody lines and lyrics ... Sexual barriers are silly. My girlfriend and I swap clothes, make-up, anything. So what? It's a shock though to read in a magazine like *Bravo* that I walk around dressed as a woman.[245]

"I don't really like it when it's played on because I don't see it as such a big thing. It's just something that I enjoy doing. I never bring the subject up myself. I think I like it because it is different and because I find male dress in general very boring. Men are very restricted in what they wear, in what is acceptable. Obviously I wouldn't go shopping in a dress but if I go out to a club I usually wear one. One thing I've noticed is that everybody considers you gay if you dress effeminately, but the thing most people seem to miss is that most girls these days – well, most girls I know – seem to prefer effeminate boys. Occasionally when I buy a new article of clothing and present it for the first time I get a few laughs, sort of 'you can't wear that' sort of thing."[246]

His sense of style really wasn't special. It was the general trend, especially among British artists at the time. When you take a look at the pop-culture of the **mid 1980s** in the UK you will find a lot of male artists dressed up in a feminine way and a lot of female artists dressed in a very masculine way – a well-known example is Annie Lennox (*Eurythmics*).

"He has totally changed," **Dave** said about Martin. "But he's just being the way he wanted to be anyway. Mart missed out on his teens, just generally going out, seeing different girls every night and getting drunk all the time, y'know, not caring. He's living all that now. It's not a bad thing. Everybody should go through that phase. Personally, I think he's just doing all the things I did when I was 16. All that stuff about boredom is exactly the attitude that I went through. I went to clubs with people much

---

[245] Taken from: Martin Gore: The Decadent Boy, No. 1, 11 May 1985. Words: Martin Lee Gore.
[246] Taken from: Are Depeche Mode Cracking up?, Smash Hits, 9-22 October 1985. Words: Chris Heath.

older than myself. I wore tons of makeup, and dresses too. But now if I go to a club I just want to have a good time, not to shock."[247]

In **1990** he claimed, "You won't catch me in a f*** dress. No sodding way! I'm the yob next door. Never worn a dress in me life. Never f*** will!"[248]

But there is a picture from **December 1980** in which he obviously wore a dress.

And it still went on and on with the clothes.

"A lot of the blokes in the audience won't even think about the fact that Martin's wearing a skirt or whatever," **Alan** remarked. "In a different situation, they'd kick the s*** out of him, but when it's onstage they love it."[249]

All this led to the suspicion they might be very decadent.

"Well, I'm not into ... pain, or any of that kind of thing," **Martin** said. "Decadence covers a lot of areas! Some of us go out drinking when we're on tour, and I know that's sort of expected of us because we're a band, but unfortunately it's a way of enjoying yourself ..."

"You do actually like decadence though, don't you?" **Dave** asked.

"Mmmm ... well, yes, I do ...," **Martin** replied. "Sometimes ... when you're doing something, even just walking down the street with your girlfriend, you get this feeling of being too normal. It's not a very nice feeling ..."

"I can assure you you're not normal, Martin!"[250] **Dave** said.

The attentive reader will have noticed that already at that time, only a few years after claiming all the partying wouldn't be attractive to them, the scenery had changed completely. Partying, going out, drinking, and going to clubs had become an inherent part of their lifestyle, and would increase over the coming years.

It was really difficult to find considerable topics this year. Dave found out that constantly touring was a very

---

[247] Taken from: Fake the Disease, NME, 5 October 1985. Words: Danny Kelly.
[248] Taken from: Depeche Mode Hip it up and Start Again, Melody Maker, 10 March 1990. Words: Jon Wilde.
[249] Taken from: Coming up Smiling, The Face, February 1985. Words: Sheryl Garratt.
[250] Taken from: The Normal Invasion, The Hit, 28 September 1985. Words: Marc Issue.

unhealthy way to live. He always lost a lot of weight and got ill very often. Nevertheless, he loved being on stage and described it as a sexual feeling, as a sense of immense power.

The big *Live Aid* festival took place without *DM*.

"It's a contradictory thing," **Alan** said. "We sit there and we think 'Oh no ... we've only got to No. 18 with *Shake the Disease*, and yet at the same time we know that if we want to make higher positions in the charts we've got to do things that we don't want to do, so at the same time we know exactly why. Trouble is, when you are very honest, when you tell the truth all the time, you can come across as just sounding a bit wimpy ... a bit boring."[251]

"Because we are on an independent label we just don't have the contacts, so we weren't asked to appear," **Fletch** remarked. "I don't think Geldof was aware of how many records we actually sell internationally. At the time we were bitter, but the whole thing has just become so tacky – all those ageing rock bands appearing solely to boost their own career – that in a way we are quite glad we weren't involved. Of course the money raised can't be criticized ... but it would have been a lot more if they had added the money that went on their cocaine bill ..."[252]

"I doubt very much that we would have accepted the invitation, had we been asked," **Alan** claimed. "My personal view is that giving to 'chariddy' should be a totally private gesture, out of which no personal gain should be made. Inevitably, nearly all the artists who took part in *Live Aid* achieved a considerable rise in record sales and being the cynic I am, I wonder just how much of the profit gained from those sales actually ended up going to Ethiopia."[253]

I wouldn't be so sure they would have said 'no' if they had been asked. The sentence "I don't think Geldof was aware of how many records we actually sell internationally" says all you need to know about how offended they had been at first. It's possible that they changed their minds afterwards. But it's a bit hypocritical nevertheless, because while they were very proud of their independence and happy about not being mixed up with the general music business, on the other hand, they were striving for

---

[251] Taken from: Aces High, Zig Zag, August 1985. Words: William Shaw.
[252] Taken from: Basildon Bond, Blitz, April 1986. Words: Bruce Dessau.
[253] Taken from: recoil.co.uk. Words: Alan Wilder.

ultimate success. Maybe they simply came to the conclusion that it was better to reach this success in a different way.

On **4 August** Dave and Jo got married and moved to a house of their own, in Essex. This was the second "big topic" of the year.

"I've met a lot of girls in my time and have been with a lot of girls and, sure, I've been in love before, but Jo's the only girl I've ever met that I could live with," **Dave** said. "I just get on with her. We have lots of arguments just like anybody else but somehow ... we cross over, there's something about it that's special. We've been going out for six years and I just got up one morning and asked her and she just sort of said 'yeah, alright'. It was that casual."[254]

One year later he added, "Obviously, we could have played on it. It doesn't bother me to be in the daily papers but so what? Who cares? Thousands of people get married every day. It's very clichéd to say that you don't feel different, but I don't. We just get on so well. Jo does a lot for me and she's always there when I need her. I miss her more and more."[255]

However, she stopped accompanying him on tour. Dave admitted that he could be a horrible person on tour because he was so locked into what he was doing. They didn't get on with each other when she was there too often and at long intervals. They even had some screaming fights. From all accounts it seems their relationship may have not been based on love.

Dave admitted that the main reason for the marriage had been that they wanted to have children. He thought that having to bring up a child would add something very special to his life and everything else would become secondary. The motivation for this may be considered as an attempt to escape himself, to try to find something to hold on to or to distract him from his deeper issues.

While Dave was getting married, **Fletch** was moving into a new flat – "a cardboard box with lots of plants" – in

---

[254] Taken from: Are Depeche Mode Cracking up?, Smash Hits, 9-22 October 1985. Words: Chris Heath.
[255] Taken from: "I Love the Idea of Wearing Leather and I Love the Idea of Being Tied up, Because I Love the Feeling of Helplessness ...", Record Mirror, 8 February 1986. Words: Nancy Culp.

London, something which the other members of the band gave him loads of stick about.

"He's lost his roots." **Alan** was rather mean here, but Fletch had said in many previous interviews time and time again that he would never, ever move from Basildon. "He's started investing in things like wine racks, you get the drift? He's even got a couple of books on caring for plants."[256]

Or another story ...

In a hotel lobby a presenter sat between the *Depeche* boys. He addressed a bored-looking Alan. "We'll start with you, Vince Clarke ..."[257] Unfortunately, Alan's response is not on record.

How is life as a pop-star?

"It's like I'm happy – I'm depressed," **Dave** replied. "There isn't really anything in between. You never just feel alright, you're either extremely happy or you're extremely depressed. There's no-one that can really understand unless they're in a successful band."[258]

Sounds as if you turn into a manic-depressive person when you decide to become a pop-star, and maybe this is the reason why so many of them become alcoholics and junkies.

And what can you do in Berlin?

"There's plenty to do in Berlin," **Alan** answered. "When you finish working at 4.00 a.m. you never feel like going to bed and so you end up in a bar or a club. *DNC* is a favourite, there's a couple of good gay clubs, *Corelles* is alright, the *Jungle* ..."[259]

Such a statement was controversial in **1985**. Much later he added: "I'm not gay but I've no problem with going to gay bars or clubs. We went there because they had the best vibe and music."[260]

From today's point of view it's very difficult to understand why the speculation that the band (or one of the band members) might be gay was so controversial. Al-

---

[256] Taken from: Are Depeche Mode Cracking up?, Smash Hits, 9-22 October 1985. Words: Chris Heath.
[257] Taken from: Coming up Smiling, The Face, February 1985. Words: Sheryl Garratt.
[258] Taken from: Are Depeche Mode Cracking up?, Smash Hits, 9-22 October 1985. Words: Chris Heath.
[259] Taken from: Alan Wilder: The Band Boy, No.1, 25 May 1985. Words: Alan Wilder.
[260] Taken from: recoil.co.uk. Words: Alan Wilder.

though I grew up in the **1980s** myself I often forget what a long way the gay community has come today. There are still many countries in which being gay is seen as a problem, but some countries try to be tolerant nowadays. This was completely different in the **1980s**. Reading through old music magazines I couldn't help but notice that they were slightly intolerant when it came to women, gay people and anyone else who was "different." Musicians had to live up to a certain image. The idea that is depicted nowadays that the media were especially tolerant with regard to artists is definitely wrong. Rock musicians especially had to be male, straight and tough. Someone with Martin's fondness for cross-dressing didn't suit the general view of that time.

Shortly after Dave's marriage they started to record *It's Called a Heart* at the *Genetic Studios*. The single was released on **16 September**. Beside the 7" mix, there were two different versions available, an extended version and the *Slow Mix* (remixed by Gareth Jones). Moreover, the U.S. version included the *Emotion Remix* and the *Emotion Dub*, both remixed by Joseph Watt. The single's B-side *Fly on the Windscreen* was available in three different versions, as the 7" mix, as an extended version and as the *Death Mix* (remixed by Gareth Jones). While the band members had agreed about *Shake the Disease, It's Called a Heart* caused some discord.

"*It's Called a Heart* has to be my least favourite, dare I say most hated *DM* single ever, and I was anti even recording it, let alone releasing it," **Alan** said. "In fact I fought tooth-and-nail on behalf of the B-side *Fly on the Windscreen* which was far superior. To me, the whole thing was a serious backward step. I felt we'd worked diligently to build up recognition for a harder sound, with more depth and maturity, and here was this ultra poppy number that did nothing for our reputation. Sadly, I was out-voted by the others although they recognised that *Fly on the Windscreen* was wasted as an additional track and agreed it should be promoted to the next album, *Black Celebration*."

Let's hope that he was still able to cope with the picture he had about himself: "I would obviously say what I thought the potential of each song was but I would hope that I was always diplomatic and never insensitive with my comments."

Likewise **Alan** hated the video for *It's Called a Heart*, answered a question about what he would change in his life if he could turn back time and do it all over again, "I don't think I'd change much, apart from some of the hair styles and those daft boots I wore in *101*. Oh, and I'd also make sure that I missed my wake-up call on the day we made the video for *It's Called a Heart*."

Asked about the intention of the video he said, "You'll have to ask Peter Care (the director) - he came up with that 'concept.' Quite how he equated 'calling something a heart' with twirling cameras around on the end of a string in a field of corn in Reading dressed in a skirt, I'll never be able to tell you."[261]

He hated that song so much that he answered the question "In your opinion, what makes up a true *DM* fan?" with "Anyone who still gives us the time of day after having heard *It's Called a Heart*."[262]

Strange enough, there aren't many quotations about *It's Called a Heart* by any of the other band members, at least not from **1985**. **Dave** simply said, "I do find it very hard to enjoy singles until a good while after they've been out."[263] And **Martin** explained, "The song is about the importance of the heart in a mythical sense, as the part of the body where good and evil are supposed to start. I'm not sure whether I believe in it but it's a nice idea."[264]

Years later **Fletch** answered the question of a fan about what their worst song was, *It's Called a Heart*.[265] And **Martin** said in **1998**, "*It's Called a Heart* is one of the worst things we've ever released."[266]

However, they must have liked it at the time otherwise there wouldn't have been such a fuss about it within the band in **1985**.

---

[261] Taken from: recoil.co.uk. Words: Alan Wilder.
[262] Taken from: Ask Alan, Bong 16, April 1992. Words: Alan Wilder.
[263] Taken from: Everything Counts (in Large Amounts), Number One, 19 October 1985. Words: Paul Bursche.
[264] Taken from: Are Depeche Mode Cracking up?, Smash Hits, 9-22 October 1985. Words: Chris Heath.
[265] Taken from: Ask Andy, Bong 17, July 1992. Words: Andrew Fletcher.
[266] Taken from: The Singles 86-98 by Martin Gore, Bong 37, September 1998. Compiled by Michaela Olexova. Words: Martin Lee Gore.

On **15 October** the compilation *The Singles 81-85* was released, mainly for the U.S. market because *DM* got more and more fans there. The U.S. version got the title *Catching Up With Depeche Mode* but had the same track listing.

With a break for a gig at *Peter's Popshow* on **9 November** in the *Westfalenhalle* in Dortmund, the band began to record *Black Celebration* at the **end of 1985**, firstly in *Westside Studios* in London, and later in *Hansa Studios* in Berlin. The idea of a "permanent session over some months to create a claustrophobic feeling" got too real all too soon.

In fact, the studio atmosphere got worse with time. While Martin was confident enough to offer his demos to those who were more focused on realising the musical aspects of his songs, it is said that the production relationship between Daniel Miller, Gareth Jones and Alan got worse. This finally led to the decision of Miller to stay outside the production in the future.

"Dan and I had grown as friends and musical associates as well as developing a mutual understanding of the territory we felt *Depeche Mode* should be exploring," **Alan** said. "For example, our affiliation had been enhanced by spending long hours finishing off the previous LP, *Some Great Reward*, when everyone else had cleared off on their holidays. With *Black Celebration*, we also ran well over our deadline but it was perhaps when too many additional voices were brought into the equation that problems seemed to arise."[267]

"There were quite a lot of arguments going on around that time," **Martin** admitted. "We'd overdone the working relationship between Daniel and Gareth Jones. That was the third album we'd done together and I think everybody'd become very lazy, relying on formulas."[268]

When I had the opportunity to chat with **Gareth Jones** I also asked him about the main reason for the tension during recording *Black Celebration*: „It was the third record we made together and obviously it was challenging and we all wanted to do something special. Daniel Miller had the idea that we should follow Werner Herzog. He had the idea we should live the album. What we did was ... we didn't have any time off.

---

[267] Taken from: recoil.co.uk. Words: Alan Wilder.
[268] Taken from: Just Can't Get Enough, Uncut, May 2001. Words: Stephen Dalton.

"At that time we all were a lot younger and we worked every day very long hours. From when we started recording the album to when we finished mixing it we went to work every single day. So that meant that we had ... in a way it brought a special pressure into the process. It was quite a high pressure process, but it was a thing we were willing to do. We all thought it was a good idea. We all felt it would be a good thing to do for this record. That wasn't something we were forced into. We discussed it and we all said, 'That's a great idea, let's do it! Let's enter the studio and don't stop working and won't have a day off until we finished.'

"And that meant that we got some kind of a claustrophobia, a claustrophobic attitude in the recording which really seemed to suit the songs and the album that we were trying to make. So, yes, it was a big tense sometimes. And when it came to the mixing Daniel and I were also tired. I remember very well the first track we were trying to mix. I think it was the title track, *Black Celebration*. We were sure we had quite a good mix and then everyone would make their comments and we decided it wasn't good enough and we tried again and again and this ... well, it drove the band nuts. Everyone was getting tired and just wanted to finish the record.

"I remember the band had a meeting and Alan said, 'Look, guys, we really need to sort ourselves out, we really have to get the record mixed! We must move forward.' I really remember it as a claustrophobic atmosphere and as sometimes dark, but it was a wonderful creative experience as well. So in a way the claustrophobia and the tensed atmosphere was really positive for the work I think."[269]

Martin obviously found the recording sessions so unbearable that he disappeared for a week, which aroused wild speculations, primarily in teen-magazines. He said he had freaked out because of the stress during the recording sessions and because he was moving house at the same time (he moved back to London).

"I think it does you good to freak out every now and then," **Dave** said. "I almost did at one point when we were recording the last album. I was moving house and then I had a bad car accident and at that point I thought 'that's

---

[269] depechemodebiographie.de.

it, it's over'." Later he told the accident had happened when he drove from a parking lot and another car rushed into his. He got hurt, particularly his knees.

"I've never actually done a runner," **Alan** added, "but I'm in a permanent state of being freaked out, I don't know who I am a lot of the time."[270]

So the year ended with some smaller and bigger disagreements. "If ever we were going to split up the band it was at the **end of 1985**," **Dave** said. "We were really in a state of turmoil. Constant arguing. Very intense. We weren't really sure where to go after *Some Great Reward* so we decided to slow things down. But it left us with too much time on our hands. So we spent most of our time arguing. Sometimes, it seems incredible that we came out of that period with the band and our sanity intact."[271]

Fletch even had a dark presentiment: "Since *Black Celebration*, I've felt our set-up could fall apart at any time."[272]

After studying all these interviews, I would also say that the point from which things started to go wrong was **1985**. Of course, they still had fun and they were very successful, but it seems to me that from this time problems started to "develop," maybe even without coming to the surface. I can imagine there was a lack of communication. Sometimes I had the feeling that they talked a lot to each other, but didn't say anything about what they really thought and felt. Meanwhile they had strict roles in the team, but didn't really talk about possible problems.

However, **Alan** didn't see this time as a real starting point. "Over the course of any 13-year period with a band, there are going to be times of high tension. I would say that by the end of recording of *Black Celebration* things were a bit difficult - but it wasn't the beginning of the end as such."[273]

It seems as if these problems were really based more on the human aspect and not so much on the musical as-

---

[270] Taken from: Are Depeche Mode Cracking up?, Smash Hits, 9-22 October 1985. Words: Chris Heath.
[271] Taken from: Depeche Mode, HMV / Melody Maker, 22 September 1990. Words: uncredited.
[272] Taken from: They Just Couldn't get Enough, Q, March 1997. Words: Phil Sutcliffe.
[273] depechemodebiographie.de.

pect, because they were all quite satisfied with the development they had achieved. *Black Celebration* "represents in many ways the end of a musical era and the conclusion of a tried and tested production liaison." Since **1983 Alan** had tried to steer the music away from its early poppy roots "to embrace a darker more tenebrous world." So *Black Celebration* was the last *DM* record "to fully salute this 'sample anything and everything' approach although the use of everyday objects as instruments would not be lost on future releases."[274]

"This is where the albums really started improving," **Martin** said. "I certainly felt very free. I wrote it in Berlin and we all started wearing black. When we're there now we're still followed by the fans; what we call *The Black Swarm*. If you get up in the morning to go to the gym, they'll be waiting in the lobby to follow you."[275]

"I think by the time we reached *Black Celebration*, a proper depth to the group's songs started to appear," **Alan** remarked. "It was partly because of the songs and partly because Martin was becoming more worldly as a songwriter along with my influence into making more of a dark sound."[276]

---

[274] Taken from: recoil.co.uk. Words: Alan Wilder.
[275] Taken from: User's Guide: Depeche Mode, Kingsize, May 2001. Words: uncredited.
[276] Taken from: Songs of Praise and Emotion, Blue Divide, Volume 2, Issue 1, 2000. Words: uncredited.

By the way ...

... Dave shares his birthday with a national celebration day in Russia, and Russian fans created their own celebration called "Dave Day."

... Gahan is Irish and is pronounced "Gaan."

... Daniel Miller studied at film school and became a film editor after leaving college in **1971**.

... I was asked by a reader what a "bong" is, and why the label (or better said: catalogue series) was called that. Well, a bong is a water pipe, used to consume cannabis. I once found an interview in which Fletch explained that they chose that name because they thought it was funny. I suppose it's the same story as with "Oberkorn," they needed a name and took the first one that sprang to mind.

... Brian Griffin used the building of the Round Oak steelworks in Brierley Hill as the backdrop for the cover of Some Great Reward. The factory was pulled down shortly after.

... Werner Herzog is a German film director whose films have often been the subject of controversy in regard to their themes and messages, especially the circumstances surrounding their creation. Herzog is known for "living" his films excessively.

... I was asked once by a very young reader why DM-fans mainly wear black. Well, this is the answer! The band wore black and released Black Celebration and The Black Swarm was born. Even today some fans still kid each other with this when blind dates are planned, especially at DM-parties and concerts. "How will I recognize you?" – "I'm going to wear a black dress." But nowadays you'll find different colours on DM-concerts as well.

1986

- Dressed in black again -

The interest in all the clothing questions finally dropped off a bit. At least half of the year music was the main topic.

With *Black Celebration*, the band mixed the third album in Berlin. "I can't work in England anymore," **Dave** said. "It's funny. The studio is right next to the Berlin Wall but none of us has ever been to the East. Martin tried once but they refused him entry. Didn't like the way he was dressed. Thought he was a hooligan." (It's true that they refused him entry, but they probably didn't think he was a hooligan.) "People imagine we work here because it's wow, you know, really heavy, but I don't feel that. The place is quite suburban. Berlin's like Brixton."[277]

Nevertheless, they came back there for the third time. "Mainly because we're too lazy to find another studio! And we know when we come here that it's going to be good. It's probably one of the best studios in the world. Working in London, it's difficult to get into it because we just have so many people coming to see us. We don't go through a manager or anything. The four of us. We are the managers."[278]

As it has been mentioned in the previous chapter, the roles were starting to be defined more clearly within the band. Something that wasn't free of conflicts.

"Martin's the songwriter," **Fletch** explained, "he's the main creative source behind the band. Alan's the chief musician, best musician in the band. Well Dave is the frontman of the group. A lot of people don't like his stage performance, but he really does get the crowd going, and you can't ignore that, basically. And he's put a lot of effort into his stage performance and into improving his singing over the years, and I think it's worked out really well. My niche is really on the organisational front, because we

---

[277] Taken from: Back to the Wall, No. 1, 22 February 1986. Words: Max Bell / Mark Booker.
[278] Taken from: I Love the Idea of Wearing Leather and I Love the Idea of Being Tied up, Because I Love the Feeling of Helplessness ..., Record Mirror, 8 February 1986. Words: Nancy Culp.

haven't got a manager and I provide all those functions." (Remarkable is that many years later – when Alan sold parts of his large *DM*-collection - Alan was turned out to be a "list-maker" as well, as someone who kept a record of everything.) "I also see myself on the morale front; getting, keeping the band together and all that sort of thing, which I think is really important. Every band's got to have that sort of person as well."[279]

"Generally me and Martin deal with the music side," **Alan** said, "and we seem to complement each other quite well. He is much more involved in songwriting and melody, while I'm more interested in the rhythms and overall production. Martin gets bored with this side of things really fast."[280]

Sometimes it bothered him that Martin didn't really care about the production, but it also gave him more space to do what he enjoyed. On the other hand, this might have been the root cause of the upcoming problems, because it was difficult for these two characters to work together, and sometimes they also had musical differences. But probably not so many relating to *Black Celebration*.

"We even have the theory that Martin is a lazy sod who writes an entire album in an afternoon but pretends he hasn't so he can take ages to think about other things and do nothing,"[281] **Alan** claimed.

And: "The *NME* made the point that we were not adventurous enough. They said that we could pull more out of the bag, that we were actually quite lazy. That is true to a point, but it comes from the problem that as a democracy we always tend to end up with a compromise between the adventurous and conservative sides of the band."[282]

Probably the "conservative sides" were Martin and Fletch and the "adventurous sides" were Dave and Alan. The only option they had when a vote was split both ways was an independent arbitration from those they respected the most, such as Daniel Miller or one of the later co-producers.

---

[279] Taken from: Depeche Mode: The Interview, Talking Music SPEEK013, 1988.
[280] Taken from: Basildon Bond, Blitz, April 1986. Words: Bruce Dessau.
[281] Taken from: Back to the Wall, No. 1, 22 February 1986. Words: Max Bell / Mark Booker.
[282] Taken from: Basildon Bond, Blitz, April 1986. Words: Bruce Dessau.

Stripped (© Ingo Bittrich)

The single *Stripped / But Not Tonight*, which was released on **10 February**, was the first result of all the cooperation, compromises and tensions. Much to the dismay of the band, the B-side *But Not Tonight* was released as an A-side in the U.S.

"The American record company just think of us as a disco band and they usually release our B-sides,"[283] **Martin** said. "We'd spent three weeks perfecting *Stripped*. *But Not Tonight* was a throwaway thing we did in a day."[284]

"The U.S. market is completely different to Europe and the rest of the world," **Alan** explained. "I don't pretend to fully understand it but whenever we 'deliver' product, they always want to do things differently to 'suit their market.' Their argument is that 'we know our own market better than you so let us decide' - perhaps they are right. Certainly, radio in the U.S. is a strange animal which dictates how the companies promote the product."[285]

In this case, *Sire Records* decided to use *But Not Tonight* for the soundtrack of the film *Modern Girls* and therefore,

---

[283] Taken from: Celebrity Squares? Sounds, 26 April 1986. Words: Dave Henderson.
[284] Taken from: Devout Moded, Vox, February 1993. Words: Martin Townsend.
[285] Taken from: recoil.co.uk. Words: Alan Wilder.

the single was flipped. Even an alternate video was filmed, directed by Tamra Davis. It was available in multiple versions.

The entire backbone of *Stripped* was based around an idling motorbike sound generated from the original *Emulator*, and a bass drone that was eventually fed through a *Leslie cabinet*. Additional sounds such as the ignition of Dave's *Porsche 911* [another source says it was a different *Porsche* type; I'm referring to Alan's website] and an array of fireworks from *Guy Fawkes Night* were recorded by Gareth Jones in the studio car park using an assortment of unusual microphones. The microphones were placed at varying distances and heights with the fireworks being let off at the appropriate angle to create the full stereophonic effect. A drum kit was used to sample individual sounds, most notably the distinctive toms with their special ambience.

Stripped was misinterpreted many times. Mainly German teen magazines offered phrases like "they dream of naked girls."

"It's not about sex," **Dave** explained. "It's to do with having nothing except yourself. The people in the song could strip off if they wanted to though."

"The idea of *Stripped* is to get away from technology and civilisation for a day and get back to basics in the country," **Fletch** said. "It's about two people stripping down to their bare emotions. In the video we're seen demolishing a car and taking a TV apart... it's a bit, er, symbolic."[286]

It was Peter Care who had the idea for this video and filmed the promo in Berlin just around the corner from the *Hansa Studios*.

"It was amazing, really," **Alan** remarked. "Just because in the video we are demolishing cars – the British can't bear to see material goods wantonly destroyed. We had lots of complaints. After it was on there was probably a film of someone having their head shot off on the news."[287]

On **17 March** the album *Black Celebration* was released. It's the only *DM*-album that has the same title as a track on the album. The voice at the beginning of *Black Celebration* was Daniel Miller's saying, "A brief period of

---

[286] Taken from: Back to the Wall, No. 1, 22 February 1986. Words: Max Bell / Mark Booker.
[287] Taken from: Basildon Bond, Blitz, April 1986. Words: Bruce Dessau.

rejoicing." The cover photographer was Brian Griffin again. Some tracks have six or eight little melodies all working together in a kind of techno-fugue which brought a completely new feeling to the songs. Some melodies were from the original demos, some came about in the studio. The sample at the beginning of *Fly on the Windscreen* is based on Daniel Miller saying 'horse' very fast.

About the title track *Black Celebration*, **Dave** said that it "sounds a bit morbid but it's a common thing. At the end of a working day you go out and drown your sorrows no matter how sh*** you feel or how bleak your future looks."

"*It Doesn't Matter Two* is very desperate. Very very morbid. There is one quite funny song called *Sometimes* which is about someone who questions their surroundings and ends up becoming tiring and over apologetic." **Martin** laughed nervously.[288]

He is known to be an autobiographical pop writer and the song was probably about himself. Or as **Alan** said, "Martin is very honest in his songs, almost embarrassingly honest."[289]

I was asked by a reader if the line "*she doesn't trust him, nothing is true, but he will do*" (*World Full of Nothing*) might be a reference to a rape. Although it's possible, it doesn't really match the rest of the lyrics. It is probably meant in a way that he is a bit rude or doesn't really watch her feelings and reactions when he does "it." This would be in line with *she doesn't trust him*. She isn't really ready for *her first boy* but he will push her. It is also possible that although *she doesn't trust him* and doesn't love him, he is good enough at that very moment. This would be the true sense of "he will do" but of course the "it" could have been left out because of the rhyme. As the main sentence of the lyrics is "*though it's not love it means something*," both interpretations are possible or maybe it is even meant in both directions.

Martin always had a strong interest in what people believe. This is probably the reason why he is so interested in religion, although he isn't religious himself. He once said he wished he could believe in something, and he said

---

[288] Taken from: Back to the Wall, No. 1, 22 February 1986. Words: Max Bell / Mark Booker.
[289] Taken from: Videointerview during Masses-Tour 1988. Media and interviewer unknown.

if he believes in something it is love. And *World Full of Nothing* deals with believing in something. Both, boy and girl, want to believe in love. That's why they are together, that's why they are doing it, that why it is so *easy to slip away and believe it all*, but nevertheless *it's not love*.

It also deals with another favourite topic of Martin's – the innocence of youth, and the way this innocence gets lost through certain events and with growing older (see **1987**.) Therefore, *World Full of Nothing* also has a connection to *A Question of Time* where he is worried about the innocence of the 15-year-old.

On **29 March** the *Black Celebration*-Tour started. It consisted of four legs. The first leg took place in the UK, comprised 13 gigs and ended on **17 April** in London.

The band played ever-fewer concerts in the UK from tour to tour because the interest in them decreased more and more in England. But at the same time the interest increased abroad.

"I think on this whole tour the band have got to all really pull together," **Dave** said. "We've talked about it, and we know that we're going to have real bad times. That's something we're good at doing, otherwise we wouldn't still be together. We've gone through a lot of bad periods. We've not really had musical differences, but just as people. It's usually between me and Fletch. We tend to argue sometimes, but, obviously, we both really love each other," he laughed, "but definitely not in a soppy way!"[290]

Many interviews with other musicians show that most bands are able to compensate for personal problems as long as there aren't any deep musical differences. But sometimes it's enough to disagree about a small detail and the whole thing might "explode." I think that both things – personal problems between the different characters, especially between Fletch and Alan, and different opinions about the way to work, especially between Martin and Alan – increased in the course of the following years, while I don't think that the arguments between Dave and Fletch were really "dangerous." The things that destroy a project are mainly those the members of a team or a band don't

---

[290] Taken from: I Love the Idea of Wearing Leather and I Love the Idea of Being Tied up, Because I Love the Feeling of Helplessness ..., Record Mirror, 8 February 1986. Words: Nancy Culp.

notice at first. So that's probably why everyone said that everything was fine at that time.

"The atmosphere backstage [in Oxford] was slightly tense but when we arrived on stage the reception we received easily calmed any nerves we had," **Fletch** told about the tour. "The gig went well with only a few hitches, the main one being when I tripped over on stage during the encore, injuring myself and nearly putting the whole tour in jeopardy. People still remind me of this incident much to my embarrassment."[291]

During this period *DM* developed into a "live-power," although they were quite a strange live band when you look at it from a traditional point of view. At first glance *DM* was a static formation, with three boys behind programmed keyboards, and a front man who was jumping around madly and didn't sing every note right. Nevertheless, they had a very special magic, which was so fascinating that even very critical people couldn't ignore it. You couldn't go to a *DM*-concert without being "blown away."

Talking about his own experience seeing *DM* for the first time live from the audience, Alan was very impressed by the way Dave was controlling the audience. This is true, and it was true back in **1986**.

Trying to compare the earlier concerts with those of today, the fans, who like the old gigs better, had difficulties explaining what was so fascinating about them. Maybe the conclusion is: "The static and unapproachable performance of an electronic band was something absolutely new. It was unique, mystical and very impressive."

In **Martin's** opinion this pushed Dave into becoming more of a frontman. "He used a lot more of the stage, ran around and got the audience participating."[292]

45% of the fans who took part in the survey of *depechemodebiographie.de* said that the "live versions were much more creative and complex" compared to today, "this is, of course, more interesting." But it isn't a real explanation I think, especially because you already could feel this magic in the very early days when they got on stage with a reel-to-reel tape recorder, wore awful clothes

---

[291] Taken from: Information Service newsletter, September 1986. Words: Andrew Fletcher.
[292] Taken from: My interview with Depeche Mode, 29 January 2010, words: oyvindholen

and Dave was moving as if he was at a dancing lesson. From this point they developed, tried different visual effects and created more and more atmosphere. With the very atmospheric and dark *Black Celebration* this magic was growing and increased until *Devotional*.

In the meantime, on **14 April**, the single *A Question of Lust / Christmas Island* was released. The cover of the single shows a kissing couple. In a teenage magazine the rumour was initiated that it was Alan who was kissing the girl. It's amazing how long such rumours stay alive, because I was recently asked by a reader if it was Alan. No, it was an actor who had been engaged for the photo session.

A Question of Lust was also a rare single with Martin taking care of the lead vocal. For the band it was usually fairly easy to predict whose voice would suit particular songs. Martin's voice tended to suit ballads and Dave's tended to suit more raucous tracks.

At the beginning of the video for *A Question of Lust* Martin appeared naked in front of the camera.

"We were in a club somewhere and, as usual, Martin managed to take all his clothes off," **Alan** explained. "The director Clive Richardson decided to bring his camera along and that's what he got."[293]

Right after that, on **24 April**, the European leg started in Oslo.

"Towards the end of the European leg of the tour I was heavily depressed," **Dave** said. "I just wanted to go home. I did a lot of sulking because, even though this is an ideal job which I love, it's also physically and mentally exhausting."[294]

It was really hard for him that the U.S. leg began right after the European leg. Nevertheless, they had their fun in the U.S. "In America we get everything thrown at us – bras, suspender belts, knickers and even shoes. After one concert we had about 40 shoes on stage and there were no pairs! Imagine all those people hopping home!"[295]

"We were visiting places where no electronic band had been before," **Fletch** explained. "Before we left these

---

[293] Taken from: recoil.co.uk. Words: Alan Wilder.
[294] Taken from: Yes, it's Two Typical Days on Tour with Depeche Mode, Smash Hits, 27 August 1986. Words: Ro Newton.
[295] Taken from: One of those Days ..., Smash Hits, 26 March 1986. Words: Chris Heath.

shores we expected to do well on the east and west coast, but in middle America we were prepared for the worst. In the end, though the whole tour was a huge success. Everywhere we went people wanted to hear our music, I don't think they had seen a band present themselves in a way like us, with no drums and guitars."[296]

"We went on a tour that just seemed to take off, particularly in America," **Alan** said. "It seemed to be where we stepped up a gear and went from playing smallish club venues through to quite big arenas. So, things moved very rapidly from that point onwards."[297]

It's interesting that at this time the general interest in the U.S. in British (electronic and pop) bands was declining increasingly, after they had had a brief wave of success a short time before. *DM* became "hip" in the U.S. when English bands were more or less out, and American rock bands were on top again. They captured a special niche, big enough to generate a kind of general interest and a huge group of followers, although I think that the most faithful fans can be found in (East) Germany and Eastern Europe, those fans who weren't able to follow the band in the early years, as if the "forbidden fruits" had doubled the special magic of the band for them.

"So with America over, next on the agenda was Japan," **Fletch** said. "A busy schedule of three gigs in three days meant all we saw were trains, hotel rooms and concert halls. Fortunately for Martin the last day fell on his birthday. After a great concert in Tokyo, we were on a TV programme where the producer gave him a video camera as a present." (There is a video of this TV show. Everyone is singing "happy birthday" to Martin, and he remarks that he's been given the "twentieth cake of the day.") "My thoughts went back three weeks earlier when I spent my birthday ill in bed in Vancouver. The World Tour was now nearing the end. While the equipment was coming back from Japan Alan and Martin had a short stay in Bali. Dave and myself feeling a bit homesick went home. The last leg of the tour was a few concerts in Southern Europe ending with a final concert in Copenhagen. This all sounds very nice but in the end we were plagued by the weather. The

---

[296] Taken from: Information Service newsletter, December 1986. Words: Andrew Fletcher.
[297] Taken from: The Story Of Depeche Mode, BBC Radio London Live94.9, 7 May 2001, Producer: Tony Wood.

concert in Bordeaux had to be cancelled because of rain."[298]

DM were seen increasingly as "dark" and "moody" by the general public at the time. In contrast, the band members enjoyed themselves and were quite self-ironic.
"As a live band we play very loud – we're talkin' *Motörhead* – but that's what it's all about. That's the power of rock 'n' roll! We've never called ourselves a 'rock 'n' roll' band; we do everything there is to do in rock 'n' roll. *It's Called a Heart* was rock 'n' roll, man!" **Dave** laughed.[299]
"We kinda subtly corrupt the world", **Martin** remarked. "Basically if you call yourself a pop band you can get away with anything."[300]
And another theory of his: "Four people is the right number for a pop group. History bears me out. Five people looks wrong and three is plain stupid. Four looks powerful."[301] (One should remember this statement for later ...)

Even at this U.S.-tour, the band began to fall into the "party-trap" and to live a real rock 'n' roll-life.
"It's exciting to be able to visit so many different places and meet new people but constant travelling and hotel life can get you down," **Alan** explained. "Obviously the social side of things is great - clubs and restaurants want you to frequent their establishments and will lay everything on for you. The downside of this kind of treatment is that it's very easy to get carried away and lose track of reality and it's very true that life on the road is like living in a bubble. As far as the shows go, it can get boring playing the same things night after night. I always found being on stage a surreal experience - at times my mind would be somewhere completely different whilst my body was on automatic pilot.
"A usual day on the road is to check out of hotel at 1 or 2pm, travel to local airfield, fly by private jet with immediate entourage (about 12 people) to next city. Arrive 4pm

---

[298] Taken from: Information Service newsletter, December 1986. Words: Andrew Fletcher.
[299] Taken from: Depeche Mode's Kinky Moods, Creem, July 1986. Words: Dave Keeps.
[300] Taken from: If You Call Yourself a Pop Band You Can Get Away With Anything, Record Mirror, 23 August 1986. Words: Andy Strickland.
[301] Taken from: Back to the Wall, No. 1, 22 February 1986. Words: Max Bell / Mark Booker.

approx. Go straight to gig for sound check, back to hotel at 6pm, quick sauna / work out if there was time, leave for gig 7.45pm. On stage 8.30 / 9pm.

"When you come from stage it is 11pm You need two hours for changing clothes and some small talk and you drink one or two beer. Now it is one o'clock in the morning and you have to go out. Before you notice it really it is 7am and you had a lot of drinks. During a tour you get used to that lifestyle so much that you are sleepless every night and drink without ever feeling drunk. This became such a normal thing that you don't recognize it as debauchery."[302]

This is the typical lifestyle of almost any band in the world. Reading thousands of interviews with different musicians I found exactly this description a hundred times. One musician described it in an interview with *depechemodebiographie.de* in this way: "It was like this: I came to the rehearsal - let's have a drink first. We settled down in the tour bus - let's have a drink. We arrived at the venue - let's have a drink. Sound-check ... After show party ... before you realise it you are caught in a vicious circle. It seems to be normal to you but it'll end up in being an alcoholic."

And another one said, "It is easy to lead a debauched way of life. I drank a lot of beer already on stage, then we partied the whole night long and I took a lot of drugs - to do it all over again the next evening. A life like this is extremely short: you'll end up in prison, you'll die or you'll stop doing that sh**!" (These interviews were anonymous.)

But before you become aware of the shadowy side to this lifestyle you of course enjoy it – and at that stage of their career *DM* definitely enjoyed it.

From **4 to16 August** the band played a small last leg, comprising 7 gigs - mainly in Italy.

"It's nice to come at this time of year when, obviously, the weather helps," **Dave** said, "but it's chaos! The actual country's in total chaos!"

"They're nice people and everything, but they're renowned for their disorganization," **Martin** agreed. "A lot of

---

[302] Taken from: recoil.co.uk. Words: Alan Wilder.

the time it's untrue what countries are famous for, but in Italy's case, it's dead true."[303]

"In this country absolutely anything can happen. The last gig we played here was in a tent and it was actually raining with condensation over the keyboards!" **Alan** remembered. "We also did one somewhere like this where the power chord ran through the crowd and just as we started the last song someone cut through the cable and everything went off. It was pitch black."

"Oh yeah, and remember that Italian TV show we did?" **Fletch** asked. "They kept saying we'd be on any minute and we ended up waiting 13 hours." (I hope he wasn't referring to the show at which they got drunk in the wardrobe and started licking each other.)

"There was that bloke poking fun at our haircuts," **Dave** added. "I said 'Well at least we've got some.' He was wearing a toupee. And when he said to Mart 'Boy or girl?' we beat him up. We're banned from that station."[304]

This is definitely not correct. You can watch this interview on *YouTube*. The presenter asked Martin whether he is a boy or a girl, but they didn't beat him up (at least not in front of the camera.)

It's just a question of time ... (© Ingo Bittrich)

In the meantime, on **11 August**, the single *A Question of Time* was released. It was mainly recorded at the *Hansa Studios* "with its unique ambience leaving its mark on *A Question of Time*," as **Alan** said. "It's difficult to say what effect the studio had on the end results but *Hansa* defi-

---

[303] Taken from: If You Call Yourself a Pop Band You Can Get Away With Anything, Record Mirror, 23 August 1986. Words: Andy Strickland.
[304] Taken from: Yes, it's Two Typical Days on Tour with Depeche Mode, Smash Hits, 27 August 1986. Words: Ro Newton.

nitely had an atmosphere about it. Even though we were predominantly working at the very top of the building in *Studio 4*, we hired out the main recording room of *Studio 2* and set up a *2K PA* system to send individual sounds through - effectively to beef them up and get the atmosphere of the room. This was done much to the annoyance of the *Hansa* cafe owner I might add, who had to endure 4's on the floor pounding directly above his head for 3 days on the trot - something akin to a road drill placed six inches from your ear. God knows what he used to put in our food as retribution ..."[305]

A Question of Time was the first promo to be directed by Anton Corbijn, who would change their image in a drastic way. With Corbijn the band finally lost their naive image. They were no longer a "young, poppy boy-band that might be gay." Their music became more matured, and Corbijn gave them a darker, more masculine style. Sometimes even a bit macho-esque (especially in later videos like *Personal Jesus*).

"We had been trying to work with Anton for quite a while, but he wasn't interested in working with us, because he felt we were too much of a pop band, and he didn't really like what we were doing," **Martin** said. "It was probably the third attempt when we sent him the single *A Question of Time*, and asked him if he was interested in doing a video for it. And finally he actually liked something we were doing.[306] We had a lot of bad experiences in the early days with videos. I think that a lot of the time directors came in, I think they just saw how young and naive we were and they were just taking the piss - 'Let's see how stupid we can make them look, see how far they'll go!'"

"Video wasn't an area where we had ever felt comfortable," **Dave** added. "We kind of stood in the background and afterwards went, 'Urrrgh, that looks really bad dunnit?' The moment we sat down with Anton and started talking about ideas it was pretty obvious that he was going to be part of the team."[307]

"In the early days it was a bit of a lottery how the video turned out," **Fletch** said. "It was kind of frustrating, be-

---

[305] Taken from: recoil.co.uk. Words: Alan Wilder.
[306] Taken from: My interview with Depeche Mode, 29 January 2010. Words: oyvindholen.
[307] Taken from: Interview with Depeche Mode, The Videos 86>98, Mute MF033 and Videos 86>98+, Mute MF042. Director: Sven Harding.

cause we felt we weren't in control. Really, up to the day we met Anton Corbijn, we were sometimes looking okay and sometimes looking terrible. We didn't have a unified image really. We didn't really look like a united band. When we started working with Anton we suddenly started to look like a cool band."[308]

But then this first promo was mainly focussed on **Alan**. "I can't really remember the circumstances but it is possible that I was the only one prepared to get up early enough. The location was two hours outside LA and I think the shoot was on a day after a gig. Directors always get you to the shoot at 5am just out of spite. Later we had to struggle with the little baskets, sorry, babies for hours before they would do what was required. There were mothers, nappies, bottles, toys - all kinds of chaos."[309]

Martin on the question about who was meant with the 15-year-old in *A Question of Time*: "Well ummm, yes, it was written about a person in particular. Full stop, no comment." He laughed.

"I think it's just looking really, observing," **Dave** tried to help out. "Rather than ... just writing about what would happen to that person, a young attractive girl who was very innocent, and obviously, once us lads get our hands on them, they change."

A horde dipped teenagers appeared exactly at that moment, and one of the girls asked whether she might kiss **Dave** on his cheek. "No, no," he said before he gave in, "oh, alright then."[310]

On **18 August** Alan released *1 + 2*, two long instrumental tracks with a lot of samples and sounds, and chose the name *Recoil* for the project.

When he was asked about where the name came from in **1989** he simply replied, "The dictionary."[311]

In **2010** he would answer the same question less ironic, "It's what happens when you shoot a gun and the power of the gun throws you backwards, that's the recoil. And I thought that was quite nice if music has that effect

---

[308] Taken from: My interview with Depeche Mode, 29 January 2010. Words: oyvindholen.
[309] Taken from: recoil.co.uk. Words: Alan Wilder.
[310] Taken from: If You Call Yourself a Pop Band You Can Get Away With Anything, Record Mirror, 23 August 1986. Words: Andy Strickland.
[311] Taken from: Ask Alan, Bong 6, July 1989. Words: Alan Wilder.

on people as well ... you don't want music to wash over people and have no effect. So I quite liked the word for that reason. But apart from that, there was no great reason, really. It's just that it sounded good at the time."[312]

About the "birth" of *Recoil* he explained, "I did a couple of refinements at home with samples and recorded them on cassette. Sampling was brand-new at that time and it was exciting for me to play around with that just for the fun of it.[313] It was a cassette demo on a 4-track *Fostex* or *Tascam*, and only ended up being released after I played it to Daniel. He said, 'could you re-do this?' I didn't really have time to do it properly, so we just decided to release it inconspicuously, as it was, and not pay too much attention to it.[314] We felt it was good to get anything out there and perhaps I didn't feel that precious about it because it was only a side project at the time."

The rest of the band didn't seem to notice it. "They didn't say much about it," **Alan** said. "And I was quite reserved about it at the beginning. The first release wasn't much more than a demo. There wasn't the impression given they had been very interested in."[315]

This didn't change with the subsequent releases, but later it became clear that all remaining band members did listen to *Recoil,* definitely. Many years later Dave would show up quite impressed by Alan's music, Fletch mentioned once that he liked *Liquid*, and there's a recording of a "hotel session" involving Martin on which he sang *In Your Room* and then added the refrain of *Control Freak* (from *Unsound Methods*, **1997**) – *you're all I need to get high*. It might seem ironic, because it was him who called Alan a control freak, but nevertheless he had listened to this record.

1986 was a year of rather unsuccessful interviews. There was one in which **Dave** simply talked and talked and ... The reporter didn't manage to put forward her questions, instead she got things like this: "I got really drunk at the last gig we did and didn't get back to the ho-

---

[312] Taken from: Recoil in Bucharest, depechemode.ro, 2010. Words: Otiliei Haraga.
[313] Taken from: recoil.co.uk. Words: Alan Wilder.
[314] Taken from: Unsound Recordings, Sound On Sound, January 1998. Words: Bill Bruce.
[315] Taken from: recoil.co.uk. Words: Alan Wilder.

tel until four in the morning. There I was lying on the bed and suddenly I wanted to go pee. I went into the bathroom and fell asleep on the loo. After about an hour I tried to stand up but I slipped on a towel and went flying through the shower – flat out on my backside, I was. I cried out for Jo who got me back to the bed. I sneaked a look down at my ankle and nearly died when I saw the size of it. It was like an elephant's foot. Huge. It still hurts me now."[316]

But no matter what kind of health related obstacles the band members faced they hardly cancelled a show – the show must go on.

"You can't just decide to have a night off just because you feel a bit tired and once on stage, a natural adrenaline rush would always see you through,"[317] **Alan** explained.

"You wouldn't believe how much money I spend on clothes," **Dave** said. "Tonight I actually ran out of leather trousers so I had to wear white cotton ones. I get soaking wet every night and the leather goes all hard. Five gigs and they're ruined. Tonight I even slipped about on stage it was so wet."[318]

And if you thought, he would look after his wardrobe himself -

"Each band member had a travelling wardrobe and a wardrobe person was responsible for making sure everybody's stage gear was washed and ready to wear etc.,"[319] **Alan** explained.

There was one interview in which the reporter wanted to know something completely different, but Dave and Fletch didn't bother at all, talked about whatever they wanted.

Dave: "Yes, I've got plans to have kids. I want to try everything. Plus I'm in a good position to look after them properly, but that doesn't mean I'll send them to private school. I want them to live and learn as I have."

Fletch: "I'm 24 now and I often get the urge – to have children that is – but my girlfriend's just started her ca-

---

[316] Taken from: Yes, it's Two Typical Days on Tour with Depeche Mode, Smash Hits, 27 August 1986. Words: Ro Newton.
[317] Taken from: recoil.co.uk. Words: Alan Wilder.
[318] Taken from: Yes, it's Two Typical Days on Tour with Depeche Mode, Smash Hits, 27 August 1986. Words: Ro Newton.
[319] Taken from: recoil.co.uk. Words: Alan Wilder.

reer and I wouldn't want to interrupt it." (He was talking about his later wife, Grainne.)

Dave: "Some people are so dedicated to their job, nothing else matters but I think that's very tunnelled vision. For example, our engineer has just had a vasectomy and he's only young. I find that really stupid." (And I find it very impolite to tell this in public. :D) "Why not take your baby into the office? What's wrong with that?"

Fletch: "Don't be silly."

Then they switched to another topic still far away from what the reporter wanted to know.

Dave: "I think that if you've got money it's wrong to feel guilty about spending it. I've always spent what money I've had whether it be a fiver or five hundred."

Fletch: "That's a ridiculous attitude. You've got to have certain values, Dave, and you need to draw a line somewhere. Personally, I think the huge amount Martin has just spent on his new sofa is completely stupid."

Dave: "But Fletch you've got to enjoy life."

Fletch: "I do."

Dave: "I know, but you only live once and it's silly to have money sitting in the bank."

Fletch: "Yeah Dave, but for you everything's got its price."

Dave: "I often don't look at prices."

Fletch: "Sure, but ..."[320]

Probably this is an example for what Dave meant when he said that he and Fletch tended to argue. As you can see it's nothing serious. They are simply different characters with different opinions and tend to talk at cross-purposes.

And there really were some articles about Martin's clothes again. Why did he wear a bra with a tin of beer on each side on stage lately? (And why did the reporter even dare to ask about it?)

"It's just something I like doing. It's a laugh, it makes me laugh when I look in the mirror, it makes other people laugh when they see me and I'm making the whole world happy!" **Martin** laughed.

"And it makes people cry," **Dave** remarked. "Especially Fletch. 'You can't wear that, oh God!' he comes in with his

---

[320] Taken from: From Lads to Dads, Just Seventeen, 19 March 1986. Words: Jenny Tucker.

new gear on and it's quite a big event because we wonder what he's got on this time."

Martin laughed loudly. "In France a couple of years ago, we'd never really had much success and I put on this gear in the dressing room when we were doing this TV programme and Fletch took one look at me and said 'Mart, we're never going to do anything in France if you go out looking like that!' The next thing we knew, we had massive hits there. That was what started it."[321]

Life in the so-called space age (subtitle of *Black Celebration*) (© Ingo Bittrich)

Legendary is the interview Martin gave in Berlin, lying on the asphalt, while the reporter wanted to learn something about Martin's ambitions as a male stripper ...

"If he carries on drinking he could strip!" **Fletch** alerted.

"It's something I never really wanted to do when I was younger," **Martin** said, "but as I've... I've not got great ambitions to be a stripper, but I quite like stripping."

What about doing it right here?

---

[321] Taken from: If You Call Yourself a Pop Band You Can Get Away With Anything, Record Mirror, 23 August 1986. Words: Andy Strickland.

"It's not a question of not being an exhibitionist," **Martin** explained. "The reason I wouldn't strip in front of *Woolworth's* in Berlin is it's just not the right place to do it."

And then she asked about the leather.

"I love wearing leather," **Martin** said. "I love wearing black, but apart from that I love the idea of ... being tied up, because I love the feeling of helplessness, and that's the only reason. I'm not really into pain. Well, it is about whips and chains, but it's not ... As in most of my songs, I hate writing about a certain subject. I like writing songs that are maybe about a certain subject, but, like, take in a greater spectrum. I hate having to describe songs because if you try and describe them in a few words, you never describe them fully. 'Cos sometimes I write a couple of lines and I'm not sure what they're about. I don't know exactly what I'm trying to say, but they fit exactly the atmosphere of the song and the music, at that point.

"I hate interviews, actually, because I find it so difficult coming across natural. I hate reading them, too. That's one reason why I don't like doing them. I don't blame journalists, I blame myself for what I say. I know it's really bad. It's just a question of ... I reckon if you interview us, a lot of the time you're going to get a lot of stuff that's real rubbish. I know when you interview me, you're going to get a lot of stuff that you're not going to be interested in at all."[322]

The journalist probably thought she had learned something about Martin's personality, but this interview is a good example for Martin's humour and for being very clever when someone was too curious about special things.

Speaking of funny things - here are two tit-bits:

Dave: "I suppose *A-Ha* will take away everyone's girl audience for a while because they're hunky good looking chaps. The problem is that they probably speak funny."

Fletch: "They probably speak better English than you do."

---

[322] Taken from: I Love the Idea of Wearing Leather and I Love the Idea of Being Tied up, Because I Love the Feeling of Helplessness ..., Record Mirror, 8 February 1986. Words: Nancy Culp.

Dave: "Rubbish. I bet they don't."[323]

Fletch: "At the beginning of this project I started taking lots of vitamins. But as soon as I stopped taking 'em I got ill. I'm not saying it's connected, mind you, but I've been ill for the last week and a half, trying to 'shake the disease.' Still it's better than being constipated, that's the worst thing!"

Dave: "Toilet talk is one of his favourite topics. It's all he ever talks about!"

Fletch: "Well, it's a weird thing. I mean you do it in private ..."

Dave: "You should interview him about toilet style ..."

Martin: "Can I just interrupt for two seconds? They need the video title now! I've thought of something I don't like very much: *Some Great Videos*."

Fletch: "Yeah, because some of our videos are pretty bad, so it's not *The Videos*, all of them, but some of 'em."[324]

Some Great Videos was released on **22 September**. For the rest of the year the band got some time off.

---

[323] Taken from: Back to the Wall, No. 1, 22 February 1986. Words: Max Bell / Mark Booker.
[324] Taken from: Depeche Mode's Kinky Moods, Creem, July 1986. Words: Dave Keeps.

1987

- Pain – will you return it? (Strangelove) -

In the **beginning of 1987** the band re-arranged Martin's demos for *Music for the Masses (MFTM)* in Alan's home studio. (According to rumours, Martin hardly took part in this phase of re-arranging. And it's not clear if the demo of *Little 15* that was released as a bonus track with *SOTU* in **2009** was the original one or the re-arranged one.)

They worked with a new team - the band on their own with co-producer David Bascombe, who would later modestly call himself "just a better sound engineer." So *MFTM* was more or less a self-produced album.

"In the earlier years everybody would be in the studio with the result often being lots of chat and mucking around with little actual work being achieved," **Alan** said. "As time went on we all realised that less people in the control room equalled more work done. On the last few albums, it would only be those that were essential or specifically needed."[325]

So, the roles within the band got stricter and stricter over the course of time. This can be a good thing for the work and the creative process itself, on the other hand, it can be difficult, because the individual team members start to drift apart without even noticing it at first.

At that time, during recording *MFTM,* and also later during recording *Violator*, the team worked quite well, and the chosen roles and the concept of the team were good for creativity. So **Steve Lyon**, who was the engineer on *Violator* and *SOFAD*, asked about the team-work as such and Dave's role in particular said, "I came in to the production of *Violator* when there was one song finished and the rest of the songs were kind of half way through but had no vocals. I didn't see Dave really much involved in the creation of the sounds or the directions of the songs. He would come in and sing and did a fantastic job, but wasn't really involved in the creativity of the material. I think he was very positive on his part and very supportive in what we were doing.

---

[325] Taken from: recoil.co.uk. Words: Alan Wilder.

"I think the team-work really worked. There weren't many conflicts. Because they had developed a style and a sound and they knew it had functioned previously on different albums like *Black Celebration* and *Music for the Masses*. They had proven that the team worked and there weren't any reasons to change it. In other scenarios I worked in this wasn't the case. Other bands operate very differently and that's why *Depeche* functioned so very well in the studio. There were never any doors closed. It was quite the opposite. The more you could bring in ... you know, I could turn to Alan and Flood saying 'What about this? What about this sound?' ... the more excited the whole crew became."[326]

Although they started to explore new ways to work, they were still searching for new samples. "Every time, before we start recording, we spend a day or four to work on or add sounds to our library," **Alan** explained. "Sometimes we even go out with some mikes and a portable recorder to, for instance, record some weird sounds at a rubbish-dump. Later in the studio we try out which sounds match best with which songs. Within the group we experiment a lot with samplers and I must say some sounds bring inspiration to melodies sometimes. Sampling has in many ways something 'vampire-ish'. You suck up what you need and throw the rest, the body, away."[327]

After the phase of rearranging the demos - a phase they would see as "senseless" later - the band moved on to the *Guillaume Tell Studios* in Paris.

Alan didn't like it very much. "From the point of view of facilities it was just about adequate. But the control room was dingy, and it just got boring after six weeks or so. Every time you go in the studio, the first couple of weeks are the most enthusiastic – by the end of a longish period, everyone's edgy, and you get less done. Last week in Paris, everyone was fed up and wanted to get home."

"We chose Paris for both studio and environment," **Fletch** added. "We work to a rigid schedule: get in at one in the afternoon and work through, with an hour's break for dinner, till one or later in the morning. And when we come out at one in the morning, we're hyperactive. In

---

[326] depechemodebiographie.de
[327] Taken from: The Jagger Reports – Interview with Alan Wilder, Backstage, April 1988. Words: Chris Jagger.

London, you have to go home to your flat and brood, but in Paris you can at least go for a drink. So you can relax."[328]

Due to their increasing success, *DM* needed professional management now, (they would still say they didn't have any, although I don't know what else Jonathan Kessler must have been) and Fletch took over the role of a kind of liaison between the band members, management and record company. According to some sources he was still a special spokesman for Martin, and according to rumours he was sometimes quite tactless in the studio.

I give in to sin (Strangelove) (© Lilian R. Franke)

On **13 April** the single *Strangelove / Agent Orange / Pimpf* was released.

"*Strangelove* was the exact opposite to a song like *Stripped*," **Alan** said. "Difficult to piece together, consisting as it did of many little parts, it was hard to find one thing to pin the track down."[329]

The single was released before the final mixing of *MFTM*. The album version of *Strangelove* became different then, basing on the original track and the 12" version (*Blind Mix*) by Daniel Miller. The single only reached No. 16 in the UK charts, but hit No. 2 in West Germany and was a Top 10 success in several other Western European countries.

---

[328] Taken from: Mode-Al, Making Music, June 1987. Words: Jon Lewin.
[329] Taken from: recoil.co.uk. Words: Alan Wilder.

The promo for *Strangelove* was filmed in Paris and directed by Anton Corbijn. He made a video for *Pimpf* as well. (While the video shows Martin playing the piano, on the recording it was Alan.) An alternative video for *Strangelove* was made at the American record company's request and directed by Martyn Atkins.

At the same time, they made fools of themselves at the attempt to get rid of their image as bores by "throwing a party" for the magazine *Smash Hits*. It turned out to be a disaster. Fletch, Martin and Dave got pissed, Fletch crawled around under the tables, Martin got undressed and **Dave** was talking and talking and ...
"The French fans are unbelievable. They sit outside the recording studio and if any of us come out they all barge up going 'Was that eet? Was that the seengle ve just heard? Was eet the seengle?' And there was one bloke, a complete weirdo who used to sit outside our hotel for literally days and nights and he never said anything, just took photos of us all the time. And he had on this combat jacket all the time and we thought he was going to blow us up or something, you know, and we'd be going, 'Well, I'm not going out the door first!' 'Neither am I!' 'Well I'm not!' and all that – he was well weird."

When Alan, who didn't enjoy the "party" at all, went to the toilet, **Dave** said, "He is enjoying himself!"
"He is! He's going crazy!" **Martin** confirmed.
"I can tell – he's gone to the loo! He got up! No, you can tell, you see, because it's his eyebrows. When he's really excited his left eyebrow goes up. Have you noticed that? And when he's depressed his right one goes down. Is he just quiet? No, no, he's the old man of the band isn't he? I mean he's 27, 28 – he's probably gone for a kip actually! Does he know that we speak about him like that? Um ... no!" **Dave** laughed.

Why do I go into this article at all? Well, it showed one thing quite clearly: The quarrels that had started after *Some Great Reward* hadn't been settled. The conflicts within the band actually seemed to be continuing, as **Alan's** statement in this article showed: "I think this is a complete farce. I suppose you think that we all get on really well together and it's like this all the time – well, it isn't! We argue constantly and that's the real us, not ... this. Yeah, I know I'm cynical but I'm also realistic."[330]

It seems that it got a bit harsher from this time onwards but I don't think it was unbearable. There were a lot of articles at this time – mainly teenage magazines – that implied conflicts that weren't there. *DM* were ascending to a peak in their career, and were definitely enjoying it. It seems that it was a time full of energy, but nevertheless the "development" of problems continued.

Because of their dissatisfaction with *Strangelove*, the band went back into the studio and worked hard on the song and the album. **Dave** recorded most of his vocals at *Konk Studios* in London to be close to his wife, who was expecting their long-desired baby. "My wife Jo is going to have a baby in **October**. I'm pretty excited about it because we've wanted one for a long time. The thing is we had a good go at it for quite a while and nothing happened. Then the minute we stopped trying so hard she became pregnant. Typical. I really hope it arrives before we go on tour. I can't imagine anything worse than being on stage and having someone whisper in my ear that Jo's just had a baby. I mean what can you do? You can't say to 10,000 people 'Excuse me my wife's just had a baby. I've got to go!' I wanna be there – definitely. Alan's girlfriend, Jeri, is really psychic, and about a week before we knew Jo was pregnant she came up to me and said, 'Is Jo going to have a baby?' It turns out she had a dream about it."[331]

In the meantime Jo had not only stopped to come on tour, but she also gave up management of the fan-club, mainly because Dave couldn't stand it anymore. When he came home he wanted to get away from *DM* and didn't wish to discuss the colour of his socks he had been wearing at a gig.

This year, **Dave** was also forced to leave Basildon and to move house to the south of the Thames. "I used to get a lot of fans outside my house. That's why I had to move with my wife, Joanne, and Jack, my son. They are fans from all over, from Germany, France, America, everywhere. They write to each other, word gets around and

---

[330] Taken from: Fzss!...Zwiing! Aargh!..Hahahah!! Smash Hits, 6-19 May 1987. Words: Sylvia Patterson.
[331] Taken from: Intimate Details, No. 1, September 12th, 1987. Words: uncredited.

when I open up my door in the morning there are all these people on my doorstep. Sometimes I open the curtains, pull the blinds and there's somebody standing there snapping away with a camera! They're not all teenage girls, though.

"There was this bloke[332] - his name's Sean – actually hired a private detective to follow me from the studio and discover where I lived.[333] I remember seeing this car parked across the road a few weekends later, and it turned out to be full of fans. They were all looking through my window, and they'd always be there.[334] It got to the point where I'd be chasing them down the road with my dog because they'd be singing our songs outside my house at two in the morning.[335] And, one day, they finally plucked up enough courage to come and see me. So they knocked on the door.[336] I lost my rag and really shouted at him. I told him, basically to f*** off. Later I sent the guy a letter saying, 'I apologize, but you must respect my privacy. I want to have some time with my wife and son.' He sent back a letter saying, 'I'm sorry I bothered you, and I won't ever do it again.' Then, right at the end of the letter, he said, 'By the way, would it be possible for me to come 'round next weekend?' I just thought, 'Well, that's it. It's time to move.'"[337]

The band moved on to the lonely *Puk Studios* in Denmark to mix the album. *DM* weren't satisfied with *MFTM* thoroughly because the demos didn't leave enough room for experiments. That was the reason for asking Martin to present rougher demos for the next album.

On **20 August** the single *Never Let Me Down Again / Pleasure, Little Treasure* was released and would become an all-time-classic. It was a relatively moderate hit in the UK, peaking at No. 22, but it was a smash hit in Western Europe.

The band, of course, was very proud of *NLMDA*, especially of the development they had taken. From that point forward – starting with *Black Celebration*, they tried to

---

[332] Taken from: Real Gahan Kid, Sky, March 1990. Words: Paul Lester.
[333] Taken from: Violator, Alligator, NME, 7 July 1990. Words: Jeff Giles.
[334] Taken from: Real Gahan Kid, Sky, March 1990. Words: Paul Lester.
[335] Taken from: Violator, Alligator, NME, 7 July 1990. Words: Jeff Giles.
[336] Taken from: Real Gahan Kid, Sky, March 1990. Words: Paul Lester.
[337] Taken from: Violator, Alligator, NME, 7 July 1990. Words: Jeff Giles.

push themselves into new dimensions without using steady formulas musically.

"Things like *Everything Counts* and *People Are People* will last forever," **Dave** said. "I even bet that in ten years' time there will be bands doing covers of those songs. Our songs always convey an atmosphere: sad or optimistic, it's full of substance. The new single *Never Let Me Down Again* really gives me goose pimples. Not all our songs have this effect on me, but this particular one is wild. People call *DM* an electronic band but it's wrong. We use anything, from the acoustic guitar to the percussion via the most sophisticated robots. The only thing we refuse are limitations and I don't think there is a single band in the world that operates like us."[338]

It's amusing that he was right with the cover songs. Today there are so many cover songs and fan remixes, you can hardly count them.

"There was one instance regarding *Never Let Me Down Again* when two separate people came up to me after a show one night and said, 'I really like that song'," **Martin** said. "One of them thought it was a gay anthem and the other one thought it was a drug anthem."[339]

He himself would tend to the drug anthem, a flight from reality with drugs. This is also the angle to follow when trying to interpret the lyrics of the album. They almost all deal with being "high" from something – drugs, love, religion.

A very ambivalent track is *The Things You Said*. It never gets clearer who "you" is. "You" said "things" which aren't clarified. "*I heard it from my friends*" who aren't clarified either. When following the angle of love, drugs and religion, there are three possible interpretations.

Firstly, an affair which ends in the lover telling wild stories, spreading rumours. But "*they know my weaknesses – you tried them*" doesn't suit this theory on the whole.

Secondly, the line "*I get so carried away you brought me down to earth*" gives a hint to the "*best friend*" in *NLMDA*. (*I hope he never lets me down again / never want to put my feet back down on the ground.*) So it's possible that *The Things You Said* is about suffering from depressions after

---

[338] Taken from: 80's, Mode d'Emploi, Best, October 1987. Words: Gerard Bar-David.
[339] Taken from: Article in Rolling Stone, 1993, Words: Marvin Scott Jarrett.

a "trip" with drugs. Someone or something, maybe even the "*best friend*" himself, spoilt this wonderful flight. But what about the "*things you said*"? The "*best friend*" won't be able to talk.

Thirdly, he might be disappointed by God. "*The things you said*" could be interpreted as the "words" which are spread "*around the world*" (*Sacred*). You can *get so carried away* by religion as well, and then notice that real life is different. But here, the line "*they know me better than that*" doesn't suit on the whole. Furthermore, it's possible that *The Things You Said* is a kind of cardinal point of the album which connects all three topics.

The things you said ... (© Ingo Bittrich)

However, *NLMDA* "stood out as an obvious single and suggested a *Stripped*-like feel," **Alan** remarked. "It has a very definite anthemic quality which is especially demonstrated when the song is performed live and the whole audience wave their hands in unison at the end - a *Depeche* high-point I think."

In addition, he mentioned the line *Promises me I'm as safe as houses, as long as I remember who's wearing the trousers* as the one that made the deepest impression on him.

And last but not least he said about the video, "This is one of my favourite Anton films. It has a very definite feel and a mood that compliments the song perfectly."[340]

---

[340] Taken from: recoil.co.uk. Words: Alan Wilder.

The band members prepared for the release of the album. It's "going to be called *Music for the Masses* which is a bit of a joke really," **Martin** explained, "when you consider how much a lot of people hate us."

"You wouldn't think it was possible to hate a band so much as the way some people hate us!," **Dave** added.

"I think our music never crosses over to the general public," **Martin** said, "hence the album title, it's a joke. It's only the fans who buy our stuff."

Likewise it was difficult for *DM* to get air-play on the radio. "We're in a bit of a dilemma," **Martin** explained, "because most of our music doesn't fit in and doesn't get played as much as others, though fortunately it does elsewhere in the world. And if we find it difficult, and we think we're quite commercial, it must be impossible if you're in a really alternative band."[341]

Neither *Ultra* nor *Exciter* was actually played by the big British radio stations later, but it had already been difficult in the **1980s**.

"Probably we're still a cult band," **Fletch** remarked, "because we find it difficult to cross over to anyone except our fans."

"I think it's nice to be more of a cult band that a hugely successful group," **Martin** said. "I think you can get more out of it and it's a nicer feeling in some way.[342] I think it's down to the intimacy of the music. People feel that the songs are personal to them. And though there is an element of contradiction when you play a concert with 17,000 people going mad, that intimacy is still there. People still feel moved by it, they feel that it's theirs. They feel that *Depeche Mode* is their cult thing, that the music shouldn't ever go mainstream no matter what it sounds like and no matter what we do."[343]

For the band, explaining why they were "cult" was as difficult as it was for the fans in the survey of *depechemodebiographie.de*. Besides the personal identification it must have been this "special magic" that let *DM* become a "power."

---

[341] Taken from: Mass Appeal, Underground, August 1987. Words: Carole Linfield.
[342] Taken from: Dep Jam, Record Mirror, 22 August 1987. Words: Francesco Adinolfi.
[343] Taken from: Faith, Hope and Depravity, Select, December 1990. Words: Andrew Harrison.

"They can't be compared, they're in their own league", "they were absolutely cool, unique and different, and when you were a fan of theirs you were unique, different and strange as well. I felt like a freak. It was something like a revolution."

The fact that they were "extremely popular without being famous" is one of the "*DM*-phenomena" that Fletch summed up with, "we find it difficult to cross over to anyone except our fans" and one fan with, "they are the best kept secret in music ever."

"*DM* is the strange antagonism of underground and mainstream, being different and identification, melancholy and hope," as one fan described this "mystery."

The same can be said about the fans. They are a strange antagonism of being individuals and a big community that connects "devotees" all over the world.

While there's a lot of communication between the fans all over the world, **Martin** explained about his lyrics that, "it's true that many *Depeche* songs deal with communication problems. There are a lot of recurring themes in my songs. One thing that always reappears is disillusionment and lack of contentment. A lot of the songs also deal with a search for innocence. I've got this theory that as you get older you get more disillusioned and that your happiness peak is when you're in your teens. As you grow older and learn more, the corners are rubbed off your life.

"I think we exploit the rut instead by writing songs about it. We're making money out of the rut that we and others are stuck in." He laughed. "In fact, we're craving for something more depressing to come along to take us out of our boredom." He laughed. "As you can see we're such an up band at interviews." He giggled. "I think that the only reason we sell more records abroad than we do in England is because foreigners don't understand us. They just hear us laughing every now and then and dig it."

About the line *What am I trying to say? / I'm not trying to tell you anything you didn't know when you woke up today* in the song *Nothing* **Martin** said, "I think that the line is true about all our songs. If you're writing a good song you're not telling anybody any new information. All you're doing is putting down hopefully shared feelings that somebody else can agree with."[344]

About *To Have and To Hold* **Alan** explained, "Martin submitted his demo in the usual way and although I liked the song, his original idea was too 'lightweight' for my taste (and I felt, the mood of the album) so I pushed it in a darker, more atmospheric direction. This was the primary version of the song which was always intended to be on the album. Martin however was very attached to his more 'poppy' demo and said that he wanted to record it too - hence the *Spanish Taster*. It wasn't a question of fighting with one another over this, it's just that Martin saw the song in a different way to me. I don't think there is a more perfect example of the musical differences between myself and Martin."[345]

It's interesting to listen to these two different versions, because they really show the different views of the two musical heads of the band. Martin's version features a bass figure, which gives the track a more filigree and lighter feel. Two melodies counterpoint each other, the basic melody and the spinet, Flamenco-like melody. The album version shows Alan's preference for rhythm, dynamics and drama (or bombast, as some people say.) It is strongly accentuated on the basic chords, which gives the track a dark, powerful note, and more depth.[346]

The speech at the beginning of *To Have and To Hold* is Russian and can be translated with: "Evolution of nuclear arsenals and socially- psychological aspects of arms race is considered in these reports."

I was asked by a reader if it was used to make a political statement. But Alan said once that they didn't even know what it meant. It sounded interesting to them, so it was used.

On **28 September** MFTM was released. The album became the band's highest-charting in the U.S. upon its release, reaching No. 35 on the *Billboard 200*. It also contained more hit singles than any of their previous releases.

---

[344] Taken from: The Dire Straits of the Synth Generation? Sounds, 5 September 1987. Words: Jack Barron.
[345] Taken from: recoil.co.uk. Words: Alan Wilder.
[346] Author of this passage: Jörg von der Fecht (Bleeding)

While Alan was still programming the keyboards for the tour, Dave became a father. On **14 October** his son Jack was born, a few days before the tour started.

The *Masses*-Tour consisted of five legs and began on **22 October** with the first European leg. On **28 December** the single *Behind the Wheel / Route 66* was released.

Route 66 wasn't planned at all, particularly not as an A-side. As such the single was released in the U.S.

"That was an accident," **Fletch** explained, "that was not meant to be, really. It was only supposed to be a bit of a laugh, and the Americans liked it and were putting pressure on, and things like that. It's a bit of a shame really, because we think *Behind the Wheel*, which was supposed to be the 'A', is a better song, but ... No, actually, *Route 66* is a really good song, it's just that we don't really like doing cover versions as a rule, especially when we've got our own songs available, it just seems a bit of a waste. This'll be the last single. We've never believed in sort of doing a Madonna or whatever and releasing eight singles off an album. We just think it's a waste: the album's the album and you take singles off to promote the album but, I mean, once enough people have bought the album, that's alright."[347] Nevertheless, there was another single release with *Little 15* later.

The lyrics and the lead melody of *Route 66* were originally written by *Bobby Troup's band*, but the music itself is similar, sometimes identical, to *Behind the Wheel*. Martin was taking care of the lead vocals on *Route 66*, maybe the most aggressive he has ever sung. On stage the song was sung by Dave.

The video for *Behind the Wheel* was directed by Anton Corbijn again.

And here are two little interesting bits at the end of this chapter:

In **1989 Martin** said, "About two years ago we did sign a very small agreement with Daniel because it was pointed out to us, what would happen if Daniel died? He was very overweight at the time, and if he died we wouldn't be paid a penny. So there's a sheet of paper which says we're to be paid on a 50-50 basis. In England we pay 50 per cent of

---

[347] Taken from: Depeche Mode: The Interview, Talking Music SPEEK013, 1988.

all our costs and get 50 per cent of all our profits. In Europe we get 75 per cent of our profits through licensing deals."[348]

Until this time there actually wasn't any official contract with *Mute*, only with the licensees. In a later interview Daniel Miller said that the first official contract was done during *Violator*-period. I tend to **1987** because in **1989** the memories were "fresher," and it made sense in hindsight of the *Masses*-Tour.

For later years this statement was interesting: "The main danger is a drying up of things to write about," **Alan** said. "There's a lot of repetition in this business, and Martin's songs ... he does repeat himself quite a lot. I think Dave has aspirations to write, but feels a bit unconfident about putting anything forward because if he did it would be in a very basic form as he can't really play any instruments. I think he has ideas about words and lyrics."[349]

This would mean Fletch, who claimed later Dave would have never had ambitions to write songs on his own, wouldn't have been informed correctly or was quoted incorrectly.

When I had the opportunity to enquire, **Alan** confirmed, "Dave did have ambitions and he did talk about songs he wished to propose, but he didn't seem to have the confidence to actually present them."[350]

Many years later **Dave** said, "I started playing around with words in the **mid-'80s**, but I couldn't take it to Martin, out of fear that it would be rejected, laughed at."[351]

---

[348] Taken from: The Unlikely Lads, Q, April 1989. Words: Mat Snow.
[349] Taken from: Mode-Al, Making Music, June 1987. Words: Jon Lewin.
[350] depechemodebiographie.de.
[351] Taken from: Interview with Dave Gahan, Mojo, 22 March 2013. Words: Martin Aston.

1988

- We're flying high (Never Let Me Down Again) -

The third leg of the *Masses*-Tour began on **9 January**, comprised 11 concerts in the UK and ended on **24 January**. Directly afterwards, on **25 January**, *Hydrology* was released, a kind of *Recoil* album with three long instrumental pieces, *Grain, Stone* and *The Sermon*, to which *1+2* were added.

"*Hydrology* was a step up from *1+2*," **Alan** said. "It was done on a half-inch 16-track *Fostex* machine. So there were limitations, but it was much more versatile than the first thing I had done. *Recoil* was still very much an aside to *Depeche Mode*, with no pressure or expectations placed upon it. It was always going to be an 'antidote' to *Depeche Mode* in some ways; a way to alleviate the frustrations of always working within a pop format. I have nothing against the pop format, but if I was going to do something on my own, there was no point in repeating what I was already doing in the group. It was intended to be completely different and experimental. It didn't matter if it was too left-field or too weird for people.[352] Naive as they sound to me now, *1+2* and *Hydrology* still say something about the idea behind *Recoil* and how the music is constructed. From that perspective, they are still interesting. The artwork was conceived by Martyn Atkins and the choice of images was down to his interpretation of the music. I thought they fitted well."[353]

From **6 February** to **13 March** the second European leg of the *Masses*-Tour took place, comprising 25 concerts. In this period the legendary gig in East-Berlin also took place, on **7 March**. DM had played some gigs in the Eastern Bloc before – in Hungary and Poland, on which their big fan-base in these countries are based - but they had never had the chance to play in East-Germany.

"We really wanted to play in East-Berlin," **Fletch** said, "but we never were allowed to. And one day it finally

---

[352] Taken from: Unsound Recordings, Sound On Sound, January 1998. Words: Bill Bruce.
[353] Taken from: recoil.co.uk. Words: Alan Wilder.

worked! We knew we had a massive fan-base in East-Germany: from letters, from friends in West-Berlin, from the media. We were told we were bigger there than the *Beatles*. Later we were told that we were used as some kind of propaganda. We heard that normal fans had no real chance to get a ticket. We didn't know this, we just were keen to play in East-Berlin. Today I would say it would have been better not have to played that gig. Nevertheless, it was a great gig - but it was also frustrating. Fans met somewhere but couldn't come closer to us. We hadn't known much about our fans in East-Germany before the gig and, unfortunately, we didn't know much about them afterwards."[354]

The interest in "western bands" in general was much stronger in the Eastern Bloc than in the "western world," because it was difficult to get their LPs, and of course almost impossible to see them live, because they weren't "invited" to play there. Socialist regimes had specific ideas about which kind of culture should be available to the youth of the nation. But in **1988** most of the regimes in the Eastern Bloc were already in trouble, and here and there they opened up a bit, maybe to give the impression of being cosmopolitan, and to distract the young people from the growing problems.

However, not everyone could get a ticket. The tickets were mainly given to leaders of organisations, and they would give them to those who had a "blameless lifestyle."

Some reports say that there had been a lot of police, and it was difficult to get closer, others say that it wasn't that difficult. But probably the venue was pretty well sealed off.

The fifth and last leg of the *Masses*-Tour started on **18 April** in Tokyo, comprising four gigs in Japan and 31 in the U.S.

At this leg the band was accompanied by the film director Pennebaker who filmed them and a group of teenagers on this "roadtrip." The film mainly shows the start of the massive success of *DM* in the U.S., using the teenagers as an angle.

---

[354] Taken from: FR Online.de, 1 November 2009. Words: Nadja Erb / Steven Geyer. (Translated from German.)

"The band had toured constantly in America and battled against a radio-play brick wall for many years until suddenly things started to happen," **Alan** said. "Of course, it was an important and exciting time for us in the U.S. and we wanted to concentrate on this territory." Only in LA things had always been a bit different. "*DM* has a massive following in the LA area which (more than anything else) is probably down to one radio station – *K-ROQ*. Of course, since **1986** or so, the band have worked that area very hard to capitalise on that success but Richard Blade and co. have been staunch supporters of the band for many years."[355]

"No-one believed an alternative band could play to so many people," **Fletch** remarked. "And again that set the ball rolling for a lot of bands after us. We were conquering the world."[356]

"After that film came out," **Dave** said, "suddenly we were this 'stadium band,' which wasn't actually true - we'd played one stadium - but the perception really changed. We started to get bigger than I'd ever imagined we'd be."[357]

I think they really felt like that, like conquering the world, and therefore the speculation in some of the media at that time that they might split up or crack up seemed almost ridiculous; you don't split up when you are successful like that. There was high tension within the band, though.

Dave's drug problems had already increased during this tour. His drug of choice at this time was cocaine. It was noticed by the other band members, but they didn't react to it. So obviously drugs weren't unknown to them or they didn't know enough about the consequences, otherwise they would have been alarmed.

At that time Dave also met Theresa [his future second wife], which was to have serious consequences later.

According to rumours things didn't run as smoothly as shown in the tour-film *101*, in which Jo and the baby also appeared. There was even one rumour saying that the tensions within the band had led to a fistfight between

---

[355] Taken from: recoil.co.uk. Words: Alan Wilder.
[356] Taken from: Just Can't Get Enough, Uncut, May 2001. Words: Stephen Dalton.
[357] Taken from: Many Smack-Free Returns! Q, June 2001. Words: Dorian Lynskey.

Fletch and Alan. This is what they said about it between the lines:

"When you come offstage the tension is very high," **Dave** explained, "you're on an emotional high but also you can get at each other. A couple of members of the band have come to blows just because of, maybe that's just because someone's not playing their part properly. And it's so extreme and you're so hyped up and you come offstage, and basically anyone gets it if they're in the way. And a couple of times there've been fights – actually real – they've been broken up and we've had to go back onstage to do an encore. I think you sense a lot of the time in the film when there's real tension in the band and possibly not getting on with each other, but then there's other times when ..."[358]

When I had the opportunity to ask **Alan** whether there had been a fight or not, he said, "Yes, there was an altercation post-gig concerning Fletch's comments about Dave's performance during the show - which I felt were rather rich in light of his own contribution."[359]

Little 15 / Stjarna / Sonata No.14 (Moonlightsonata) was the last single release, on **16 May**, although it wasn't released worldwide.

Sonata No.14 is a piece of Ludwig van Beethoven, an unusual choice for a pop band. It was Martin who had the idea to put it out as a B-side, and it was Alan who interpreted it on the piano. At that time he was obviously practising the piano regularly, and was very interested in composers like Philip Glass, who combine classical and modern music.

Little 15 was never intended as a single. They hadn't even been sure about whether the track would be recorded at all. Encouraged by Daniel Miller, an experimental approach in the studio gave rise to a simple ballad based around a Nyman-esque opening string arrangement.

It was the French record company who later insisted the song was perfect for their market, resulting in a release geared towards this territory only. Ironically, *Little 15* didn't chart in France, but when it was released in other countries as well it finally became a success.

---

[358] Taken from: In Movie Mode, "TV-AM", ITV, February 1989.
[359] depechemodebiographie.de.

The video for *Little 15* was directed by Martyn Atkins, but it fits well in the way of the Anton Corbijn-videos with its black and white image and narrative or implied storyline.

In the course of time **Alan** answered a lot of questions about touring with *DM* while he was a member. Taking all his answers together, it gives a good insight into the "tour-machinery" of the band.

Even at the time of the *Masses*-Tour, *DM* had "a crew of a couple of hundred people to take care of" all kinds of things that were needed on tour. But some of the planning was still done by themselves together with "our agent and Jonathan [Kessler.] Between us all, (taking into account many factors) we would decide which countries and cities to play and when. Once we had a general plan, the specific routing would be optimised, again depending on travel times, venue availability, local promoter advice, record release dates and other logistical considerations etc."

For the backing-tapes they used two identical machines which ran in sync - one was purely a back-up to the other in case of breakdown. The machines would be started by the keyboard technician at the beginning of the set and were only stopped and restarted inbetween encores. **Alan** was responsible for re-working the tracks, so they could be used as different live performances. "There are many subtle differences one would apply depending on the nature of the track, what you're trying to achieve with it, and where it comes in the set etc. Generally, live versions can take more dynamic contrast, longer dance sections and a big ending!"

He usually worked out "8 separate tapes - basically 4 different setlists (red, green, blue and yellow I think) which were each split into two halves and broken up by an acoustic song somewhere in the middle - which allowed for the tape change. Effectively therefore, we could mix and match any combination of 1st and 2nd half tapes. Along with a few different alternatives for Martin's acoustic songs, this gave us the opportunity to perform many different running orders although all of them had the same overall shape and structure. So, for example, a quick chat beforehand might result in 'let's play the blue / red set tonight with *Somebody* instead of *I Want You Now* in the middle.' We could also change tapes for the encores, if necessary."

They also improved their appearance on stage, began to use guitars and other instruments because they thought it would add something "to the dynamics of the show as well as giving Martin and myself an opportunity to move away from standing behind keyboards all the time. As *DM*'s popularity increased, it was necessary for the music and shows to grow - it would have looked pretty ridiculous to have 4 blokes bleeping away on little synthesisers in a massive stadium."

About 50% of the music was played live while the rest was pre-recorded music. "Our policy was to always play as much as we could manage (without bringing in lots of extra musicians). For me, I can't stand being on stage with nothing to do. I would feel uncomfortable, so I always gave myself plenty of parts to play. I liked the challenge of having to remember lots of things. There were no special rules" about who had to play which musical parts. "It was a question of logistics. I would just spread the sounds over the two keyboards [Martin's and mine] as conveniently as possible."[360]

It's remarkable that he left Fletch out and was talking about using only TWO keyboards. I assumed it was some kind of mocking remark because he wrote this many years later, but I found an article from **1988** in which he also spoke about using just two keyboards. "I divide all important melodies among Martin and myself, so we don't have to program anything for those. Most of the time we use an *E-Max Emulator*. We split the keyboard in six parts so we can play 6 sounds at one time."[361]

It was quite easy to choose the positions on stage. "Being short with a bizarre appearance, Martin always seemed to look better in the middle. I always chose the position nearest the monitor desk for communication with the sound engineer." From the mixing board, there were always recorded some "rehearsals and the first few shows of a tour. These don't always give you an accurate balance but are good for checking performance etc."

For other bands it has never been easy to open for *DM*. "Daniel [Miller] always tried to encourage *Mute* bands for

---

[360] Taken from: recoil.co.uk. Words: Alan Wilder.
[361] Taken from: The Jagger Reports – Interview with Alan Wilder, Backstage, April 1988. Words: Chris Jagger.

obvious reasons but we would consider anyone who seemed to vaguely fit the bill. As always, everybody had different opinions as to who was most suitable. I must admit, it wasn't something that I felt very strongly about so Martin or Dave usually had final say."[362]

One of the opening acts for the *Masses*-Tour was *Nitzer Ebb*. Several collaborations date from these days, especially between Alan and Douglas McCarthy, the singer of *Nitzer Ebb*.

The tour ended on **18 June** with the legendary 101st concert in the *Rosebowl* of Pasadena, California. It became the band's biggest success so far, and was described by the band members as one of the greatest moments of their career, but not as their best performance due to monitoring problems.

"It was a turning point for us in the U.S. and in alternate music,"[363] **Fletch** remarked, and **Dave** said, "When the curtain goes down and you see that amount of people going crazy it's very, you know, lump in the throat stuff. Towards the end of the concert it got so emotional that I actually found myself having trouble singing. That sounds probably a bit twee – but it was really like that. And I went backstage afterwards and just felt really upset that it was all over."[364]

All band members would recall *Rosebowl* as their highest point and best memory for a long time. It was obviously difficult for them to move onwards from this point. Especially Dave, who was getting more and more into trouble, had the feeling that not much could come afterwards. He thought that they just couldn't climb any higher.

During this last leg of the *Masses*-Tour, a tradition was founded that has survived until today - fans waving their arms in the air during the end of *Never Let Me Down Again*. It wasn't "developed" at the *Rosebowl* as such, but had happened before, but of course the *Rosebowl* concert was filmed, and the picture of all these people waving their arms was very impressive.

---

[362] Taken from: recoil.co.uk. Words: Alan Wilder.
[363] Taken from: Masters Of Their Universe, The Times, 3 May 2009. Words: Uncredited.
[364] Taken from: In Movie Mode, "TV-AM", ITV, February 1989.

The number 101 also became a symbol for *DM*-fans worldwide. Many of the "die hard" fans still try to get a number plate / hotel room / flat / house with number 101 on it.

101 (© Ingo Bittrich)

On **12 July** *Strange* was released, a video collection with mainly Corbijn-videos that was important for the image of the band. For the rest of the year they finally got some time off.

1989

- Dangerous – know I will come to harm -

On **13 February** the single *Everything Counts Live* was released. It had been recorded at the *Rosebowl*. On **13 March** the album *101 - Live* was released, and on **12 June** Martin released his solo album *Counterfeit e.p.* with cover songs.

The internal problems increased slowly, although it wasn't obvious to the public, and maybe even still not obvious to the band. So Alan would say later that the atmosphere was good around then. Martin also would depict the **late 1980s** as being absolutely great. He loved the feeling of being in a real gang. He said that he had a feeling of being invincible, and conquering whichever city they arrived in. But from this point onwards this could be true only partly, because the excess became more serious - also in public. They became known as the band that was able to drink a whole bar dry in one evening. I remember an article that began with meeting the band in a bar, and the band members were frustrated because it was a milk bar or something like that, so no alcohol was available.

This became particularly noticeable at the beginning of the recording of *Violator* in Milan. Dave's marriage ran into trouble. He frequently called Theresa, mostly drunk. During the rehearsals for *Worldviolation*, he met her again, and he thought he had fallen in love with her.

"Dave was increasingly living in his own world," **Alan** said. "The most unsettling thing was that his drug use adversely affected his personality, either through enhanced aggression or the loss of his greatest asset, his sense of humour. I think I noticed it during the period of recording for *Violator* in Milan. I remember, for no reason, he deliberately picked a fight with about 10 locals just walking down the street. I was petrified, expecting to be knifed at any moment, but somehow he always got away with that sort of behaviour."[365]

They recorded *Violator* about three weeks at *Mute* in London before they moved on to Milan. They spent about

---

[365] Taken from: Just Can't Get Enough, Uncut, May 2001. Words: Stephen Dalton.

six weeks there, but most of the time they weren't doing anything. Instead, they went out partying. Concentration levels were low, and in some ways the tensions were exacerbated by Alan's and Flood's (the co-producer on *Violator* and *SOFAD*) desire to spend more time constructing intricate sequences and involved sounds.

"Studios can be incredibly claustrophobic places - even more for those who perhaps don't play a big part in the nuts and bolts of the process," **Alan** remarked. "Boredom is an especially powerful and destructive force. For example, one of the most annoying things is if I'm working on a complicated sample (which I want to cut up into many pieces and reconfigure into something new), the process is inevitably complex and until the procedure is complete, things will usually sound chaotic and meaningless to anyone listening in. If someone who doesn't fully understand this procedure interjects negatively at an unfinished stage, it can be really irritating."

Additional tensions were brought in by Francois Kervorkian who brought with him an excitable and at times quite 'difficult to work with' personality, as **Alan** said. "He was quite loud and opinionated as well as being prone to mood swings for no apparent reason. I liked him though, and his methods. We never took him or his stroppiness too seriously and a healthy amount of piss taking would usually force a smile to his face. He looks something like the British athlete, Fatima Whitbread, so her poster ended up on the studio wall (much to his disgust.) He liked to work long hours and is something of a perfectionist - again, something I admired. For him, it must have been as strange an experience to work with us as it was for us to work with him. However, the tension that resulted from this was good for the record and provided the individual tracks with some extra touches, as well as a much-needed new angle."[366]

Later they mixed the whole album with Kervorkian in London.

In Milan only the single *Personal Jesus / Dangerous* got ready and was released on **29 August**. It would become one of their most successful singles although many people misinterpreted the song.

---

[366] Taken from: recoil.co.uk. Words: Alan Wilder.

"Our problem is that we've never been banned," **Martin** said, "just relegated to the evening shows. We did have a few problems with *Personal Jesus* but in America they took it as a religious tribute. Ha! It seems you can get away with anything if you've got nice pop tunes!"[367]

"We were always very, very pessimistic as a band, we were always afraid the worst could happen," **Fletch** added. "We always think the record gets bad, that it has a bad chart entry, isn't played on the radio. Martin wrote *Personal Jesus* and we loved it. It was an excellent song, sounded excellently, we recorded it ... and we thought: 'This record will never be played.' We wouldn't say our songs are controversial. They do cause controversy, but Martin would say all he does is write about life. Martin's a classic songwriter and he's a great pop fan. When he presents songs to us they're songs he's dead sure about. We're like a family really, so usually what he writes about is the sort of thing we're experiencing too. Martin doesn't get us around the table and say 'Listen lads, this is what this one's about.' He never explains the lyrics at all. I've heard about 10 different interpretations of *Personal Jesus* and that's what Martin really likes."[368]

Martin mentioned that *Personal Jesus* is based on Priscilla Presley calling her husband Elvis by that name. "It's a song about being a Jesus for somebody else, someone to give you hope and care. It's about how Elvis was her man and her mentor and how often that happens in love relationships; how everybody's heart is like a god in some way, and that's not a very balanced view of someone, is it?"[369]

In another interview (a video interview during the recording session at the *Puk Studios*) Dave said that the lyrics are about "TV-preachers" in the U.S., who you just have to phone to get rid of all your sorrows. Probably the title of the song and the figure of "Personal Jesus" itself refer to what Martin said, while the lyrics suit the story about the TV-preachers.

Personal Jesus was the band's first gold single and their first Top 40 hit in the U.S. since *People Are People*.

---

[367] Taken from: Sin Machine, NME, 17 February 1990. Words: Stuart Maconie.
[368] Taken from: Breaking the Silence, Record Mirror, 17 March 1990. Words: Lisa Tilston.
[369] Taken from: Pop a la Mode, Spin, 4 July 1990. Words: Marisa Fox.

About the acoustic version of *Personal Jesus* **Dave** said, "That's, I'm sure, how the song was originally written. Martin and I just went in the studio, and he strummed away while I was singing. I think it's a really good feel, actually - it's the song at its bare minimum. And a very different sort of sound of *Depeche Mode* as well."[370]

And **Fletch** about the video, "*Personal Jesus* could have been my worst experience because we was actually in this desert town in Spain, it was one of these cowboy towns where they make all the westerns and stuff. And all day, they'd been telling me, 'Well, Fletch, you know, you've got to ride a horse later,' and things like that. And I was like, 'Aw, f***. You know, I can't ride a horse.' You know. 'Don't worry, you'll be OK. He's nice, he's calm ... he's big, but he's OK.' And it came to this bit and everyone was with me to watch me ride this horse, you know. It turned out it was a rocking horse. It's like one of those sort of nice wind-ups, but it did spoil my whole day thinking about that."[371]

Personal Jesus (© Ingo Bittrich)

With *Violator* the band tried to improve the recording and the production process, although **Fletch** probably exaggerated it a bit too much when saying, "In the past we were basically re-recording Martin's demos with better

---

[370] Taken from: The Wherehouse 3/20/90, Sire/Reprise/Mute PRO-C-4329.
[371] Taken from: Interview with Depeche Mode, The Videos 86>98, Mute MF033 and Videos 86>98+, Mute MF042. Director: Sven Harding.

sound, better production and Dave's vocals. For this album we said to Martin, just present the demos on acoustic guitar and organ, only lyrics and chords, so we could decide the direction of songs as a group. It's also the first time we've used a producer rather than an engineer / producer."[372]

Well, they probably didn't just "re-record Martin's demos with better sound, better production and Dave's vocals" in the past. (E.g. *Pipeline* is quite different from the demo, while the demo to *Shake the Disease* is close to final result.) Or as **Alan** said, "If we had recorded them as they were I could have gone on holiday for a year." But: "It is probably fair to say that from *Violator* onwards, the final results bore less resemblance to the original demos."

They had already had a co-producer with David Bascombe at *Music for the Masses*, and Flood with whom they recorded *Violator* and later *SO-FAD* was also only a co-producer.

So this statement is more specific: "We did something that was extremely strange to us - we simply went into the studio and played. It might sound funny but it was really strange for us," **Alan** explained. And about Flood's role, he said, "Flood and I worked well together. Our styles complimented each other - my musical angle coupled with his technical prowess."

While Martin would reflect *Violator* as "Alan's album" (and remarkably as his "favourite record") later, Alan wasn't satisfied completely, favoured *SOFAD* much more. Dave was quite self-critical as well.

"There were times when it was obvious that Dave would have liked the band to 'rock out' more," **Alan** said. "Even though I wouldn't have necessarily advocated the use of more guitars, I could sometimes share his sense of frustration at the lack of dynamics - something I go on about a lot as well because I believe it is so important within music."

Dave tried to bring himself more into the production, and they used some of his playing on the guitar as sound effects in one of the cross-fade sections of *Violator*. "He has his own 'special' style, when he plays the guitar."[373]

---

[372] Taken from: Breaking the Silence, Record Mirror, 17 March 1990. Words: Lisa Tilston.
[373] Taken from: recoil.co.uk. Words: Alan Wilder.

The next recording session for *Violator* took place in the *Puk Studios* in Denmark, before they mixed the album in London. The *Puk* period was much more prolific, although some tracks like *Clean* and *Policy of Truth* went through many guises before the final versions were settled upon.

"We had a lot of problems with recording *Policy of Truth*," **Martin** recalled. "We actually recorded it twice, two totally different versions. For a long time it sounded ... some kind of stupid ... it had no surprises or anything. But in the end we really liked the result of it.[374] I remember the original demo of *World in My Eyes* being slightly faster and maybe slightly more obvious. While we were recording it in Milan, Dave was going away for a couple of days, so we worked on it and turned it into this really moody piece. I can remember Dave arriving back in the studio, slightly jet-lagged and being totally shocked, thinking that we just ruined the song, but half a day later he came back and said 'that's really good, the way it's turned out.' It always takes a while to get used to things."[375]

"There was a song called *Mother Me* which we also recorded during this period but never finished," **Alan** added, "and for a long time *Happiest Girl* was going to be on the LP. As for singles, *Halo* was on a shortlist but was never really a major contender. We ended up using it in a roundabout way by making a video (as well as one for *Clean*) to fill out the *Strange Too* compilation."[376]

Whereas this recording session had been a very successful one, another problem arose. Fletch suffered from a serious depression and became convinced he was physically ill. Finally, he had to depart to see a doctor. His band mates first thought that he was joking, had no idea that he was going through depression, but finally they had to realise that it wasn't funny at all.

For a while Fletch went to several doctors who tried different kinds of anti-depression medication. These changed his personality and made things worse. It took long before the right therapy was found.

---

[374] Taken from: TV-Interview, 1990. Unknown media and interviewer.
[375] Taken from: The Singles 86-98 by Martin Gore, Bong 37, September 1998. Compiled by Michaela Olexova. Words: Martin Lee Gore.
[376] Taken from: recoil.co.uk. Words: Alan Wilder.

Violator (© Ingo Bittrich)

On **14 November** the film *101* was finally released. *Mute* released it as a double DVD. Disc One included the film, Disc Two showed parts of the *Rosebowl* gig.

Not everyone liked the film, and some journalists wanted to know why it had been made at all.

"The problem with this country [UK] is that we've always been underrated artistically," **Dave** remarked. (Well, not only in the UK. I recently found some reviews about *DM*-albums in old German music-magazines and was pretty surprised at some so-called music-experts.) "That's one of the reasons to make this film; we wanted to be portrayed as we really were, and if we're still considered dickheads, then fair enough."[377]

"Well, I think with us it wasn't really a serious analysis of our career," **Martin** said. "And on the other side, this was the right time to do a film. I think *101* is quite inter-

---

[377] Taken from: The Unlikely Lads, Q, April 1989. Words: Mat Snow.

esting although I'm still very sceptical as to whether it's gonna work in the cinema. But it will definitely work as a video cassette for fans. I hope the fans understand us. We try to put some realism into our music – if people see the film, they would see that we are not the serious people that they imagine. There's a lot of humour in *101* and there aren't any scenes where you see us sitting down and discussing philosophy. We have fun, but we take our music very seriously. We are very realistic and because of that we get accused of being a depressive pop band. I can't understand that."[378]

"Well the film is something that we've been working on for a long while, all in all about six months," **Dave** said. "We started to work on it during the tour – the tour lasted around ten months – and so we felt we had to sort of document the whole thing, because it was such a big thing that we were doing in our career. And then we decided to do this big show at the *Rosebowl* to finish the whole tour off ..."

The last quote was taken from a TV interview, and the following conversation developed:
Interviewer: "The *Rosebowl* where?"
Dave: "In Pasadena."
Interviewer: "In California?"
Dave: "In California, yeah, and that was like the biggest crowd we'd ever played to, and we felt that we should really get it on film."
Interviewer: "And the film is called *101*?"
Dave: "Yeah."
Interviewer: "Why?"
Dave: "Well it was in fact the hundred and first concert of the tour ..."
Interviewer: "Oh really?"
Dave: "We were hoping it to be a hundred, but somewhere another one got added."
Interviewer: "Oh, I think '101' actually has a lot more ring to it than 'one hundred.'"[379]

Just as an example for some journalists' questions ...

---

[378] Taken from: Boys on Film, Melody Maker, 15 April 1989. Words: Francesco Adinolfi.
[379] Taken from: In Movie Mode, "TV-AM", ITV, February 1989.

After all these years it's still not clear how many people actually were at the concert.

"There was actually about 70,000 people," **Dave** said, "there have been various different people saying different amounts – but there was actually about 70,000."[380]

"I think we were more nervous about the recording and filming of the show than the actual number of people at the *Rosebowl*," **Fletch** remarked. "Personally, I'm blind so I can only see the front row."[381]

Whether there were 70,000 or 60,000 – the *Masses*-Tour had been very successful and set the ball rolling for a new development. *DM* had become a huge event, and suddenly earned more money with T-shirts than with anything else.

"When you tour America, suddenly things like merchandising are far more important than ticket sales," **Dave** said. "Merchandise finances tours. People talk about million dollar deals with merchandisers. Before you know it, you may as well be running a chain of T-shirt shops. To tour in America you need to sell T-shirts."[382]

Not all fans as well as not all members of the band were happy about *101* completely.

"To be honest, I could have done without the 'fans on the bus' angle which I felt gave the whole film too much of a pop feel," **Alan** said. "That's not to say I didn't like the fans, I just think Pennebaker was limited because he had to make the film from the only perspective he had - a pop band playing to massive audiences of screaming kids. For that reason alone the film works but from my personal perspective it's not all that interesting. I would have liked it to have offered something more in-depth."

He also found it "all pretty embarrassing actually" to see himself acting in this film, "especially the premiere in London with my parents and friends sitting there watching us make fools of ourselves in massive cinemascope."

---

[380] Taken from: In Movie Mode, "TV-AM", ITV, February 1989.
[381] Taken from: Ask Fletch, Bong 5, May 1989. Words: Andrew Fletcher.
[382] Taken from: The Unlikely Lads, Q, April 1989. Words: Mat Snow.

1990

- Though we may deserve it, it will be worth it (Halo) -

On **5 February,** the single *Enjoy the Silence / Memphisto / Sibeling* was released. *Sibeling* is referring to the Finnish classical composer Jean Sibelius, *Memphisto* is, according to Martin, the name of an imaginary film about Elvis as a devil that he created in his mind.

Enjoy the Silence became the band's best known song and most successful single to date, reaching No. 6 in the UK, No. 8 in the U.S. and earning the band a second gold single. It was in the Top Ten of many West European countries and earned gold in Germany. It won "Best British single" at the **1991** *Brit Awards*.

Enjoy the Silence had actually been a ballad, before **Alan** had the idea to make it more upbeat. "When I listened to the demo of *Enjoy the Silence* the first time it occurred to me that Neil Tennant could sing it. Something at the line *all I ever wanted* sounded like hamster ... er ... *Pet Shop* to me. Martin's demos always had a complete set of lyrics but musically they varied from sometimes being quite detailed to often very simplistic. I felt that to have taken the simple ballad approach for this song would have been to criminally pass on its massive commercial potential. It was a great tune crying out for the kind of treatment it eventually got. Flood and I worked on the backing track before calling Martin in to play the guitar riff."[383]

At first **Martin** wasn't keen on this version. "I thought the very nature of the song was, you know, enjoy the silence, so it ought to have a very serene atmosphere. It took me a while to get used to the idea, but as we took it further that way with the guitar riff, it really pulled together."[384]

"I remember him sitting there and playing it, and he came up with this riff, and then I sang the song and everyone was surprised that I sang it so well – including myself." **Dave** laughed.

---

[383] Taken from: recoil.co.uk. Words: Alan Wilder.
[384] Taken from: Faith, Hope and Depravity, Select, December 1990. Words: Andrew Harrison.

"It's the first time ever in our whole career that we've actually thought we've got a hit single," **Fletch** added. "We just knew straight away."[385]

The same can be said about the video, although *DM* didn't like Corbijn's concept at first. Especially Dave was very sceptical, and the band even asked Corbijn to come up with another idea, but later not only **Dave** changed his mind: "*Enjoy the Silence* was Anton [Corbijn] at his best."

The filming in the studio just took about an hour, but Dave and the crew spent about a week filming in Portugal, in Scotland, at Balmoral, and in the French Alps.

"There's shots in that video that actually weren't me," **Dave** said. "Towards the end of filming there's this one shot and I'd really had it, I just wanted to go back to the hotel. We'd taken this helicopter which we had on standby at the top of this mountain, and Anton wanted me to do this shot where I was like way way away, and there was this beautiful scene, it was just all snow ... And so I thought, 'You know what, Richard?' I took the crown off, I put it on his head, I took the robe off, I put it on him, I said, 'You f*** do it.' And I got in the helicopter, went down and had a cup of hot chocolate in the hotel."[386]

Well-known is also the promotional video for *Enjoy the Silence* featuring the band lip-syncing the song while standing atop the *World Trade Center* in New York. This clip was filmed by a French TV station.

In these days the band had to face something they hadn't known before, at least not in such a massive dimension: being hip.

Dave and Alan gave an interview for a radio station in Madrid on **1 March**. When they came back to the car they were received by about 500 fans. The driver wanted to take a shortcut quickly, but was held back by a lorry which blocked the street, so that the fans could catch up with the car and surrounded it. They almost knocked it over.

On **19 March** *Violator* was released. It would become the most successful album in *DM*'s history. In **2010**, *Viola-*

---

[385] Taken from: Depeche Mode: A Short Film, EPKMUTEL5, included with The Singles 86>98 promotional box set, PBXMUTEL5. Director: Sven Harding.
[386] Taken from: Interview with Depeche Mode, The Videos 86>98, Mute MF033 and Videos 86>98+, Mute MF042. Director: Sven Harding.

tor had sold more than 15 million copies, and remains the band's best-selling album worldwide.

One day after the release date, *DM* appeared at *Wherehouse* (a big record shop) in LA, to sign *Violator*. According to reports, about 5,000 fans had already been camping outside the shop for four days. Then, about 20,000 people came to the autograph session. The traffic snarled up, and the police tried to get the situation under control, but they gave up after 90 minutes, and escorted *DM* back to their hotel to prevent anything worse happening. Nevertheless, there had been quite a number of incidents and even some injuries.

"It actually got quite scary," **Dave** said. "The whole thing got a little bit out of control. There was no way we could have known that there was going to be so many people turn up. They have these huge glass windows and fans were pushing up against the window. You could feel the atmosphere in the place building up. We just all kind of looked at each other and said, 'We gotta get out of here!'"

"Eventually it got so out of hand that the police told us to leave," **Martin** added. "So we went back to the hotel, switched on the TV and there we were all over the nationwide news."[387]

"All sat down together and we flicked through all the news channels and it was like, 'English rock band *Dee-Pesh Mode* tonight stopped the traffic!'" **Dave** laughed. "It was really funny watching it all."[388]

Ironically this incident was the reason *DM* became really big in the U.S. from this day onwards. A lot of the media became aware of them, which in turn created a general interest.

I often receive emails from readers asking me about the interpretation of song lyrics. Sometimes Martin's lyrics are quite obvious, but mostly they are ambivalent and difficult to interpret. (It's not true – by the way – that you can interpret them in any way you want to, as I have often read in message-boards. Interpretation means to prove a possible meaning with every line of a song. E.g. you can't say

---

[387] Taken from: User's Guide: Depeche Mode, Kingsize, May 2001. Words: Uncredited.
[388] Taken from: K-ROQ radio, February 1997, DJs: Kevin and Bean.

lyrics are about drugs when half of the lines don't suit this theory.)

Some main topics always appear in his lyrics, so when trying to interpret the songs you can base your interpretation on these issues and try to find your angle. Nevertheless it's difficult, because it's not easy to understand what kind of person **Martin** really is, and because he doesn't like to talk about his songs. "I just write about things that affect me. I find it very unappealing to write songs that are safe, that go nowhere, that do nothing. I know that *Clean* has a lot of holy imagery, and that intertwines with the sex theme, which are two ideas I find interesting to mix together. But I don't try to analyze things."[389]

It's interesting that some people tend to think that *Clean* is about drugs. Looking at the lyrics, you will discover three of Martin's favourite topics – religion (*I don't claim to know where my holiness goes*), losing/searching for innocence when you become older (*as the years go by all the feelings inside they twist and they turn as they ride with the tide*) and sex (*I just know what I like that is starting to show sometimes.*) So "clean" is meant in the way of inner clarity, peace or holiness.

"I was never a Christian but I did go to church regularly for about two years and it's certainly rubbed off on me. I'm almost obsessed with the idea of good and evil. I suppose my songs do seem to advocate immorality but if you listen there's always a sense of guilt. On *Halo* I'm saying 'let's give in to this' but there's also a real feeling of wrongfulness. Then there's *Blue Dress* – that's the pervy song! – the idea of watching a girl dress and realizing that this is *what makes the world turn.* On the opening track *World in My Eyes* you seem to be saying 'just for this moment pleasure and gratification are all that matters.' It's a very positive song. And I don't mind you bringing up existentialism because I am influenced by that. I'm probably as influenced by Camus, Kafka and Brecht as I am by pop songs."

Being asked about *World in My Eyes* very often – it's not only a positive song, it's the ambivalent way to describe a positive sex experience.

---

[389] Taken from: Faith, Hope and Depravity, Select, December 1990. Words: Andrew Harrison.

As the years go by all the feelings inside they twist and they turn as they ride with the tide (Clean) (© Ingo Bittrich)

"Perhaps we should have described ourselves as a rock group," **Martin** went on. "Maybe if we'd done that people might have taken us a bit more seriously. But we aren't. We are a pop group and proud of it. The only songs I can write are pop songs, no matter how dark and pervy some people might find them. We called [the album] *Violator* as a joke. We wanted to come up with the most extreme, ridiculously Heavy Metal title that we could. I'll be surprised if people will get the joke. However, when we called an album *Music for the Masses*, we were accused of being patronising and arrogant. In fact it was a joke on the uncommerciality of it. It was anything but music for the masses!"[390]

The "connection" between *DM* and Metal is quite funny indeed. While Martin had his bit of fun naming three *DM*-albums (*Violator, Ultra* and *Exciter*) in a "metal" way (there are lots of bands in the Metal scene who use these names as a band name or an album title), but you can also find lots of *DM* titles used by Metal bands. Just to give one example of many: In **1991** the metal band *Massacra* re-

---

[390] Taken from: Sin Machine, NME, 17 February 1990. Words: Stuart Maconie.

leased an album with the title *Enjoy the Violence*. There is also a metal tribute album to *DM* with some amazing versions. When you talk to "metalheads" you'll find many who like *DM* because "they have substance."

One of the reasons for it might be that *DM* never jumped on any bandwagons or tried to go along with the trendies.

"Even though we're into our second decade, it still seems very fresh," **Dave** said. "We never wanted to be big for five minutes and that's it. Plus, we've changed, and all the changes have been natural. No one has ever pushed us in any direction - we do exactly what we want, the way we want. There's still that naivety of learning, of trying to better ourselves, and it's all done with an intense energy, a power and urgency that's lacking in so many other bands around. We're off in our own little world, really.[391]

"Nowadays, I think pop and rock is a lot more normal and controlled. That's sad. I think the music business itself is partly to blame for that because of the way bands are manipulated. The way management sells bands. Yeah, it's sad that the rebellion has gone out of pop. That's what interested me in the first place in bands like *Sham 69*, *The Clash*, *The Damned* and *The Banshees*. That's what made me want to be in a band, y'know. For me, that was the most exciting period of my life. At the time, nothing else mattered. I did the classic thing - dropped out of school, not bothering with exams. Now I look back and wish I'd done it. I wish I'd got a better education. Learned some languages. When I got to France, Italy or Germany, I realized how thick I am. Just another stupid Englishman who hasn't learned another language. An ignorant bastard basically."[392]

At this time the band's state of mind was much more serious than in previous years, indeed. But still there were some funny moments from time to time. Sometimes the band members were to blame for it themselves.

So **Alan** entered a hotel bar in Florida, in which they had an appointment for an interview, and he immediately said, "I've been called a faggot about twenty times today. Mostly from guys leaning out of trucks. This is a sort of backward place, isn't it?"

---

[391] Taken from: Real Gahan Kid, Sky, March 1990. Words: Paul Lester.
[392] Taken from: Depeche Mode Hip it up and Start Again, Melody Maker, 10 March 1990. Words: Jon Wilde.

"It's the haircut," **Dave** explained to him. "In America, people think you're homosexual just because you've got short hair. Except for the marines. We'll just have to hang out with the marines."

Later Dave sent his bodyguard for an orange juice. A fan used his change to approach him: "Martin, can I have your autograph? Have you got a pen?"

"Sure," **Dave** replied smiling, "but my name is Dave."

The scene recurred with another fan a little later: "Martin, can I have your autograph?"

Dave rolled his eyes, irritated obviously. "To begin with, my name's Dave, and I don't have a pen."[393]

On **7 May** the single *Policy of Truth / Kaleid* was released.

Compared to the *Masses*-Tour the *Worldviolation*-Tour was much shorter but nevertheless, about 1.2 Mio. tickets were sold. It consisted of three legs. To capitalize the success in the U.S., they began with the U.S.-leg, which kicked off on **28 May**.

Even today, many fans wish there would have been a DVD about the *Worldviolation*-Tour. On the reasons why a DVD hadn't been released after the tour, **Alan** explained, "After *101*, to have released another live record or even live B-sides would have been milking it too much. The *Worldviolation*-Tour was too soon after the *Music for the Masses*. The *101* LP + film seemed to sum up *DM* live very well and we felt it was time to give the live tracks a rest. I'm sure there are some recordings from *Worldviolation* but I don't know if they will ever be released."

According to insiders, *Worldviolation* was a very wild and debauched tour, during which all band members took Ecstasy. Although it's obvious, and one biography quoted Martin talking about taking Ecstasy, it's nevertheless something to be treated with caution. While the same biography quoted Fletch as saying he'd never taken Ecstasy, an inside source alleged that he had.

They themselves – except Dave – were always a bit vague when it came to this topic.

"The more Martin drinks the more affectionate he becomes," **Alan** said who at least admitted once that he had taken psychedelic drugs in his youth. "He collects com-

---

[393] Taken from: Violator, Alligator, NME, 7 July 1990. Words: Jeff Giles.

plete strangers around him and tells them his life-story, but different to Dave he has never left an expanse of rubble. Perhaps Dave must make trouble to humble himself. Martin remains cool and many things never come to the light. To be honest, the alcohol was worse than any other things, but drugs played a large role during the *Violator*-time: Ecstasy, cocaine - everything apart from heroin - then Dave began with heroin during *Worldviolation*. I think it must be up to his personality. He simply needs the ultimate extreme."[394]

"To be honest, I don't like talking about drugs too much," **Martin** warded off that topic. "It's something that doesn't sit comfortably with me in interviews. We did go to raves in those days. I discovered them in **1988**, just before I started writing *Violator* ..."

"I think the answer is yes, maybe!"[395] **Fletch** remarked.

"Everybody has a honeymoon period with drugs where everything's fine and you can bounce back the next day," **Martin** said in a different interview. "But that didn't last very long for me. I was always depressed for weeks afterwards."[396]

So I think the answer is yes, maybe. ;)

Besides that, there are inside sources who say that the band members had a lot of groupies on both tours - *Worldviolation* and later *Devotional* as well - but here the same applies: only Dave admitted he had some. The other three are much more diplomatic here, talking about "having their fun," and there was one interview in which a "girl" appeared too early for a "date" with Martin (during *Devotional*.)

According to interviews with other musicians, it was extremely easy to have as many groupies as they wanted in the **1980s** and **early 1990s**. One musician remarked in an interview with *depechemodebiographie.de*: "In the **1980s** and **1990s** it was much easier to have sex with groupies. Nowadays this is more difficult. It's not because of the girls, but everything is more distanced. And you are observed much more. If you take a groupie with you to

---

[394] Taken from: recoil.co.uk. Words: Alan Wilder.
[395] Taken from: Mode Ahead, Muzik, July 2001. Words: Ralph Moore.
[396] Taken from: Just Can't Get Enough, Uncut, May 2001. Words: Stephen Dalton.

your hotel room, the next day someone will post it on some f*** message-board."

Waiting for the night to fall (© Ingo Bittrich)

That there aren't any girls who sold their stories to the media isn't surprising to the fans who took part in the survey of *depechemodebiographie.de*. 41% think that *DM* "aren't mainstream enough to create a general interest" so that "the tabloid press wouldn't have been interested in stories like these."

However, their lifestyle became more and more debauched, and Dave was no longer that relaxed. At parties he increasingly lost control, and often overdid it.

"I think he just felt that performing was the only thing he could do right," **Fletch** said. "He was very emotional with all of us. I personally tended to steer clear of him."[397]

In **1990 Dave** still tried to express himself very carefully and didn't define things clearly: "Our lifestyle does have its ups and downs, and it's sometimes a struggle to

---

[397] Taken from: In the Mode, Details, April 1993. Words: William Shaw.

keep things together because I'm away so much. That's a massive pressure, trying to maintain a family and do year-long tours at the same time. I definitely want to have more children but at the moment it's really difficult. When Jack was born two years ago, I was with him for his first three weeks and then I was off on tour for the whole of the next year.

"It's a schizo life and it can cause arguments, but I love both parts of my life so much that I carry on. It'd be a lie to say we haven't done those things, whether in the past or the present. I think we've experienced pretty much everything. You can get tempted by things, certainly, like drugs or girls, but they can't help but affect your relationships, marriage, whatever. I've been through this myself, and it's only when I saw how I could lose the things that were really special to me that I realized how superficial those on-the-road attractions really were. I'm talking from personal experience here, but I don't really want to go into it.[398] You go through these extremities - playing the field, excesses of alcohol and stuff - and you come out of it a lot wiser. I'm a family man now. I like to go back home and be with my wife and little boy."[399]

At that time he was still trying to save his marriage. But when there wasn't anything to save anymore, things sounded quite different.

"I cheated my wife. Often. You make yourself blind and you go out there. It's great to meet lots of different girls and have fun, but then you realise what a s*** you are and how you're destroying other people's lives – or life – with it. Well, I know, well ... I think pretty much I know ... that my wife, my previous wife, was completely faithful to me. And I'd go back to her and ... not lie, because Joanne wouldn't even ask me things. I'm sure she suspected it. She wasn't stupid.[400] I felt trapped by everything that was around me. The last go round was great, we had a lot of success and *Violator* was huge round the world – and I should have been on top of the world, and I wasn't. I had everything I could possibly want, but I was really lost. I didn't feel like I even knew myself anymore. And I felt like s***, cos I constantly cheated on my wife, and went back home and

---

[398] Taken from: Real Gahan Kid, Sky, March 1990. Words: Paul Lester.
[399] Taken from: Depeche Mode Hip it up and Start Again, Melody Maker, 10 March 1990. Words: Jon Wilde.
[400] Taken from: In the Mode, Details, April 1993. Words: William Shaw.

lied.[401] I was really bored and really safe. I felt really safe in my life in England in lots of ways, and I didn't like it. There I was with a loving, caring wife, a new baby, a big house in the country, a couple of cars in the drive, and it just didn't feel right."[402]

Besides, he thought he had fallen in love with Theresa. "It was like being smashed on the head with a hammer. You look at yourself in the mirror one morning and suddenly everything's very, very different and the whole perspective has suddenly changed. Teresa brought out some emotions in me that I hadn't discovered, like love. I think I was just denying my true feelings a lot of the time, having to lie my way through a lot of my life with people I was supposed to respect and love and care for."[403]

Also in **1990**, Dave's biological father died - another heavy blow for him, and it pulled the rug right up from under him.

From **31 August** to **12 September** the "world-leg" with 8 concerts in Australia and Japan took place.

On **17 September** the single *World in My Eyes / Sea of Sin / Happiest Girl* was released, before the European leg started on **28 September**.

On **6 November** the video-compilation *Strange Too* was released, another collection of Corbijn-videos. Anton Corbijn directed all promotion videos for *Violator*. *Strange Too* contained the videos for all singles (two slightly different versions of the video for *World in My Eyes*) as well as videos for *Halo* and *Clean*.

The band had a break after the end of *Worldviolation*, a break that wouldn't do them any good.

"I think we need to [have a break]," **Fletch** said. "If we're to stay this good, or hopefully even improve, we need to conserve energy for a while. That's necessary in order to get inspiration, new ideas. So there may be a couple of years before a new *Depeche Mode* record comes out."[404]

---

[401] Taken from: "I Never Wanted to Destroy Depeche Mode", Melody Maker, 3 April 1993. Words: Jennifer Nine.
[402] Taken from: The Basildon Bond, The Times Magazine, 14 April 2001. Words: Paul Connolly.
[403] Taken from: In the Mode, Details, April 1993. Words: William Shaw.
[404] Taken from: Depeche Mode – Interview with the band, ULTRA Magazine, May 1990. Words: Jan Gradvall.

As if with hindsight to this and to the future **Dave** said, "We'd wonder if we'd still be around in another five years. It comes down to whether we'll carry on being friends and how long we'll want to record together. *Depeche Mode* is a group of four people, those four people make the sound of *Depeche Mode*. If one of those people left the group, it wouldn't be *Depeche Mode* anymore. If we split up, that would be it."[405]

Of course, fans know that he would change his mind later. But it has to be noted that at that time Alan was already losing interest increasingly in touring. I think it's one of the reasons why he finally left the band. He was thinking about if he wanted to do touring (and also working in a pop format, in a band) for the rest of his life.

"I don't really miss [touring]," **Alan** said in **1992**. "Often, when you're actually involved in a very long tour you start to wonder if you'll ever want to do it again."[406]

He was interested in exploring new paths – personal and musical – and **1990/91** was a point at which he started to develop in a different direction than that of the rest of the band.

---

[405] Taken from: Depeche Mode Hip it up and Start Again, Melody Maker, 10 March 1990. Words: Jon Wilde.
[406] Taken from: K-ROQ radio, 17 April 1992. Interviewer: Richard Blade.

1991

- I'm coming home (Death's Door) -

A "year out" like that is awful for a biographer. You can leave it out and pretend it had never existed because not much material about it can be found, or you wonder if it might be THE year in which the ball really began to roll.

In the case of *DM* I would say it was the latter. For an outsider it is difficult to understand what exactly was so awful about the subsequent *Devotional* time. Don't get me wrong: Of course, Dave's drug abuse was awful, and it was certainly hard to be with him after this break. But was this really the reason why ALL relationships were broken off, and why wasn't there "any diplomacy going on" as an inside source described the situation?

For a long time I couldn't get rid of the impression that there's something that hasn't been mentioned in any interview or biography so far. Some fans, who took part in the survey of *depechemodebiographie.de*, also think the existing sources are not enough. 24% answered the question whether there's actually a *"DM* mystery" for them, said they would like to know the exact background details of this period.

But over the course of time, I came to the conclusion that there probably isn't a big secret behind the whole story, all the information is out there, although the explanation that the changes in their private lives had been so drastic that they simply couldn't stand each other afterwards sounds strange on first hearing, especially because - except for Dave - nothing special happened.

Therefore, you could get the idea that there is something missing. But maybe it really is that simple. Each band member changed in some way, and developed in a different direction, especially according to their personal interests. This might have changed the feeling of the group completely.

A lot of people might know this situation: You work on a project very intensively and then take a longer break. When you come back, you notice that things that have always been like that suddenly get on your nerves. You just hadn't realised it before, because you were used to it.

But you have changed because of experiences you have had in the meantime, so you can't stand the old things anymore. You don't like some things that have changed in the time you were away either, because you feel you should have been consulted. You find the people are still basically the same, but nevertheless different somehow. Suddenly you don't like the behaviour you were used to anymore. Sometimes you find your way back into the team, sometimes you realise you have to quit.

Let's have a look at the changes in the lives of the members of *DM*.

Dave sought divorce from Jo, and moved to live with Theresa in LA. At first he tried to present this as diplomatically as possible: "It's great! I'm really enjoying it here. I'm just kind of living here for the moment, and I'm actually still keeping my place in London, and I'm just ... To tell the truth, I just recently got divorced from my wife, and I'm just trying to set up a new life. But as I said, I'm keeping my second home. I'm spending my time between both places. I'm lucky enough to do that. I just needed to get away and get some space, and think about what I wanted to do. ...

"We've worked really hard for the last 11 years or something. Al's in the studio at the moment with *Nitzer Ebb*. He's producing their new album. Mart's living in London now, and just kind of enjoying himself. I think he's going to be working on another 'Martin Gore solo thing.' I don't know what Fletch is doing at the moment. I think he's just kind of hanging out. I think he's thinking of opening a bar or something. I don't know what it's going to be called, but he's definitely thinking of that." (He opened a restaurant indeed, but meanwhile gave it up because it was too much work and took too much time.)

"Well, the thing is, it's fun to be working and doing stuff, and to be in the studio and creating music, and to be on tour and going out there and playing to people, but there are times when it's incredibly lonely. I mean, I'm not moaning about it. I love it. I wouldn't do anything else. It's the most exciting thing you could possibly be doing. I wouldn't change it for the world, but there are times when you lose contact with your friends, and it can be incredibly lonely and you go, yeah, I want to have some fun."[407]

He actually wasn't well at all. He suffered from the divorce from Jo and from having left his son. He admitted this within later years.

"In the space of six months everything just piled on top of me.[408] I just packed a case and split. Went off and rented a place in Los Angeles. During the *Violator*-Tour, I split from my wife. My year was really spent doing a lot of soul-searching and trying to find out what had gone wrong in my life, and thinking, to be quite honest, about whether I wanted to come back and do the whole thing – records, tours, fame, *Depeche Mode* - again."[409]

His band mates had a different view on this whole thing. So Alan would say that it was easy to influence Dave, and **Fletch** had a similar opinion: "Dave tends to adopt the personality of the person he's with. Theresa liked drug-ravaged skinny men with tattoos, so he became that person."

Maybe there's some truth in it. "For as long as I can remember, I've had this shield between me and life," **Dave** said. "As a teenager it was music. Then it was *Depeche* – that was my identity. Then that identity stopped working and the drugs and booze really kicked in as a new identity. I became so lost I was really unsure whether I could find my way out."[410]

So Dave really changed. He must have been an almost completely different person when his band mates met him again in **February 1992**.

Although Fletch used to say that he had been the one who kept the band together - why not think about what kind of role Dave had in the team? Could it be that he was the one who brought in some kind of balance to the team, especially to the team-spirit? Think about the "conservative and adventurous sides" of the band. If Fletch was a kind of spokesman for Martin, maybe Dave was the one who brought the two sides together?

---

[407] Taken from: K-ROQ radio, 9 May 1991, Interviewer: Richard Blade.
[408] Taken from: In the Mode, Details, April 1993. Words: William Shaw.
[409] Taken from: I Never Wanted to Destroy Depeche Mode, Melody Maker, 3 April 1993. Words: Jennifer Nine.
[410] Taken from: Songs of Innocence and Experience, Mojo, November 2005. Words: Danny Eccleston.

When I had the opportunity to chat with **Steve Lyon**, I asked him about Dave's role within the team, and also about the balance he might have brought in. "Well, a band is a balance. And when the balance becomes difficult ... unfortunately, the band fell apart ... but, yeah, Dave and Alan were the more adventurous in the material.

"I can remember sitting in Spain and chatting with Dave about the *Red Hot Chili Peppers* in which Alan also was very much into, the stuff coming from Seattle, American rock bands, hearing *Nirvana* on *MTV* the first time, Perry Farrell's band *Jane's Addiction*. Their album came out when we were recording *SOFAD*. Dave was a big fan and I sat down and listened to together with Dave, and that was something Martin and Fletch never listened to.

"Flood also was influenced by many things. It was a pretty impressive team I have to say. My job was to make the sounds more adventurous and creating a platform for Alan and Flood to work on. I think it was a very creative time.

"Fletch can be a very negative person about what can happen next, and I think he was worried a bit about the change from *Violator* to *SOFAD*. Alan, Flood and myself were not and nor was Dave. I think Martin was kind of middle ground ... but we all knew there's was something good in what we were doing. Later they were very much surprised by the success of *SOFAD* considering what had been spoken about during the making of the album. Like 'Is it too far away from *Violator*?' But if you ask any *Depeche* fan about his favourite albums, he will probably say *Violator* and *SOFAD*.

"When I started working with them I was completely unaware of the back catalogue. I knew some old singles and old songs, but I really didn't know them at all. And I remember we took a break at the recording in London and I got a delivery from *Mute* with the whole back catalogue of *Depeche* stuff and I sat down at the weekend and I was completely blown away. I was like, 'Wow, why I never knew this?' And I remember I was talking to Alan and Flood about it, and for them this was a good thing. On a creative side this is a good thing because you are not afraid to propose ideas or change sounds and do things. When you are aware of the band's history and their success you can get scared and on a creative side that can be bad. You can always get backwards. The step forward is the most difficult thing."[411]

Remember Alan saying that Dave wanted the band to "rock out more" – long before *SOFAD*. For Dave it had also always been very important to move on, to take a step forward, to develop further. So he might really have been the one who supported Alan when it came to discussions within the band about making experiments. But although Dave was very enthusiastic about *SOFAD*, and tried to contribute as much as possible, he was ill, and thus not able to fulfil his role in the team completely.

Making of: Violator-rose for this book. (© Ingo Bittrich)

It took a while before **Martin** started to write new songs. He had overdone the partying on *Worldviolation* a bit, so he was burnt out. For a while he was thinking about doing a solo album, but then something new stepped into his life, that gave him back his creativity - his first child.

"The new album [*SOFAD*] has a very uplifting feel to it and I'm sure that is due to my daughter. You see a life being born and growing, it's just wonderful, it moves you."[412]

Viva-Lee was born on **6 June**. Before that, his mother had told Martin the whole truth about his real father.

---

[411] depechemodebiographie.de
[412] Taken from: The Life and Loves of Depeche Mode, I-D, October 1993. Words: Michael Fuchs-Gambock.

"Actually, his Dad is American," **Fletch** said, "and he's black and lives in Virginia. Since then, Martin's met his Dad."[413]

It seems that this was quite a shock for Martin, and that the first meeting with his father didn't go very well. Maybe these things made him more sensitive to the "emotional violence" of the situation in **1992**, until it finally all became unbearable for him.

Also Fletch and long-term girlfriend Grainne became parents, when they had a daughter, Megan.

Fletch was suffering from depression during the recording sessions in **1992**, so he couldn't fulfil his role in the team either. Maybe the team collapsed because Dave and Fletch were ill, and couldn't liaise as usual between the two musical leaders.

For Alan, things settled down a bit this year too. He married his long-term girlfriend Jeri, although he would say about her later that she was "someone who thought she was descended from the lost city of Atlantis and of alien origin."

Nevertheless, they bought a house in the Sussex countryside, and a house for his own studio.

"I've invested a lot [of the money I made] back into my music via my studio and all its equipment and also into my house and estate. I also bought my parents a house."

The studio, *The Thin Line*, is in a house built in the **mid. 19th century**, adjacent to the bigger residential house. It was intended to become "a living, breathing space designed not necessarily for controlled sound but with the feel of a workshop, with plenty of light."

During **1991** a team of expert builders, electricians and steel workers spent 6 months gutting, reinforcing and rewiring the building. "It was always my intention to design this studio so you could simply remove all the gear and be left with a really interesting open-plan building."

At that time he also was busy with a lot of other projects. He was co-producer of *Nitzer Ebb* (album *Ebbhead*), together with Flood (before he left to produce *U2*) and Steve Lyon, and he recorded the first bigger *Recoil* project,

---

[413] Taken from: Blank Celebration, Revolver, May-June 2001. Words: J. D. Considine.

Bloodline, again together with Steve Lyon - but not in his new studio, because it wasn't ready yet.

"It was recorded at my house in London. My studio there was just a small back room with too little space and too much equipment."[414]

Some people think he bought his studio AFTER his decision to leave the band. But as you can see, he had bought it long before that, and he was obviously interested in exploring new directions. He didn't use this break to hang around and have fun, he kept on working. He actually ran out of time. He probably wasn't thinking about leaving the band at that point, but it is possible that the process that finally led to his decision had already started at the end of the *Worldviolation* (or maybe even earlier, when he started *Recoil* in **1986**.)

"What happened was, last year *Depeche Mode* decided to take a year off," **Alan** said in **1992**, "and I didn't want to just stop and do nothing for a year, so the obvious thing for me to do was to just do some work on my own. To me, it's as important as working with *Depeche Mode* even though *Depeche Mode* is still my main thing. But to me it's just important to make music and be creative. I can't stand just sitting around watching the clock tick by. I always feel guilty I should be doing something."[415]

I think the last sentence is the most important one. It shows how eager he was to work, to be creative, and to make music. Seeing himself confronted with a changed team a little later, which slowed down the whole process, must have been frustrating for him.

In this year there the only contact between band members was between Alan and Martin, who met in **spring 1991** to record *Death's Door* together, engineered by Steve Lyon, a single song that was released on **10 December**, as part of the soundtrack for *Until the End of the World*. (Martin sang the lead vocals on this track.)

"We literally did nothing for a whole year apart from the song for the Wim Wender's film, which only took us about 2 days to do, so we really had about 363 days off." **Martin** laughed. "I think that [*Death's Door*] was actually the first showing of a gospel direction, I think it had a real sort of

---

[414] Taken from: recoil.co.uk. Words: Alan Wilder.
[415] Taken from: Depeche Mode Spinoff Band Releases First U.S. Album, Chicago Tribune, 28 May 1992. Words: Jim Sullivan.

gospel feel to it that pointed the way to this album [SO-FAD]."[416]

Also in **December**, Dave decided to carry on with *DM*, because Martin's demo-tracks to *SOFAD* seemed to suit his current lifestyle perfectly.

1992

- You're blind from the facts (Curse, Bloodline) -

Apart from a questionnaire in *Bong* magazine published in **April 1992**, there was nothing in the media about the band that year.

Question: "You always seem so easy-going, but do you ever get in a temper and start shouting? If so, what is usually the cause?"

Alan: "Sometimes, for various reasons."

Question: "If one of the other band members showed up drunk for a show, what would you do?"

Alan: "Nothing. Each band member is aware of his responsibilities."

Question: "Do your parents listen to your music and if so, what do they think of it?"

Alan: "Yes they do, but I don't think they like it much."

Question: "What or whom do you miss most when you're on the road?"

Alan: "My independence, family, QPR [*Queen's Park Rangers*] home games, cooking for myself and driving."

Question: "Which do you prefer, working in the studio or playing live?"

Alan: "Working in the studio."

Question: "Do you see yourself being in *Depeche Mode* for the next ten years?"

Alan: "No."

Question: "What are your feelings now that you're faced with recording and touring again?"

Alan: "Apprehension."[417]

---

[416] Taken from: Dave & Martin interview, K-ROQ radio, March 1993. Interviewer: Richard Blade and Jed the Fish.
[417] Taken from: Ask Alan, Bong 16, April 1992. Words: Alan Wilder.

But when were these questions answered? In **April**? Or before the band's first meeting in **February**? Unfortunately it's impossible to tell from the *Bong* article.

The rest of the story appeared in later years and was anything but pleasant. The first meeting of the band in a villa near Madrid to record *Songs of Faith and Devotion (SOFAD)* was a disaster. During two sessions - each about six weeks long - with a break of a month in between, the band lived there together.

"In theory, it was a really good idea," **Dave** said, "but we found that our personalities clashed incredibly when living together 24 hours a day, seven days a week. I didn't mind it so much, but Alan detested it and Fletch had a hard time.[418] However, I'd changed, but I didn't really understand it until I came face to face with Al and Mart and Fletch. The looks on their faces battered me."[419]

Alan tried to be diplomatic. "The fact that we took a break away from each other, that people went and did things with their own personal lives - had children and moved to different parts of the world - has given us all a different perspective on what the group was and is, and what it means to us all. Coming back together has taken a long time to get used to. I think, for a long period this year, there were a lot of disparities between the different members of the group."[420]

"Dave would come forward on a real burst of energy, do a vocal," **Fletch** described the situation, "then disappear to his room for a couple of days. It was a bit odd."[421]

"A lot of the time it was hard for them to even want to be in the same room as me,"[422] **Dave** said.

"It was an absolute disaster," **Martin** explained. "We all hated it there, because it wasn't really in the centre of Madrid. It was about 30-40 minutes outside. So every time we wanted to go out, we had to get cabs into town. Also living on top of each other became difficult. We never had space from each other."[423]

---

[418] Taken from: Mode Three, Future Music, April 1997. Words: Uncredited.
[419] Taken from: They Just Couldn't get Enough, Q, March 1997. Words: Phil Sutcliffe.
[420] Taken from: Devout Moded, Vox, February 1993. Words: Martin Townsend.
[421] Taken from: They Just Couldn't get Enough, Q, March 1997. Words: Phil Sutcliffe.
[422] Taken from: In the Mode, Details, April 1993. Words: William Shaw.
[423] Taken from: Mode Three, Future Music, April 1997. Words: Uncredited.

Some of their statements seem to be a bit contradictory at first glance. Alan felt disturbed by lots of acting up, as he said once, on the other hand, it is said that Dave was in his room most of the time and Martin was out partying. What did he mean exactly? The only one who obviously was often in the studio was Fletch because he felt his privacy was disturbed. The same here: if Dave wasn't around and Martin wasn't around – how could he have felt his privacy was disturbed? Martin's remark about never having space from each other seems strange too. I saw pictures of the villa: It's very big. Of course, they weren't alone, there were also members of the crew there, but it's nevertheless a bit strange because the band members were just referring to the presence of the other band members, not to crew members.

Now one could think that Fletch was disturbing Alan when he was spending most of the time in the studio, but his depressions were known to Alan meanwhile. It is said that Fletch wasn't well. Sometimes he was hyperactive when he had taken anti-depressive tablets. Sometimes he didn't say a word, and just sat silently in a corner of the room.

However, the main point was probably that Alan was eager to work while no one else in the band seemed to show much interest.

"Alan was angry that he spent 12 hours in the studio while Mart was getting drunk somewhere and I was doing something different," **Dave** explained. "He was the one who was trying to keep things together while everyone else was busy with their ego-sh***. But nobody thanked him."[424]

Alan confirmed, "It's fair to say that the majority of the production/sound-shaping side of things on the last few albums was down to me and Flood with Martin bringing in a few keyboard and guitar lines from his original demos.[425] A lot of the time it's myself and Flood who are left there in the early hours of the morning, doing what we call 'screwdriver' work. It's sifting through bits of performance and restructuring it, which bores Martin most of the time and

---

[424] Source can't be found anymore
[425] Taken from: Alan Wilder Interview, Future Music, Issue 62, November 1997. Words: Andy Jones.

Dave to an extent.[426] In fact, it's been suggested that I was unsociable, spending too much time in the studio. The truth is that the job just wouldn't have gotten done otherwise. It disappoints me that anybody would think that wanting to achieve the best possible results isn't worthwhile."[427]

And why exactly Martin didn't feel well? He knew the depressions of his friend, he knew how fixated Alan was on studio work. So what exactly was different or worse in comparison to *Violator*? Why did something not work anymore that had worked before?

"I felt totally distanced from the rest of the band," **Martin** said. "I really didn't want to be there. Up until that point we always felt like a gang - then suddenly it felt really wrong for the first time.[428] I think when we first got together in Madrid it became obvious that there wasn't a real feeling of band unity."[429]

So, obviously the changes of the individual team members in their personal development led to a loss of teamspirit. And as it has been mentioned before - you'll find people basically the same but nevertheless you can have a different view on them when you've stepped back for a while. Living so close together they probably found out some things about each other they didn't want to know ...

The band members also had very different ideas of how the album should sound, so the studio work took a lot of time. It needed some jam sessions to find a basic sound for it.

"With all *DM* albums, we tried to move away from the previous one and after some discussion between myself, Flood and the others, we agreed that our approach should be more towards performance and to try to push ourselves into areas we hadn't explored," **Alan** explained. "Some of the songs like *I Feel You, In Your Room* and *Rush* suggested a looser, more 'live' feel."

---

[426] Taken from: Biography, International Music Publications, 1993. Words: Uncredited.
[427] Taken from: Alan Wilder Interview, Future Music, Issue 62, November 1997. Words: Andy Jones.
[428] Taken from: Just Can't Get Enough, Uncut, May 2001. Words: Stephen Dalton.
[429] Taken from: Many Smack-Free Returns! Q, June 2001. Words: Dorian Lynskey.

But it was a difficult process, before they were able to get in a creative working flow.

"Everybody tries to pull a record in their preferred direction. Sometimes those tensions help but normally they slow down the process while the person who has a problem argues their case, after which either a compromise is reached or they lose the debate and go off and sulk for a bit. Personally I find continually having to put your ideas to a committee wears you down after a while and ultimately stifles the creative flow."[430]

This is what **Alan** said later, after leaving the band. It shows the main point of his frustration with the teamwork at the time. From a certain point, he didn't like making compromises anymore.

Try walking in my shoes ... (© Ingo Bittrich)

---

[430] Taken from: recoil.co.uk. Words: Alan Wilder.

In **1993** he explained, "Martin gets bored very quickly in the studio, Dave gets very enthusiastic, but he's not a musician as such, so he can only contribute to a degree, and Fletch doesn't have a musical role at all. Martin always errs on the melodic side, he's a pop merchant, so he pulls in one direction a bit, and I always try to pull it in a darker direction 'cause that's the music I tend to listen to. We meet in the middle and end up with pop music that's got an edge to it, so it's more interesting, it's got more depth plus it's all melodic."[431]

This is the best description of what made *DM*'s music special "in the old days," and that is what the "old fans of the *DM* with Alan" mean when they're trying to explain why Alan was such an important part of the band for them. The point is not that Alan is such a great musician or producer, but that he was a counterpart to Martin.

"Their musical tastes were quite different," **Steve Lyon** said about Alan and Martin. "And I think that this blend of what they were doing made it work to be honest. I remember being in the studio in Spain and I went to see Martin in his room and he was listening to soul music, gospel, Elvis, 80's electronic music, he had a very wide taste. And the same was with Alan. When you listen to *Recoil* stuff ... the track we did with Moby, [*Curse*], when you listen to Moby's solo records they are almost identical to what he did with Alan. I don't think they had really a different musical approach. It wasn't too much of a problem."[432]

Maybe not the different musical approaches as such, but obviously the compromises, and especially the communication about it. It seems that Alan enjoyed the work with the production team very much, but not the work with the band. This might be an explanation for his contradictory statements about having fun and finding it unbearable at the same time.

This time it really was difficult to "meet in the middle" and so they finally did something that for them was quite unusual: "I can remember the first time we recorded *Walking in My Shoes*," **Alan** said. "It was the first, and possibly only, time the band has ever jammed together. We were never that kind of group; we just meticulously programmed music. Yes, there would be performance ele-

---

[431] Taken from: The Highs and Lows and Rise of Depeche Mode, FHM, June 1993. Words: Andy Darling.
[432] depechemodebiographie.de

ments, but they tended to be over-dubs and single-person performances. We were getting nowhere; we had tried different ways of recording that track, and none of it sounded any good. So after the third or fourth time, Flood finally said, 'Look, just all sit down, pick up an instrument and play something together.' And that was met with derision. 'What? What are you talking about? Play together?' Alien concept to *Depeche Mode*. So Martin had a guitar, I had a bass, someone else had a tambourine, we had a little rhythm box going, and we just made this noise. And after that, we got the main groove for that song, the bass line and guitar lines. I'm not saying it was anything special. All I'm saying is that the process was so different and so unusual, and we did get a result from it. I wish we had done more of that kind of thing."[433]

Alan's main problem was obviously with Martin, because about Dave he said, "With this record we've tried to make Dave sing in a different way. In simple things, like raising the register of the song so he has to sing higher than he would normally, forcing him to approach songs differently and making him go over and over things, trying different environments in which he hasn't sung before, not using headphones like we normally do, anything to try and get a different performance. He's responded really well. Dave has a very good attitude. He's willing to try things even if he doesn't understand why he's being asked to at the time."[434]

On the other hand, when he was longing for some rest after studio work, **Alan** had to bear Dave's exercises on E-guitar next door.

"Although Dave was filled with enthusiasm by the idea of a new album actually, he committed himself no longer strikingly soon. But he came down into the studio now and then and praised Flood's and my work as the only one. He was at least worried about the group, in which constitution he himself identically was."[435]

This constitution got worse in the course of time.

"Alan was the first who confronted me with that," **Dave** remembered.

---

[433] Taken from: Bullz-Eye, 10 May 2010, Word: Dave Medsker.
[434] Taken from: Biography, International Music Publications, 1993. Words: Uncredited.
[435] Taken from: recoil.co.uk. Words: Alan Wilder.

"Then we had our first ultimatum-meeting with Dave," **Martin** said. "We said to him, 'You've got to sort yourself out. You're putting yourself in danger.'"

"They were genuinely concerned about my health," **Dave** explained. "Of course, I couldn't see that. I said to Mart, 'F*** off! You drink fifteen pints of beer a night and take your clothes off and cause a scene. How can you be so f*** hypocritical?'"[436]

(It was a serious situation but I can't help laughing, though, every time when I read, "You drink fifteen pints of beer a night and take your clothes off and cause a scene." It's probably the best description of what you got when you went out with Martin in the **1980s**.)

At the meeting Alan had organised in London, Martin finally realised that Dave was taking a lot of heroin at the time. But it was too late to take appropriate measures.

In the meantime - almost overseen - on **9 March**, the single *Faith Healer* was released, followed by the *Recoil*-album *Bloodline* which was released on **13 April**. *Bloodline* was markedly different from *Hydrology*, particularly since **Alan** had gone in a new direction musically. So he worked with some vocalists like Moby, Toni Halliday and Douglas McCarthy. He worked out a piano improvisation (*Freeze*) and an homage to *Kraftwerk* with the song *The Defector*, and he gave a new tune to recordings of Bukka White.

"The original Bukka recording is virtually acapella - he is actually singing to an acoustic guitar but the guitar is just about inaudible. It therefore seemed to be a very interesting source of material to try and do something unusual with. I also loved the sound of his voice - particularly when he talks in his own unique language / babble. Certain lines were sampled, re-structured and then filtered."[437]

He didn't feel any pressure to make an album which was more conventional, but he felt he couldn't produce ongoing experimental instrumental music either.

"However, I didn't really see it through in the way I should have done; I think I lacked the energy. I had *Depeche Mode* commitments, and I was really fitting *Bloodline* into the first real break the band had taken in 10

---

[436] Taken from: They Just Couldn't get Enough, Q, March 1997. Words: Phil Sutcliffe.
[437] Taken from: recoil.co.uk. Words: Alan Wilder.

years. By the end of that year – while also producing a *Nitzer Ebb* album – I'd just run out of energy. I think the album suffers a little bit because of it, especially the vocals."[438]

For a while, it was planned to release *Edge to Life* as another single, but by that time, Alan had already moved off into the production of *SOFAD* so he wouldn't have had the time to promote it.

In **April** Dave got married to Theresa. No other band member attended the ceremony. He had a lot of tattoos done, motivated by Theresa. Within the later years some biographers and journalists tried to represent the relationship as if Dave would have influenced Theresa more than the other way around, because she was willing to fulfil his desires for drugs and sex. Dave isn't a "milk-and-honey-type" (as Alan once remarked) at all, but reading between the lines you come to another conclusion about who had influenced whom.

"I mean, my wife's American, and you know, she's really aggressive, and I've definitely picked up on that," **Dave** said. "And most of the time she's dead right about what she thinks. She's said things to me over the last year that've completely changed my view about a lot of things I was doing, and she's done nothing but encourage me."

He saw his drug abuse as a lifestyle choice, a lifestyle that didn't suit his band mates, so he often felt like it was him against them. He frequently shut himself up in his room to paint.

"I remember when I'd finished, Martin said to me, 'Oh yeah, you know, I didn't realise you could paint.' And I said, 'Well, yeah, that's what I used to do, Mart, that's all I could do. I was in art college for three years, and the only thing I was even any good at was painting.'"

Although he often felt isolated from the group, the demos for *SOFAD* and the lyrics were completely appropriate to the way he felt at the time. It was almost as if Martin had written the songs just for him.

"I think *Condemnation* is by far my finest vocal performance. When I came into the control room everybody went all quiet and turned around, and suddenly Flood

---

[438] Taken from: Unsound Recordings, Sound On Sound, January 1998. Words: Bill Bruce.

said, 'That was f*** great!' And Alan and everybody said, 'That's probably the best vocal you ever did' – and I thought, 'yeah, it was.' It was completely breaking me up inside, and, at the same time, it was really optimistic and uplifting."

He claimed that it had been his idea to use live drums. "I kept pushing and pushing and, in the end, Alan got on the drumkit and said, 'Well, I'll f*** do it, then!'"[439]

Alan had a different memory to this: "I'd been considering it for a while and eventually mentioned it to Dave who thought it was a good idea."

I was asked by a reader whether Alan learned to play the drums for *SOFAD*. He had learned to play them long before (he played the drums on *Clean* e.g.), but did special exercises for *SOFAD* and the *Devotional*-Tour.

About Dave's vocal performance **Alan** said, "I worked personally with Dave for many years to get the optimum performance out of him and I actually believe that some of his best vocals are on the *SOFAD* album. Dave's voice on tracks such as *In Your Room, Condemnation, I Feel You* and *Walking in My Shoes* absolutely mirrors the intensity of the music. Obviously there is a degradation in his vocals during some of the live performances from *Devotional* but this is purely down to the stresses and strains of extensive touring and perfectly understandable. That said, I would rather hear a cracked and 'rough' sounding voice that is full of emotion, to one that is technically perfect but bland and lifeless."[440]

Later **Dave** explained that he had planned the transformation of simple Dave from Basildon to a monster. And he did during *Worldviolation*. "There were a couple of ingredients missing: a companion in doing everything it took to be a rock 'n' roll star - which turned out to be Teresa, my second wife – and ... the drug. I wanted to lead that very selfish lifestyle without being judged. She was joining in. In fact, she introduced me ... she didn't make me take heroin, she gave me the opportunity to try it again. I'd actually played around with it back in Basildon, didn't inject it at that time, however."[441]

---

[439] Taken from: I Never Wanted to Destroy Depeche Mode, Melody Maker, 3 April 1993. Words: Jennifer Nine.
[440] Taken from: recoil.co.uk. Words: Alan Wilder.
[441] Taken from: Tears of my Tracks, Q, March 1997. Words: Phil Sutcliffe.

In the meantime, the relationship between Fletch and Alan collapsed.

"Alan really didn't get on with Andy," **Martin** said. "We've always been honest about the fact that Andy's not really musical. And Alan around that time was heavily involved with what made *Depeche Mode*, in production and arrangement. I think he felt that it was wrong that he was making the same money as Andy, who basically doesn't do anything in the studio."[442]

An inside source told me that money had definitely been an issue, but I don't think that money was the main point.

From the production of *Violator* onwards, the band started to fall apart. Fletch's depressions and Dave's drug abuse were both increasing and having an impact on the team-spirit. Martin took a backseat, while Alan was heavily involved in the studio work. It seems that he had the increasing impression of being the only one who was working, and that he felt forced to take over the tasks of the other members of the team. In a situation like this one can get the idea of being overworked and underpaid. But it was probably mainly about being disappointed that no one seemed to notice how much work had to be done, and how much work he was providing.

Alan says about himself that he is sometimes quite cynical. It is said that there were a lot of arguments going on between the band members during the recordings of *SOFAD* and during *Devotional*. It's not known what these arguments were about, but it's easy to guess when reading between the lines. Alan said he was accused of being unsocial, and one of his answers to this might have been: "At least I'm doing something in contrast to this lazy sod that never does a single thing in the studio. I wonder what he's paid for." With this you are right in the middle of a money-discussion although the main point is something completely different.

While some fans share **Martin's** opinion - "Andy, I think, finds it most annoying when he goes into interviews and has to basically just talk for the whole interview about the business side of the band. Everybody thinks that he's totally incompetent as a musician, and think that even

---

[442] Taken from: Just Can't Get Enough, Uncut, May 2001. Words: Stephen Dalton.

when he's onstage playing with us that he doesn't play a note 'cause he's not capable"[443] (although Martin often said something completely different, see the quotation above, but note that it dates from **2001** while this one dates from **1993**, and might be a result of arguments of this kind) – Alan, Fletch himself and some other fans think that Fletch's role really is a different one. (He even said once that he was in the band by accident, and wasn't interested in making music that much.) But, of course, it will hurt you badly, especially in Fletch's state of mind at that time, when there's someone who gives you the feeling of being useless, lazy and overpaid. In Alan's view (he said it between the lines or even directly) Fletch never had any musical role. It's obvious that Alan didn't take Fletch seriously at all (understandable from his point of view) and probably Fletch couldn't deal with that (which would be also understandable.)

However, I think Fletch's role in Alan's decision to leave the band and the fact that Fletch earned the same money as Alan are overrated. There are still many fans who believe Alan left the band because of Fletch. Some even believe Fletch mobbed him out. But I don't think Alan is someone you can mob out that easily. He probably never really got on with Fletch, but hadn't been bothered by it for more than ten years.

Of course, that these two characters couldn't get on with each other anymore in this tense recording situation didn't make things easier, especially when you remember that Fletch was a kind of spokesman for Martin. Alan said once that he had to talk to Fletch when he wanted to talk to Martin, so the problem might now have been that there wasn't much communication going on between these two musical heads anymore.

The relationship between Alan and Dave - maybe not real friends, but good mates at least - suffered from an event, too, when Dave provoked a group of *Hell's Angels* in a bar in Madrid.

"I think Dave's words to one of them were: 'What are you looking at, you fat c***?'" **Alan** remembered. "About 10 minutes later, all hell broke loose with several resulting

---

[443] Taken from: Plugged In, Creative Loafing, 2 October 1993. Words: Katherine Yeske.

'autographs' in the form of bruises and black eyes - none received by the bikers though. Miraculously, none were received by me either. I have an uncanny knack of making myself invisible during times of extreme violence."

He was disappointing when he found out that Dave was taking heroin. "Not for any moral reasons but because his drug use adversely affected his personality and more specifically his greatest asset, his sense of humour. There was also an increase in general apathy. It didn't necessarily turn him into a monster or anything but, obviously, Dave was in his own world. Consequently this made normal communication more difficult, which was an added pressure in an already quite tense group relationship. It was just a bit sad from my point of view because he wasn't really 'there' a lot of the time and I missed his sharp wit." (Maybe Dave's previous role in the team had been solving problems and diffusing tension with his humour.)

"Nobody else in *DM* has ever taken heroin as far as I know so I imagine Dave felt alien to the rest of us at this time. A distance arose between Dave and me which made me sad, particularly because he is actually an enthusiastic and vigorous person. Dave is also very generous and frank but perhaps this is the problem, and yes, of course, everybody tried to help him but I don't think that someone of us really understood what the matter was actually. It isn't easy to help someone who's on a mission."[444]

I'm not quite sure whether **Dave** was referring to the same story about that bar in Madrid, when he told many years later that he had been suffering from withdrawal symptoms once during their stay in Madrid. "Everyone scrabbled around to find what they thought I needed - booze, coke, hash, pills. But heroin wasn't provided. I went looking in some subterranean club. I approached some guys who looked like they might be in that vein, but I got a severe beating outside instead. I remember rolling under this car, snow on the ground, and Martin trying to intervene and promptly getting punched."[445]

From the context the impression was given that it was an incident which caused a distance to Martin. It seems as if Martin lost his faith in him because Dave said it had taken him a long time to earn his trust back.

---

[444] Taken from: recoil.co.uk. Words: Alan Wilder.
[445] Taken from: Interview with Dave Gahan, Mojo, 22 March 2013. Words: Martin Aston.

The band had a break and then met in Hamburg again, where they worked from **10 to 29 August** in the *Chateau du Pape Studios* (today *Home Studios*). Things ran a little more smoothly there.

"Fletch went back to England and booked himself back into *The Priory* [because of his depressions]," **Alan** said. "Dave only really showed up to do his vocals, and that left myself, Flood and Martin to get on and knock the album into shape."[446]

DM in Hamburg (the picture was taken in Berlin, though ;))
(© Ingo Bittrich)

But according to rumours Martin also went on pub crawls lasting days at that point, and Dave sometimes disappeared for days on end. His drug addiction was so obvious by then that there are rumours about some quarrels about it.

Other sources say that the band almost never left the studio (it's, of course, a question of how well these persons know them and to whom they were referring when saying that they never left the studio) and that things between Alan and Martin went well in this period, and that they often had some "hotel bar gigs" with Alan playing the piano and Martin singing. The latter was, however, nothing special.

"We had hundreds of imprompu sessions around barroom pianos the world over," **Alan** remembered. "It was

---

[446] Taken from: Just Can't Get Enough, Uncut, May 2001. Words: Stephen Dalton.

quite a common thing for myself and Martin to take over the piano in hotel bars. My sight reading is poor (mainly through lack of practice) but it's never been a problem for me to play by ear or from memory. I've always been able to improvise quite easily and Martin seems to know the words to every song ever written."[447]

Things like these seem to be contradictory to the "very bad relationship" between these two characters. In one statement Alan differentiates between the "human side on which we got on well" and the "working / musical side," but there's also a later statement (around *SubHuman*) when Alan said that Martin might never have liked him. According to doubtful sources Martin said that Alan was more communicative in Hamburg so it had been easier for him to get on with him, while Alan said that the "smaller producing team" made things easier.

Maybe these things are so contradictory because journalists and biographers quoted or translated them wrongly. Maybe it is just a complex thing – Alan and Martin have some things in common and might get on well here, but they differ on some points and might get on badly there.

It really seems that it was a constant up and down, and not a permanent tension, because there are also statements from this time saying that it wasn't that bad. It also really seems to be a problem within the band itself, not so much a problem within the whole crew that was working on *SOFAD*.

So **Steve Lyon** said, "Well, certainly towards the end of the time I was working with them or during the time in Spain and then a little bit in Germany it was quite obvious that Dave was having a bad time. He had a lot of support from everyone, from the band, certainly from me, certainly from Flood, from Daniel Miller. Everyone could realise that he was having a difficult time. But it didn't really stop the creative work. When I look back at this time, *Violator*, *Violation*-Tour, pre-production of *SOFAD* ... I wouldn't say it was a dark, difficult period. Completely opposite, I had a great time. They are really nice guys, they are brilliant to hang out with. I can remember walking around the *Reeperbahn* in Germany, with the band and the whole crew, having a great time! We weren't worried about fans

---

[447] Taken from: recoil.co.uk. Words: Alan Wilder.

or anything, just having a good time. Going back to the hotel, where we stayed there in Hamburg, sitting around the piano, playing, singing, fans coming in, watching ... it was a very happy, creative period. Unfortunately Dave had a difficult time but it hadn't an influence on what we were doing."[448]

The last recording session took place in the *Olympic Studios* in London. They worked together with a gospel-trio - Hildia Cambell, Bazil Meade and Samantha Smith - a pipes-player, Steafan Hannigan, and a string-orchestra.

"We got the choir in and I was just sitting at the back thinking 'this isn't going to work, I don't know why we're trying this'," **Martin** recalled. "I was really nervous about the whole thing. But the moment they started singing, for me, it lifted the track onto another level, it was just up there somewhere, and so then I decided I shouldn't be so closed-minded about the whole thing."[449]

"Once we decided we wanted 'real' strings, there was only really one or two choices as to who should arrange them," **Alan** said. "Will Malone arranged the strings for *Massive Attack*'s *Unfinished Sympathy*, a particular favourite of both myself and Martin. The strings were recorded at *Olympic Studios* in London, using a 28 piece string section, to which Martin sang the vocal 'live' - thus equalling the fastest ever recording of any one *DM* track, the other being *Somebody*."

While they agreed about *One Caress*, they didn't about *Judas*.

"We actually recorded that track in three or four different ways," **Alan** explained. "The final version was completed very late in the day and Martin didn't say much about it which is his way of indicating he doesn't like something. I think Martin was quite attached to his demo version but I felt it needed more atmosphere. He in turn didn't like the sequencer end-section. It was omitted for the live version because it wasn't really suitable in that particular context."

At the **end of December**, the album was finally ready, far behind schedule.

---

[448] depechemodebiographie.de
[449] Taken from: The Life and Loves of Depeche Mode, I-D, October 1993. Words: Michael Fuchs-Gambock.

1993

- Well, I'm down on my knees again (One Caress) -

On **16 January** Fletch married his long-term girlfriend Grainne. On **15 February** the single *I Feel You / One Caress* was released. *I Feel You* peaked at No. 8 on the UK Singles Chart and also made No. 1 in many countries. It was the band's highest charting single worldwide.

On the cover of the single there are four symbols, each representing a member, the top left corner represents Alan, the top right corner represents Dave, the bottom left corner represents Martin and the bottom right corner represents Fletch.

"In typical fashion, the US record company wanted a different release," **Alan** said. "So they insisted that we stand outside all day in the freezing cold and make a video for *One Caress* which in the end they decided not to release at all."

Directed by Kevin Kerslake, it was shot just outside Chicago and included an unusual cast of animals and insects.

"The only amusing part of the whole event was when half of these creatures escaped into the trees and the crew had to spend the rest of the night coaxing them down."[450]

The video for *I Feel You* was directed by Anton Corbijn.

The album *Songs of Faith and Devotion (SOFAD)* was released on **22 March**.

The single *Walking in My Shoes / My Joy* was released on **16 April**. Again, the video for *Walking in My Shoes* was directed by Anton Corbijn. At the beginning of the second verse, there's a shot of Martin, Fletch and Alan with naked women on their laps. This was removed in the *MTV* version in the U.S. and replaced by footage of the three members standing still.

The band tried to talk about the new album and to draw the attention to it.

"It's been a difficult album at times, there's no doubt about it,"[451] **Alan** said, but "I don't agree at all that *SOFAD*

---

[450] Taken from: recoil.co.uk. Words: Alan Wilder.

is a dark album - it's the only *DM* album that leaves you feeling really uplifted. *I Feel You* for example, or *Higher Love, Rush* etc. all have an overriding sense of optimism. If I remember correctly, everyone else felt *I Feel You* should be the first single. The main reason for the choice was that the track had attitude and was radically different to what we had done before. We hoped it would surprise people and make them curious about the rest of the album.[452] To me, *SOFAD* is quite a complex album. It was hell to make at times. When you're in that situation, you just don't see that. You can't imagine that when things are going wrong and everyone hates each other that some good music can be coming out of it. You just think everything sucks and everybody sucks. So it's only in hindsight that you see it."[453]

"It's still one of my favourite albums of ours," **Dave** remarked. "It felt like we were trying desperately to challenge ourselves and break out of everything we had done on *Violator*, which was very controlled, very polished, very clean - a perfect pop album. We wanted to blow all that stuff away."[454]

Alan was quite satisfied with the overall artwork for *SOFAD*, but not with the cover. "I have to agree it wasn't one of the greats but nobody wanted to hurt Anton's feelings having given him the job of artistic direction - one of his problems is that he is quite inflexible once he has an idea for something. When it comes to cover art, I always felt that Anton should have really focused exclusively on his photography (which is what he does best) and let others take care of layout and graphics."[455]

"Anton suggested that as the music was becoming more human, that we should use our images on the cover," **Martin** explained. "We weren't too sure about it but we told him if he could come up with a good idea then we'd

---

[451] Taken from: Devout Moded, Vox, February 1993. Words: Martin Townsend.
[452] Taken from: recoil.co.uk. Words: Alan Wilder.
[453] Taken from: Songs of Praise and Emotion, Blue Divide, Volume 2, Issue 1, 2000. Words: Uncredited.
[454] Taken from: In the Mode for Love, Time Out, 4 April 2001. Words: Omer Ali.
[455] Taken from: recoil.co.uk. Words: Alan Wilder.

think about it. He came up with a design that used our faces and obscured them enough for our liking."[456]

"*Walking in My Shoes* was certainly one of Anton's more surreal promos and the actual filming was quite a different experience for us," **Alan** recalled. "I remember how odd it was being surrounded by all these people with every manner of deformity - especially at meal times. It brought a smile to my face standing next to a hunch-back, dressed like a gothic nightmare and hearing him ask the catering girls: 'Have you got any ketchup, love?'"

Despite the difficult recordings they decided to undertake a long tour. It seems strange to do something like this when everything is in a mess. Maybe they simply did it because it had already been planned (as early as **April 1992** Alan had said in a radio interview they would tour for a year.) Maybe they didn't realise what they were doing to themselves. Maybe they thought things could be fixed during the tour. They had always enjoyed touring and partying together, so maybe this was really the idea they had in mind. Nevertheless, they weren't sure if Dave was able to do it.

"We had a couple of meetings where the question of Dave's drug usage was addressed," **Alan** said. "It was put to Dave that if he didn't clean up his act, we wouldn't make it through such a long tour. He agreed."[457]

They believed in his agreement, something that seems quite naive. But in the music business drugs are a normal thing, and on the other hand, they obviously weren't used to the habits of a real junkie.

"I'd like a life outside rock," **Dave** said before the tour started. "But, at the same time, I'm in it right up to my f*** neck, and I'm going to remain in it. My wife would back me 100 percent, even if it meant us spending a lot of time apart. What we have is much stronger than that."

"My wife and I have been together a long time and it's become so normal," **Alan** explained. "It doesn't seem weird to her when I go away."[458]

---

[456] Taken from: It's Just Devotion, Press Magazine, 2 March 1994. Words: Andrew Mast.
[457] Taken from: recoil.co.uk. Words: Alan Wilder.
[458] Taken from: Devout Moded, Vox, February 1993. Words: Martin Townsend.

The marriage would break during the tour at which Alan started an affair with his later second wife Hepzibah, who was a violinist of the opening act *Miranda Sexgarden*.

Jeri's son Jason appeared as the lead singer of the band *Parallax* as an opener for the *DM* concert in Liévin.

"*Parallax* released some singles on *Mute* before changing their name to *Hoodwink* who also released one or two more," **Alan** said. "They never got around to completing their debut album and are no longer on the label."[459]

Dave tried to explain how it feels when one tries to find one's way back to everyday life after playing in front of so many fans. "You're in this funny little world where you can do whatever you like whenever you like. You start getting a bit crazy. You really get into it. You're a gang and there's all the crew ... and then suddenly you gotta go to the supermarket and get your groceries."

"You've got to sort of come back to reality and do all kinds of normal things," **Martin** admitted.

"You find yourself pacing around the room hating to talk in the evening," **Alan** added. "Then you realise the reason is you're supposed to be on stage."[460]

Some reporters obviously weren't aware of the tension within the band. Instead, they preferred to concentrate on putting forward the eternally same questions to **Martin**, whether he is gay - maybe just a little bit -, and whether he likes BDSM and pornography. (On the other hand, it has to be said that it was difficult to talk to the band at the time. They were careful and tended to pretend everything was fine.)

"I've always tried to write from a personal point of view. I don't see any of the things I write about as being pervy, you know? I actually really like the imagery of S&M, and the clubs and things like that, but I wasn't just glorifying it. It's also a topic on this album. We had someone down the other day, and it was really funny because he was talking about this pervert thing as well. We played him four or five tracks and when it got to *One Caress* and it started off, *Well I'm down on my knees again*, he went, 'Oh good!'." He laughed.

---

[459] Taken from: recoil.co.uk. Words: Alan Wilder.
[460] Taken from: Mode Squad, Creem, April 1993. Words: Jeremy Helligar.

"I think, probably, 70 percent of our songs are about, or touch on, sex. Personally, I find it an important thing, I find it amazing when I talk to people and they consider it a secondary thing in life. For me, it isn't something that's very secondary.[461] Maybe it's very naïve, but the only religion for me is love. I believe in love. So that's why the songs touch on love, sex and religion; for me they're the same thing.[462]

"I should imagine from reading the lyrics they'd think I was dark and moody with quite a perverted sense of things. The BDSM reference comes up so often in songs that I must be interested in but if I practise it I think that's personal stuff, really. If pornography is well done I like it. It always amazes me that so much pornography is done badly. If it's done well ... You have to choose your words carefully here, you're always treading on dodgy ground. I think I like the idea of androgyny. Maybe it's to do with my dislike of normality. I've always thought a macho image really boring. I think a lot of people think that I'm gay, which doesn't offend me or worry me in the slightest. People can think what they like."[463]

And here are some answers from Martin which are quite funny or interesting with hindsight of the future:

Question: "Do you sometimes get fed up with being in *Depeche Mode*?"

Martin: "Yes."

Question: "What would you do if one of the other three said they were leaving?"

Martin: "Give up." (We all know he wouldn't.)

Question: "Would you prefer it if the other three wrote songs as well as you?"

Martin: "I like being in control of the music." (And we know that he had to give in when Dave forced him to let him contribute songs.)

Question: "What one thing couldn't you live without?"

Martin: "Two things equally – sex and alcohol."[464] (I don't know about sex, but he would quit drinking a couple of years later – and he's still alive. ;))

---

[461] Taken from: Devout Moded, Vox, February 1993. Words: Martin Townsend.
[462] Taken from: The Life and Loves of Depeche Mode, I-D, October 1993. Words: Michael Fuchs-Gambock.
[463] Taken from: In the Mode, Details, April 1993. Words: William Shaw.
[464] Taken from: Ask Martin, Bong 18, April 1993.

"I'm not passionate about anything other than music," **Martin** admitted. "I bore my friends to death with music! I often invite friends to come and stay with me, and I get drunk and I play then every one of my favourite records. At the end of the night, everybody is crawling to bed, and I'm still left saying, 'But you have to listen to this one!'"[465]

(© Ingo Bittrich)

"I think we've lost a lot of the naive enthusiasm," **Fletch** said. "You gain experience, but you lose enthusiasm. Because of that we won't be making as many records in the next 10 years. There won't be as many tours because we've lost that bubbly enthusiasm."[466]

Fletch told the others about the budget suggestions for the next video.

Dave: "How much?"

---

[465] Taken from: The Life and Loves of Depeche Mode, I-D, October 1993. Words: Michael Fuchs-Gambock.
[466] Taken from: Mode Squad, Creem, April 1993. Words: Jeremy Helligar.

Fletch: "A hundred thousand."
Dave: "Pounds or dollars?"
Fletch: "Pounds."
Dave: "F*** hell!"
Fletch: "And it's only black and white!"[467]

Some people noticed, however, that something was going on and asked questions like whether the band members still got on well with each other.

"I think most successful groups have a unique blend, if you like, that chemistry thing," **Alan** replied. "And I'm sure we do have that, but we also have had the type of problems that you talk about, it's just that you don't hear about it, I'm sure. You always have internal wrangles; you always have internal problems. There isn't a group that exists that hasn't had that, and we're no different in that respect, but we tend to keep that kind of thing fairly private because it's not for anyone else's ears really."

"I think ... obviously we have our disagreements, and after thirteen years you know everybody's personality so well, and when there are disagreements you can predict how they're going to go," **Martin** said. "But I think we get on as well as we can after thirteen years, which is ... That makes it sound bad, but we actually get on well."

Even **Dave** tried to be diplomatic. "To be honest I find it a little bit sad that I haven't become much closer to the other people that I work with, and have worked with for a lot of years. I'd like to have changed some of the things that we done, in that ... you know, our relationship: to me it's really important, what we have, the whole atmosphere that *Depeche Mode* creates when they're in a room together, as much as, sometimes, I hate it, I love it so much as well. And each person I love, as well."[468]

On the whole, Dave was sometimes much more honest than his band mates, who tried not to publicly air the band's internal problems.

Dave also admitted that his marriage to Jo went wrong from the beginning. "Over the years, I think I was a pretty sh*** person. I'd been with my ex-wife, Joanne, for a long while, and we used to be really great friends, and that had deteriorated - mostly on my part. Ninety percent of that

---

[467] Taken from: In the Mode, Details, April 1993. Words: William Shaw.
[468] Taken from: Songs of Faith and Devotion EPK / Interview CD, 1993. EPK: taken from The Videos 86-98+, MF042. Interview CD: VERBONG1.

was my doing, definitely. But I now know that it had to end. There's a big difference between what you believe is love and what hits you as actually being love."

Now, he claimed to be overjoyed with Theresa, but a moment later his thoughts would switch to the son he left behind. "My dad left myself and my sister when we were very young, in a very vulnerable position, and I've done the same thing with my son.[469] It's a heartache. I want to influence him, but I'm not there, so get real, you know? I don't want him to grow up with the same feelings I had when my stepfather died, wondering what was going on. I want Jack to know that he has a father.[470]

"I'm determined, much as he might hate it, to force myself on him. I'm going to see him next week, actually. I'm going down to his school next Friday to meet all his teachers and that kind of stuff. And Joanne's really good about all that - she understands the importance of me seeing him and Jack being able to see me. She's been really good about it. What I hope, what I really hope, is for her to meet somebody and fall in love and realise that, probably, we weren't in love at all. That would be the best thing for me, because it would remove a lot of the guilt that I now feel."[471]

A journalist cautiously asked whether alcohol and drugs were in his PAST, but you only had to look at Dave's condition at the time to know the past was nothing in comparison with the present.

Dave only heard what he wanted to hear: "Drinking? Yeah. When you're in a band, you're in a gang. And when you go out, you rule. You hit a town and take over. You can go to any club. Whatever you need you can get. And you do."

And on the question whether he had been addicted to drugs: "Mmmm. Not really. No, no. I was drinking way too much, but then I think most people do when they get to that age."[472]

---

[469] Taken from: Devout Moded, Vox, February 1993. Words: Martin Townsend.
[470] Taken from: In the Mode, Details, April 1993. Words: William Shaw.
[471] Taken from: Devout Moded, Vox, February 1993. Words: Martin Townsend.
[472] Taken from: In the Mode, Details, April 1993. Words: William Shaw.

Meanwhile, Alan and engineer Steve Lyon were working on the tapes for the tour. They worked alone, without the other band members. First they worked in the *Olympic Studios* in London, and then later in Alan's studio *The Thin Line*.

"While the earlier tours included some tracks that were recycled to some extent for the last couple of tours (*Violator* and *Devotional*) they were re-worked from scratch," **Alan** explained. "All the live tracks were restructured by myself although the running order for the show was a collective decision. It's a lot of hard work and involves imagining the songs in a different way from the album versions. But it also was fun. The motivation was that if I was going to play those older songs for 18 months on the road, then they had to be revitalised to make it an enjoyable task.

"Unfortunately, putting the *Devotional* live show together proved to be more of a handful than either myself or Steve had bargained for. It isn't just about revamping the songs. There are a million other jobs to be tackled like deciding what will be on the backing tapes and what will be live, or who will play what parts and how that will effect the way I program the keyboards (which is a logistical nightmare in itself!)

"There are also questions about the track running order and the different set lists themselves - this was to be a long haul and to play exactly the same songs night after night for 15 months would have been agony. You also have to consider each different country because every audience reacts differently, preferring favourite songs that have been particular to their territory. Consequently, we had 4 setlists - red, green, yellow, blue - with a similar overall structure but some variation in terms of which ballads and encores we'd perform.

"We knew when we started that we didn't have a lot of time on our hands and it didn't help that the *Roland* sequencer was giving us continual problems. However, we persevered and had nearly completed the work when disaster struck. The machine couldn't handle the sheer volume of traffic we were demanding from it and one day the whole system just crashed - we lost everything. Three and a half months of work. Luckily we had had the foresight to back up all the music onto multitrack but the edits had gone."[473]

It was **Steve Lyon** who had the idea to back up the music. "Alan and I had finished our time at *Olympic* [in London] but still had an enormous amount of work to do, Alan also wanted to play some live drums, so we went to his house. I remember on our last *Olympic Studio* evening we said, 'ok Pub!' But I said, 'Wait, I'm going to record from the *Roland* samplers onto 32 *Mitsubishi* as a back up.' So, I set it up, hit record and we went for a beer. Thankfully that saved us as the system crashed a week later and we would have lost everything, 2 months of work."[474]

Then there were only two weeks left to get ready, and they had to work day and night.

On **19 May** the *Devotional*-Tour started. It consisted of five legs. Additional background singers on stage were Hildia Cambell and Samantha Smith (much to the dismay of some fans).

"Before that, wherever we went, it used to be the four of us together," **Martin** said about the problems on this tour. "We were a gang, we'd go out – always go out together, and that just didn't happen so much anymore. Dave was definitely off somewhere on his own, Alan was definitely off somewhere on his own."

"And we agreed to do this year-and-a-half tour – straight from the album, straight off on tour, and then ... it was probably the worst two years of our lives," **Fletch** added.

"I went through periods when I thought 'What am I doing?', you know, 'What is the point of all this?'" **Martin** recalled. "This is supposed to be about enjoyment and nobody seems to be enjoying it anymore."[475]

It wasn't just a very excessive tour it was a different tour, different to the previous tours. So Dave added stage diving to his performance.

"I think Dave had a very demanding job to go out there every night and engage the audience so it would be unfair

---

[473] Taken from: recoil.co.uk. Words: Alan Wilder.
[474] depechemodebiographie.de
[475] Taken from: Depeche Mode: A Short Film, EPKMUTEL5, included with The Singles 86>98 promotional box set, PBXMUTEL5. Director: Sven Harding.

to criticise him for stage diving, no matter how much of a rock cliché it was," **Alan** said. "He never announced that he was intending to do it but you could see the idea brewing in his mind over the course of several gigs so it was no surprise when he went for it."

And it saw **Alan** on the drums. "I only started playing drums more seriously for the *Devotional*-Tour but I'm really glad I did because it was very enjoyable. It was prompted by a desire to challenge myself on stage and to try to make the *DM* live show a bit more varied."

But of course, he didn't like that some journalists described him as the "drummer of *Depeche Mode*" after that. He wasn't just the drummer, but also the musical director, keyboard player and "I had many different bits to play in quick succession that occasionally led to having to cross hands to play a part (with my left hand) at the top of the keyboard, whilst also playing a part with my right hand as well as changing a preset with a foot pedal."[476]

"It's just a completely different feel," **Dave** explained. "Alan's playing a lot more live drums. He's right behind me on stage; I can feel him, hear him. Martin's playing guitar right next to me on stage. We wanted more emphasis on us playing and doing the songs, with the energy more coming from the band rather than the lights and theatrics of a modern-day rock show. It's a lot sleazier, a lot more live, basically a lot more fun."[477]

The journalist Gavin Martin accompanied *DM* on the tour for a couple of days (whoever had this idea - it was a bad one) and published two long articles about his experiences in the magazine *NME*. These are the saddest articles one could ever read about *DM* and they presumably give a good insight into this time. On the other hand, one has to be careful because it is, of course, a subjective sight.

David Gahan is breathless, still on that adrenalin-surging, post-showtime high, he has just come offstage after a performance in front of a 25,000 crowd at a football stadium in Budapest, Hungary.

Notice, that the concert in Budapest took place on the very first leg of the tour! It is also remarkable that Dave tried to make people to call him "David" at the time. Al-

---

[476] Taken from: recoil.co.uk. Words: Alan Wilder.
[477] Taken from: Future Unknown, L.A. Daily News, 21 May 1994. Words: Mark Brown.

most no one did, though. Gavin Martin was at least polite enough to do so.

He described Dave's dressing room as a "darkened coven." *Candles burn on table tops, on flight cases and other surfaces provided by his make-shift road furniture. Loud music blasts from his hi-fi.*

Gavin Martin was well aware of what was going on. *His "problems" have become* Depeche Mode*'s dirty little secret - everybody in the camp knows about them but no-one mentions them. Gahan talks about them in vague terms. He doesn't look or sound like a well man. His skin is sickly grey in the half light, his eyes sunk into bluish sockets. Beneath his vest, tattoos embellish his biceps and torso, but the inside of his long skinny arms are all bruised and scratched.*

He had his back tattoo with the wings done two weeks before they went on the tour, because, "everybody has wings. You just have to fly."

And for **Martin** being on tour was like being in a film or in a fantasy land.

Are there any dangers in that?

"I'm sure there are."

What frightens you?

"I think death for some strange reason. Death in general, specifically my own death, that's why I'm a total hypochondriac. I can't work out if it's normal to be a hypochondriac. I think it's normal for men to be hypochondriacs. Every now and then on tour I have these panic attacks where I think my heart is beating too fast, my pulse seems strange in my arms and I think I'd better get a doctor, I think I'm going to die at any moment."

Furthermore, Garvin Martin described the atmosphere in the hotel bar in Budapest.

Andy Fletcher has thrown caution, and Yoga tea, to the wind and is taking his chances with a sizeable draught of lager. The last time Fletcher was interviewed by the NME *the journalist started out by asking if he drank a lot on the road. The press officer was livid: sat behind the journalist, he started signalling to Fletcher to terminate the interview. Alan Wilder is knocking back double tequila shots and his face is becoming a well-worn road map of rock 'n' roll excess. When he left the hotel for more tequila at the disco club, a group of Hungarian fans clambered outside at the* window. Wilder staggered up towards them. "Go on, f---off!" he said. "Get away from the f---ing window."[478]

To this **Alan** explained, "I remember being chased through the streets of Budapest. It started out as a few fans seeing us eating outside a restaurant and following us back to the hotel asking for autographs. Then, as onlookers became more inquisitive, the crowd began to grow. My security man Joel started getting nervous and said, 'One, two, three, RUN!!!', and we had to leg it back to the hotel with a crowd of excited Hungarians hot on our trail. When we eventually made it inside, they were all banging on the windows of the bar so I went out to have a word. I explained that we weren't the only guests in the hotel and it may be slightly unsettling for other people in the bar to feel like they were in 'Night of the Living Dead' but that I'd sign a few autographs if they promised to leave us in peace. This was subsequently translated as, 'Alan Wilder told us all to f*** off.'"[479]

It's up to every reader to draw a conclusion from these two different stories. Maybe Gavin Martin exaggerated his story. He's a journalist, and journalists sometimes tend to make stories more interesting than they actually were. On the other hand, he was a neutral observer, not integrated into the crew, and it's difficult to think up a situation like this from nothing. He described Alan as being drunk, so maybe the "control freak" had lost control in this situation and was wrong in his self-assessment. And maybe both descriptions are correct in some way.

One should never forget that, besides all the debauchery, there were a lot of people saying that they had fun, and that the band was always able to run a professional tour and sell its products. They even became famous for it.

"At the height of our partying, everyone in the band was on something," **Dave** said. "We became known as a band who could party into the early hours, but still get the job done on stage."[480]

He described them as being a "band on stage," but offstage everyone being on their own. It's amazing that he

---

[478] Taken from: Penance Extra, NME, 18 September 1993. Words: Gavin Martin. / Tattoo Unlimited, NME, 25 September 1993. Words: Gavin Martin.
[479] Taken from: recoil.co.uk. Words: Alan Wilder.
[480] Taken from: They just can't get enough: One-time synthesiser sissies Depeche Mode are back on song, Mail Online, 3 April 2009. Words: Adrian Thrills.

once said that Martin, Fletch and himself went out to get drunk or get high separately while Alan did the work. But it's known – not only from articles by Gavin Martin – that Alan drank a lot as well. Maybe he started drinking after he had done the work. It would suit him.

In **August** Alan mixed the sound for the live album and for the video, together with Steve Lyon, who was the co-producer for these, so he couldn't go on holiday.

The North American leg started on **7 September** in Quebec.

In the meantime, on **13 September**, the single *Condemnation* was released. The single's B-Side was the *Jazz Mix* of *Death's Door* of which the original track had been released in **1991**. The video for *Condemnation* was directed by Anton Corbijn. It didn't appear on *The Videos 86-98* in **1998**, was replaced by the live version from *Devotional*. (The reason is unknown to me.)

Also in **September**, Dave and the chief safety officer were arrested because of a fight in Quebec and were set free, however, the next day. "The staff was very rude to us and wanted us to leave," **Dave** explained. "We tried to convince them we were guests in the hotel. I ended up smacking one of the guys. Nothing really out of the ordinary. We just happened to get arrested this time, that's all. No one was really hurt in the end."[481]

In the same month Alan and Martin were on their way on a short holiday trip from Dallas to the Caribbean when their aeroplane got caught in a hurricane.

"The only thing that was going through my mind at the time was that my daughter's not going to ever know me!" **Martin** recalled. "She was only two at the time."[482]

"After 20 minutes or so, there was a loud bang and I think all the oxygen masks came down," **Alan** added. "It was some kind of pressurisation problem. There was a fair amount of panic and the air-hostesses, tearfully embracing one another, didn't exactly inspire confidence. I tried to keep calm, and Martin was like one of these decline prophets: 'Oh God, we'll all die!' The pilot had to turn around and we sat through a hair-raising 20 minutes as the plane tried to make it back to Dallas. Later on, we

---

[481] Taken from: Future Unknown, L.A. Daily News, 21 May 1994. Words: Mark Brown.
[482] Taken from: Flaunt, May 2001, Words: Tom Lonham.

were reliably informed that had we been at our proper cruising altitude, this would have been a major incident. We ended up getting blind drunk in the airport, eventually hiring a private plane at great expense and woke up in the sunshine of the West Indies with a headache."[483]

In a different source Alan is quoted further on as saying that Martin had been the one who had hired the private jet, and that he had mixed a sleeping-pill in Alan's drink because Alan had been so scared of flying.

If this quotation was correct it would be slightly contradictory to Alan's statement "the relationship that never worked was the one with Martin." And it's also difficult to understand why Martin said that "Alan definitely was off on his own." Their relationship was good enough to go on holiday together and to look after each other. But as it has been mentioned before, maybe it was a relationship that sometimes worked and sometimes didn't.

In **October Dave** suffered from a circulatory collapse. "At the end of the gig I couldn't go back for the encore, Mart had to do a song solo while all the paramedics rushed me off to hospital. I'd overdosed, I'd had a heart attack. Next day, we didn't think any more about it."[484] It's almost sure that it was a circulatory collapse or maybe cardiac arrhythmia but no heart attack.

In **November Martin** was arrested because of disturbance of the peace. "I had a party in my room and there were about 50 people and it was really loud. The night of the arrest, it was me and a friend and the music was really quiet. They rang me and asked me to turn it down, so I did. They rang me again and asked me to turn it down, so I turned it off. Next thing I know there's complete silence and the police knocked on the door. I stupidly opened it. They burst in, threw me on the bed and handcuffed me. There was no music whatsoever playing. I think they were out to get me for the night before. I can't remember much about it. I was really drunk at the time and it seemed like fun."[485]

According to rumours, all relationships were broken off, everybody was either stoned, drunk or depressed, and it is

---

[483] Taken from: recoil.co.uk. Words: Alan Wilder.
[484] Taken from: They Just Couldn't get Enough, Q, March 1997. Words: Phil Sutcliffe.
[485] Taken from: Pavement, 16 April 1997. Words: Uncredited.

said that only swear words were used about Dave behind his back. It's possible that all these things are correct.

A psychiatrist was in attendance during the first part of the tour. "When I look back, it seems incredible that we paid an on-the-road psychiatrist $4,000 per week to listen to our ramblings - something I think I instigated," **Alan** remembered. "The idea was that he could provide some kind of support for those people who wanted it - although the real reason was to try to persuade Dave to come off smack because we weren't confident he was going to make it to the end of the tour. Ironically, I think everybody went to see the shrink at some point apart from Dave."[486]

Dave once said that the psychiatrist told them that they had really bad problems and then left saying he couldn't help them.

The band adhered to their "bunker mentality" whatever might be published about them, and they sometimes gave an impression of being a bit blundering.

"In Germany, they're writing these stories at the moment that Dave has AIDS or he's dying or he's on heavy drugs, and it's so funny because it doesn't actually do us any harm, it sells more records." **Martin** laughed. "Anyone reading it must think 'that sounds really interesting, I've got to go and buy that'!"[487]

On **23 November** the video *Devotional* was released. It had been filmed by Anton Corbijn in Barcelona, Spain (*Palau Sant Jordi*), Liévin, France (*Stade Couvert Régional*) and Frankfurt, Germany (*Festhalle*.) It was nominated for the *Grammy Award* for *Best Long Form Music Video* in **1995**. The soundtrack was recorded in Liévin on **29 July 1993**.

The album *SOFAD Live* was released on **6 December**. It had the same running order than the studio album. It was a marketing tool instigated by the record company. Having the identical running order meant that it could be given the same catalogue number, hence the elongated chart position.

---

[486] Taken from: Just Can't Get Enough, Uncut, May 2001. Words: Stephen Dalton.
[487] Taken from: The Life and Loves of Depeche Mode, I-D, October 1993. Words: Michael Fuchs-Gambock.

Another five concerts were played in the UK from **12 to 20 December**.[488]

Directly after **Christmas** Steve Lyon and Alan spent three weeks in Milan programming the tapes for the next leg - because there wasn't any end in sight. They replaced the intro song *Higher Love* with a dynamic version of *Rush* that started with a frenetic techno sequence. Alan also worked out a kind of a trip-hop version of *I Want You Now* which the other members of the band didn't hear until it was played on stage, another point that shows how much work Alan put into the project while no one else in the band seemed to show any real interest.

1994

- Will you let the fire die down soon? (In Your Room) -

The last single of the album was *In Your Room*, released on **10 January**. The single version of *In Your Room* is the *Zephyr Mix* (remixed by Butch Vig, additional guitars by Doug Erikson.) It is radically different from the original version on the album.

"The worst memory about *In Your Room* is the making of the video," **Martin** recalled. "We spent a whole day in the studio filming and I probably had lunch at some point, but it was just something really small, like half a sandwich. We finished filming at about 8 o'clock, and went back to the hotel and I forgot to eat. We went to the bar and I didn't eat ... We went out to a club,[489] met some guy who gave me some stuff, so I was up all night until probably 9 or 10 in the morning. We had a band meeting at 12 o'clock and I managed to sleep for about an hour. Then I got up and I've never felt so dreadful in my life. I managed to literally crawl to this meeting, I had to lay on the floor just saying 'Yes' or 'No', that was all I could muster.[490] And that was when I went into a seizure. So whenever I see

---

[488] Dates and events on tour were taken from: Devotional Diary II, Bong 23, December 1994. Words: Daryl Bamonte.
[489] Taken from: The Singles 86-98 by Martin Gore, Bong 37, September 1998. Compiled by Michaela Olexova. Words: Martin Lee Gore.
[490] Taken from: Just Can't Get Enough, Uncut, May 2001. Words: Stephen Dalton.

this video, I just think, 'Oh, God' ... It brings back terrible memories."⁴⁹¹

As indicated in the articles of **1993**, Martin had some seizures on tour (he said it had been just two) as well as panic attacks.

In your room where souls disappear ... (© Ingo Bittrich)

The video for *In Your Room* wasn't broadcasted by *MTV America* because of its BDSM reference. Furthermore, Anton Corbijn cut in scenes from former videos because he thought it might be the last video with Dave. Obviously, Corbijn was more familiar with drug abuse and its consequences and saw that Dave was in a really bad condition.

"We would usually reach a consensus to form a shortlist of potential singles," **Alan** explained. "For example, *Higher Love* was on this list for the *SOFAD* singles but never made it and there were differences of opinion about in which order they should appear. Dave felt very strongly that *Condemnation* should have been the first single but he was outvoted. I wanted *Walking in My Shoes* as a second single and got my way but I really wanted the original

---

⁴⁹¹ Taken from: The Singles 86-98 by Martin Gore, Bong 37, September 1998. Compiled by Michaela Olexova. Words: Martin Lee Gore.

version of *In Your Room* [instead of the *Zephyr Mix*.] This is all a good example of the problems of democracy - somebody usually ends up disappointed."[492]

I've been asked very often about the meaning of the lyrics of *In Your Room*. This is a really difficult question. On the one hand, it's quite obvious. The lyrics seem to have a BDSM reference. *Your favourite slave* is in the hands of a person whose will is absolute. The point people are confused about is that Martin said it is about sitting in a child's room. But there isn't any real reference to it in the lyrics. For example "*your burning eyes cause flames to arise*" doesn't suit a child at all.

Maybe Martin had the IDEA for this song while sitting on the bed of his eldest daughter (who was a baby when he wrote the song), but the lyrics turned out differently. Lines like "*only you exist here*" and "*living on your breath*" might refer to a situation sitting on the bed of a child watching it sleeping and breathing. In this moment all your concentration is focused on the child. Maybe he connected this experience with a BDSM-situation which is quite similar because the concentration of the "sub" (slave) is focused on the "top" (master). He is watching every single move and is *hanging on your words*.

On **9 February** the next part of the tour started, called *Exotic*-Tour this time. Until **19 April** the band played 28 concerts in South Africa, Australia and Asia as well as in Latin and South America.

"That trip to South Africa was very memorable for us," **Fletch** said. "We had all of our rehearsals in Cape Town and were in the country for six weeks."[493]

But it wasn't a good trip on the whole.

In **February Alan's** wardrobe was stolen. "Considering the building was securely locked and patrolled by guards, we concluded that it must have been an 'inside job.' I lost about £10,000 worth of clothing, some very personal bits and pieces and of course most of my stage outfits which had to be re-made."

He himself had to have an operation to remove kidney stones in the same month.

---

[492] Taken from: recoil.co.uk. Words: Alan Wilder.
[493] Taken from: Masters Of Their Universe, The Times, 3 May 2009. Words: Uncredited.

There were different opinions about a second U.S. leg that introduced added tension. **Alan** was one of those who were for this additional leg. "The second leg should take in outdoor venues (sheds) which attract a summer crowd and are very different to the indoor arena shows. Actually, Dave also wanted to do another leg and the others didn't object at the time."

Contradictory to the statements before and after *Devotional* that he had no intention of touring anymore and to the rumours he wanted this second leg because he knew it would be the last thing he would do with the band, he said, "I didn't think about it being the last time touring for me as I didn't decide to leave the band until 18 months later."[494]

True, but he also said once that he had begun thinking about leaving the band during the recording of *SOFAD*, respectively during *Devotional*, but as it has been mentioned before it was probably on his mind for longer, although it wasn't a real decision.

Allegedly Dave and Alan told Martin that they couldn't bear Fletch's depressions any longer.

"It was very difficult," **Martin** said. "Andy's been my closest friend since we were twelve. But, for the others, he'd become unbearable. I justified it by thinking that it would be better for him if he went home and got professional advice."

But Fletch also wanted to go home, having had enough of the tour. So in **March** it was decided that Fletch would leave the tour, to be replaced on stage by long-term friend and companion of the band, Daryl Bamonte.

"With the targets, the deadlines, the partying, the excess, I just lost it," **Fletch** recalled. "I had an obsessive-compulsive disorder which made me displace this stress into worries about bodily symptoms. This sounds terrible, but I thought I had a brain tumour. I couldn't sleep. I couldn't think, this headache wouldn't go away. I had tests. It wasn't a brain tumour, it was a breakdown."[495]

Allegedly Fletch left the tour saying he would never go on tour with Alan again. This quotation isn't confirmed and it's not known if there was a special incident to which he referred. Maybe it was just because of his illness.

---

[494] Taken from: recoil.co.uk. Words: Alan Wilder.
[495] Taken from: They Just Couldn't get Enough, Q, March 1997. Words: Phil Sutcliffe.

Maybe it was because of some of Alan's cynical remarks. Alan's later statement that "there are things that better never come to day-light"[496] according to a biography, might refer precisely to those arguments.

The others still tried to remain diplomatic. When asked how the band members are, **Dave** replied, "Really good." Some persistent questioning resulted in the admission "Andy will not be playing with us for the rest of the tour. He's in New York at the moment. He's not been feeling well and his wife's about to have their second baby and he's got to sort some stuff out so he won't be doing it.[497] Being away from the people you want to be with for a long while probably had a lot to do with Fletch's feelings."[498] (Fletch's and Grainne's son Joseph was born on **22 June**.)

"While everyone else was sunning themselves on the beach and enjoying a well-earned rest, Daryl and I spent a week cooped up in a hotel room in Hawaii where I taught him the entire set," **Alan** said. "He subsequently played it perfectly for the rest of the tour - pretty good eh, considering he'd hardly ever played a keyboard before in his life."[499]

One could see this as a mocking remark at Fletch, and maybe this is an example of those things that made Fletch feel that Alan was the one who was unbearable.

On **12 May** the last leg of the tour started in Sacramento - without Fletch.

According to rumours, the relationships got worse and worse, and meetings ended in scuffles (although the reasons are unknown.) Further on, Dave, being totally stoned, allegedly bit a journalist in the neck. No rumours are that there were separate limousines and separate hotel floors.

"That was a practical necessity in case individual band members threw raucous parties,"[500] **Martin** admitted. Like the Berlin aftershow party which ended in a police raid and a ban from the *Intercontinental* hotel. "We lost the

---

[496] Taken from: recoil.co.uk. Words: Alan Wilder.
[497] Taken from: Modern Rock Live, 10 May 1994, unknown radio station, DJ: Tom Calderone.
[498] Taken from: Future Unknown, L.A. Daily News, 21 May 1994. Words: Mark Brown.
[499] Taken from: recoil.co.uk. Words: Alan Wilder.
[500] Taken from: Just Can't Get Enough, Uncut, May 2001. Words: Stephen Dalton.

plot. But it's really difficult for us, at our level, to just decide to do a few key dates around the world. I think those extra 30 to 40 gigs were the straw that broke the camel's back." He laughed.

"The intensity of the partying had gone to a new stage," **Fletch** recalled. "It had just been steadily getting worse and worse and worse and worse, until on that tour in particular it was just one huge party. Every night. Martin says he only went to bed early one time on the whole tour."

"About 12," **Martin** said. "You don't get offstage usually 'til 10.30, 11, so to get to bed by 12 you've really achieved something there."[501]

"What people have heard about that tour is all pretty much true," **Alan** admitted. "Everyone was indulging in their own thing, sometimes with destructive results but it's all part of the private way you deal with such a bizarre and unreal world. Of course, everybody was concerned about Dave's welfare but addicts are notoriously difficult to dissuade from their cause unless they themselves really want to change.

"At the time Dave wasn't in that frame of mind and therefore any advice given to him fell on deaf ears. In spite of all these things, there were loads of good moments too. Not only was it the most successful tour with some of the best shows we'd ever played, but personally, I can't see what all the fuss is about - I had a great time. The myth that has been building up around the second U.S. leg of the *Devotional*-Tour seems to be now fully out of control. It wasn't really any more 'rock 'n' roll' than any other *DM* tour over the years - everyone had their own little 'on tour' world which existed alongside a fully professionally run live show."[502]

"What we discovered was that we enjoyed playing together this time more than any other time before," **Dave** explained. "We pulled everything together and decided not to be so separated on the stage. We wanted to get rid of some of the theatrics and be less of a big, swamping show. I think now at the moment we're having a lot of fun. I think we've been having more fun on stage this time then

---

[501] Taken from: Synth and Sensibilities, NME, 25 January 1997. Words: Keith Cameron.
[502] Taken from: recoil.co.uk. Words: Alan Wilder.

we've ever had before. Everything seems a lot more organic and a lot more powerful."[503]

I don't think it was just a phrase. I think *Devotional* really had different facets – the debauchery, the fun, the suffering, the tensions and the great and professional show.

Nevertheless, over the course of time Dave increasingly presented a picture of misery when he danced or rather staggered over the stage, stoned and just being skin and bones. But when you listen to bootlegs of the time, the concerts were amazing. Some people say that Dave's voice suffered more and more from his drug consumption, but I don't agree that it was really weak or broken. The set on the *Exotic*-Tour was very dynamic and full of energy, with a lot of amazing, dynamic live versions.

On **18 July 1994** the insanity reached an end, at least as far as the tour was concerned. Whether Dave fell off the stage or wanted to do stage diving is unclear, anyway he crashed against the barrier during the encore, breaking two ribs and suffering internal bleeding. He was so stoned and drunk that it took 24 hours until he realised what had happened. He was told to stay in hospital for a couple of days but he didn't want that. Instead, he and Theresa rented a little hut at Tahoe Lake in California.

It's almost funny that this happened at the last planned concert, so no gig had to be cancelled because of it (not even this last concert. Dave was able to get back on stage and finish the concert.)

It's not known if the rest of the band was really aware of what had happened to Dave. They enjoyed themselves with some last gig pranks - "Jez Webb - the guitar tech. - emerged, to my surprise, from the shell of the piano during *Somebody*," **Alan** said. "Another favourite was when someone dressed as a cleaner came on stage and started sweeping the floor – during a dramatic point in the show." - and had "an end of tour party at *St. Andrew's Hall* in Detroit that was pretty much on a par with the reputation the band had acquired (at least all the standard *Depeche Mode* requirements were met - scantily-glad girls, erotic dancers, Martin dressed as a woman.)"[504, 505]

---

[503] Taken from: Modern Rock Live, 10 May 1994, unknown radio station. DJ: Tom Calderone.
[504] Taken from: recoil.co.uk. Words: Alan Wilder.

As for the reasons how it could have come to this exaggerated excess (and especially to the breakdown of all relationships), you'll find very little in the quotes from the band members. "We overdid it and couldn't stop it" or "a rock band isn't a church choir" is all they said. Many fans also see it as "a normal part of the music business, it was part of the zeitgeist." – "It was absolutely hip to overdose. It was the Grunge-era, absolute nihilism was hip." And really, you have to see that Grunge didn't mean pain, suffering, drugs and being close to death. It didn't mean to die for your art. When these bands went on stage they only had one thing in mind: fun. Maybe a very egoistic and destructive kind of fun - but still fun.

But most fans see success as the main reason for why things got out of hand for the band. It seems as if they didn't know what to do after the huge success of *Violator* (or even after *101*.) Well, I think there must also have been some other reasons as well for losing one's footing momentarily, even for a rock musician - a person with an extreme job, extraordinary lifestyle and the permanent temptation of alcohol and drugs. Dave especially shows nowadays that you are able to do this job without being an alcoholic or a junkie. And the "boys" weren't in the beginning of their 20s anymore, but family men turning 30, an age at which you would guess they were "mature and grown up."

So "I did it because everyone did it" would be a cheap alibi. Not only Dave wanted to "lead this egoistic lifestyle," as he admitted, the others wanted it too. If that had not been the case, they would have stopped it. I think Fletch had tried to, but it was difficult for him because of his illness. In the end only two people are left: Alan and Martin. What kind of "alibi" do they have?

Alan surprisingly said that he had had his fun. Although he didn't look like he had. In pictures and videos of that time he often looked morose and peeved. So what? Was it so awful that he finally couldn't take it anymore and left the band, or did he have his fun? Probably both things are correct. Working on a project there are always some things you enjoy and some things you don't like or even suffer from. A world tour is a special event on which you probably turn a blind eye to many things.

---

[505] Some dates and information about events on tour were taken from: Devotional Diary III, Bong 24, March 1995. Words: Daryl Bamonte.

However - at least some fans assume that private problems could have made things worse, a "close to the 30s crises," no support from their families or real friends, no team-spirit within the band, a lack of communication - or as one fan said, "maybe they hoped they would forget their personal problems on tour, but it went 'Wrong'." This is probably correct. As it has been mentioned before – they might have thought that the team-spirit would return and the problems might get solved.

After *Devotional* they were asked how long it took until they found their way back to everyday life.
"I actually think it didn't take me very long," **Martin** said. "I got into some very bad habits on that tour. I was taking sleeping tablets every day and when I got home from the tour I still had a couple left and so it gave me a few days of good sleep ... sleep is a key to happiness." He laughs. "After that I ran out of those tablets and I was totally back to normal."[506]
"I didn't," **Dave** replied. "I was functioning only with the use of drugs, without them I couldn't even move. I came back from the tour and I wasn't playing music and singing anymore but I really threw myself into using drugs."[507]
"I was just so emotionally knackered after the tour and that's why I didn't do the last American leg," **Fletch** said. "I think we just set ourselves too much of a target and I think we all suffered in different ways."[508]
And on the question whether they had kept their contact, **Martin** replied, "Because Dave went back to America we didn't see him very often and we didn't speak on the phone very much, maybe not as much as we should have. We didn't speak to Alan at all even though he was living in London which we felt was quite strange and we were totally prepared for his decision to leave the band. We actually predicted that months and months before it happened. Andy I see all the time because we have the same group of friends and so if I'm in London I'm almost bound to bump into Andy at some point."[509]
"Not really," **Dave** said. "But no-one is to blame really, because the phone rings both ways. The only time that I

---
[506] Taken from: Catching up with ... Martin, Bong 30, December 1996.
[507] Taken from: Catching up with ... Dave, Bong 30, December 1996.
[508] Taken from: Catching up with ... Fletch, Bong 30, December 1996.
[509] Taken from: Catching up with ... Martin, Bong 30, December 1996.

heard anything from anyone was really if I was kind of hurting myself and it got in the press. Then I got a call from somebody, usually Martin or I'd call him. I got a call from Alan at one point when he decided he wanted to leave. But I didn't really react in any way to that because I was deeply into using drugs by then."[510]

While Martin married Suzanne in **August**, **Alan** separated from his wife Jeri and went on holiday with his new partner Hepzibah in the **beginning of September**, and was almost killed. "I was in a remote part of Scotland driving on the A85 just beyond Lochearnhead. As I approached a sharp bend in the road, the sound of an *Royal Air Force* Tornado appeared behind me and as I looked up, I saw the underside of the aircraft above me. Within a split second to my complete astonishment, the plane had crashed beside the road into the Glen.

"As I swerved off the road onto a farm track, I heard the sound of the impact and witnessed an enormous explosion from which the smoke and debris almost engulfed me. At the same time, particles of carbon etc. began to 'rain' down onto the open- top car. Beyond the bend I witnessed the road full of the wreckage of the aircraft and the parts of dead airmen's bodies which were clearly visible in the road. After the police arrived I decided to leave the scene; there was nothing further to do. It was only at this point that I realised what an incredible escape I'd had. I would have surely been killed or worse, severely maimed, had I been 10 seconds further into my journey."[511]

The aircraft was on a routine training flight. It wasn't confirmed whether the exercise involved low-flying, but the area was frequently used for low-level training. When the Tornado crashed a crater was formed which Alan described in the song *Black Box* (released on the album *Liquid* in **2000**) with, *"Then we saw for the first time what had happened in the crater. We saw nothing but black ice covered with ash and then water with floating ice blocks and ash at the bottom."*

Later **Alan** admitted he still had nightmares about this incident. "The thing that struck me was that such an instantaneous tragedy is immediately followed by the banal-

---

[510] Taken from: Catching up with ... Dave, Bong 30, December 1996.
[511] Taken from: Near Miss, Bong 22, September 1994. Words: Alan Wilder.

ity of continuing life. As two dead airmen were splattered across the road, the sun shone, the birds sang and no music played."[512]

It's possible this was another factor in his decision to leave the band. Events like these often show there are many more important things in life than making music with a difficult team.

Meanwhile **Dave** lost control completely. "After the tour ended, I spent a few months in London and that's when my habit got completely out of hand. In fact, Teresa decided that she wanted to have a baby and I said to her, 'Teresa, we're junkies. Let's not kid ourselves, when you're a junkie, you can't s***, p***, c*** ... nothing. All these bodily functions go. You're in this soulless body, you're in a shell.' But she didn't get it."

He developed paranoia, carrying a .38 at all times. He thought somebody would come and get him, without knowing who "somebody" was. Being so scared and in a truly bad condition, he toyed with the idea of "the big one" - that one last hit that would end it all.

His condition got worse when his ex-wife Jo wouldn't let him see their son anymore. She decided to stop Jack visiting him after he and Dave's mom had been in LA and Dave overdosed one night. When Dave woke up, his mother and son were in the kitchen - and his stuff was gone.

"I said, 'What did you do with my stuff, mum?' She said, 'I threw it in the rubbish outside.' I ran out the door and brought in six black bags. If you can picture this insanity, I'm with my son and my mother and I brought in six bags, five of which were my neighbours' and emptied them out on the kitchen floor. I was on my hands and knees going through other people's garbage until I found what I needed."

Now he couldn't deny it any longer. His mother rang up Joanne, who came and picked Jack up.

Around **Christmas Dave** went into rehab for the first time. "When I came out, Teresa met me. We went to get some lunch and she said, 'I'm not gonna stop drinking or using drugs just because you have to. I'll do whatever I

---

[512] Taken from: Just Can't Get Enough, Uncut, May 2001. Words: Stephen Dalton.

want to do.' At that point, I knew our relationship would have to be over if I was gonna have any chance. I'd thought we loved each other. Now I think the love was pretty one-sided. Actually, she soon left me to get her life together, as she put it. She always used to say to me, 'It's all about you, Dave - if only you could love yourself.' Well, that's come full circle now, because she's suing me for a ridiculous amount of money, claiming I'm responsible for her life."[513]

He soon reverted to his old habits. "I was then give the excuse to go out and get even more f*** up. My wife had left me, friends were disappearing and so I was left surrounded by a bunch of junkies. And I knew exactly what was going on - y'know, I had the money, I had the drugs and that's why they were around. I knew it, and that fuelled my anger even more. I didn't know whether I wanted to get clean. It was becoming very apparent that the party was gonna be over pretty soon. I was either gonna die or I was gonna get sober."[514]

---

[513] Taken from: Tears of my Tracks, Q, March 1997. Words: Phil Sutcliffe.
[514] Taken from: Dead Man Talking, NME, 18 January 1997. Words: Keith Cameron.

1995

*- Ah, they shutting down the factory now
(Coming Back to You, Tribute to Leonard Cohen) -*

Alan decided to leave the band and called a band meeting in London. It took place without Dave, who didn't react to Alan's telephone call, or to a fax.

"Alan just told us that he didn't particularly get on with us anymore," **Martin** said. "He felt that our relationships had all gone down the drain and, because of that, it was time to leave. But there were a lot of things he didn't tell us at that meeting that came out later. He made a very big press statement saying that he felt the workload had been unfairly distributed over the course of the last album or two, and that he wasn't getting enough appreciation and gratitude from the rest of the band.

"What he failed to say in that press statement is that he is a control freak who decided it should be that way. We were all quite happy going home at midnight or one in the morning when we were in the studio. But Alan is one of those studioheads who loves being there until four in the morning. He focuses on every minute detail. Or overfocuses. And also, for the last tour, he took it on himself to prepare all the backing tapes. He said he wanted to do it. Since the rest of us don't particularly enjoy that task, we said, 'Fine, if you want to do it, go ahead.' Maybe we didn't thank him enough at the end."[515]

Alan's statement read: "Due to increasing dissatisfaction with the internal relations and working practices of the group, it is with some sadness that I have decided to part company from *Depeche Mode*. My decision to leave the group was not an easy one particularly as our last few albums were an indication of the full potential that *Depeche Mode* was realising. Since joining in **1982**, I have continually striven to give total energy, enthusiasm and commitment to the furthering of the group's success and in spite of a consistent imbalance in the distribution of the workload, willingly offered this.

---

[515] Taken from: Ultra Sounds, Guitar World, May 1997. Words: Alan di Perna.

"Unfortunately, within the group, this level of input never received the respect and acknowledgement that it warrants. Whilst I believe that the calibre of our musical output has improved, the quality of our association has deteriorated to the point where I no longer feel that the end justifies the means. I have no wish to cast aspersions on any individual; suffice to say that relations have become seriously strained, increasingly frustrating and, ultimately, in certain situations, intolerable. Given these circumstances, I have no option but to leave the group."[516]

Later he explained, "The reason I made a statement when I left the group was to try to summarize succinctly in my own words some of the reasons for my departure, rather than have the press speculate and inevitably draw the wrong conclusions."[517]

It seemed as if especially Martin was angry about this statement. The question here is whether Alan told some uncomfortable truths or if Martin felt that it wasn't the truth.

I'm quite sure that everything Alan said is true; it's just a question of putting it in the right context and of not forgetting that there are always two sides to every story.

Alan was willing to provide everything and – when he noticed that he didn't get anything in return – probably seized almost the whole project, leaving no room for the other members of the team. Martin, however, was willing to let him seize the project. He was fine with going out partying, leaving Alan behind working in the studio. He was also fine with letting Alan work out the backing tapes and the new live versions, without even listening to them before they were played on stage.

Alan enjoyed what he was doing, but he felt forced to provide more than he wanted to provide, because it was no longer "work sharing," but became a "working while the others enjoy themselves and sometimes deliver something" situation. Martin obviously didn't try to involve himself or to sit down and talk to Alan to find a solution; however, Martin is known to be shy. Maybe he felt pushed aside and wasn't able to tell Alan what he wanted, especially because Alan was so focused that he might not notice small hints.

---

[516] Taken from: press statement. Words: Alan Wilder.
[517] Taken from: recoil.co.uk. Words: Alan Wilder.

Here we are again at the question of how important Fletch and Dave were for the balance and the team-spirit, because at that time the band was (more or less) reduced to Alan and Martin, and evidently it became clear that they couldn't work with each other on their own. Thus, maybe Alan felt Martin didn't value his work, while Martin felt Alan had taken over such an important leading role that it wasn't a team situation any longer.

At that time Martin was sure that this was the end of *DM* because they didn't want to go on without Alan. But we know that he would change his mind later.

"Martin shook my hand and looked a bit embarrassed and Fletch got quite defensive and seemed to take it rather personally," **Alan** remembered. "Some of the comments that were made during the promotion for *DM*'s last album [*Ultra*] were disappointing although not unsurprising and I can understand a bit of why they might have been said. The simple fact is that most people just do not understand or appreciate that 'producing' a record properly requires an enormous amount of energy and concentration. Anyone can go into a studio for a couple of hours a day, take loads of drugs, twiddle a few knobs, whack it all on a CD and call it a finished album but invariably the end result sounds like what it is - lazy and ill-judged. I can't just roll into the studio at 5 o'clock in the afternoon with a raging hangover and expect to be able to work effectively. This doesn't mean that I never take a break during a session but as a rule, I like to keep work time and play time separate so I can give my absolute best to whatever project I'm involved in. If this makes me boring then fine ... I'd rather be boring but have a really good record."[518]

If his words about rolling "into the studio at 5 o'clock in the afternoon with a raging hangover" were a description of the recording sessions of *SOFAD*, one gets closer to the reasons why he found it unbearable.

Martin and Fletch made some caustic statements around this time, indeed.

"We were never in contact with him anyway when he was in the band," **Fletch** said. "It's almost like he never existed."

---

[518] Taken from: recoil.co.uk. Words: Alan Wilder.

Martin tried to be a bit more diplomatic. "I don't think we should ever get into a slanging match with Alan, because he was an integral part of the band who had a lot of input and a lot to say in what the band was doing.[519] It wasn't totally unexpected. Alan's always been very private and secretive, so it's very hard to know exactly how he's thinking at any given point. But it became very apparent to us that he wasn't happy. It wasn't a shock at all when he left. I think he took too much upon himself. I think even he would readily admit he's a control freak.[520] I think Alan was very set in his ways. I'm sure if we ever suggested something to Alan, and he didn't particularly like what we were suggesting, he would make sure it didn't work."[521]

Interestingly enough, **Alan** thought none "of them were aware that it was coming and even if they were, I don't think they thought I'd actually go through with it."[522] It's yet more proof of how bad the communication was between the band members, backed up by **Martin**'s remark "It's hard to know exactly how" Alan's "thinking at any given point," because Alan said almost the same thing about Martin.

"I think he felt the band would split up, what with the state Dave was in," **Fletch** said. "I think he wanted to be the first one to jump ship."[523]

This is a statement that you still find today on some message-boards. "Alan wanted to destroy the band / he thought it would split up when he left." And although an inside source told me that Alan really said something like this – that his departure should come down on Martin like a ton of bricks, and that he felt it would be the end of *DM* – I don't think one should overrate this just as one shouldn't overrate the statements of Martin and Fletch at that time. All of them were angry, and angry people tend to say such things.

---

[519] Taken from: Synth and Sensibilities, NME, 25 January 1997. Words: Keith Cameron.
[520] Taken from: Pavement, 16 April 1997. Words: Uncredited.
[521] Taken from: Ultra Sounds, Guitar World, May 1997. Words: Alan di Perna.
[522] Taken from: recoil.co.uk. Words: Alan Wilder.
[523] Taken from: Many Smack-Free Returns! Q, June 2001. Words: Dorian Lynskey.

Ah, they shutting down the factory now (Coming Back to You, Tribute to Leonard Cohen) (© Ingo Bittrich)

"It sounds arrogant, but if I could do everything myself I would," **Alan** admitted. "I like to work alone – though this doesn't mean that I don't ever want other people's input. I enjoy collaborating, but not on a permanent basis. With *Depeche Mode*, what I learned over the years from working with other people has been invaluable. It's left me in a position where I know what I want in terms of production. Nowadays, I find that working with other people slows that process down, and sometimes turns it into a battle. At this stage in my life, I feel I don't want that anymore."

He described himself as being quite diplomatic in the studio and as being able to put people at ease, and encourage them to bring the best out of themselves. "Dave loved being driven hard, even to the point where he would become frustrated; but then the next day he would say, 'I'm so glad you did that, because I'm really pleased with how my vocal sounds.'[524] I wouldn't say I left *DM* because of the mass of the work. I enjoyed doing this, the production and the programming, I didn't have any feelings of resentment against it. I only had the feeling that it was taken as a given thing."[525]

Martin once said Alan's tensions with Fletch might have been the key for leaving the band. This is also something that still appears in message-boards very often.

But **Alan** said, "The relationship that never really flourished was between myself and Martin. I felt that it was mainly he who didn't really value the effort I put in, and that disappointed me, because generally we got on OK and I respected his talent as a songwriter."[526]

When I had the opportunity to talk to **Gareth Jones** I asked him about the relationship between Alan and Martin in the **1980s**, especially around recording *Black Celebration*, because I was curious to find out if there was any sign of a difficult relationship between these two characters before *SOFAD*.

"I just remember everyone was working very hard. At that stage Martin wrote all the songs, and Alan was a huge part of the studio-team. He was there every minute. Martin, Dave and Fletch might come in a bit later sometimes, on some days. Alan was there with me, Daniel Miller and the assistant every minute of the whole thing. We were all working in a very loving way, I think, with a lot of love and respect for the songs. We all felt we were working on the songs, even Martin had written them. Once he had written them they became a life of their own. And the responsibility of the production-team as a group of musicians was to make the songs as good as we could. To me it seems that Alan and Martin had a great relationship. Alan was working incredibly hard and focused to make the best out of the songs."

Of course, **Gareth Jones** can't say anything about the relationship between them during the time of *SOFAD* because he didn't work with them at that period. "I don't know if there was particularly a problem between Martin and Alan. Clearly there was a problem in the group some-

---

[524] Taken from: Unsound Recordings, Sound On Sound, January 1998. Words: Bill Bruce.
[525] Taken from: recoil.co.uk. Words: Alan Wilder.
[526] Taken from: Just Can't Get Enough, Uncut, May 2001. Words: Stephen Dalton.

how. Y'know, it's like in a family, isn't it? In a family, if one member starts behaving badly then you have a family problem. You can't just blame one person, the whole family is something that needs to be looked at. And I guess it's a bit like in a band, it's a complex relationship. And when it goes wrong it goes badly wrong sometimes."[527]

There's a lot of truth in it. Each member of a team is "guilty" of something, and no one particularly can be blamed for the whole situation.

"During *Devotional* I decided to leave *DM*," **Alan** said. "However, I had already thought about it during the work on the album. The relationships within the band had got very bad. Generally I never wanted to be in a band my whole musical life, and I thought this would be a good time to do this step forward."[528]

Remember the previous chapters. There are quotes of him, saying that he decided to leave the band 18 months after the tour. As it has been mentioned before it probably was a kind of process. At a certain point you start being dissatisfied. This dissatisfaction grows over the course of time, nevertheless there are things you still like. So you actually enjoy what you do most of the time, but basically you are not satisfied, and think about changing things. So Alan probably means that he started to consider leaving the band much earlier, but the final decision was not made before **1995**.

In **1997** he named one of the songs on his album *Unsound Methods - Control Freak* and was asked whether he did this because Martin called him that name.

"Yes, but it doesn't refer to the lyrics, it's just the name of the song," **Alan** replies. "I found it funny somehow. However, it doesn't have a deeper meaning."[529]

According to my statement that I'm definitely a control freak myself because I want a project to be as good and perfect as possible, he admitted, "It's true that I am a bit of a control freak. I think that anyone who is deeply passionate about what they do will have that element about them."[530]

---

[527] depechemodebiographie.de.
[528] Taken from: recoil.co.uk. Words: Alan Wilder.
[529] Source can't be found anymore.
[530] depechemodebiographie.de.

Once **Fletch** was quoted with, "Alan never did like us as people. Well, he doesn't like anyone as people, really – he hasn't got friends and things like that."[531]

It's not certain whether he really said it in this way, but Martin also once called Alan a misanthropist.

"There's probably an element of truth in this but 'misanthropist' is perhaps a little harsh," **Alan** said. "I don't have a huge army of so-called 'friends' because I don't suffer fools gladly and I'm also not so insecure that I need an entourage of sycophants singing my praises all the time. I'm very selective about the people I socialise with. I suspect Martin meant that I was cynical and sarcastic which is pretty much right! It takes quite a lot to really get me rattled actually and I've consistently found that humour (or more specifically, sarcasm) is the best method of diffusing difficult or confrontational situations."[532]

Later **Martin** said that it is maybe, "false intimacy when it's all based on partying, but I think Alan would have to admit that he had fun with us at times."[533]

He certainly had, but this sentence again clearly shows how little they talk to each other about essential things. It seems as if Martin was well aware that some of their statements were a bit harsh, and over the course of time he would retreat increasingly from this position.

For a long time this "battle" was fought between Martin, Fletch and Alan, while Dave said little.

"I didn't hear back directly from Dave but he did send Hep and me a huge bunch of flowers when Paris was born and we saw him on a couple of occasions quite soon after," **Alan** said. "I'm sure he understands exactly why I left and he has been nothing but a perfect gentleman regarding the whole situation."[534]

At first, **Dave** evaded the questions about Alan or humoured Martin and Fletch a bit. So he said in **1997**, "I think it was happening around when we were making SO-FAD. Alan put in a lot of work, and the thing is, if you're going to put in all that work, fine, do it. But afterwards,

---

[531] Taken from: Long and Winding Mode, Details, May 1997. Words: Gavin Edwards.
[532] Taken from: recoil.co.uk. Words: Alan Wilder.
[533] Taken from: Many Smack-Free Returns! Q, June 2001. Words: Dorian Lynskey.
[534] Taken from: recoil.co.uk. Words: Alan Wilder.

don't kind of turn around and say, 'Hey, I did all this and what do I get back for it?' There's a lot of ego stuff goes on, as we know, in these bands. It just got to the stage where it was like, 'I do all this, and I don't think I'm respected.' And that's really sad, but I think Alan had to do what he had to do. You know, I love Alan. I mean he was in the band with us for like, fifteen years or something. I mean, it's a family. It is a brotherly thing. Sometimes you hate your brother, and it's like, 'Get out of my face', but there's something there that's really special."[535]

He is concordant with Gareth Jones on this. Probably many successful bands feel that way because they share experiences that aren't easily experienced by "normal" people.

In **2001** he said according to *Ultra*, "I felt a big part of what we were doing was missing - a leader, musically, and for me Alan was that. The others would say he was too controlling, but he just worked his a*** off because he really believed in it and the idea of pushing himself musically, which you can hear on his own records. I find that really inspiring. I miss him."[536]

And in **2003**, "I really miss Alan's input on everything we do musically, but I miss him as a friend. He was probably the person in the band I felt supported by the most and I wish I'd fought harder for him to stay. What Alan really wanted was for Martin to turn round and say, 'You've really contributed something great,' but Martin's not someone who hands out compliments very often."[537]

"Dave is very generous and I think he is honest at his comments," **Alan** said. "I think it seemed strange to him to work with so many new people. He said such nice things about me which gives me a good feeling. Although I'm happy with what I do now I also miss it not having him around."[538]

To understand why Alan left, it's necessary to put his different answers together and not to look at a single statement. As we have seen, there were 26 different an-

---

[535] Taken from: K-ROQ radio, LA, February 1997, DJs: Kevin and Bean.
[536] Taken from: In the Mode for Love, Time Out, 4 April 2001. Words: Omer Ali.
[537] Taken from: Cash for Questions: Dave Gahan, Q, June 2003. Words: Paul Stokes.
[538] Taken from: recoil.co.uk. Words: Alan Wilder.

swers to the question in the survey of *depechemode-biographie.de* about why Alan had left the band. This shows how much Alan had said about it over the course of time. Maybe he said TOO much but the reasons that led to his final decision were probably so complex that he could talk about it all day and still wouldn't be able to sum it up, as he once said.

Not even people who are close to him are able to understand and explain it.

"I don't know really why Alan decided to leave the band," **Steve Lyon** said. "I knew before it became a common knowledge. I don't know if he told anyone else but I knew that he was going to leave. I really think it's really unfortunate because the working relationships and the success that they had were good. When we were working together it was incredible. It's a real shame that he left. Sometimes things have to break and then go together again. So let's wait and see. They had been together in the band for a long time. And he took a very, very lead role in the band and it's a shame that they are not working together again."[539]

But probably this lead role is the crux. All the problems and tension seem to be based on it.

Some fans and journalists have their own theories about Alan's departure. "I don't believe him when he says it had been a well-thought out decision. I think it was an irrational act because he was burnt out, hurt, disappointed and angry" is one of these theories.

Being burnt out, and thus coming to the conclusion that he had had enough of the whole thing, so that it would be the right time to do something that had been brewing on his mind for longer would be an explanation that makes sense. There is even a statement by Alan that could prove this (see **1997.**)

Later, not only the remaining band members but also **Alan** watered their statements down. But I think that "I never expected to remain in a band all my life. There's something quite sad about being in a 'pop' group when you hit middle age" and "one of the reasons I eventually left was so that I'd be able to spend more time at home

---

[539] depechemodebiographie.de

with my family"[540] as well as "I wanted change and wanted to do something different. It was at a time in my life when I needed to clear out a lot of baggage and I just felt it was time to move on"[541], and the additional wish to focus on his own project shouldn't be seen as alibis, or as back-pedalling as some people do, because he had mentioned some of these things long before *SOFAD*.

I think these reasons were a kind of background. Only "My decision to leave wasn't as a direct result of tensions anyway"[542] sounds a bit strange, because it doesn't match his official statement at all. Because the main point, of course, was the team-work fraught with problems. If he had still been happy in the band, the other reasons wouldn't have become that important for him, or he would have found a way to combine the band with his own projects, and with family life.

Both points are probably correct again – it was a well thought-out decision and an irrational act at the same time. The well thought-out decision followed a line of consideration and personal / musical development from *Violator* (or even earlier) onwards, but in the end it was probably based on being burnt out and being disappointed, because his official statement sounds a bit like that, while everything he said afterwards is much more moderate.

But maybe he was simply slightly unhappy with his official statement – perhaps because of being angry about the reactions of Martin and Fletch at the meeting, (maybe he had expected they would try to change his mind), or possibly because he was over-accurate in writing down the reasons. Everyone might know this: you are trying to write down something very important, write, edit, think, write, edit ... and end up leaving out something essential, or coming across in the wrong way. This caused angry reactions from Martin and Fletch, and that raised speculation in the media and among fans - a typical knock-on effect.

The speculation got out of control here and there, and some fans still think today that Alan got paid less than the other band members. But **Alan** said, "The publishing royalties go to whoever wrote the song (and are obviously split if there was more than one writer.) Record royalties are

---

[540] Taken from: recoil.co.uk. Words: Alan Wilder.
[541] Taken from: Alan Wilder Interview, Future Music, Issue 62, November 1997. Words: Andy Jones.
[542] Taken from: recoil.co.uk. Words: Alan Wilder.

divided equally between all group members at the time of the recording. Just as I receive royalties from any recordings I was involved in, I have certain rights regarding their release. Leaving the band does not stop me receiving a 25% share of royalties from record sales of all the work I was involved in - that means everything from *Construction Time Again* through to *SOFAD*. I will continue to earn for as long as the records keep selling."[543]

Hear a voice in the hall, echoing in my mind (Useless)
(© Ingo Bittrich)

This had been one of the big topics of that year. The other was **Dave** again. In **August 1995** he made another detox. When he got home he found it had been looted. Everything was gone, his *Harleys*, studio equipment, the stereo system, everything down to the cutlery. The house had a coded alarm system, so it must have been an inside job. He didn't know what to do, so he checked into the *Sunset Marquis* (a hotel in LA and a meeting point for junkies.)

"I rang my mother and she said Teresa had told her that I hadn't been to any rehab, I wasn't even trying to get clean like I'd promised - and I was trying, I was doing the best I could. I quickly got loaded and drank a lot of wine, took a handful of pills. I went into the bathroom and cut

---

[543] Taken from: recoil.co.uk. Words: Alan Wilder.

my wrists. Uh, there was a friend with me. ... In fact I remember now, I was in the middle of that phone call to my mum and I told her to hold on, I'd be back in a minute, went to the bathroom and cut my wrists, wrapped towels round them and came back to the phone and said, 'Mum, I've got to go, I love you very much.' Then I sat down with my friend and acted like nothing was going on. I put my arms down by my sides and I could feel them bleeding away."[544]

There is also another version of this story. According to that version he was alone, but knew a friend would come over. However, probably at the behest of the record company or the band, he later said he had just injured himself "by mistake" and it hadn't been a suicide attempt.

"Anyway, I woke up the next morning in a psychiatric ward, strapped up, the full padded cell. First of all, I thought I might be dead, then this psychiatrist came in and informed me that it was a felony to take your own life in California - so I was busted for trying to kill myself!" He laughed. "I'm glad I can laugh about it now. Things went from worse to worse. There were loads of other occasions of overdoses, waking up outside dealers' places downtown, on the lawn with no clothes on, robbed. But there were always people to pick me up. I'd go to these meetings and be f*** high as a kite among all these sober people. And you can't imagine a worse place to be when you're loaded! I used to go to the bathroom and shoot up then come back and raise my hand and say, 'I got 30 seconds clean!'"[545]

At one of those meetings or at a detox he became acquainted with Jennifer, his present wife, a New York actress and scriptwriter, who had also been addicted to heroin once.

"I met her in Arizona," **Dave** said. "Jennifer went back to New York. I went to LA and we kept in touch. I'd visit her and her kid, who is now my stepson, and we remained friends. I could see something in her I wanted. She didn't give a crap about the band I was in. She just genuinely cared about what I was doing to myself and I saw that right from the start. That was unusual because I was usu-

---

[544] Taken from: Tears of my Tracks, Q, March 1997. Words: Phil Sutcliffe.
[545] Taken from: Dead Man Talking, NME, 18 January 1997. Words: Keith Cameron.

ally suspicious of people, particularly myself. When you can't trust yourself it's impossible to trust others."[546]

Despite all these circumstances, the band started to record *Ultra* in **September 1995**. It seems as if it was something like an act of defiance. Martin realised that Alan wasn't even an original member of the band, as he said, and that perhaps it would be right to go on without him. So he decided to do so – and maybe he wanted to prove to Alan that he was able to make a good *DM*-record without him.

Fletch confirmed, "I think there was a feeling of us having to prove ourselves, a bit like after when Vince left. It gave us a new challenge and I think in some ways it's spurred on us to do better things."[547]

Quotes from that time show that it wasn't as simple as they sometimes pretended it was, and they went on saying things which weren't always diplomatic.

Martin tried at least, however. "Alan was a very important part of the band, especially the last two albums. He was the one who would spend the most time at the computer, sometimes until 4 in the morning. And he took on a lot of the production side of things. So, um ... it was very important for us to find the right kind of person."

The "right person" he was talking about was Tim Simeon, whom they chose as producer for *Ultra*.

And while the first sentence was friendlier and a little step towards Alan, the next one ruined it: "Since Alan left, we are working so much more as a complete unit. We ... we do describe ourselves as a family these days.[548] Alan left at a very strange time. It was when we were actually doing nothing. He didn't leave us at the end of the last tour, and he didn't leave when we got together and decided to actually start working again. I think, after that last tour, he probably felt that he'd had enough and wanted to leave the band, but he wanted to give himself time to reconsider."[549]

---

[546] Taken from: Facing my Monsters, Daily Mirror, 27 June 2003. Words: Gavin Martin.
[547] Taken from: Andy Fletcher Interview, Dotmusic, 4 May 2001. Words: Uncredited.
[548] Taken from: Modus Operandi, Detour, May 1997. Words: Shari Roman (Ed: Trent Buckroyd).
[549] Taken from: Ultra Sounds, Guitar World, May 1997. Words: Alan di Perna.

"I wasn't sure whether I could work in a band without him anyway," **Fletch** added. "I felt he didn't have too much respect for the other members of the band. In the end, it made the decision-making process a lot easier. When there are three people, there has to be a decision."[550]

By the way ...

... NLMDA is the most played song live. Although there are some setlists missing, it's clear that NLMDA is on the top with about 720 times played live, followed by Enjoy the Silence, Personal Jesus, A Question of Time, Stripped and Everything Counts (all played about 620 times). [The statistic was done after TOTU, but as NLMDA was also played on every single Delta Machine and Global Spirit gig only the numbers have changed.]

... Violator is not only the most successful album, but it is also at the top of the favourite albums in almost all polls of several message-boards and fan-websites. Taking nine different polls together, Violator is alone at the top, above SOFAD, MFTM, Black Celebration and Ultra. These are the Top 5. A Broken Frame is in the last place. (Note that some of these polls were done before the release of SOTU, but they all included Playing the Angel. Newer polls, including Delta Machine and Spirit, also showed Violator at the top.)

... it was nothing special that the band spent time in the villa in Madrid. At that time (at the **beginning of the 1990s**), it was "hip" to rent a house, live there like a kind of family and produce an album.

... the German Heavy-Metal band Helloween and DM were recording at the Chateau du Pape Studios in Hamburg at the same time. Helloween's Michael Weikath said that, „there were girls everywhere but they weren't there because of us. We had to fight our way into the studio through lots of 15-year-old girls. Depeche Mode were nice, we often talked to them." (Taken from: Helloween in Hamburg, Metal

---

[550] Taken from: It's a Mode Mode Mode Mode World, Hits, 28 April 1997. Words: Janet Trakin.

Hammer, Issue 3, 2010. Words: Marc Halupczok. (Translated from German)

... in **2013** Alan sold the car with which he had been on the road to Lochearnhead.

... there is a quote from Daniel Miller in which it is claimed that there had been a meeting right after the tour and that Alan wanted to get full control in the studio. Alan said that there had never been such a meeting and that he had never said anything like that. Of course, it's not sure whether Miller had ever said anything like that.

... the only release in **1995** was Coming Back to You, a cover song recorded and performed by Martin. (It was a solo release of his.) It was released on Tower of Song, a Tribute to Leonard Cohen.

1996

- When the longing returns (Sister of Night) -

In **spring 1996** the band, now reduced to three members, met in New York for a recording-session for *Ultra*. They spent six weeks there, during which in the end only one song was completed. Dave was taking heroin and cocaine at the same time, because taking only one of them didn't work anymore.

"But he was hiding his habit from us again - lying to us, saying 'now I'm clean'," **Martin** said. "We got one usable vocal out of him in four weeks and we told him, 'Go home to LA and sort yourself out. We'll record you later in the year.' Dave seemed quite happy to go along with it. Of course, I felt sympathy but I also thought, how seriously is he taking this? We're slogging away and he's so ... ill that he's never going to be fit to carry on."[551]

A thought which might have come to him before they started to record the album ... And it's strange that he said that Dave had been able to hide his habit from them. There's an unaired radio-interview from **December 1995** in which Dave was definitely high, unable to speak in complete sentences, giving the impression of being confused, and not sure about what he was doing or saying (probably the reason why this interview wasn't aired.) It's difficult to imagine that Martin didn't notice that – or this:

"When we started this album, 90 per cent of the time I was still strung out, and the rest of the time I was sick from kicking," **Dave** admitted. "It became very obvious that physically I wasn't able to stand up in front of a microphone for more than an hour without wanting to lay down and die."[552]

The only vocal which they recorded in New York was *Sister of Night*. Dave sang it when he was loaded. Nevertheless, he liked that song very much and felt appealed by the lyrics. He felt that it took him through something

---

[551] Taken from: They Just Couldn't get Enough, Q, March 1997. Words: Phil Sutcliffe.
[552] Taken from: Depeche vs Drugs, Winnipeg Free Press, 1 May 1997. Words: Mark Brown.

wonderful like love, and then, by your own actions, how it was destroyed."

"It's all been done in London, basically," **Fletch** summed it up. "Started **September '95**, then we had a six-week period in New York last spring, then Tim went to LA after that ... after Dave's ...thingy ... to record Dave's vocals for three or four weeks, then we came back home and finished here."

Martin laughed. "That's the best I've heard it described! Dave's thingy!"[553]

The "thingy" meant that Dave was arrested after an overdose because of cocaine possession and because of being under the influence of heroin.

"Police and paramedics were called to the *Sunset Marquis* hotel in Hollywood, popular with musicians, and found Gahan, aged 34, unconscious on the floor of a hotel room," *The Guardian* reported, "the people with him, who summoned help, said he passed out 10 minutes after injecting a 'speedball' – a mixture of cocaine and heroin."[554]

First he was taken to hospital and then later to the police station. He spent two nights in prison before he was dismissed on bail.

Later he would recall that time as very scary because he was in a cell with some other men, some of them accused of murder. But it didn't stop him. As soon as he came out of prison he got straight back into taking heroin. But then it wasn't working anymore. For the first time of the couple of years that he had been in and out of detox, he picked up the phone and asked for help. If he kept off drugs, the charges against him would be dropped. He had to go to a urine test twice a week within the next two years. If one test was positive, two years in prison would await him.

"All I can do is hope my actions will speak much louder than the crap that's come out of my mouth the last few years," **Dave** said. "When I left the hospital, I said to someone that I'd overdosed, and they said, 'David, you died. They revived you three times.' I could have had permanent brain damage. People seem to believe the myth that if you just do it once you're fine, and now many peo-

---

[553] Taken from: Dead Man Talking, NME, 18 January 1997. Words: Keith Cameron.
[554] Taken from: Pop Singer Arrested, The Guardian, 29 May 1996. Words: Uncredited.

ple seem to be going straight to heroin, bypassing pot and all that and going straight to the devil. It's really scary. I saw this happening in London - lots of kids smoking a joint in the loo are smoking heroin in it and are chasing the dragon. They think that because they're not mainlining it won't get them. I don't want to be any kind of preacher. I'm in a rock 'n' roll band, and I love to do that and just want to be David. I'm happy to get in touch with that little kid that was lost inside."[555]

The apple falls, destiny calls – I follow you (The Bottom Line) (© Ingo Bittrich)

So he finally underwent a serious detox, and went into therapy.

The band's statement was quite simple at first: "As you may know, Dave accidentally overdosed on drugs in Los Angeles on **28 May**. Upon release from the hospital he was arrested for possession of a controlled substance and being under the influence. Following his release on bail, Dave moved into a live-in rehabilitation centre for four weeks. He has since entered a 'sober living house' which gives him more flexibility to work on upcoming projects."[556]

---

[555] Taken from: I'm Hanging on by my Teeth, Melody Maker, 27 July 1996. Words: Steve Hochman.
[556] Taken from: Introduction, Bong 29, August 1996. Words: Uncredited.

Again, as previously in Alan's case, when they issued a brief statement that he had left, but the band would continue, one had the feeling they shouldn't have said anything else. Later interviews didn't help to get rid of that feeling, especially because they showed up many of the conflicts within the band.

Martin on the question whether it sometimes seemed funny to him when Dave interpreted his lyrics: "No, because Dave is like another instrument. He's the voice of the band. His voice is particularly suited to a lot of the songs. I can't sing the way he sings."[557] This is one of the statements Dave was irritated about. It seems he doesn't like being seen as an instrument, although it is a typical view among musicians.

Furthermore, they were asked whether it influenced their relations that Dave was in LA and Martin and Fletch in London.

"I think the fact that there is such a great distance between us sometimes raises more communication problems," **Martin** replied. "We are realising that we should keep in touch more often."[558]

"There's no difference really because even when Dave was living in England we hardly saw him at all," **Fletch** added, "and the same with Alan, we never saw him and he only lived 20 minutes away."[559]

"I don't really have much of a relationship with the others outside of the band," **Dave** said. "When you're on the road for that long, and that was nearly two years, I think the last thing you want to do is hang out together." He laughed.[560]

They were asked whether they found it difficult to be in the studio again. (Attention: Joke of the year is following!)

"This record has been really easy for us to make,"[561] **Martin** replied.

"We had to satisfy ourselves that Dave wanted to do it," **Fletch** said. "I think there's a strong bond between us all. I think Alan thought that when he left the band it was

---

[557] Taken from: Rolling Stone, 1993, Words: Marvin Scott Jarrett.
[558] Taken from: Catching up with ... Martin, Bong 30, December 1996.
[559] Taken from: Catching up with ... Fletch, Bong 30, December 1996.
[560] Taken from: Catching up with ... Dave, Bong 30, December 1996.
[561] Taken from: Mode Three, Future Music, April 1997. Words: Uncredited.

going to be enough to split us up but I think the bond is much stronger than he believed."[562]

Dave was more critical about the whole stuff. He felt that things were getting more and more difficult, "because when you know each other so well, little things become really big things. There is a lot of outside things ... everyone's got families and they've got other interests outside of the band so less and less time really gets spent on making music together. The roles are very defined: Martin writes the songs and I sing them. We have Tim Simenon working with us on this record and a number of other people playing music, programming and stuff like that. Tim is playing a really big role in it. I wouldn't say that he replaced Alan because it's completely different thing, but he fulfils that role. I think Martin is working a little bit harder in pushing himself further and working in the studio because there's nobody else to do it.[563] In retrospect, I wasn't ready and it was more important for me to take heroin than being in the band, but I think that in the last few months I feel like I've done some of my best work. I've thrown myself into it, I've been working with a vocal coach, Evelyn. It's a long process and I'm trying to put all my energy into doing that ..."

And when he was asked whether he found it easy to sing the new songs, he said, "I never find it easy to sing. It is a very emotional thing to do. Everything else is pretty much programmed and it's all what I call 'head-work.' When I sing I sing from my heart and it's the human element in *Depeche Mode*."[564]

Obviously, the "programmed stuff" was a very emotional thing to do as well. In these days, when **Martin** was asked about production you could foresee what he would answer.

"In the past, Alan was almost a control freak. I think he'd even admit he's a bit of a control freak. He tended to really focus on the production and it's something that didn't interest me as much. Obviously, I cared about what was going on and what the end result was. If I liked what he was doing then I would let him get on with it. If it came

---

[562] Taken from: Catching up with ... Fletch, Bong 30, December 1996.
[563] Taken from: Mode Three, Future Music, April 1997. Words: Uncredited.
[564] Taken from: Catching up with ... Dave, Bong 30, December 1996.

to a point where I really didn't like something, then I would say I don't think that works."[565]

Here he named exactly what Alan criticized, and Dave would do later as well, without seeing that Alan was not the only one being "guilty" of the conflict. If you stay back most of the time and only say what you DON'T like it'll probably irritate the other one. But it seemed as if **Martin** was suffering from a "blind spot" here.

"We have never worked with a programmer before, we've always done it ourselves." (He meant: Alan did it.) "We've never had outside musicians constantly in the studio with us before." (He meant: They didn't need any because Alan was able to play almost every instrument.) "Dave Clayton, the musician we are working with now, in a way fulfils Alan's role, but it's far easier to manipulate him. If Alan didn't like something, I am sure he wouldn't actually play it badly, but if we say to Dave, 'Can you try this out for us?' he'll try it, and he'll try his hardest to make it work for us."[566]

"I think that Alan was trying to gain control of everything towards the end of the project, and because I wasn't very well, he was doing that," **Fletch** said. "He was able to take control, and I think I deal with things a bit differently. I don't think the roles have changed at all ... we just replaced Alan with a team of people."[567]

It's amazing how many people they needed to replace one single man ...

"It was important for us to fill his shoes," **Martin** remarked. "I think that Tim and his team helped to fulfil that role. The musicians in Tim's team were very important. Because Alan was always the so-called musician in *Depeche Mode*. The classical trained one. It's a fine line. What's a musician? I can play a guitar and I can play keyboards, but I was never classically trained."

"He can read music scores as well," **Fletch** bitched about Alan.

Martin tried to cool it down a bit: "I never had any music theory, I just know what sounds good and what moves

---

[565] Taken from: Catching up with ... Martin, Bong 30, December 1996.
[566] Taken from: Mode Three, Future Music, April 1997. Words: Uncredited
[567] Taken from: Catching up with ... Fletch, Bong 30, December 1996.

me when I write it, when I try out things. So this was a totally different way of working for us."[568]

Some fans tend to label Alan as a victim. But - as we've already seen – there are two sides to every story. Therefore it's too simple to see him as the unfortunate victim, (or "fluffy bunny-wunny" to say it with his own words.)

Some fans tend to see him as a traitor, as the one who committed the crime of leaving "the sinking ship," as the one who left his friends in the lurch. I think this view is unfair, because you have realise the amount of work he put into this band.

Where would *DM* have got without him? Would they have been able to produce albums like *Violator*? Would they have been able to play in front of 70,000 people at the *Rosebowl*? I wouldn't be so sure.

But it would also be wrong to say that the entire success was due to him, (like some other fans do.) It was the success of this special team. Alan alone wouldn't have gotten far without Martin's songs and Dave's distinctive voice and charismatic live performance.

Fans also tend to stress the role of the co-producers too much. In message-boards you often read sentences like "if they worked with Flood again, the album would be great."

But a producer is never the driving musical force of a production. Talking to Gareth Jones and Steve Lyon both said that as producers they always try to do what the band / artist wants. They might bring in ideas and some kind of style, but the basics of an album are always up to the band themselves.

"This is what they wanted and this is what they got," **Steve Lyon** replied on the question whether it was wanted or accidentally that the album *Host*, which he produced, by the band *Paradise Lost* (a metal band in their basics) turned out their so-called "*Depeche Mode* album."

"It was a very different kind of record for them. If you had listened to the demos to this album, the final result wasn't so different. So, that's the album they wanted to make. A band always knows what they want. A producer is the person in the middle to bring in an external voice."[569]

---

[568] Taken from: Depeche Mode: Respect To The Originators, unknown media and date. Words: René Passet.
[569] depechemodebiographie.de

Although Martin and Fletch were to stop bitching about Alan after a while, the band nevertheless tends to deal rather unfairly with Alan's role.

Staring down the barrel of a gun.
(© Ingo Bittrich, model: Denise Eichberg)

1997

- I'm talking to you now: the fire still burns (Insight) -

At the **beginning of 1997**, after recording for the album had been completed at the **end of 1996**, everyone was tired and longing for some rest. Producer Tim Simeon found it so extreme that he only recorded one more single with *DM* after that, and then never worked with them again. According to rumours he was completely burned out after those long recording sessions.

This is contradictory to **Martin** saying, "There was this easy atmosphere. And this friendly, nice atmosphere hasn't always been there in the past. Tim knows exactly what has happened before and where we should be going, as we do. He just helps push us in the right direction."[570]

Apart from Martin, no one would ever say that recording *Ultra* was easy. So it's difficult to understand why he stressed it so often. To prove to Alan that this band was able to make a good record without any tension?

"After the album Tim suffered from what is known as *P.A.D.: Post Album Depression*," **Fletch** admitted. But it has to be said that, "he is the coolest man in the world as well. He knows how to get access to all the clubs."

"Until he met us." **Martin** laughed. "We just did *Top of the Pops* ..." (where not only Tim Simeon was seen on keyboards but also Anton Corbijn on drums.) "Just before we got on stage I said to Tim: 'you realise that you now become among the ranks of the uncool, being seen on stage with us.' I think he got really nervous."

"Anton is taking it really seriously," **Fletch** said. "He told me he's been the happiest he has been in the last ten years."

"We are getting becoming slightly worried about our new videoclip. We haven't seen the full script yet and we are worried that it will focus on the drummer for about 99%." **Martin** laughed.[571]

---

[570] Taken from: Pavement, April 16th, 1997. Words: Uncredited.
[571] Taken from: Depeche Mode: Respect To The Originators, unknown media and date. Words: René Passet.

On **3 February** the single *Barrel of a Gun / Painkiller* was released.

The single *It's No Good / Slowblow* was released on **31 March**.

On **10 April** a release party took place in London, before the album *Ultra* finally was released on **14 April**.

Ultra debuted at No. 1 in the UK Albums Chart and at No. 5 in the *Billboard 200* with sales of 90,000 copies in the first week. So it went well. But whatever the band released and whatever they did - the media was interested in anything but music.

It was the year of confessions and public "therapy meetings." Dave even hugged journalists after he had "cried on their shoulder." But they were still interviewed separately, or Dave alone, because it seemed to be difficult for him to talk frankly in the presence of the other two. Symptomatic of that was an unsuccessful interview in which Dave began to speak and then fell silent when Martin cast a meaningful glance in his direction. Martin and Fletch opened up a bit too, but here and there you couldn't ward off the impression that Dave's "soul striptease" got on their nerves.

"Well, it's no secret that I've been drinking and using drugs for a long time," **Dave** said. "Hash. Amphetamines. Coke came along, Alcohol was always there, hand in hand with drugs. Then all of a sudden I discovered heroin, and I'd be lying if I said it didn't make me feel, well ... like I've never felt before, I felt like I really belonged. I just felt nothing was gonna hurt me, I was invincible."[572]

Many people asked why no one of the band members or their environment had done anything to help him.

"There were a lot of people telling me I needed help. But I didn't want to listen. To be honest, Martin, Fletch and Alan were pretty naive. They thought that I had decided to become more reclusive and become this strange rock star. And I was pretty strange. One of my biggest problems is being a people-pleaser. I want the whole world to love me. If people seemed like they weren't having fun, I would try to become the centre of attention. I tried so hard that I forgot about loving myself."

---

[572] Taken from: Tears of my Tracks, Q, March 1997. Words: Phil Sutcliffe.

Although he would have enjoyed to tour *Ultra*, he didn't dare to because he was afraid of not being strong enough to do that at the time.

"When I got off the last tour and tried to go back to my normal life, I found that I had lost David completely. I was just Dave. David is a very scared person who lost the ability to trust, to love or to be loved, or to feel anything at all. The only feeling that was comfortable was to be in pain. I do pain really good. It's one of my big problems." He laughed.[573]

While Martin demoted Dave to an instrument, **Dave** liked to claim Martin would write about him. "Martin says he's not. I think he's subconsciously looking at himself. I'm not passing judgment on him, but I think he has a bit of an alcohol problem, and I think he knows it. So I think Martin is writing these songs and he can't help but think about what's been going on with me and then maybe look at himself in the mirror."[574]

At that time he often accused Martin of being an alcoholic, (although he admitted being an alcoholic himself), something Martin wasn't happy about at all. But Dave was correct. Many years later he said that Martin had been drinking like a fish at that time, and even Martin admitted it.

However, it was very difficult for **Dave** to be together with people who drank alcohol or took drugs. Not because he wanted to get drunk, but because he didn't feel part of it. He was struggling hard to keep sober.

"I don't wanna go back there, I've got too much to lose now. And I don't mean the band, I mean myself. There's little bits of David that come back every day, and he ain't such a bad guy. I sit and I watch Harry Enfield and I laugh my arse off. Or I cry at some soppy movie - I didn't do that sh*** for a long while! I didn't have those normal feelings! I would sit and watch the f*** weather channel for 12 hours of the day. I wanna see my son grow up. Just this weekend I got the opportunity to spend time with him. It was great.[575] How can you expect to be there for any-

---

[573] Taken from: Dave's Addiction, Spin, May 1997. Words: Barry Walters.
[574] Taken from: Synth and Sensibilities, NME, 25 January 1997. Words: Keith Cameron.
[575] Taken from: Dead Man Talking, NME, 18 January 1997. Words: Keith Cameron.

body else? And I'd want to be there for somebody else, but at the moment I have to look after David."[576]

Institutions, jail, death? I've been there and done them all.
(© Ingo Bittrich)

Martin and Fletch were seldom lucky with interviews at that point. I think it was really difficult for them. They belong to the generation of English men who were told from early childhood that "real men" don't have any "strange feelings," and they have always been really bad at communication. And now everyone looked at them, asking difficult questions like, "How could it happen that you lost a member and another one almost died?"

"I've only actually thought Dave was dead twice which is not bad going," **Martin** said. "If you get a phonecall and it's your manager or somebody saying, 'I need to speak to you about Dave, something really bad's happened,' the

---

[576] Taken from: K-ROQ radio, February 1997, DJs: Kevin and Bean.

first thought you have is 'Oh my God, this time it's the big one.' And that's only happened twice. And it's really bad."

"He should have been dead, honestly," **Fletch** added. "I don't know how his body actually kept up with it."

"What's that phrase? 'Institutions, jail, death?' And Dave says, 'I've been there and done them all.' And he's still walking. He's still singing. So it's a miracle, praise the Lord." **Martin** laughed.

"People of our label must have had a few heart attacks in the last couple of years," **Fletch** said and Martin laughed again.

I think laughing helps Martin to get through situations he doesn't feel comfortable with. So, when it is reported by journalists, that Martin was laughing, it gives a slightly false impression, because it probably doesn't mean he really laughed in situations like these.

"Six months ago, I was really p*** off about it, because all that really seemed important to Mart and Fletch was if I was dead there'd be no *Depeche Mode* anymore," **Dave** recalled. "I didn't get any support at all, verbally, from Fletch or Mart at any point. In fact, I've maybe heard from Mart once or twice in nearly three years. To be fair, I don't think they knew how bad it really was. They only saw me sporadically, and I tried to get it together enough to fool them. But I still am a bit resentful, especially of Mart. He rang me just before I went into the detox unit and he was angry with me. I came off the phone in tears, because I realised, 'F***, they don't really give a shit about me, it's the fact that there might not be any *Depeche Mode* anymore.' Really selfish. I was the most selfish one of all, by far, and I claim that, but it would have been nice if there had been some support from my so-called friends. Fletch used to tell me a lot of his friends were like, 'Why don't you just boot him out?' Which is a pretty funny concept, coming from Fletch!" He laughed.[577]

"When Dave was ill some people were asking why we couldn't get rid of him, get another singer," **Fletch** said. "But Dave would never come to me and say, 'Gore's being

---

[577] Taken from: Synth and Sensibilities, NME, 25 January 1997. Words: Keith Cameron.

a pain, let's get another songwriter.' His voice and Mart's songs are *Depeche Mode*."[578]

It's amazing that Fletch was able to adapt to the given situation so easily. At this time it was only a few years after the last time he had said that *DM* was Dave's voice, Martin's songs and Alan's music. It's a repeated sentence, like the one that the current album is the best they have ever made. (I've just read in a message-board that maybe he never said this. He did! There really are some interviews in which he said the current album was the best.)

Maybe you become a caricature of yourself after a period of years. Fletch is humorous enough to admit it; he even did once. One reason why people probably like *DM* so much is that the band members are not glamorous pop stars, but ordinary people with "normal" strengths and weaknesses. The survey that was done for *depechemode-biographie.de* shows that most fans see them mainly as musicians, but there were also many answers like, "they are people who are part of my life in some way", "they are kind of relatives you don't know much about but feel connected with" or "they are old chums you used to know at school" and "you seem to know them although you never met them."

At some points during this promotion tour the band felt they had to put some things right. They said that they hadn't had a full paid drug dealer on the staff during the *Devotional*-Tour. Furthermore, they said that they had supported Dave. But it had been difficult because he had isolated himself.

Besides, **Martin** emphasised, "I'm not an alcoholic. I don't particularly like to vocalise about my personal problems. I drink quite a lot. But virtually everybody I know does. Even if I do drink too much, it's a personal thing. Dave has come to realise that he may not have made the right decision to go into interviews and open his heart about his private life, especially the drug aspect. It's getting very boring. Every interview he goes into now, all they want to talk about is drugs. The fact that he happens to make music seems to be irrelevant for most people."

---

[578] Taken from: They Just Couldn't get Enough, Q, March 1997. Words: Phil Sutcliffe.

He also denied that his lyrics are about Dave and his problems. "I always write from a first-person perspective. I don't know what's going on in someone else's head. He does seem to get some therapeutic value from singing the songs. He does definitely feel passion for the songs and obviously feels some connection."[579]

"I don't actually believe that, to be honest," **Dave** said, confronted with Martin's statement. "I think he has a deeper sense, and knows that some of the things he writes about are what's going on all around us. That's how I feel connected with him. We don't talk much."[580]

And of course they were asked about the *Devotional*-Tour and its consequences over and over again, a topic that you find up to now.

"At the end of it, obviously Alan had had too much," **Martin** summed it up, losing his patience more and more. "He left the band. Andy had to leave the tour. He was going through terrible depression. Dave had various heart murmurs along the way; he was rushed to hospital. It was just too much. But once you've decided to do a tour of that length and all the dates are booked, it becomes a commitment."[581]

While he had thought right after Alan's leaving that this had to be the end of the band, he now declared over and over again, that there had never been a point at which *DM* would have almost split.

"There were times when we thought it was very probable that we would. We always stuck through the bad times because we felt we did something very special together. The closest it came to coming apart was after the New York recording session, where we got one vocal out of Dave in six weeks. We heard two weeks later on the radio that he'd OD'd. I did a lot of searching to decide what to do with the band because at one point I thought it was better for Dave if the band didn't exist anymore because it wasn't doing him any good."[582]

After all, he showed consideration for Dave with respect to a possible tour: "We've decided not to. I don't think it

---

[579] Taken from: Article in Pavement, 16 April 1997. Words: Uncredited.
[580] Taken from: Many Smack-Free Returns! Q, June 2001. Words: Dorian Lynskey.
[581] Taken from: Article in Pavement, 16 April 1997. Words: Uncredited.
[582] Taken from: It's a Mode Mode Mode Mode World, Hits, 28 April 1997. Words: Janet Trakin.

would be a very healthy environment for Dave to be in, with his problem. He gets really bored on tour for the 22 hours he's not onstage. And when he gets bored, that's when it gets worrying."[583]

Years later they weren't able to remember. So this is a funny bit.

"*Ultra* was a very important record to finish in retrospect," **Dave** said. "You know, we didn't tour with that record. That was probably the best decision that we made. Probably the only studio record that we ever didn't tour with, actually."

"Did we actually make that decision?" **Martin** asked.

"I don't know," **Dave** replied.

"Yeah, we did, didn't we?" **Fletch** said.

"Yeah," **Dave** recalled. "I seem to remember sitting in a meeting and everybody's going ..."

"I think when we couldn't answer," **Martin** guessed. "I think they took it as a no."

"Yeah," **Dave** said. "And I might've gotten arrested again or something like that."[584]

Almost desperate, Martin and Fletch tried to stress that there was a new album, but the media still wasn't interested in it. For them, of course, drugs, near-death experiences and a lost member were much more interesting than music.

"We got more press over Dave's suicide and overdose than at any time in our whole career. We got a double page in the *Sunday Times* magazine! Now, if we tried to get into the *Sunday Times* magazine for our music there'd be no way on this earth ...," **Fletch** said and Martin laughed.

"But Dave OD's and he gets the whole thing!" **Fletch** added.

"One thing we should always remember is that Dave and drugs is a small facet of this band," **Martin** emphasised. "It's a big part of Dave's life but, of course, it makes headline news and it's always over-focused upon. But there are so many other interesting facets to this band ..."

"Not much!" **Fletch** chipped in.

---

[583] Taken from: Ultra Sounds, Guitar World, May 1997. Words: Alan di Perna.
[584] Taken from: The Complete SXSW 2013 Interview, NPR, 25 March 2013. Words: Jason Bentley.

Martin laughed. "Obviously we know that people are going to be interested in the Dave-drugs angle, but hopefully they'll also be interested in the fact that we've finished an album."

On **16 June** the single *Home* was released. The video was directed by Steve Green. The painting on the *Home* cover was designed by Anton Corbijn's daughter Emma who was five years old at that time.

On **20 October** the single *Useless* was released. The video was the last one to be directed by Anton Corbijn for some years.

Dave recorded a cover song, *A Song for Europe*, for the sampler *Dream Home Heartaches* which was released on **4 September**.

Although anyone – except the fans – seemed to be interested the band tried to talk about music.

"The title – *Ultra* - really fits in with our new line-up. We lost a member along the way and now it's the new, improved, slimmed-down version." **Martin** laughed. "I think it's a great, positive title.[585] I think this is the album with the least religious connotations. It's hardly *SOFAD*. I think religion is one of those things that's so important – it's a crux of life – that you can't help cutting on it every now and again. But I think we have overdone it in the past. So I am consciously trying not to get involved with it every time I pick up a pen. It's just too easy for me to fall into writing about religion, because it is one of my fascinations."[586]

Nevertheless, there are some religious references, especially in *The Love Thieves*. But mainly, the lyrics on *Ultra* deal with frustrating relations, love and hope.

Martin's explanation about *Barrel of a Gun* is an angle for possible interpretations. "It's about understanding what you're about and realising that you don't necessarily fit into somebody else's scheme of things."[587]

"The song sums up the way I was treating myself and everybody around me," **Dave** added. "That's what life had

---

[585] Taken from: Synth and Sensibilities, NME, 25 January 1997. Words: Keith Cameron.
[586] Taken from: Ultra Sounds, Guitar World, May 1997. Words: Alan di Perna.
[587] Taken from: Synth and Sensibilities, NME, 25 January 1997. Words: Keith Cameron.

in store for me every day. It's a really powerful statement. When you're in that kind of row, the last thing on your mind is dying."[588]

I doubt that Martin wrote about Dave but nevertheless, the lyrics to especially *Barrel of a Gun* and *Useless* suit the given situation.

"*Barrel of a Gun* - we shot that in Morocco," **Dave** said about the video. "The interesting thing about that video was that I had eyes painted over the top of my eyes. There's this wall round the old city of Morocco, this huge wall, which to the Moroccans is basically a bathroom. It's like where they go and take a s*** and stuff like that, right? I had to walk all the way along this wall down one side where they was filming me so there's the wall on one side and I'd be like, 'Left ...right ...' because every time they came along to some guy that was, like, doing his business there - I had no idea, I'm blind you know! I'm walking through all this stuff, this s***!"

And about the video for *It's No Good* he said, "I think [it] was probably one of the most fun videos that I've ever made. Anton took it to the extreme. I got to really kind of like play a role, and play a part that Anton wanted me in - the real has-been rock 'n' roll star that ends up playing these places but he still thinks he's larger and bigger than life itself."[589]

I was asked by a reader if *Home* is about death. The answer is quite easy this time because **Martin** confirmed it. I think he was asked about it because the video referred to it. But it's also obvious from the lyrics. He said also, "I think at the time I was drinking way too much, and it was about accepting that fact."[590]

And while some lyrics on *Ultra* are a bit dark and depressing, the album ends with the very positive song *Insight*, which is full of hope. *The fire still burns.*

The fire also still burnt for the band that left behind the dark years. **1997** ended on a positive note.

---

[588] Taken from: It's a Mode Mode Mode Mode World, Hits, 28 April 1997. Words: Janet Trakin.
[589] Taken from: Interview with Depeche Mode, The Videos 86>98, Mute MF033 and Videos 86>98+, Mute MF042. Director: Sven Harding.
[590] Taken from: A La Mode, Gaywired, 2 November 2005. Words: Lawrence Ferber.

During a radio-interview wild things were brought to daylight ...

Interviewer: "You have a ring ... in your scrotum!? I hope you were strung out on dope when you got that done - you didn't do that consciously, did you?"

Dave: "You know what? I wasn't and it really hurt!"

Interviewer: "Well no, duh, Dave! Ah, what a surprise!"

Dave: "It's not actually in my scrotum, it's called a guiche, and it's the - you know that little bit ... in between?[591] It was that bit of skin that men have between the b*** and a***h*** - that really thin line."[592]

Interviewer: "Yeah ... that doesn't make it sound any the less painful though!"[593]

Dave: "Supposedly you get more sexual energy from it, but it was the most painful thing I've ever done. As it was being done I was in stirrups for half an hour with this girl staring at my a***, lining the needle up.[594] And it was kind of like, um ... I got a '10-9-8-7-6-' ... BAAANNGG! It was like somebody kicked me really, really hard. I earned that!"

Interviewer: "And do you still have it there?"

Dave: "Yes I do. And it's a lot of fun. Hey, if you can do that you do anything.[595] I don't think I touched my d*** for ages afterwards, I couldn't even sit on a hard chair for six months, although I showed everybody." (I don't want to picture the scene when he was going to show everybody ... Did he really get undress saying, "Look I've a ring in my a***"? :o)

In **1994**, when the guiche was done, **Dave** explained that it was done a day after his wedding with Theresa because he wanted a ring, but he didn't want to WEAR a ring. He doesn't have it anymore. In a later interview he said he had taken it out, after one of his children had asked him why he had had an earring in his a***. "But I've still got the holes - you can have a look if you really want."[596] (Er, no thanks.)

---

[591] Taken from: K-ROQ radio, February 1997, DJs: Kevin and Bean.
[592] Taken from: Cash for Questions: Dave Gahan, Q, June 2003. Words: Paul Stokes.
[593] Taken from: K-ROQ radio, February 1997, DJs: Kevin and Bean.
[594] Taken from: Cash for Questions: Dave Gahan, Q, June 2003. Words: Paul Stokes.
[595] Taken from: K-ROQ radio, February 1997, DJs: Kevin and Bean.
[596] Taken from: Cash for Questions: Dave Gahan, Q, June 2003. Words: Paul Stokes.

On **13 October** the *Recoil*-single *Drifting* was released. B-sides were *Control Freak* and *Shunt*. All three tracks were also released on the album *Unsound Methods* which was released on **27 October**. It had been recorded in Alan's own studio *The Thin Line*.

Alan presented himself now as a father of a little family together with his wife Hepzibah and their daughter Paris, who both joined in the video for *Drifting*. He admitted, though, that he had had a very bad time before.

"I had been burned out completely. There were a couple of things in my life that I had to change, very important things. I got divorced, I became a father, I left the band - a lot of decisive things happened, and I was much happier than before when I finally left this tunnel behind. This was a good moment to work creatively again. My enthusiasm was back."[597]

He started to work "last **September** and finished in **June** so it took about 9 months with a couple of breaks. Essentially I'm happy with the result. I think it is the most focused thing I've done and the most completed. There is always a side of me that thinks I could have done something better, but I think that's a natural reaction. You always feel that you can do more and do better."

It was important to him to work with new people, very different musicians to explore new areas. "Most of the time in *Depeche Mode* we didn't work as a group and we didn't used to bring people in. The last album we done we did have some extra musicians but that was the only one."

Now, "I can bring in people and I always try to find someone new to work with and think it's a real challenge. It makes you do things differently if you work with a stranger, somebody new, so I like to give myself that challenge to find interesting new people each time."[598]

For *Unsound Methods* he worked together with different vocalists, following his own musical instincts. "My starting point is often a combination of tried and tested guide sounds that evoke a particular feeling or mood in order to get the ball rolling. Then, by trial and error, I keep throwing ideas at the track until a theme or concept emerges which I like to keep in mind to focus the direction. From

---

[597] Taken from: Article in Orkus Magazine, November 1997. Words: Collette Stritzke.
[598] Taken from: Chatting with Alan Wilder, September 1997. Words: Hendrik Wittgren.

that point I usually park the idea and move on to another track until I have built up more of an overall picture. Whilst keeping this in mind, I then bring the music to a point where it accurately demonstrates the atmospheres I want to create and is acceptable to play to vocalists. I am looking for vocalists who present something either out of the ordinary and unique in some way or who are incredibly powerful singers. I gave each track to more than one vocalist to see how they perceived it. As a result, I actually got different interpretations of the same song. I 'ghosted' parts of some versions onto others."[599]

Nevertheless, the interviews at that time were more about *DM* than about *Recoil*. And of course, **Alan** was asked what he thought about *Ultra*. Mostly he refused to answer, but there's one reply on the record.

"I can't hear it in the same way as a record I was involved with, but I certainly don't feel a yearning to be involved again, and I've no regrets about leaving at all. The album is difficult for me to comment on, though I do have something of a stock answer, which is: you can probably work out what I think about it by listening to *Unsound Methods* and then *Ultra*, because the two records tell you everything you need to know about what the musical relationship was between myself and Martin. It's almost as if we've gone to the two extremes of what we were when we were together. What the band had before was a combination of those extremes."[600]

When doing what Alan suggested and listening to *Unsound Methods* and then to *Ultra*, you have to notice that these two albums aren't that different in their overall sound. But while Martin wrote pop songs, which aren't lightweight but more direct and straight to the point, Alan wrote a kind of soundtrack songs, more landscape-y, more filmic, with lots of unusual ideas and song structures.[601]

Even at this early stage of his solo career, **Alan** had to notice that it wouldn't be so easy to be successful with *Recoil*, although he never expected to be successful because he wasn't trying "to make a commercial, radio-friendly record, but of course it can be frustrating when you're trying to get the music across to people and the

---

[599] Taken from: recoil.co.uk. Words: Alan Wilder.
[600] Taken from: Unsound Recordings, Sound On Sound, January 1998. Words: Bill Bruce.
[601] Author of this passage: Jörg von der Fecht (Bleeding)

reaction you get is, 'oh, it's difficult music for weird people.'"[602]

1998 H 1999

- *Just another sacrifice to love's eternal fight (Surrender)* -

On **9 March 1998** the Recoil single *Stalker / Missing Piece* was released.

On **2 September** - yes, up to this date nothing was to be seen or heard of the band except for a press conference at the *Hyatt Hotel* in Cologne to announce the tour - DM started the *Singles*-Tour with the concert in Tartu (Estonia.) This tour was the first one to feature two backing musicians in place of Alan – the Austrian drummer Christian Eigner, and the British keyboarder Peter Gordeno. This is still the live line-up up to today.

Because *Devotional* had been so disastrous the band was careful not to let the *Singles*-Tour get out of control.

"We've got rules that we keep," **Martin** said. "I only drink two days a week – you may laugh."

Dave was very nervous before the start of the tour. "Well sitting here, desperately stopping my body from shaking ... But I think it is good to be nervous, you know nervous energy can be put into performing. For me personally, it is pretty important. If I wasn't feeling nervous then I would think there was something wrong, but yes, I am really nervous."[603]

Then he, however, could manage it quite well and got accustomed to go to bed immediately after the concerts.

"I've reached a certain level in life where I can trust myself, but not completely. To be honest I'm so tired after the shows that I'm asleep within five minutes of my head hitting the pillow."[604]

The tour went very well then. During the sound-check of the first show in Tartu the following conversation took

---

[602] Taken from: Unsound Recordings, Sound On Sound, January 1998. Words: Bill Bruce.
[603] Taken from: 20 April 1998 Depeche Mode Press Conference, Bong 36, June 1998.
[604] Taken from: Cleaning Up, Q, November 1998. Words: Nick Duerden.

place: "Good crowd tonight ... and lots of flags. I might grab the *Union Jack* and wrap it round myself." - "Oh, very patriotic, Dave." - "Not really, it's the nearest one and I'm f*** freezing."

This time there were only small incidents like being held at a small Russian village for nearly six hours while a customs point "sorted out" some paperwork, a small cold went through the touring party, trouble for the trucks at the border to Austria, heavy rain in Berlin, voice-problems in Zurich, and there was the concert in Birmingham in which near the end of the show Martin realised the zip on his trousers had been undone.[605]

In the meantime, on **7 September**, the single *Only When I Lose Myself / Headstar / Surrender*, for which they had worked together with Tim Simeon again, was released.

On **28 September** *The Videos 89-98* and *The Singles 89-98* were released. For these releases Alan was involved, but he didn't talk to any of the remaining band members (just to the record company and management, etc.), although he had his input on the box sets, which versions were to be used, artwork, label copy, promo items, marketing ideas, etc. Nevertheless, he was ignored by most journalists.

"I never pushed myself forward as a member of the band and the media tends to concentrate on lead vocalists and songwriters - to a lot of people, the 'techno-nerd' in the studio isn't really that glamorous," **Alan** said. "I also haven't been to death's door and back and more importantly, I committed the heinous crime of leaving the band - so, out of sight, out of mind. I can accept all these things but I was annoyed in particular with the *DM Singles E.P.K* (a short film) which I thought was extremely imbalanced - to have 10 years of one's hard and dedicated work represented by about 30 seconds out of a 20 minute piece is pretty insulting. I was also excluded from (and not even advised about) the interview with Anton Corbijn where the other band members discussed his videos for the singles - the same singles that I worked and performed on."[606]

---

[605] Information were taken from: Singles Diary, Bong 40, June 1999. Words: Jez Webb.
[606] Taken from: recoil.co.uk. Words: Alan Wilder.

The American leg of the *Singles*-Tour started on **27 October**, comprised 33 concerts and ended on **22 December** in Anaheim.

"Before we went on that tour I thought maybe this is going to be the last thing that we do together," **Dave** said. "I was ready to move on and felt totally okay with that. During the tour I realised how much I loved performing. It was overwhelming every night how much support I felt from the fans."[607]

"It was great," **Fletch** added. "A real buzz. We felt like a band again, no stupid arguments, no ego-ridden rubbish."[608]

One can and should see this as a general remark, not least because all band members admitted at a certain point to being ego-driven during *Devotional*. But one can also understand it as a mocking remark to Alan. Taking all these remarks from the *Ultra* period together, one shouldn't wonder that some fans think Alan had been mobbed out, because it sometimes seems as if he had been blamed for everything that went wrong.

For some fans the new presentation of "sober," (from the second half of *Touring the Angel* onwards even completely, when Martin gave up drinking) meant that *DM's* live performance wasn't exactly brilliant. There were a lot of changes: Alan was no longer in the band, a permanent live drummer, a new stage keyboarder, the whole thing became rockier and more conventional. Many fans think that "they lost something of their former magic" and many more people are not really happy with the current live versions of the songs.

But although there are fans who say that "Gordeno gets on my nerves", "the visual effects were much more impressive in the old days," that it is "a too often seen play without any spontaneous ideas" and that "Dave's voice was much better in former days," they will nevertheless go to the concerts.

The band is still fascinating and there's something magnetic. It must be the reason why the "old" fans can't get away from them - as much as they might moan. And it

---

[607] Taken from: In the Mode for Love, Time Out, 4 April 2001. Words: Omer Ali.
[608] Taken from: The Basildon Bond, The Times Magazine, 14 April 2001. Words: Paul Connolly.

must be the reason why there are many new fans, people who didn't know *DM* with Alan at all. They are tempted by this special charisma that some people tried to explain by saying "interaction with the fans and on stage is much better today" and "Mart has really developed." It's on the whole "still a great event to see them live."

Some fans say that *DM* is a "philosophy of life," I have the suspicion that it's a kind of drug. They are able to attract a large audience and this is a fact that can't be ignored when it comes to discussions about *DM*'s live performances.

In **1999** Dave got married for the third time, to Jennifer, and became a father for the second time, to Stella Rose. He also took on Jennifer's son Jimmy, (he adopted him officially in **2010**), so that he calls the three children "his own" now.

Also in **1999**, Martin got the *Ivor-Novello Award,* awarded by the British academy for composers and songwriters - probably the only good award *DM* ever got, because they are often ignored and neglected when it comes to awards.

2000

- Done with the black cotton mafia (Chrome, Liquid) -

On **6 March** the *Recoil*-album *Liquid* was released. On **3 April** the single *Strange Hours / New York Nights / Don't Look Back* was released, and on **21 August** the single *Jezebel*, of which *Black Box Complete* was the B-Side, was released. There were videos for *Strange Hours* and *Jezebel*.

Similarly, like its predecessors, *Liquid* was rather unconventional and wasn't received with enthusiasm everywhere, leading to speculation that **Alan** might be a little depressed. "I can't really put my finger on why I gravitate towards that kind of music, but I just suppose that the dark side of human nature is much more interesting.[609] I don't think that I'm a gloomy type, I'm quite funny and not too serious. They are mistaken if people think due to the music I'm morbid or serious. People always talk about the darkness in the LP. I see it as dramatic rather than dark. I don't know why my music always sounds that way, I simply follow my instincts there and this is what comes out. Perhaps this is a side of me that only comes through in the music, I don't know, I can't give any reasons for."[610]

With this project he showed that some of the criticism from his former band mates was valid. "I'm a perfectionist and that tends to make each project that little bit harder - you feel you must improve upon what you've done in the past. Making *Liquid* was probably the most grueling time I've ever spent in the studio. I was encamped there for sometimes 20 hours a day, for a year or so. Naturally, the rest of your life suffers as a result."[611]

The 14 minute version of *Black Box* "was the original version, albeit having been through many changes along the way. I always imagined that the opening sequence was an onlooker's reflection of events and when the electro section kicks in, the listener would find themselves actu-

---

[609] Taken from: Songs of Praise and Emotion, Blue Divide, Volume 2, Issue 1, 2000. Words: Uncredited.
[610] Taken from: recoil.co.uk. Words: Alan Wilder.
[611] Taken from: Recoil aka Alan Wilder – On hold for the time being, Side-line.com, 21 March 2004. Words: Bernard van Isacker.

ally on the 'plane at the beginning of its fatal journey.' In the end, the 'journey' section (which is very long) didn't seem to fit with the rest of the LP and I preferred the idea of splitting the 'reflection' and the 'aftermath' into two parts while replacing the middle section with the rest of the LP, acting as a man's life memories."

So this became the concept for the album, which was awarded as best album by the *Charles Gros Academy*.

Last Call for Liquid Courage (© Ingo Bittrich)

As usual, there was hardly a *Recoil* interview without *DM* being mentioned.

"I still have a little contact, mainly to Dave," **Alan** said. "However, since he lives in New York, we don't see each other often. When I was in New York on promotion tour I met him. Dave is in fantastic shape and we had a good laugh about lots of things - old and new. He is obviously besotted with Stella Rose and seems very content all round. I don't have really much contact to Martin and

Fletch. It's just a business affair. At least I'm proud and happy about my years with *DM*. They were good years. Of course, we had some problems but I have so many good memories in me that are important to many people and to me, and also for what I'm doing now."

But when asked whether he could be thinking of having Dave sing on a *Recoil*-album, **Alan** replied, "I don't think it would feel right. I like Dave very much but I want to work with different people. Did you think about that he perhaps couldn't be interested in collaborating with *Recoil?*"[612]

Even at that time - only three years after *Unsound Methods* - some people noticed that Alan didn't look happy, although he said he was again and again, and also that he had no regrets about leaving *DM*.

In **2001** he became a father for the second time and wanted to "enjoy family life." He obviously did at first. In **2004** he said that he was travelling around Europe, rekindling relationships with his family, spending time with his children, entertaining friends, playing tennis, etc. But then - according to his own words – he spent most of the time "on the sofa, drinking and watching sports." The reason for it was - according to him - that he was frustrated, having put so much work into his albums, but having to hear that people say they haven't been able to find his records in the shops.

Maybe he was also starting to realise - he was very interactive at this time and answered many fan questions (mainly about *DM*) - that he would never get rid of the ghost of *DM* whatever he did (as well as *DM* would never get rid of the ghost of Alan.)

There's no real connection, but nevertheless it's quite interesting that Dave once said about the *Devotional* period that they had created a kind of mafia for themselves – and that Nicole Blackman sang about *the black cotton mafia* in *Chrome*. When you listen to the lyrics you might get the impression she had been there.

On **5 June** *DM* went back into the studio and started to record *Exciter*. It was more or less the beginning of a new *DM* era. While *Ultra* had been a kind of outstanding experiment and a "project in between," with the remaining band members trying to face their demons and form a new

---

[612] Taken from: recoil.co.uk. Words: Alan Wilder.

band, *Exciter* marked the start of new working methods, and producing formulas that became typical for this and the following albums.

The sessions lasted until **January 2001** and took place in London, New York and Santa Barbara, where Martin had moved to in the meantime. This was one of the new formulas. The following albums were also recorded in these three cities.

They changed their working times to make it more enjoyable than in the past, when Alan used to work all night. "We all come in about 12:30 and get something to eat," **Fletch** explained. "I buy and read my newspaper. Then we tend to work all the way through till about 7 o'clock when we eat and then go back and finish. Then go out maybe or go home."[613]

After they had worked with Tim Simeon as producer on *Ultra*, they chose Mark Bell this time, and also had a different team. While they were looking for a producer, they were forced to realise that there weren't that many suitable producers for *DM*.

"When Alan left us, he was kind of our musical director he would help to take Martin's songs and develop them and push them to another place," **Dave** said. "When he left, we kind of had a hole there, you know, we didn't have anybody to do that. With the last album it was Tim Simenon and a crew of people working as well. And this one was just basically Mark Bell. And Martin seemed to be a lot more open to Mark, like, giving his influence, and he was a lot more open with me, as well, like experimenting with my voice more. On this album I kind of like do some different things with my voice that you wouldn't expect from me. And, you know, try to challenge myself a lot more, with songs like *Goodnight Lovers* and another song called *When the Body Speaks*. It's not typical of what I might sing on a *Depeche Mode* album. And then you also get Dave Gahan doing Dave Gahan in his gothicness on songs like *The Dead of Night* which is, you know. I get to play out all my favourite sort of roles."[614]

---

[613] Taken from: Interview with Fletch – Santa Barbara studio, California USA, Bong Magazine (U.S.), 31 October 2000. Interviewer: Michaela Olexova.
[614] Taken from: Interview with Dave, K-ROQ radio, 19 February 2001. DJs: Kevin and Bean.

Mark Bell "sees a voice as just another instrument." Something Dave probably didn't like that much. On the other hand, he felt encouraged and relaxed in a positive, creative way.

"I really liked the atmosphere Mark created for Bjork. After having worked with him, we realized how essential he was to those records,"[615] **Martin** said. "He can visualize sounds in his head. He goes to a keyboard, and he creates that sound. It's not even just about the keyboard sound - it's the whole vision of a song.[616] Mark is so good with sound, that I tend to take a background seat from that stage, and I'll tell him what I like and what I don't like, which is in a way kind of how I worked with Tim [Simenon] as well. Me and Tim would conceptually talk about the songs, and then put ideas out to the team, whereas this time I can leave Mark to do stuff. I can say 'I like that', 'I don't like that', 'I think that's good because of this or that' or 'That's not working because I think that's wrong for this song' ... just working like that."[617]

Martin is right when he says that people stay basically the same. I think he was used to working like that before, taking a back seat and acting as a kind of a director, and it was probably something Alan didn't like. ("We never worked as a group.") And evidently Tim Simeon and Mark Bell didn't like it either, otherwise they wouldn't have refused to work with them again.

Talking to **Steve Lyon**, he confirmed that Martin used to act like this back in the **1990's**. "Sometimes Martin would come in saying, 'I don't like this' and 'I don't really like that,' and then we would work on things to get a different version but he would trust a lot in the three of us, Alan, Flood and myself. And Fletch as well, y'know. Fletch would come in, say his thing but leave it to us because he knew something good would come out."[618]

Yes, he clearly trusted in the people he was working with but as Alan said, and also Dave said several times in later years that he sometimes seemed to forget to tell those

---

[615] Taken from: Q&A: Depeche Mode, Mean Street, May 2001. Words: George A. Paul.
[616] Taken from: Article in Keyboard, May 2001, Words: Robert L. Doerschuk.
[617] Taken from: Exclusive Martin Gore Interview, depechemode.com, 12 December 2000. Words: Daniel Barassi.
[618] depechemodebiographie.de

people that he valued what they did, although I'm sure he did value it. Remember him calling *Violator* "Alan's album," and naming it as his favourite one. So it's probably just a question of communication again.

It took a while before things got started because **Martin** had no ideas. He had six months in which he basically did nothing because he wasn't inspired. So he decided to get two friends in the studio to kick-start him. These two friends were Gareth Jones, who took over the role of the engineer, and Paul Freegard, who took over the role of the keyboard programmer. So, in the end, the songs were actually a lot more finished when they were brought to the studio stage.

According to **Gareth Jones**, the pre-programming took them about eight months. "Basically we were playing around with Martin's compositions. Martin would always come with a set of chords, vocal melody, and most of the lyrics for a song, and we would take it from there — trying different tempi and different timbres and atmospheres. Later we changed the keys for Dave."[619]

Again, they had a big production team, and some additional musicians were brought in.

"This time we did actually work with somebody that was really a totally off the wall coincidence," **Martin** said. "While we were recording in Santa Barbara, we were trying to put a percussion loop in time, and it was very complicated because it was a 4/4 loop over a 3/4 beat. This percussionist just happened to walk into the office, and Jonathan, our manager, was there and said, 'Oh, you're a percussionist. Maybe you can go in there and help him try and put this percussion loop in time.' So anyway, he came in and just introduced himself. He said, 'Oh, I'm a percussion player. My name's Airto. If you ever want me to do any percussion, just give us a call.' So we did a bit of research on him, and he's one of the top percussion players in the world. Apparently he can play a month at *Ronnie Scott's* in London." He laughed. "That one wasn't necessarily someone that we earmarked to work with, but it just happened to turn out that way."[620]

---

[619] Taken from: "Two-plus decades of platinum synth hits" - Interview with Gareth Jones, Keyboard Magazine, November 2001. Words: Greg Rule.
[620] Taken from: Exclusive Martin Gore Interview, depechemode.com, 12 December 2000. Words: Daniel Barassi.

As he had done on *Ultra*, **Dave** wrote some songs for *Exciter*, and played the demos to Martin. Both times he failed.

"The only time really that I plucked up enough courage to do that was during the making of *Ultra*. I had that song, actually, which then was called *The Ocean Song* and I played it to Martin, it was a really rough demo, I mean it's basically me tapping my foot and singing the melody and singing some words. I played it to Martin and he really liked it. And then for whatever reason during the recording it was presented to me that the song didn't really fit in with the theme."[621]

The Ocean Song would later end up as the B-side of the *Paper Monster* single *I Need You* in **2003**, titled *Closer*.

Almost the same thing happened when he played some demos to Martin during the making of *Exciter*. "He nodded his head and let me know that they were pretty good, but he never turned around and said, 'Great, let's record some of these for this album.'"[622]

This would lead to *Paper Monsters* and some internal problems. Strangely enough Fletch would blame Dave for Martin not reacting, because he had played the demos to Martin when he was drunk, and Dave hadn't asked him directly if the songs could be used for the album. This is probably more proof of their inability to communicate.

---

[621] Taken from: Dave Gahan: Paper Monsters Interview, EPK, Mute IPKSTUMM216.
[622] Taken from: Gahan Ditching Depeche Mode?, Rolling Stone (US), 20 August 2003. Words: Corey Levitan.

2001 H 2002

- Can you feel a little love? (Dream On) -

The first track they worked on was *Dream On*, the single that was released on **23 April 2001**. It suited the album's programme: a mixture of electronic beats with an acoustic blues guitar. As has become usual over the last few years, there are many different versions of this song available. The B-side was the instrumental track *Easy Tiger*. While the version on the album is a short interlude, the version on the single has an extended intro, and continues the song with a similar melody underpinned by a beat.

The video for *Dream On* was recorded in the desert in California. It's a kind of driving video. It was directed by the French film maker Stéphane Sednaoui. One of the special aspects of the video is that it was filmed on *Route 66*. Although Anton Corbijn didn't make the videos, he was nevertheless the art director for the sleeves, cover and stage design.

Allegedly, the atmosphere within the team had been excellent (which was to prove to be not quite true a little later.)

"In the past we weren't getting on as a band or as people," **Fletch** explained. "These days, we are getting on better than ever. It's a bizarre situation for *Depeche Mode* to be happy.[623] We did have a chat together at the start of this album. And any problems that we had with each other we sorted out." (Evidently they didn't because Dave wasn't happy with the situation.)

"We can say we had a really good time. I must say I didn't think a few years ago that I'd ever be able to say that. But don't worry, we still argue. We still have those tensions, but a band has to have tensions. Martin is one of my top three, top four friends. Dave I'd consider a brother. I don't have to be Dave's best friend to be in a band with him."[624]

---

[623] Taken from: Mode in Britain, Hot Tickets, 12-18 October 2001. Words: Andrew Panos.
[624] Taken from: Just Can't Get Enough, Uncut, May 2001. Words: Stephen Dalton.

Can you feel a little love? (Dream On) (© Ingo Bittrich)

"Dave and Andy are much more on the same wavelength," **Martin** said. "I don't know if they'll ever be close buddies, but they definitely get on better these days.[625] I think for the recording of this album, the inter- band relations were particularly good. We were actually able to sit down in a room and discuss things and make decisions, which sounds like a very simple and basic process, but it's something that we at one point would have avoided doing. Often our manager would have had to come to each one individually and talk to us about things; there was all kinds of weird stuff going on like that.[626] We got to a stage where we couldn't make any decisions because it would always end up in a fight. Now band meetings are actually

---

[625] Taken from: Hard drugs, alcoholism, nervous breakdowns at last Depeche Mode find, The Sunday Herald, 11 April 2001. Words: Uncredited.
[626] Taken from: Article in Virtually Alternative, April 2001, Words: Sat Bisla.

pleasant affairs. I took my daughter to one recently. I wouldn't have considered that a couple of years ago."[627]

"It's like a family thing, really," **Fletch** claimed. "On this record there are four songs with the word 'love' in it. It seems like *Exciter* is a love album, in a way."

"That is the main theme for the record - all of my songs are about relationships,"[628] **Martin** explained.

According to rumours, the working title of the album was actually *Love*. So much love was almost unbearable, especially for a biographer because it's boring to be honest. ;) There are tons of material from this time but it is all about getting on well. You read through 20 different interviews without finding any quote of interest. This was and is also part of the "new *DM*." This is, of course, nice for them after all the bad times they had had. One could raise the theory that this band probably needs some tension to produce a good album, but a good album is something different for everyone. Some fans didn't like *Exciter*, and it caused a lot of discussions but it's still a question of taste, and nothing you can have a real theory about.

On **14 May** the album *Exciter* was released, for which *DM* received the *Q-Award* for innovation. Although some fans didn't like it, it sold well. It debuted at No. 9 on the UK Albums Chart and at No. 8 on the *Billboard 200*, selling 115,000 copies in its first week in the U.S.

The plant that Anton Corbijn photographed for the cover of the album belongs to the genus Agave.

"We liked *Ultra* and *Violator*, we like to have some kind of theme throughout the years of *Depeche Mode*," **Dave** explained the title of the album. "Martin actually came up with the title [*Exciter*]. And what we did is we had a couple of other titles going on and stuck them up on the wall in the studio and kind of lived with them during the recording. And yeah, it just stuck. It sounds good."[629]

On **4 June** the *Exciter*-Tour started with the U.S.-leg.

In between, on **20 July**, the single *I Feel Loved / Dirt* was released. In **2002** *I Feel Loved* was nominated for two *Grammy Awards*, for *Best Dance Recording* and the *Danny*

---

[627] Taken from: Hard drugs, alcoholism, nervous breakdowns at last Depeche Mode find, The Sunday Herald, 11 April 2001. Words: Uncredited.
[628] Taken from: Article in Virtually Alternative, April 2001, Words: Sat Bisla.
[629] Taken from: Interview with Dave, K-ROQ radio, 19 February 2001. DJs: Kevin and Bean.

Tenaglia Remix for *Best Remixed Recording* but lost out. The single's B-side *Dirt* was originally written by *The Stooges*. It was used on the soundtrack to the film *Resident Evil* which was released in **2002**.

"I make life hard for myself," **Dave** said about *I Feel Loved*. "I'm in a band, and that's a compromise, and I bring something to *Depeche Mode* that I think is important and I express myself through somebody else's songs, which has been normal for years for me."[630] Being part of a family became a very important part of his life. He felt loved by his children and his wife although he felt he still had to work on himself. "I miss Jennifer [my wife], and my baby daughter Stella. I really have a life now. I have a life separate from *Depeche Mode*. It's the first time I've had that in years and I'm determined not to f*** it up. I still make mistakes but I'm there for it. I'm not running away any more."[631]

He seemed to be more relaxed than in previous years, although he wasn't satisfied with *Exciter* on the whole. He would be the one who brought back some tension into the band. (Probably he also couldn't stand all this love floating around. ;))

About *The Dead of Night* **Martin** explained, "We once lured into the privileged upstairs rookeries of London's poshest after-hours drinking establishments like *Soho House*, the *Groucho Club*, and *Brown's*. And it was a really sad scene. You had three levels - the regular bit downstairs, the slightly VIP but on the second floor, then upstairs the total VIP-VIP bit, which at *Brown's* was called the *Red Room*. And you got there, and everyone was taking so many drugs because it was commonly known that it was perfectly cool to take drugs there. So the *Red Room* for me was the *Zombie Room*, because everyone in there was always talking way too fast, saying nothing and just staring. And while you're there, all these people in the room are your best mates in the world. But the next day, if you bump into one of them on the street, you won't even know their name."[632]

---

[630] Taken from: In the Mode for Love, Time Out, 4 April 2001. Words: Omer Ali.
[631] Taken from: Many Smack-Free Returns! Q, June 2001. Words: Dorian Lynskey.
[632] Taken from: Article in Flaunt, May 2001, Words: Tom Lonham.

Some journalists shared the feeling of boredom, and dared to ask about "darker topics." For Alan for example, what consequences his departure had, especially on the sound of the last two albums.

"I do feel that Alan was a very important part of *Depeche Mode* and we do miss his input quite a lot," **Fletch** replied.

"That's very humble and kind of you, I'm sure Alan would appreciate that comment a lot." **Dave** laughed.

"To be honest, I think we got well-rounded by working with some interesting people that perhaps have got more involved because of Alan's departure," **Fletch** said. "Alan would have tended to take more control in the studio; it meant we had to rely on other people coming in, and so far we've been lucky."[633]

As it has been mentioned before – Alan was one of those topics that were repeated constantly. The band tried to fend it off, and finally one could get the impression that Alan had never been a part of *DM*. The same happened to the drugs theme.

"I'm bored to tears with talking about drugs," **Martin** said. "It seems anyone we ever talk to these days just wants to talk about drugs. Everyone's drug-obsessed. And, yeah, there have been drugs but, you know, that all happened so long ago - it's just so boring now. I don't know why you always have to talk about drugs. We did some interviews with some magazines and when they printed them, they were just all about drugs."[634]

At a certain point the band would claim that they couldn't remember anything about that time. This is understandable, as it is wearying to be asked the same questions all over again. On the other hand, they sometimes came across as rather impolite.

Growing older, they made quite a journey of self-discovery.

"In the old days, we'd come into L.A. for seven or eight days, and we'd immediately be checking out where every party is, every happening club," **Fletch** said. "But last night was different. I woke up this morning and thought,

---

[633] Taken from: Article in Virtually Alternative, April 2001, Words: Sat Bisla.
[634] Taken from: Time for a clean living Mode, Sunday Express, 22 April 2001. Words: Dominic Utton.

'God, I wish I hadn't had those extra two drinks!' I can't do my best on a hangover."

It's amusing that he was using almost the same words as Alan when asked, "why are you so f*** boring in the studio?"

Martin agreed. "In the past, we would've been out partying every single night that we were here. But last night was the first night this week that we actually ventured out of our hotel rooms, and only because of that one Grammy party. And I'm not saying that I didn't drink more than I should have, but I was aware of it. In the past, I would not have been aware of it. My main goal would've been to get as wild as possible and not care about the following day."[635]

Dave was realising now that he had put himself in a position to speak too openly about himself during the promotion for *Ultra*. "It came across like I was the first and the only junkie in the world that had been through it - but I lived like that. I take great comfort today in knowing that I'm one of millions of people desperately sadly looking for someone in their lives to make them feel good about themselves. The way I felt was so new to me, being clean and stuff, that's all I wanted to talk about because I wanted everybody else to feel that and there was a different way."[636]

About his tattoos, he said that he "regret all of them. I think I had some weird sense of putting myself through a lot of pain and, from that, I thought I was becoming stronger."[637]

Nevertheless, he's still showing them off whenever there's an opportunity. ;)

This reminds me of a quotation of **Ron Young** (*Little Ceasar*): "Musicians are exhibitionists. What any other reason they should have to show off themselves in front of so many people? Tattoos are for people who like to show off themselves – these two things go hand in hand. It's the same with a great soul-singer who shows off lots of emotions. Tattoos show off parts of your soul on your skin."[638]

---

[635] Taken from: Article in Flaunt, May 2001, Words: Tom Lonham.
[636] Taken from: In the Mode for Love, Time Out, 4 April 2001. Words: Omer Ali.
[637] Taken from: The Survivor, FHM, June 2001. Words: Caroline Rees.
[638] Taken from: Metal Hammer, article and author can't be found anymore. (Translated from German.)

Besides, **Dave** said, "From the start of *Depeche Mode*, Fletch and Martin were obviously real friends. They went to school together and I was the odd one out, and basically I've continued to be the odd one out throughout the whole life of *Depeche Mode*. We're very different personalities and I know Fletch and Martin hang out, but I don't think we'd ever hang out as a band. We do occasionally go to the pub and have a drink together, but that's it really. But that's alright, I'm OK with that now.[639] I have a feeling that Martin respects me as much as I respect him but he has an inability to actually acknowledge it. Martin's not the sort of person who turns around and pats you on the back and goes, 'that's fantastic.' To be honest, I wouldn't know what to do with that anyway."[640]

They also wonder about their fans and what would happen when both – themselves and the fans - grew older.
"I find it stranger every single time we put a record out and wherever we go we're followed by these obsessive fans. I mean they are so obsessive, and it's a real sort of compliment. But, I don't know, as you get older, maybe around sixty, I wonder if they'll still be there." **Martin** laughed. "Cause they're not much younger than us. We'll have grannies following us."
"We do have," **Dave** said. "In the hotel, there's a couple of fans that have their baby with them. There was another couple of fans that told me they wanted to come, and they have children, and their children were at home with babysitters and stuff like that. So I don't know, it's like, this little baby was already wearing black. It was a bit worrying!"[641]

Towards the end of the chapter a little tit-bit – Dave was on a radio show, a snippet of *Surrender* was played to him and he was supposed to guess which song it was.
Interviewer: "And you can't even identify it?"
Dave: "I haven't got a clue what it is."
Interviewer: "But it really is you, Dave?"

---

[639] Taken from: The Basildon Bond, The Times Magazine, 14 April 2001. Words: Paul Connolly.
[640] Taken from: Many Smack-Free Returns! Q, June 2001. Words: Dorian Lynskey.
[641] Taken from: Depeche Mode - Press Conference, Valentino Hotel, Hamburg, 3 March 2001.

Dave: "Yeah. That is me. Yes ..."
Interviewer: "You should see the look on his face. He's like, 'I can't figure out what this is.'"
Dave: "I ... you know ..."
The question was given to the audience and finally, someone phoned the radio station.
Dave: "It's probably Martin." (All laughed.)
But it was a girl who knew the right answer.
Dave: "*Surrender*! That was it! I knew that! I knew that ..."
Interviewer: "You SHOULD know that. You sang it!"
Dave: "I was getting there."
Girl: "Yeah. What a beautiful song it is. It's so beautiful, I always listen to it."
Dave: "Which album? Or ... was it like a B-side or?"
Girl: "Right. It comes out on *Only When I Lose Myself*."
Dave: "There you go. It was the B-side."
Interviewer: "She came up with it, right there. One mystery solved, right there."
Dave: "I knew that. I was just testing." (All laughed.)[642]

The European leg of the tour began on **28 August 2001** in Tallinn.

On **5 November** the single *Freelove / Zenstation* was released. The single version of *Freelove* is completely remixed from the album version. It was done by Flood although he had previously said he never wanted to work with *DM* again but of course, you don't need to when remixing a song.

Before, on **3 September**, *The Singles 81-98+* had been released.

In **2002** *Mute* was sold for £23 million to *EMI*. (Daniel Miller stayed managing director of the label, though.) And so finally, *DM* ended up as an *EMI*-act, something they had always tried to avoid. Nevertheless, they kept some of their independence.

At the same time, Fletch founded his own label *Toast Hawaii*. He mainly was busy to market the band *Client*.

On **11 February 2002** the single *Goodnight Lovers* was released. The single did not qualify for the UK Singles Chart because it had too many songs on it. Singles with

---

[642] Taken from: Interview with Dave, K-ROQ radio, 19 February 2001. DJs: Kevin and Bean.

more than one unique track need no more than three tracks while this single had four.

On **27 May** the concert video *One Night in Paris* was released, and on **25 November** *The Videos 89-98+* were released. *One Night in Paris* was directed by Anton Corbijn and was filmed at the *Palais Omnisports de Paris-Bercy* on **9 and 10 October 2001**.

2003

- There's a devil waiting outside your door (Loverman, Counterfeit 2) -

This year, Martin as well as Dave released solo records. It was the start of a partly quite amusing "bitch alarm." You had to fear there would never be another *DM* album ...

Martin began and released the single *Stardust / Life Is Strange* on **14 April**, followed by the album *Counterfeit 2* on **28 April**, and the single *Loverman* on **17 November**. From **24 April** to **7 May**, he went on a little solo tour, comprising 7 concerts.

Contrary to the years before, **Martin** was much more diplomatic but nevertheless, he made some statements which would lead to some trouble with Dave later. Like his answer to the question whether he had listened to Dave's solo album. "I was just this minute speaking to our manager about it. I've tried to pick up a package Dave has sent me three times but it seems to have got lost in the post."[643]

Some journalists seemed determined to dredge up old news, such as how his family had reacted to his clothing style in the **1980s**, and whether or not he was gay (okay, this was asked by a gay magazine ...)

"I think my father probably disowned me more than my mother. But it was the **1980s**: Everybody had a strange look pretty much – there was something funny in the air. I still think to this day that everybody assumes I'm gay, well, not everybody, but a lot of people assume that. It doesn't bother me. I never questioned my sexuality. I al-

---

[643] Taken from: 60 Second Interview: Martin Gore, Metro, 28 April 2003. Words: James Ellis.

ways felt totally heterosexual, very comfortable with my sexuality, very comfortable dressing like that – it wasn't a big deal for me. It seemed to be a big deal for everybody else."[644]

At the time, **Martin** had been living in Santa Barbara, California, for a while - with his wife Suzanne (the marriage broke down shortly after), their two daughters Viva-Lee and Ava-Lee as well as their son Calo Leon, who was born in **2002**.

"Well, I think I lead two totally separate lives. There are times when I have to slip into rock star mode and the majority of the time I'm at home with my family and nobody particularly knows who I am. I play football – soccer, they call it in America – three times a week, and for the first six months nobody in my team even knew who I was. And that's quite nice."[645]

Asked for his motives doing a record with cover-songs he explained, "When I was a kid I used to really love the Bryan Ferry cover records, so I quite liked the idea of doing this series of counterfeit records, just because I think it gives people an insight into my influences. It's not like when I do a cover version I expect it to live up to the original, they're just songs I like and that have in some way touched me on an emotional level.[646] I've been thinking about it for a long time but we had a lot of commitments with the band and I started to value my free time with my family. It's hard enough to combine having a family and being in a band at the best of times, so I put it on a back burner. Last year, I found out Dave was doing a solo album and so I thought it would be ideal."[647]

He went to see one of Dave's concerts, when Dave was touring *Paper Monsters*. While Martin said that it had been a strange experience for him because Dave had played a lot of *DM*-songs, **Dave** said, "He came to one of the LA shows, I hadn't seen him for a while, and afterwards - he'll probably hate me for this - he said, 'I really feel like I'm

---

[644] Taken from: The Return of Martin Gore, Boyz, 12 April 2003. Words: Uncredited.
[645] Taken from: Martin Gore: Counterfeit 2 Interview, Mute ICDSTUMM214
[646] Taken from: The Return of Martin Gore, Boyz, 12 April 2003. Words: Uncredited.
[647] Taken from: 60 Second Interview: Martin Gore, Metro, 28 April 2003. Words: James Ellis.

following you around now,' which shocked me because I'd been following him for so long."⁶⁴⁸

Obviously, it encouraged him to do what he did ...

Dave released the single *Dirty Sticky Floors / Stand Up / Maybe* on **26 May**, followed by the album *Paper Monsters* on **2 June**.

According to rumours Dave had asked Alan to play the piano on some songs or even to produce the album. There's one source saying, Alan refused because of having no time, while in this one the impression is given that **Alan** had never heard about it: "I'm not aware actually that Dave was after any of my so-called production skills. As you know, I try not to comment too specifically on the newer works of *DM* but I'm pleased for David. I'm sure it feels mighty fulfilling to have got some of his own writing off his chest and it's indicative of his state of mind that he got it done and is out on the road, which he clearly loves."⁶⁴⁹

Of course, **Dave** talked much more than Martin. "I just got the feeling, during the last band album, that it was something I had to do, and that it wouldn't be possible within *Depeche*.⁶⁵⁰ This album has helped me get rid of my insecurity."⁶⁵¹

About *Black and Blue Again* he said, "My wife and I had a huge fight, and I walked out of our apartment. I was on my way to the studio when it suddenly dawned on me that I was the one in the wrong. That song is basically me admitting that I'm not always a very nice person. I realized that relationships weren't easy, and I had to change."⁶⁵²

About *Dirty Sticky Floors*, "I had these huge *Wizard of Oz* statues in my Santa Monica apartment - the *Tin Man* and the *Cowardly Lion*. They pretty much became my companions. On any given night they'd begin talking to me. I ended up actually shooting the *Tin Man* ... he was

---

⁶⁴⁸ Taken from: Interview with Dave Gahan, Mojo, 22 March 2013. Words: Martin Aston.
⁶⁴⁹ Taken from: Recoil aka Alan Wilder – On hold for the time being, Side-line.com, 21 March 2004. Words: Bernard van Isacker.
⁶⁵⁰ Taken from: The Uncut Questionnaire: Dave Gahan, Uncut, July 2003. Words: Chris Roberts.
⁶⁵¹ Taken from: Facing my Monsters, Daily Mirror, 27 June 2003. Words: Gavin Martin.
⁶⁵² Taken from: Depeche Frontman in New Mode, Daily Mail, 2 May 2003. Words: Adrian Thrills.

the worst. It was complete paranoia. I mean, I'm laughing now, but it really was heavy at the time. Anyway, this song - I wanted to reflect the stupidity of addiction. To say, look, this is where it ends up - hanging out with the toilet bowl, with your head down it most of the time. Crawling around some dirty sticky floor, usually your own, on your own."[653]

From **5 June to 30 November** – with a break in **September** - Dave went on a solo tour. In the meantime, on **18 August**, the single *I Need You / Closer / Breathe* was released.

In **June 2003** Dave met Gavin Martin again who had described the shattering conditions behind the scenes of *DM* ten years before.

"Did I get aggressive with you?" **Dave** asked. "I remember reading what you wrote and it p***ed me off. But I was glad you did it. There were people like you who said 'Forget the music, this guy is sick and needs help.' But at the time I was beyond receiving help."[654]

At the beginning of the promotion tour, Dave was in a good mood. On the question whether he got a free subscription to *Mode Dépêche*, the French magazine they took the name from, **Dave** replied, "I don't, but they once wanted to do a photo session with us. Years before that there was a period of time where there were lawsuits flying around because we'd copied the name. Once we became more successful they let it go because we probably helped them to sell more copies. I always see it in the shop where I buy my magazines in New York and it's funny because it's similar to *House and Garden*."

And when questioned whether it was true that a few years ago a bloke had approached him for an autograph in the toilets while he was having a piss and he turned round and pissed all over him, **Dave** admitted, "Yeah, that is true. I can't remember where it was though. I don't mind signing autographs but when you're at the urinal and someone's standing next to you shaking with a pen it's a bit strange. I actually gave the guy an autograph, but I was still pissing so it splashed all over his feet and he did-

---

[653] Taken from: The Uncut Questionnaire: Dave Gahan, Uncut, July 2003. Words: Chris Roberts.
[654] Taken from: Facing my Monsters, Daily Mirror, 27 June 2003. Words: Gavin Martin.

n't notice because he was just so hell-bent on getting me to sign his bit of paper. I think now I'd just say, 'Piss off'." (Sorry for the unrefined expressions, but I like the pun ;-))

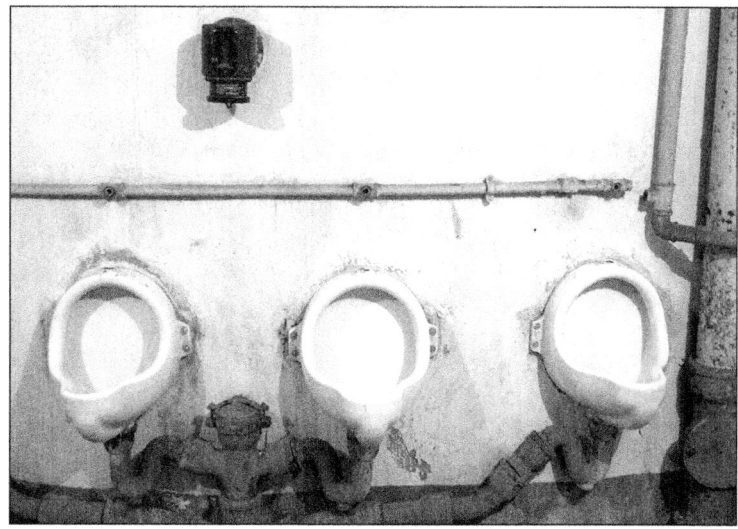

Never ask Dave for an autograph when ... (© Ingo Bittrich)

But over the course of time **Dave** had to realise that it wasn't so easy to release a solo record without any *DM* connection. Whether this was the reason or not – he started a kind of slugfest against Martin.

"Has Martin heard *Paper Monsters*? He called me and said, 'I've just got back from holiday and I've got a message that there's an album at the post office which I'll pick up, but what I'm ringing about is have you got a number for a chiropractor?'[655] I'm writing new songs, working with new musicians. I'm open to that, and if there's to be another *DM* record, Martin would have to be open to it as well. If he's not prepared to work as a team, I can't see that there's any point.[656] I don't know at the moment whether I could work for *DM* under the same conditions as before. I don't think so. One should let me have my say, listen to me and give me the feeling that my ideas are as important as Martin's. I sent Martin a copy of my album, I

---

[655] Taken from: Cash for Questions: Dave Gahan, Q, June 2003. Words: Paul Stokes.
[656] Taken from: Q&A Dave Gahan, Metro, 27 October 2003. Words: Rob Haynes.

had to ask for his. And Mart said, 'I asked my manager to send you one.' I said, 'You asked your manager for it? Move your a***, take a CD, put it into an envelope and send it to me, you arrogant a***!'"[657]

And it got even worse. In the course of time **Dave** reacted increasingly irritated and thin-skinned. "I'm not here to be judged by Martin Gore. I'm not his marionette. If Martin can give me what I have given him with his songs within all the years, then we can work together. I have a solo album ..."

But when he was asked about the perfect mode of operation with Martin and Fletch: "Well, listen: There aren't any plans, okay? Is that enough now? And Andy doesn't do anything in the studio, even the fans know this. He hasn't contributed musically to *DM* perhaps since *A Broken Frame*. It was Alan, Martin and me. Alan left the band and now it's Martin and me. I'm not going to carry on with *DM* just because it's such a big name. A new album must fill me with enthusiasm. It must come from our hearts. But at the moment I find it rather outrageous to ask me all these questions. I'm working with a cool band ..."

And when one dared to ask him about Alan ... "Alan left *DM* ten years ago. You should get over it. I do something else now and enjoy it!"[658]

Sometimes the media reaction was almost as bitchy as his, calling him an "insulted diva," comparing his lyrics with Martin's and sneering at "cliché afflicted cross rhymes." On the other hand, it was often his own fault. So there was an interview on an Austrian TV-show which was first shortened from twenty minutes down to ten minutes, and was finally broken off because Dave was in a very bad mood.

While Martin kept quiet at first (good decision), **Fletch** shot back. "Dave's talking nonsense. He has just released his first solo album and he's very proud of it with good reason. Therefore, he's on cloud nine at the present. But basically he knows, of course, that Martin is the songwriter. Martin's songs and Dave's voice - that is *DM*."[659]

---

[657] Taken from: Depeche Mode Am Ende?, Musikexpress, Juni 2004, Words: Albert Koch. (Translated from German)
[658] Taken from: Ich bin nicht Martin Gores Marionette, Laut.de, 6 November 2003, Words: Michael Schuh. (Translated from German)
[659] Taken from: Dave Gahan schwebt auf einer Wolke, Laut.de, 30 October 2003, Words: Michael Schuh. (Translated from German)

But **Dave** insisted on his opinion, "It's just not fun in the studio if you've got an idea for something and the person you're working with can't even be bothered to pick a guitar up. It seems to me like a waste of time. Unless he's open to both me and him coming into the studio with a bunch of songs and supporting each other, I don't see that there's any point in going on and making another *Depeche Mode* record. You know what? At this point, I don't really care."[660]

2004

- All alone with someone, and I should be so glad (A Little Piece, Paper Monsters) -

On **27 October 2003**, with *Bottle Living / Hold On*, another single of Dave was released, followed by the single *A Little Piece* on **9 February 2004**. Also, on **1 March**, the concert video *Live Monsters* was released.

In **2004** the bitching still persisted for a while, until peace was restored, and *DM* announced that there would be a new album.

"Unfortunately, Dave uses interviews as a therapy substitute sometimes," **Fletch** said. "He always talks a lot about things which are burning issues to him. He always tells journalists a lot to inflate his self-esteem, this is rather obvious. 'Why are you suddenly writing songs, Dave? Why didn't you do this before?' His answer was of course, 'Because Martin didn't let me.' This is complete rubbish because Dave had never shown any ambitions to write songs."[661]

This is the quotation in request. Already in **1987**, Alan had talked about Dave having song ideas, and there is a radio interview from **1994** in which Dave was thinking about making a solo record. Didn't Fletch know this? Maybe this quote is wrong, or it might have got lost in translation because it's only available in German. But

---

[660] Taken from: Gahan Ditching Depeche Mode?, Rolling Stone (US), 20 August 2003. Words: Corey Levitan.
[661] Taken from: Depeche Mode: Das ist Demokratie, Intro, October 2005. Words: Jürgen Dobelmann / Thomas Wenker. (Translated from German)

Dave also played demos to Martin during the recordings of *Ultra* and *Exciter*. He didn't ask him directly whether the songs could be used for these albums, but playing self-written songs to someone meant that "he had never shown any ambitions to write songs"?

"I was trying to let Martin know through the press that this was not something that was going to work for me again,"[662] **Dave** said.

One could wonder now why he didn't tell him directly. Why did he use the media to tell him? Well, the answer is always the same – this band isn't able to communicate.

"I want to know what Martin feels about me," **Dave** admitted, "but at the same time, I don't, because I feel like it's going to be the worst. He's really extroverted, but in other ways introverted — we're all like that. I really admire and respect him, and I see him having a hard time in his life right now," (Martin went through divorce from Suzanne at the time), "and I sympathize with him. After all these years, you'd think we'd know each other a lot better, but I don't think we really do."[663]

"It was a question of having to accept that or not carrying on with the band," **Martin** realised. "I wouldn't call it an ultimatum, but it was obvious to everyone involved that if Dave wasn't going to be contributing then he probably wouldn't be interested in carrying on."[664]

But he was also a bit offended and worried. "During the press for his solo record, he went a bit too far, saying stuff like he felt like a puppet and I was a dictator, and he felt he had a right to contribute. I realised during that period that if the band were going to continue then I would have to allow that to happen up to a point. But I didn't think it was right that after 25 years he should step in and write 50 per cent of the songs."[665]

"I said, 'I contributed to everything you've done all these years. I want some back now'," **Dave** said. "I said, 'let's shake it up a bit. I'm going to bring in my stuff.' Martin said, 'well, how many songs? How much?'"

---

[662] Taken from: Pop: It's good to talk, Sunday Times (US), 18 September 2005. Words: Dan Cairns.
[663] Taken from: Fighting Mode, Music Article, 14 October 2005. Words: Chris Willman.
[664] Taken from: Heroes of their degeneration, Times (UK), 30 September 2005. Words: Stephen Dalton.
[665] Taken from: Songs of Innocence and Experience, Mojo, November 2005. Words: Danny Eccleston.

"Dave came to that project with a lot of bravado," **Martin** said. "He wanted to write half the album! We were all a little cautious of that. He had just put out his first solo album and had really only just started writing."[666]

"Martin said, 'I think it's going to be very hard for *Depeche Mode* fans to take this'," **Dave** recalled. "I was like, 'Bulls***!'"[667] But he also said that he had known it would end up with a compromise.

So, is Martin a totalitarian dictator? ;)

"Yes, Dave called me a totalitarian dictator." **Martin** laughed. "Which was a little unfair because I'm not like that. Everyone who knows me knows that I'm not a totalitarian dictator."

"Oh, but you have your moments," **Fletch** chipped in. "But, yes, Dave said some strange things. But that's how Dave is. He always says what he thinks."

"Even in *DM* interviews he sometimes says things that let me think: 'What?!' But we know what he is like," **Martin** said. "He doesn't always say what he means."[668]

(Sometimes I think the same about some things Fletch says. Recently I found an article quoting **Fletch** with, "It was sad the way things turned out eventually, especially with Alan leaving. I miss him terribly; he is a good friend."[669] It made me think: 'What?!' Things definitely calmed down over the course of time but Fletch calling Alan a good friend, missing him terribly, really sounds strange to me.)

As an outsider it's difficult to consider if Dave's hurrying ahead was warrantable. Sure, Martin isn't exactly an innocent "fluffy bunny-wunny" either and it might be difficult to work with him, especially as he seems to consider the band as his in some way - but a dictator? But I don't know why Dave thought the solution might be to write songs on his own. Some fans had their difficulties with that. So Martin was quite right worrying about the idea of letting Dave write half of the album.

---

[666] Taken from: Depeche Mode in Mature Mode, Los Angeles Times, 28 March, 2009. Words: Chris Lee.
[667] Taken from: Songs of Innocence and Experience, Mojo, November 2005. Words: Danny Eccleston.
[668] Source can't be found anymore
[669] Taken from: Depeche Mode returns to basics with latest Album, Channel News (Asia), 14 October 2005. Words: Zul Othman.

At least Dave had realised that the band had a problem, especially after *Exciter*, which really divided their fanbase, (and the band had never been closer to split up as at that point.) And he tried to find a solution. Indeed, he preferred the Alexander method (cut the Gordian knot with a sword), but the bottom line is that he gave a new impulse to the band.

2005

- I thought we'd managed but words left unspoken (Precious) -

On **17 January** recording for *Playing the Angel* began in Santa Barbara, continued in New York and London, and like during *Exciter*, they noticed once again that they got on with each other much better now.

"The strangest thing that's happened is that we're all getting on pretty well," **Dave** said. "With the last album, it all felt a bit dead. This time we're all pulling together a lot more."[670]

Even **Martin** opened up a bit, although it was difficult for him. "The first line," he said about *Damaged People*, "is *we're damaged people, drawn together by subtleties we're not aware of*. And I think that happens all the time with dysfunctional people, me included."[671]

In later articles it became obvious that the atmosphere wasn't as great as they had claimed.

"Martin was drunk most of the time,"[672] **Dave** said and admitted that making *Playing the Angel* hadn't been enjoyable. "When he came in the studio we knew we had a few hours: he's a little drunk right now, he's going to get drunker. Ben Hillier put a guitar around his neck and ran around getting as much out of him as he could."[673]

---

[670] Taken from: In the Studio: Depeche Mode, Q, July 2005. Words: Uncredited.
[671] Taken from: Fighting Mode, Music Article, 14 October 2005. Words: Chris Willman.
[672] Taken from: Depeche Mode on synths, drugs and Basildon, The Times (UK), 21 March 2013. Words: Ed Potton.
[673] Taken from: We're dysfunctional. Maybe that's what makes us tick, The Guardian (UK), 28 March 2013. Words: Dorian Lynskey.

Because later Martin would pass out and wasn't able to work anymore.

So, at least there weren't that many changes.

The original title of the album was *Pain and Suffering in Various Tempos*. It was based on Dave joking about it when asked about a title during the first recording session. In the end, it was printed on the back of the album. The title which was finally chosen is referring to the line *oh, you sad one, playing the angel* in the track *The Darkest Star*.

While the way of producing the album and the main topics weren't so different to *Exciter*, it was new that **Dave** contributed three songs to the album. "It's about that I still can't allow any feelings. There is this side in me that is a bit strange. I could never write a song about the euphoric beginning of a relationship. It's difficult for me to handle the love that is given to me whether of my family or of my friends. Perhaps I have been disappointed once too often in my life. I have actually everything. I feel loved but I often don't use this wonderful supply because it's hard for me to let anyone get close to me. I'm afraid of opening my soul and give myself completely to someone else. Through this my life is more difficult than it has to be. Maybe the reason for it lies in any debt in my subconscious, deep dug in my childhood. I don't know. My wife tries to cheer me up then. We are very similar in this regard. It's not by chance that you surround yourself with people with whom you can share such feelings."[674]

They also had a new producer, Ben Hillier, a choice that parts of the fanbase didn't really like, the music fans especially weren't that happy. The band had – of course – a different view on this issue.

"*Depeche Mode* has always had a specific sound and it's not necessarily easy to detach oneself from it," **Dave** said. "It just exists there. But Ben Hillier took us to a whole different new direction. And that is exactly why it is so exciting and thrilling to work with people like him. We wanted to work with someone who would push us further and experiment more."[675]

---

[674] Taken from: The Dark Side of the Mode, Kulturnews, October 2005. Words: Stefan Woldach.
[675] Taken from: Radio interview with Dave and Martin, Eins Live, 17 June 2005. Interviewer: unknown.

"Ben came to the table not really even being a fan of our music," **Martin** added. "He knew a few songs and we had to actually get him the whole catalogue for him to listen to. But he really had an idea of how he wanted to approach this and he was aggressive with that and I think we needed that."[676]

He was also great at "breaking down the shit that forms between family members," **Dave** explained. "Seeing very quickly the sort of roles we had devised for ourselves and going, 'This is ridiculous.' We wanted to have somebody who was a headmaster-type figure. But he was like the art teacher - you know, the one who would let you into the storeroom to bum a cigarette."[677]

And it seems as if **Dave** also used him as a kind of accomplice for pushing through his idea of shared songwriting because Hillier had to choose the songs for the album. "At that point, Martin had maybe written five songs, and I had, like, 15. That kind of became the catalyst to make Martin write more songs. And there was one point where I was like, 'You need to write some more songs, or we're going to have to use mine.'"[678]

Obviously, he put some pressure on **Martin** who wasn't well at the time, suffering from his divorce. "When people meet me I think they're surprised to find out I'm not always angst-ridden. But I think anything that I write comes from the soul. I don't write poems and put them to music. Just let things flow."[679]

He tried to work differently, put more importance to the atmosphere of the songs. **Dave**, on the other hand, was still at a learning stage and had to find a good working process for himself.

"I'm not patient," he admitted. "That's my problem. And I forget stuff really quickly. I have this guy in New York who helps me out, and he has lists for me everywhere of like, 'This is how you record a vocal,' 'This is how you set up your mic,' or 'This is how you access the keyboard.' I've got all these lists everywhere, and I still manage to fuck it

---

[676] Taken from: Mode Turn Angelic, Manchester Evening News, 24 March 2006. Words: Kevin Bourke.
[677] Taken from: Pop: It's good to talk, Sunday Times (US), 18 September 2005. Words: Dan Cairns.
[678] Taken from: The Long Ride Home, Remix Mag, 1 November 2005. Words: Robert Hanson.
[679] Taken from: A La Mode, Gaywired, 2 November 2005. Words: Lawrence Ferber.

up. Christian [Eigner] and especially Andrew [Phillpott]," with whom he was working out his songs for this album, "are a lot more technical, and I kind of leave that up to somebody else so I can just kind of be free and go wherever I want to go with the song or with the melody."[680]

And what was **Fletch** doing? "The truth is, I don't write songs," he replied. "I have no interest. I play a bit of keyboards but I took an interest in the business side of the band, dealing with the record label and our daily affairs. Martin and Dave are the backbone of the band, I suppose I'm the guy who brings them together."[681]

On **3 October** the single *Precious / Free* was released. There were several different versions of *Precious* available, while there was only one different version of *Free* available. The B-side was unavailable in the U.S., aside from importing. *Precious* was a quite successful single. It made No. 1 in some countries, reached No. 4 in the UK and No. 71 on the *Hot 100*. The video was directed by Uwe Flade. An early version of the video (with unfinished rendering and many sketch placeholders) was leaked on the Internet long before the song was released, so most fans were able to listen to it about two months ahead of the release.

On **17 October** the album *Playing the Angel* was released, for which *DM* won the *MTV European Award* in the category best group. All songs were written by Martin, except *Suffer Well, I Want It All* and *Nothing's Impossible*, which were written by Dave, Christian Eigner and Andrew Phillpott. Dave took care of the lead vocals on all tracks, except on *Introspectre*, an instrumental interlude, and on *Macro* and *Damaged People*, which were sung by Martin. An additional musician was Dave McCracken (piano.)

The character on the album cover is a little creature called *Mister Feathers*. (The band calls it *Tubby Goth*.) It was designed by Anton Corbijn.

The media didn't believe in the sudden harmony, therefore the previous "bitch alarm" was picked up again (among all the other well-known topics – weird clothes in the past, being gay, drugs, Alan's leaving ...)

---

[680] Taken from: The Long Ride Home, Remix Mag, 1 November 2005. Words: Robert Hanson.
[681] Taken from: Depeche Mode returns to basics with latest Album, Channel News (Asia), 14 October 2005. Words: Zul Othman.

"I find a quarrel very healthy and beneficial if it's about ideas," **Dave** said. "But not if it's about ego. This was my problem in the past. I have never said clearly enough: 'Here, I have some ideas, I want you to help me.' I simply couldn't say it. For this album I formulated it for the first time and was greeted with open arms."[682]

But there still was some tension, about the concept of the video for *Precious,* e.g. "The director was just going through the concept of the video, and that he wanted us to be playing in this futuristic ballroom," **Martin** said. "And Dave said, 'Well if it's a ballroom, Andy, I think you should play a piano,' and Andy said, 'Well if it's a futuristic ballroom maybe it would look better if I play an old synth.' Suddenly Dave's shouting, 'Well I only want what's best for the band!' and he's stormed out."[683]

Speaking of funny things, there were some amusing moments this year.

Hilarious interview with Martin and Fletch which was published on *aol.de,* shortly before *DM*'s appearance at *TOTP* on **8 September** and which, unfortunately, can't be found anymore. Therefore, the name of the journalist who met the two for a wheat beer is unknown.

Martin: "The beer was my condition for this interview."

Fletch: "He's been drinking non-stop for 14 hours."

Martin: "A new journalist comes in every half an hour, and I get a new beer every half an hour. That's the deal. I have to be fit tomorrow, though, because of *TOTP*. We're alone at the show. We are even a bit angry that we won't meet Nena this time."

Journalist: "Do you like her?"

Martin: "She was quite cute 20 years ago."

Fletch: "She has four children, one more than you, Martin. And she's shaving her armpits now."

Martin: "Every journalist comes in, saying, 'I like the album.' In the past, there used to be real discussions with the rock journalists, heated discussions about what the songs are worth. This was extremely more fun. To take the cassette recorder from a journalist and throw it out of the window was fun, too. Good old days. In the **1980s**, we

---

[682] Taken from: The Dark Side of the Mode, Kulturnews, October 2005. Words: Stefan Woldach.
[683] Taken from: Songs of Innocence and Experience, Mojo, November 2005. Words: Danny Eccleston.

were at least hated. Now, everybody accepts electronic music, and we are in the pop shelves. We're terribly mainstream. We wouldn't make any albums anymore if we weren't sure they're important and relevant beyond their time. It would be really sad to be like the *Rolling Stones*. Everybody wants to see them, but then they only want to hear *Paint It Black* or *Satisfaction*."

Fletch: "But, Martin, people also come to us because of *Just Can't Get Enough*."[684]

During an interview with a German radio station Martin and Dave were asked whether they speak German.

„Ich habe Deutsch in der Schule gelernt. Und ich habe eine Weile in Berlin gelebt. Ich hatte eine deutsche Freundin." **Martin** laughed. „Ja, ich spreche nicht gut Deutsch, aber ich spreche okay Deutsch." [I have studied German at school. And I have been living in Berlin for a while. I also had a German girlfriend. Yes, I don't speak very good German, but I speak okay German.]

"I'll stick to 'Spiegelei mit Bratkartoffeln, ohne Toast'." **Dave** laughed. [Fried egg with fried potatoes, no toast.][685]

In another interview the band members were asked to say, separate from each other, what they liked about the other two.

"Martin, I've known him since the age of 11, and he's one of the nicest men I've ever met," **Fletch** said. "Dave, he staggers me with his performance every night."

Martin also managed this task well. "Dave is extremely disciplined. And Andy's excessively organised."

But **Dave** was apparently caught unprepared. "Um ... tell you something great? Oh, that's much harder than I thought. I couldn't tell you something great about myself. Well, Martin ... You know what? That's a really difficult question. You just landed that one on me. ... Well, Fletch is, um ... I can't think of anything. Do I get to hear what they said?"[686]

---

[684] Taken from: Interview on aol.de. Source can't be found anymore. (Translated from German.)
[685] Taken from: Radio interview with Dave and Martin, Eins Live, 17 June 2005. Interviewer: unknown.
[686] Taken from: Showtime! Q, February 2006. Words: Johny Davis.

2006

*- Even the stars look brighter tonight
(Nothing's Impossible) -*

On **28 October 2005** *Touring the Angel* began in New York.
"Any tour is a mixture of excitement and fear," **Martin** said. "Andy always says that if you don't get some kind of adrenaline rush then there is something seriously wrong. And that is true. Being on tour tends to be very grueling. For me the shows themselves are not particularly grueling but for Dave as the front man they are extremely so. Dave is very good front man and he expends a lot of energy every night. It is not the shows that I find taxing, it is everything else that revolves around the tour. It's the travelling and the different hotels every night. There is always someone trying to take you somewhere. We are all a little bit older this time and I think we will have to start declining a few of these offers."[687]

I was asked by a reader when Martin started wearing wings on stage. It was during *Exciter*-Tour. Obviously he has a crush on angels. The same reader asked whether the band member have special designers who make their stage clothing. Yes, each member has his own designer, in Martin's case it's mostly Sara Freegard.

On **12 December** the single *A Pain That I'm Used To / Newborn* was released. Although *Better Days* was mentioned to be the B-side for the single in its press release, it ended up being the track called *Newborn*. *Better Days* went on to be the B-side of the following single, *Suffer Well*. The single was only physically released in Europe. Again, the video for *A Pain That I'm Used To* was directed by Uwe Flade.

On **13 January 2006** the European leg of the tour started in Dresden.

In the meantime, on **27 March**, the single *Suffer Well / Better Days* was released. It was the first single that was written by Dave. It was nominated in the category *Best Dance Recording* at the **2007** *Grammy Awards* but lost

---

[687] Taken from: Angels by Design, Santa Barbara Independent, 17 November 2005. Words: Brett Leigh Dicks.

out. The video was directed and filmed by Anton Corbijn in **mid-December 2005** in California. It was the first time after some years break that Corbijn made a video for *DM*.

About the line *where were you when I fell from grace* in *Suffer Well* **Dave** said, "It was definitely a little dig at them. I didn't write it like that but when I sang it, I did picture Martin. It was, 'What didn't you understand that I needed you the most then. Where was the f*** answers when I needed them most?' When I finally hit a wall, of crawling across the floor of that apartment in Santa Monica, I felt myself dying. I felt my soul had gone and inside I was screaming, 'Where the f*** are you?!'"

I suppose this is one of those statements about which Martin said he'd think, 'What?!' And I don't think Dave meant it as he'd said it. He just jumped on a suggestive question from the journalist because it sounded so nice at that moment.

"I've been accused of being closed, emotionally, and it's true up to a point," **Martin** admitted. "Sometimes I find it difficult, dealing with life in general. Music helps me there. It's some kind of therapy. There are obviously things I feel guilty about in my life. I'm in the middle of my divorce at the moment. I've got three children." – That's what the lyrics of *Precious* are about. – "I feel like I've failed in my marriage. I feel guilty about that because of the children. Maybe the marriage was partly a charade for a while anyway. Maybe I felt guilty about that for ... I don't know how many years. We're a very non-talkative band. I think, deep down, we all want the same thing, but it only takes one person to say something slightly off the beaten track for someone to take it wrongly and for it all to go off. But why not look at it another way? We've been together 25 years, so we must be doing something right."[688]

From **27 April** to **21 May**, the band returned for 12 concerts to the U.S., Canada and Mexico. On **2 June** the second European leg started.

In the meantime, on **5 June**, the single *John the Revelator / Lilian* was released. It was the first double A-side release since *Blasphemous Rumours / Somebody* in **1984**. *John the Revelator* is based on an **early 20th century**

---

[688] Taken from: Songs of Innocence and Experience, Mojo, November 2005. Words: Danny Eccleston.

gospel/folk song performed by Son House, Blind Willie Johnson, and later by *The Holy Modal Rounders*, *The Blues Brothers* and John Mellencamp. It's not a cover song as such but is working with several elements of the original track.

On **25 September** the concert video *Touring the Angel: Live in Milan* was released. It was directed and filmed by Blue Leach on **18 and 19 February 2006** at the *Fila Forum* in Assago near Milan, Italy.

On **30 October** the single *Martyr* was released. It was linked to *Best of Depeche Mode Volume One* which was released on **13 November**. The song, originally titled *Martyr for Love*, is a missing track from the *Playing the Angel* sessions. It was considered to be the first single but in the end it did not make it onto the album.

"It isn't a release for the big fan," **Fletch** said about the *Best of*. "This one has the songs anyway. The record is aimed more at people who only have a few *DM* records, or even none at all. We discussed the selection of the songs a lot. It was difficult. Every big *DM* fan probably has a completely different list of favourite songs. I associate many memories with every song, for example how we recorded it and whether we had good or bad times."[689]

Altogether *Playing the Angel* (including the tour) was a great success. Many fans liked the livelier and "edgier" *Playing the Angel* better than *Exciter*, and it brought many new fans to the band. The internet helped, too, or the fact that in **2006** many more people had internet access than in **2001**. Many fans are in networks nowadays talking about their collections and interests and making appointments for parties and concerts. The "devoted community" (or *Black Swarm*) came alive a second time, although in a different way than in the **1980s**.

Sometimes it doesn't work at all because some "old" fans, who still hang on to "their" band but have increasing problems with what *DM* is doing and releasing today, get into trouble with "new" fans. And the difference gets bigger so there are almost two communities today – "the fans who want Alan back moaner community" and the "I like most what they do who the f*** is Alan community."

---

[689] Taken from: DM: Das haben wir uns verdient, ZEIT Online, Tagesspiegel, 6 November, 2006, Words: Nadine Emmerich. (Translated from German)

While the "old timers" often have their difficulties with the newer stuff from the band, the younger fans often don't understand the real old stuff, but it's interesting that most of them nevertheless often name *Black Celebration, MFTM, Violator* or *SOFAD* as their favourite albums, along with the newer ones with which they found their way to the band. There are only a few who say that they have difficulties with *Violator* or *SOFAD* because of "all the drug stories."

Every album from the "post-Alan-era" had its critics, (although critics of the critics say that even an album like *Violator* got bad reviews) and these critics get louder from album to album. The highpoint was reached at *SOTU* which divided the fans more than ever before. Of course, the fans are still devoted, but it's noticeable that in the survey of *depechemodebiographie.de* most answers (34%) applied to "the former days." Of those there are 24% saying that "the sound (without Alan) is not longer that complex / rich / bombastic / atmospheric / orchestral". And 24% - applying to "today" - said that the "quality isn't as high anymore." It is also noticeable that 77% of the answers applying to former times are positive, while there are only 54% positive answers applying to today. That they "lost their typical sound" is one of the central points in the endless "Alan-discussion."

I found an interesting statement from **Bruce Dickinson** (*Iron Maiden*) about this. Of course, he is referring to *Iron Maiden* but it nevertheless suits *DM* as well. "I think that fans are very old fashioned in general – whatever they are fans of. In that very moment you discover something you like you want to keep this for you. If you like a painter who tells you one day that he won't paint anymore but works as a sculptor, you'll be disappointed. It is the same with the music business. Musicians are always trying to find something new so as not to get bored. But fans are only entertained by songs they really like. They don't want completely new things, but consistency."[690]

---

[690] Taken from: Article in Metal Hammer, April 2002. Words: Matthias Mineur. (Translated from German)

2007

*- I'll take a line of everything you've got
(Intruders, SubHuman) -*

After having released *Liquid* Alan announced that he would release another album quite soon. But it took until **25 June 2007** before the single *Prey* was released, followed by the album *SubHuman* on **9 July**, for which he got the *IGN-Award* (best electronic album.)

SubHuman (© Ingo Bittrich)

The media was astonished by the long break, so almost every interview would start with the question as to why **Alan** had been away for such a long time. His answers varied from that he wanted to spend more time with his family to "I did make some feeble attempts to write music on a few occasions but didn't posses the will to battle through - which I took as a sign that I needed a longer break"[691] and ended with explanations that he had been a bit frustrated about having put so much work into *Liquid*, but people had difficulties finding the albums in the shops.

There were also interviews in which he – between the lines or directly – admitted that he hadn't done much during that time, until his wife had had enough of all this hanging around, drinking, watching sports, doing nothing ..., and "encouraged" him to go back into the studio. He realised then that he was more pleasant when he was creative.

After a technical update in his studio, he started to work on *SubHuman*. He had no real idea where the album was headed when he started. It soon became clear that the basic of the album was a mix of electronic and swamp-blues.

Therefore, he was looking for an intensive, authentic blues singer. He found Joe Richardson (a white blues singer from New Orleans) via the Internet and started to work with him. He sent him some music to which Joe worked out some lyrics and then finally, they met in Texas.

"I think one of the most exciting moments was going over to Texas to record with Joe," **Alan** recalled. "He's such a fantastic musician anyway. He was able to give me even more than I expected because he's also a great guitarist and harmonica player and has a wonderful voice. We recorded in a very very special sort of semi-commercial studio, it's really open to only friends, really, with a guy who had massive of old vintage equipment. There were moments then when I thought: 'This is what *Recoil* is all about.' The mixture of musicians from completely different areas coming together to make something modern and new in an interesting way, you know. It was great."[692]

---

[691] Taken from: Article on Shout!, 7 July 2007. Words: Alex Davie.
[692] Taken from: "Recoil in Bucharest- Interview with Alan Wilder", depechemode.ro, 2010. Words: Otiliei Haraga.

After this recording session, Alan was looking for a second voice to bring in a balance to Joe's very distinctive voice. It took some time before he found Carla Trevaskis.

Finally, the title was found – *SubHuman*, which led to some speculations whether it might be a "political" album.

"I do not have some great political message to bring to the world - the *SubHuman* concept is much more to do with human nature," **Alan** explained. "The title is designed to be slightly provocative but not directed towards any specific group - it can also apply to racism and homophobia, class or politics and so on. It represents a repeating pattern of human behaviour where subordination occurs in a seemingly endless cycle, often with tragic consequences, and where people are rendered as worthless. The artwork design came from Jesse Holborn who came up with various ideas and I was attracted to the mannequins, shown in everyday situations to represent recyclable lifeforms."[693]

In **2007 Alan** also collaborated in the re-releases of old *DM* albums. "I don't think that any other band member would have had the time or the interest to get involved with this project. I'm interested in everything that has to do with records, recordings or production. But the main reason why I was asked was: I had all the rare sounds." He laughed. "But the aim wasn't to produce radical new mixes of the old songs. I was involved only sporadically, just listened to the songs, saying 'yes', 'no', 'yes' ..."[694]

He also provided some of his private film-material for the re-released documentary. While he didn't really like the commentaries (I can see why: they tend to brighten things up. They don't lie! They just understate things in a way the band members wish they had happened) he enjoyed the short films nevertheless.

"It's something we started years and years ago, like twenty years ago," **Dave** commented on the rereleases. "It's kind of interesting because you get to give your music that you've finished to somebody else to mess around with and put their own input into it. Yeah, it's something we've always done. It's become a part of what we do."[695]

---

[693] Taken from: Article on Shout!, 7 July 2007. Words: Alex Davie.
[694] Taken from: "Youtube ist einfach klasse", laut.de, 2007. Words: Michael Schuh. (Translated from German)
[695] Taken from: Depeche Mode conclude reissue series with Ultra and Ex-

Building a tower of fear by the river (21 Days)
(© Ingo Bittrich)

Speaking of Dave - on **8 October** he released his solo-single *Kingdom / Tomorrow*, followed by the album *Hourglass* on **22 October**. Again, he had worked together with Andrew Phillpott, who belongs to the *DM*-Team, and Christian Eigner, the live-drummer of the band.

The album was some kind of "accident" or "occupational therapy" because after the end of *Touring the Angel* **Dave** didn't know what to do with so much free time.

"I went home and tried to get back in the swing of things. It's always quite difficult after a tour - you're kind of waiting for somebody to put a note under your door with what it is you've got to do that day." He laughed. "You create new obsessions, like how to load the dishwasher correctly and stuff like that.[696] All the big fights with my wife start with the dishwasher. It shows you how it's supposed to be loaded: knives and forks go pointed-end downwards. You get more in if you put everything where it's supposed to go. If Jen goes out of the room and I get

---

citer, ArtisanNewsService, 30 July 2007. Words: Uncredited.
[696] Taken from: Article in Prefix, 25 March 2008, Words: Jen Zipf.

the chance before it goes on, I will fiddle with it.[697] It's like you get locked into this type of personality that functions pretty well in the performance mode, but is not what you want to take home," he explained. "It's like, 'I want it all, I want it now, I'm going to take it whenever I want it, and I don't really care what you think about it.'"

He also admitted that he, "still can be the kind of person that's like, 'F*** it! You know what? This ain't working, it's over.' I jump straight to that rather than, 'Let's talk about this.' It's very childish. My wife often says to me, 'God, you're like Jimmy! You're acting like a teenager!' And I'll stomp around the room saying, 'So what?!' But it doesn't work."[698] After he had annoyed his family for about a month, as he said, it was suggested to him to do some work, so he planned to get together with Christian and Andrew to do some writing.

The first song they worked on was *Saw Something*. "The lyrics are about sitting, waiting for something to come - protection of some kind, or some kind of answer. What I've come to learn is that you've got to go find it, take some action. I prefer to sit and wait, but it just doesn't work. It sounds kind weird, but I do believe in that sort of divine intervention, if you allow it. If you allow life to happen, not try to push it in the direction you think it's supposed to go in — which is what I spend a lot of time doing — then really amazing things happen, things that you didn't expect. But you've got to take some action."[699]

Otherwise, there wasn't any concept at first. "When we started, we had a few musical ideas, but nothing song-like in any way. We really wrote as we went along. After two weeks, we looked around and realized we weren't just demoing, so we thought, 'Why don't we just make a record?'[700] We decided to produce it ourselves, which was a lot more work than we thought."[701]

Nevertheless, they finished the recording process in a speedy eight weeks.

---

[697] Taken from: "This much I know", The Guardian, 28 October 2007. Words: Johnny Davis.
[698] Taken from: I don't want to lose what I have, Scotsman, 29 September 2007. Words: Paul Lester.
[699] Taken from: Article on Shout! 28 January 2008. Words: Alex Davie.
[700] Taken from: Gahan Digs 'Deeper' On Second Solo Album, Billboard.com, 2007. Words: uncredited.
[701] Taken from: Article on NME.com, 6 September 2006. Words: uncredited.

And not *Saw Something* became the first single but *Kingdom*. "It's this idea that there's a better place, and it's not up there in the clouds, it's right here," **Dave** said. "And it's about becoming more accepting of life and the way it is. I would be lying if I said the world didn't affect me. I have children and I want to protect them; and sometimes I don't really have the ability to do that."[702]

After *Paper Monsters* had been a very personal album, one could suspect that *Hourglass* also contains autobiographical elements.

"I'm becoming more accepting of the fact that I'm getting a little older," **Dave** admitted. "It always seems to be a theme in my life that I'm racing against time. I'm a 25-year-old in a 45-year-old man's body. I wrote about those themes more, like, this is who I am and these are my frustrations.[703] My inspiration comes from the life that I have around me - you know, being part of a family and desperately trying to do better at that," he laughed, "and falling flat on my face most of the time. And New York is a great place to feel inspired all the time. I quite often spend time walking around being among people here.[704] My little studio is on one of the busiest streets in the city so you get the flavour of New York all day and all night long: On the track called *Endless*, you can hear the street in the background. At one point you'll hear the 'woop' of a cop car. But we just left it."[705]

So maybe he used it as some kind of therapy? "Well, I'm not in therapy - I actually now have a run-of-the-mill psychiatrist. I've moved away from the 'be gentle with yourself' kind to, like, getting down to the nitty-gritty. I actually find it a lot more ordered. With a psychiatrist, it's more like, 'So, what do you think that means, David?' That kind of stuff. 'I don't know, I'm paying you to tell me what it f***ing means!'"[706]

---

[702] Taken from: Depeche Mode's Dave Gahan Returns With 'Hourglass,' Starpulse, 11 October 2007. Words: Uncredited.
[703] Taken from: Gahan Digs 'Deeper' On Second Solo Album, Billboard.com, 2007. Words: uncredited.
[704] Taken from: Article in Prefix, 25 March 2008, Words: Jen Zipf.
[705] Taken from: Article on NME.com, 6 September 2006. Words: uncredited.
[706] Taken from: I don't want to lose what I have, Scotsman, 29 September 2007. Words: Paul Lester.

On **14 January 2008** the single *Saw Something / Deeper and Deeper / Love Will Leave* was released. Dave decided not to tour because on **5 May 2008**, *DM* started to record *SOTU*.

2008

- Do we believe in love at all? (Kingdom, Hourglass) -

In **spring 2008** *DM* began to record *Sounds of the Universe (SOTU)*. Again, they recorded in three different cities – Santa Barbara, New York and London. Again, they worked with Ben Hillier as producer – "We thought that it worked very well with *Playing the Angel*, and we were very comfortable with him,"[707] **Fletch** said - and again Martin and Dave shared the songwriting.

Once more, they had a "nice friendly atmosphere" and a lot of fun in the studio. Again, these were the main topics in the media. After you had read one article about it, you didn't need to read another. (I nevertheless did it of course. ;))

"Dave was in quite a strange position — it's rare for a frontman not to write lyrics," **Fletch** said, "but now he's been writing songs for the last two albums and he feels more a part of it.[708] I think generally Dave writing songs has really glued him a bit more to the group, and he's so much more confident and fulfilled. It's one of the main reasons the band is really gelling together. Dave's songwriting is improving all the time. You know, it's sometimes hard to actually distinguish between Dave's songs and Martin's songs."[709]

This time Martin did go about the whole song writing process in a totally different way. The actual writing process he did on a lap top which was much quicker. He wrote about 18 or 20 songs this time. With Dave's songs included they had 22 songs of which they recorded 18.

---

[707] Taken from: Catching Up With ... Depeche Mode's Andrew Fletcher, Paste, 7 May 2009. Words: Grant Shellen.
[708] Taken from: Masters Of Their Universe, The Times, 3 May 2009. Words: Uncredited.
[709] Taken from: Interview on Dmdotcom, 23 January 2009. Words: Daniel Barassi.

Sounds of the Universe (© Ingo Bittrich)

There were only a few new things that happened. One was that Martin stopped drinking – a topic you could find in almost every article in that time. Of course, it was at least more interesting than getting on well, although Martin had already given up drinking three years previously during *Touring the Angel*.

"He is a changed man," **Dave** said. "There's a different side of Martin that has always been there, but sometimes it gets clouded when the drinking and stuff becomes more important than anything else. I think it got to that phase on the last tour, and Martin was the one that stood up and said, 'You know what? I've got to stop this.'"[710]

"It was just a decision I made," **Martin** explained. "I didn't go to AA or any of that stuff. I've found that I've got plenty of things to do with my time. It was all part and parcel of being in a band. It's almost encouraged for you to be drunk almost all the time if you're in a band. People are disappointed if you're not!" He laughed. "There's always someone somewhere who wants to give you something![711] I think I am more spiritually connected now. More a part of the universe, no pun intended. I feel like I'm more in touch

---

[710] Taken from: Article on CNN, 12 May 2009. Words: Denise Quan.
[711] Taken from: Depeche Mode Interviewed: Universal Truths And Sounds, The Quietus, 20 April 2009. Words: John Doran.

with my emotions. You have to be careful when you talk about spirituality and stopping drinking in the same breath. You start sounding a bit holier than thou. That's the last thing I want to do - come across as some new-age guru."[712]

Now **Fletch** is left over as the last one who sometimes likes to have a drink. "I've cut down but ..."

"He's under pressure," **Dave** remarked.

Fletch obviously doesn't like being under pressure. "These things are happening to make the atmosphere better. So it's got to be good."[713]

The second new topic was that Martin swapped alcohol against buying old analogue synthesizers and other stuff on *eBay*. Although he bought the stuff under his real name only few people commented on it – and it didn't even make the round.

The band members had their fun with all the drum machines, synthesizers and sequencers which were arriving every day.

"That was quite an inspiration," **Fletch** said. "Generally, I think it's more of an electronic album. There is guitar on it, of course, but much more electronic than *Playing The Angel*."[714]

They warded off the prejudice that this album was "retro." For **Martin** it was more a kind of "yesterday's future." "I started buying these old, vintage synthesisers, and the sounds they produced conjured up images of the universe and space travel. That's how we came up with the album title."[715]

Later it became clear that the band – or at least **Dave** – wasn't happy with *SOTU* and the way it was recorded throughout. "*Sounds of the Universe* was a bit too much production, too smooth, too much was going on. You cannot force out good music. It is a delicate thing. So it is

---

[712] Taken from: Depeche Mode in Mature Mode, Los Angeles Times, 28 March 2009. Words: Chris Lee.
[713] Taken from: Article on CNN, 12 May 2009. Words: Denise Quan.
[714] Taken from: Interview on Dmdotcom, 23 January 2009. Words: Daniel Barassi.
[715] Taken from: They just can't get enough: One-time synthesiser sissies Depeche Mode are back on song, Mail Online, 3 April 2009. Words: Adrian Thrills.

with *Depeche Mode*, albums come when they are supposed to. And they are not like they were planned to be."[716]

Nevertheless, he felt that it was more landscape-y, more filmic, very driven, and very out front. Maybe this was one of the reasons why they wouldn't play many of these songs live later. It was too difficult to transpose the complex studio versions into live versions.

2009

- I'm channelling the Universe (Little Soul) -

After the new single had been represented at the *Echo-Awards* in Berlin on **21 February**, the single *Wrong / Oh Well* finally was officially released on **6 April**.

There were several different versions of *Wrong* available, while there was just one different version of *Oh Well* available, the *Black Light Odyssey Remix*. The video for *Wrong* was directed and filmed by Patrick Daughters in **December 2008**. The actor in the video was *Liars* drummer Julian Gross. The video was nominated for a *Grammy Award* for *Best Short Form Video*.

At a fairly early stage, the band had decided to release *Wrong* as the first single because it was quite different to anything they had released before. And it really stood out of the album tracks.

"*Wrong* was the song of which we thought it would make a big impact," **Fletch** said. "We thought it would be good to come back with a bang. The first single has to be challenging to the audience, something to makes them react."

They thought the same about the video. "Anton Corbijn normally does our videos, and we had an idea from Anton and we had ideas from for other people. One of them was Patrick Daughters. And Patrick's idea didn't include the band very much, and Anton's idea did include the band. And, y'know, I think on these days *MTV* doesn't play many videos anymore. So finally we decided for Patrick's idea because we thought it had more effect on the audience.

---

[716] Taken from: Sanger på tro og ære, dagsavisen.no, May 2012. Words: Geir Rakvaag.

We don't like making videos anymore, so it was quite enjoyable."[717]

Oh Well was the first track to be released which had been co-written by Martin and Dave. Although it wasn't like they sat in a room and wrote it together. It was rather written by Martin as an instrumental track, but Dave heard it and liked it. So he took it back to his hotel room and wrote some words and a melody over the top. Unfortunately, some demos leaked out, and finally the whole mastered album. They took it as it came, and comforted themselves in the knowledge that the fans would buy it anyway. They were less happy about the leaked demos, as it seemed to them like showing someone an unfinished painting.

And the truth is – you're miles away (© Ingo Bittrich)

On **20 April** the album *Sounds of the Universe (SOTU)* was released. A year later they received the award for *Best International Group - Rock / Pop* at the **2010**-*Echo-Awards* in Germany for it.

The band, of course, tried to explain the album, said things like that they wanted it to sound as if they drove with a car in a tunnel by night and that this album was

---

[717] Taken from: Interview Depeche Mode - Sounds Of The Universe, 2009, fnac (Videointerview). Interviewer: unknown.

less "dark" than *Playing the Angel*. Again, they tried to point out that there was a lot of humour in their lyrics.

"There's definitely more on this one," **Martin** explained. "It's mainly dark humour but this time it's sometimes more obvious. In the song *Little Soul* there's a small musical break, and every time I hear that I laugh. I hope the listener will laugh when they hear this too.[718] Well, I think *Jezebel* is a good name for an exotic booze. I imagine it would taste like a strong-smelling perfume. There must be a perfume called *Jezebel*."

Fletch was shocked. "You can't drink perfume!"

"Well, you can," **Martin** insisted, "but they take it away from you if you go to rehab."

"It would be quite good for goth girls, wouldn't it?" **Fletch** suggested. "Women are different now," **Martin** claimed. "They like wearing T-shirts with things like *SLUT* and *WHORE* and stuff. I'm sure a bottle of *Jezebel* would go down well."[719]

While Martin changed the title *Footprint* to *Little Soul* and was worrying that *Miles Away* was a Madonna song title, and wanted Dave to change the title to *Miles Away/The Truth Is*, he wasn't worried about *Jezebel*. Of course it's a biblical figure, but nevertheless it's also a song title on Alan's album *Liquid*.

On the *SOTU*-box set they also released some old demo tracks. "Initially it was my idea to put the demos on the box set," **Fletch** said. "I was convinced that this was unique content that people would appreciate and that would make the purchase of this box set worthwhile. Martin didn't mind at all. He was fine with it. The main problem we encountered was to actually find the demos. Basically the five people that you'd think who would logically have the demos would be Alan, Daniel [Miller], Dave, Martin and me. But as it ended up, Alan had them somewhere tucked away and couldn't find them directly and that was also the case with Daniel, Martin and Dave. I knew I had lots of demos but they were in storage so I dug them up. In the end I recouped about hundred demo songs - which also means that there are hundreds that we don't have

---

[718] Taken from: Videointerview, FG5, 2009. Interviewer: unknown.
[719] Taken from: Songs of faith and commotion, The Guardian, 21 March 2009. Words: Peter Robinson.

anymore ... and that includes for instance the demo for *Personal Jesus* which seems to be lost forever."[720]

He promised that they would release some more demos in the future. (They didn't when *Delta Machine* was released, but they had some problems with the various labels, on the other hand, they also didn't when *Spirit* was released.)

Then they prepared for the tour. There was no question of not touring the album, because especially for Dave this is the thing that makes sense for him. And of course they were aware that you sell a record by touring today.

"We've done a lot of touring for a so-called 'electronic band,' and we've proven that electronic music works in a live format and in a huge live format," **Martin** said. "In a way, what we're going to do now is a landmark like the *Rosebowl* gig. We're going out to play our first stadium tour. There's not another electronic band that has gone out to play a stadium tour."[721]

Although for them it's always a bit of a nightmare to pick a setlist, in the end the setlist turned out like most previous setlists. This caused lots of discussions on several message-boards about the question whether *DM* might have become too *"Rolling Stones."* In fact, *DM* had never played as many different songs on a tour as on this one, although all of the all-time classics like *Personal Jesus*, *Enjoy the Silence* and *Never Let Me Down Again* appeared. That the live versions aren't as varied as they used to be in former times is probably mainly a problem for the hardcore fanbase. People who sometimes listen to *DM* and have been to one concert on a tour probably wouldn't notice it. But it is noticeable that although the band had announced that they wanted to play as many songs from the new album as possible, they didn't play many from it in the end.

At first, the band explained it with the variety of their audience. In their view they were aware of their legacy and not repeating themselves. They said they would stop making music the day they don't think they were achieving something or stop enjoying it. This led to the question

---

[720] Taken from: Article on Sideline, 16 April 2009. Words: Bernard Van Isacker.
[721] Taken from: Depeche Mode in Mature Mode, Los Angeles Times, 28 March 2009. Words: Chris Lee.

whether this was the last album and the ultimate tour (as they had been asked before during the promotion for *Playing the Angel.*)

"We've been together for 29 years and we've had ups and downs, but I think if *Depeche Mode* ended tomorrow we'd end on a positive note," **Martin** said.

"It's hard to think about your farewell gig and where it would be," **Fletch** added.

Martin has a clear idea about it. "It would have to be the Pyramids."

On **6 May** the *Tour of the Universe (TOTU)* began in Esch-sur-Alzette in Luxembourg as a warm-up gig. The first real gig was played in Tel Aviv. They started the tour there because they were supposed to end *Touring the Angel* there but unfortunately, the Israel/Lebanon war got in the way of it.

"We had to make the decision not to fly in and do the gig because there were missiles flying around and to make up for that we're starting this time in Tel Aviv,"[722] **Martin** explained.

It was astonishing to read in some comments in the internet that they were blamed for cancelling the gig in **2006**. Some people thought it would have been a political statement to play there, no matter if there was a conflict going on or not. I think it's harsh to demand playing a gig in a crisis region. You not only endanger yourself and your crew members, you also endanger everyone in the audience.

DM has never been a political band. They did not even react to the attack on **11 September 2001**, although they were on tour at the time. While other artists cancelled gigs, made a speech or asked for a minute's silence, *DM* did nothing. They simply played their gigs (**11 September** in Vienna and **12 September** in Budapest) without saying or doing anything special. Some people thought it was a strange, even a cold reaction. But maybe it was the best reaction to show. If you don't have words for something, it's always the best to say nothing at all and carry on as usual, showing that *the world still turns* (from *Insight, Ultra.*)

---

[722] Taken from: Songs of faith and commotion, The Guardian, 21 March 2009. Words: Peter Robinson.

Some political statements were made from the recording of *SOTU* onwards, like supporting gay rights. But you couldn't get rid of the feeling that their way of not mentioning political issues, as they had done before, was the better one.

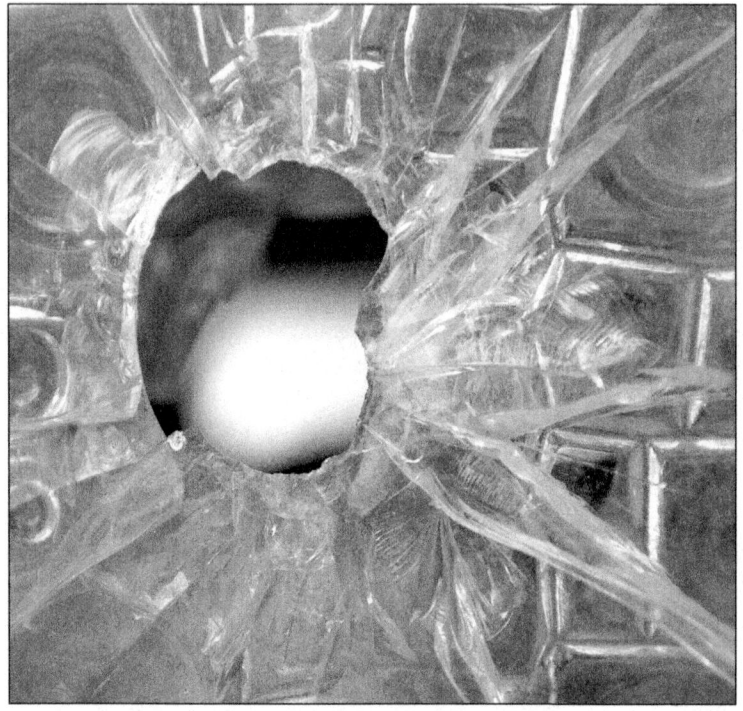

Hole to Feed (© Ingo Bittrich)

However, it seems that Tel Aviv and *DM* weren't a good combination, because with this gig some problems started.

"Actually on the first gig of the tour in Israel, I had the first bit of bad news: My father died,"[723] **Fletch** said.

The gig in Athens had to be cancelled because Dave fell ill. It was said it was a severe bout of gastroenteritis. While in hospital, further medical tests revealed a low-grade malignant tumour in Dave's bladder.

"Actually, Dave was very lucky because he had gastroenteritis and they found this tumour very early,"[724] **Fletch**

---

[723] Taken from: Pop Quiz: Andy Fletcher of Depeche Mode, sfgate.com, 9 August 2009. Words: Aidin Vaziri.

said. "It was low grade. It was just a question of zapping it out. I said to Dave the other day, 'I can't wait for your autobiography. It's quite a story developing.'"[725]

This information was released very late. Too late. Instead, an extremely bad new policy was in practice. While Dave had a surgery in New York, fans thought the concert in Poland might still take place. While he was recovering from surgery, fans thought other planned concerts might take place. A lot of rumours were floating around, it seemed to take ages before it was confirmed that the gigs were cancelled. The band apologized, saying that they hadn't known how things would continue. Sure, but if someone undergoes surgery, it's obvious that they won't be able to play a concert on that day, and that they will need some time to recover afterwards.

With the release of *Exciter* in **2001** the band had established a presence on the Internet. The *Bong*-magazine that had been used for information and interaction until then was stopped in the same year. Instead, they now had a website and a message-board. And while they had shown some interest in this new way of communication, it was now diminishing increasingly. Around the time of *SOTU* the band remarked that their official forum was a "big moan" because people were complaining about a lot of things, and Dave even wondered whether the people posting there had a job at all.

And while other bands are using the Internet a lot, providing news, using *Facebook* and *Twitter*, and being interactive with their fans, *DM*'s official website and *Facebook* site got less interesting over the course of time. They went retro, and they became much more retro with the next album, *Delta Machine*, at least as far as their way of communicating was concerned.

The tour was re-started in Leipzig on **8 June**, comprising 18 concerts in Europe, until **9 July**, when another concert had to be cancelled because Dave injured his leg.

In the meantime, on **15 June**, the single *Peace* was released. It charted at No. 57 in the UK charts; this was the band's second lowest UK singles chart position since *Little*

---

[724] Taken from: Six Questions for ... Depeche Mode, Washington Post, 28 July 2009. Words: David Malitz.
[725] Taken from: Pop Quiz: Andy Fletcher of Depeche Mode, sfgate.com, 9 August 2009. Words: Aidin Vaziri.

15. In Germany *Peace* reached No. 25. It was not commercially released in the U.S. The video was filmed in Romania by French duo Jonas & François. It featured the Romanian actress Maria Dinulescu and was the first video without any of the band members, but this was due to Dave's illness.

On **24 July** the American leg started in Toronto. In **August**, they had to cancel some concerts again, this time because of **Dave**'s voice-problems. He wasn't well at all, but this turned out much later. At every break they took he had to go to hospital for some more treatment. Nevertheless, "I was very lucky. The cancer hadn't spread through the walls of my bladder so all the chemo was localised. It still made me sick but I didn't lose all my hair."[726]

Despite all these problems, **Martin** did enjoy this tour, the first one he experienced sober completely. "It was difficult as we were on the road and that's always difficult to avoid drinking. I just got to a point where I knew if I carried on then I wouldn't be alive for much longer. I was drinking all day — literally getting up and drinking with breakfast. I'm just thankful some of the madness missed the age of smartphones. Back in the day when I was drinking and out of control I would have been all over *YouTube*." He laughed. "Just for the fun of it I'd just get naked in hotel bars. Can you imagine doing that now?"[727] (Oh, I think lots of people would have enjoyed this. ;)) But this time "I'd really been lucid enough to take in everything and enjoy the concerts and then enjoy the cities the next day."[728]

From **1 to 17 October** they played nine concerts in Central and South America, before the second European leg started on **31 October**, which comprised 27 concerts and ended on **18 December.**

In the meantime, on **7 December**, the single *Fragile Tension / Hole to Feed* was released.

---

[726] Taken from: We're dysfunctional. Maybe that's what makes us tick, The Guardian (UK), 28 March 2013. Words: Dorian Lynskey.
[727] Taken from: Depeche Mode: Brits wouldn't show our set so we said 'f*** them', The Sun, 22 March 2013. Words: Uncredited.
[728] Taken from: Depeche Mode, 'pessimists at heart,' never imagined longevity, Reuters, 14 March 2013. Words: Corrie MacLaggan.

2010

- I'm the ghost in your house -

The last leg of the tour - another European one - started on **9 January 2010** in Berlin. Luckily on this leg there weren't any incidents.

The concert on **17 February** was a very special one. It was the first time in their career that *DM* did something they had never wanted to do: they played a charity concert.

It's "something we should have done long time before," **Martin** said. "A friend of us is part of the *Teenage Cancer Trust* and asked us to join in."

I don't know if they should have done this before. They never wanted to be one of those bands who "push their career with charity." Many fans liked *DM* because of their being consistent, and different to mainstream bands. Although the good cause was appreciated, the new opinion of the band about charity nevertheless caused some discussion among the fans. (It became even more charity with the next release, *Delta Machine*.)

However, everything was special about this concert. It took place in the *Royal Albert Hall* (funny when you think about what especially Dave thinks about British symbols – nothing good) in London, and they had a special guest.

"We asked Alan to join us on stage," **Martin** said. "It's a long time ago that we saw him. I think it's nine years ago that I saw him the last time and we asked him to play one song with us tonight and he very kindly agreed."[729]

"Well, I got a call from Dave and he just said: 'we would like to invite you to take part at this event, the *Teenage Cancer Trust*'," **Alan** explained. "And my reaction was that I hoped, it was the whole band who wanted it not just Dave. So, I asked him that question and he said, 'Yes, definitively.' And so I didn't think twice about it because it's a great thing to do for many reasons, y'know, the good cause, getting together after such a long time ..."

So he joined Martin on stage for *Somebody*. It was a natural choice because they hadn't much time to re-

---

[729] Taken from: A video interview at the RAH-gig, 2010, dmdotcom. Interviewer: Daniel Barassi.

hearse. It seems that the band and especially **Alan** enjoyed the show.

"The reaction of the crowd was a bit special, very heart warming, emotional, I got goosebumps ... it was a great day. It was not only that moment, it was seeing Martin and Fletch and Dave again. We had a good chat and it was good to see them again. I haven't seen Martin and Fletch for a long time, it was really interesting to catch up. And Martin was on very good form I thought, not just vocally but in himself. He seemed sharper, more focused and more open than I have ever known him. It's a little piece of history for us, y'know. Being on stage with *Depeche* since ... **1994** ... the end of the *Songs of Faith and Devotion*-Tour ... about 16 years."

That the reaction of the crowd was "a bit special" is the understatement of the century. People hadn't known before that Alan would be on stage, so the crowd almost "exploded" when they realised that he was playing the piano. They screamed, shouted, cried and were difficult to silence. Maybe it was the most emotional *DM* moment ever.

A few days later **Alan** had the opportunity to watch a *DM* concert for the first time in his life from the audience, something he had never wanted to do.

"It was a very interesting and enjoyable experience. Y'know, I had feelings for every song because I know them all so well ... so ... y'know when you hear the versions they play now you remember the versions we used to do. I thought some of the versions were really good, and some I wasn't so keen on. I felt the same about the stage set, too - some things looked great, and some didn't work for me. The sound balance was poor unfortunately, but neither that nor the staging could be blamed on the band. Their own performance was impressive. Dave was on good form and everyone seemed to enjoy themselves. Martin's song *Home* sounded especially good. The after-show was fun and I was able to catch up with all kinds of people I hadn't seen for a long time. I missed Dave, however, as he always disappears as soon as he leaves the stage."[730]

They talked about "mainly usual things that you chat about with people, you know, families, what their habits are these days, do they still drink as much as they used to

---

[730] Taken from: Interview With Alan Wilder, 20 February 2010, dmdotcom. Interviewer: Daniel Barassi.

do, how is the partying situation on tour ... I mean, things have actually changed quite a lot with *Depeche Mode* since I was in the band. Martin doesn't drink anymore, Dave goes home after every show so he doesn't go out anymore. We used to go to big parties after every concert. So, it must be a very different thing for them to be on the road these days. But in their personal lives things have changed a lot, I think. I was very impressed with Martin because he has been sober for four years and he is like a new person, someone I almost didn't recognize."[731]

I'm the ghost in your house (© Ingo Bittrich)

Dave left the venue right after the concert and didn't talk much to Alan but nevertheless, he appreciated Alan's input. "I think *Playing the Angel* was great but Alan always brought something extra to Martin's songs. We email each

---

[731] Taken from: Recoil in Bucharest- Interview with Alan Wilder, depechemode.ro, 2010. Words: Otiliei Haraga.

other and when he joined us on stage for the *Teenage Cancer Trust* concert at the *Royal Albert Hall* in **2010**, it was awesome. When Alan left we missed him and it became apparent on the next couple of albums for sure."[732]

This is a good reason to do some surveys about how much Alan is still present to the fans. The result of a survey in a big message board was that 69% want him back as a band member, and 20% at least as a producer. The survey of *depechemodebiographie.de* had similar results. For 71% he "still belongs to the band somehow" (at least as a legend), and for 21% he is even still a part of the band today, "because he was part of them at their highest point and had a big influence on their music and success." For the minority, however, he is the "most nerve-racking discussion whenever it comes to *DM*."

The appearance at the *Royal Albert Hall* and the promotion for his own tour took place almost at the same time, so one could come to the conclusion one fan had: "It's amazing that it is mostly Alan, who is using the history of *DM* for his own project."

An inside source also remarked that there had been a business meeting at the day of the concert in *Royal Albert Hall*, and the band and Alan would have met anyway. The band has owned several different companies from the beginning of their career to run their business affairs for their different projects (albums, touring, merchandising, etc.), and at that day they met to discuss some issues. According to rumours it wasn't a really good meeting.

Alan had had a difficult time after the release of *Sub-Human* in **2007**. He separated from his wife, and now had a new partner, Britt. "I share custody of my children so you have to plan 6 months ahead in your diary, who is going to have them when etc, and I have to fit the music somewhere in the gaps.[733] That has made working on a new album almost impossible, although I have made a

---

[732] Taken from: Depeche Mode: Brits wouldn't show our set so we said 'f*** them', The Sun, 22 March 2013. Words: Uncredited.
[733] Taken from: Recoil / Alan Wilder - I'm not naive, Sideline, 31 March 2010. Words: Bernard van Isacker.

start on new material but it's a long way off being near to completion."[734]

Instead, he went on the *Selected*-Tour. The first leg started on **12 March**, comprising 24 events, mainly in Europe, and ended on **18 May**.

The idea to tour *Recoil* evolved when **Alan** decided to undertake some promo visits. But he didn't want to keep making personal appearances to sign CDs and shake hands. So he decided to do a kind of audio/visual presentation, a mixture of DJing and playing live, while showing special films.

On **19 April** *Selected* was released, a kind of Best of *Recoil*. The project started when *Mute Records* approached **Alan** with the idea for a compilation, but the project soon got bigger. "I had to decide which were my favourite tracks and which ones worked together. I really wanted to avoid a mish-mash which most compilations are."[735]

Nevertheless, the most frequently-asked question, of course, was whether there might be a reunion with *DM*. **Alan** got tired of it quite soon. It started with a friendly "I doubt you'll see me in the *Depeche Mode* line-up in the near future. They haven't asked me being their producer. It would certainly be weird",[736] went on to "Well, we've not discussed anything like that so there aren't any plans. But you never know"[737] then to "It's just boring - it's the question I get asked more than any other",[738] and ended up in saying nothing at all when the question was put forward again.

The second leg of the *Selected*-Tour started on **16 October**. This time it was more concentrated on the U.S. and South America, but there were also some more events in Europe afterwards. The tour ended on **4 December** in Budapest.

---

[734] Taken from: Recoil / Alan Wilder - February 2010, Reflectionsofdarkness.com, 5 March 2010. Words: Janos Janurik.
[735] Taken from: Alan Wilder: A Selected Interview, stevenwilsonbeales.com, 14 April 2010. Words: Steven Wilson-Beales.
[736] Taken from: Recoil / Alan Wilder - February 2010, Reflectionsofdarkness.com, 5 March 2010. Words: Janos Janurik.
[737] Taken from: Alan Wilder: A Selected Interview, stevenwilsonbeales.com, 14 April 2010. Words: Steven Wilson-Beales.
[738] Taken from: Recoil / Alan Wilder - I'm not naive, Sideline, 31 March 2010. Words: Bernard van Isacker.

The reunion rumour was fed with Martin DJing at the event in Santa Ana on **24 October**, and Dave appearing as a guest at the event in New York on **1 November**.

The discussions about whether Alan might re-join DM again or at least might produce their new album eased off when it became clear that DM would produce Delta Machine with Ben Hillier again. But it never really stopped.

The reasons why Alan had left the band were brought up again – each time a different one – and were used to substantiate the different opinions as to whether Alan might or might not re-join the band.

Even if you left out all his other reasons – family, his own projects, not wanting to be in a band anymore – the "driving force" in his leaving the band after Devotional, the bad team-spirit, would be the main reason for not rejoining. Why should something that didn't work anymore 20 years ago suddenly work again? Because everyone had grown older, become wiser? I don't think so. In fact, the working methods of DM and Alan have become more different over the years than ever before. They would find the same situation again, with Alan focused on studio work (maybe more than ever, remember what he said about recording Liquid), while the others aren't really interested or meanwhile have become interested, but nevertheless use different working methods.

Martin has started to develop a fondness for studio work. "I love being in the studio. If I'm at home, I will go to the studio pretty much every day anyway. It's just something that I like to do."[739] I don't think this new passion would work with Alan's passion for studio work.

The former musical heads, Alan and Martin, have developed in different musical directions over the course of time. They are farther away from each other in their musical interests than ever before. Listening to SubHuman and then to Delta Machine is all you need to do to know how these two see "electronic with Blues elements."

Comparing 5000 Years (SubHuman) and Slow (Delta Machine), you have to notice that some of the Blues elements are quite similar, but again, Slow is more direct and straight to the point, so that it can't develop such

---

[739] Taken from: Martin Gore on new Depeche Mode CD, Frank Ocean, Associated Press, 26 March 2013. Words: Uncredited.

huge depth and variety as *5000 Years* or *Prey*. Of course, there are some generally accepted guidelines for pop songs – defined length (about 3:30 to 4:30), a certain ease, not too many instruments, and the known structure of verse – chorus – verse – chorus. Alan doesn't abide by these rules, but use a whole Blues song as a base for *5000 Years* and *Prey* as well, instead of repeating certain elements. Besides, he works with a lot of different sounds, and still has a fondness for dramatic elements.[740]

Although some people think that the most interesting thing about *DM* was the combination of these two extremes, that it was this "that made it work" as some people say, I doubt that they are really interested in trying it again. Maybe both sides thought about it at one point or another, especially after Alan's appearance at the *Royal Albert Hall* (and insiders say not all rumours about a reunion were baseless), but it's hard to say if it was a heart's desire. It also would be still difficult to define the lead roles of Alan and Martin.

And what would happen to Dave and his new role as a songwriter? Maybe he would be the one who would benefit most from working together with Alan. On the other hand, it's probably much too late. It would have been interesting to know what would have happened if Dave had played his early demos to Alan, and had asked him if they could work them out together. Maybe the whole story of *DM* would have taken a completely new direction. But he didn't, and found his own formulas to write songs now. Although he is open to collaboration and to new ways, it might be difficult for him to work with an over-accurate musician like Alan, especially because he says several times during the recording of *Delta Machine* that he would prefer not to overproduce, but rather to make things simpler and more direct. That wouldn't suit Alan's working methods at all.

The only one who probably wouldn't care at all is the one who is mostly accused of being against a reunion – Fletch. The only reason I can think of why he should be against it is that he might fear new tensions.

Another point that hasn't changed at all is the communication. They didn't talk to each other in the old days, and they still don't. Sometimes you find some friendly remarks about Alan from Dave, and even from Fletch and

---

[740] Author of this passage: Jörg von der Fecht (Bleeding)

Martin, or about the band members from Alan, but there aren't any signs that they sat down at a certain point and really talked WITH each other.

2011

*- I gave you everything you ever wanted
(So Cruel, Tribute to U2) -*

In **2010** *Mute* became independent again, but *DM* stayed signed to and marketed worldwide by *EMI Music*. In **2011** this contract ended with the release of *Remixes 2: 81-11*. Alan and Vince were both involved in *Remixes 2: 81-11*, which was released on **6 June 2011**.

"Toward the end of the last tour I asked Alan if he would come onstage at London's *Royal Albert Hall* and he agreed," **Martin** said. (This is an interesting new perspective because until then everyone said that Dave phoned Alan and asked him to join.) "Then he came on tour in America. It seemed natural to ask him"[741] to collaborate at the remix album. At the time, he also collaborated with Vince, so it seemed natural to ask him to do a remix as well. So Vince remixed *Behind the Wheel*, and Alan remixed *In Chains*.

"It was the *Depeche Mode* manager Jonathan Kessler who suggested it," **Alan** said. "It had been suggested a long time before that, by the guys at *Mute* organizing the whole remix album." (Hasn't Martin just said that he asked Alan to contribute? Hm, maybe it was Martin's wish, but he told Dave to phone and Kessler to ask. ;) Or it's really true that they planned to meet at that day anyway, and Alan's contribution in the concert was a common decision, maybe even a decision for business reasons.) "They never came back to me. I thought: 'oh well that's not going to happen.' I wasn't bothered by that at all and then I was speaking to Jonathan about something else, I think it was about Martin DJing at one of the *Recoil* nights and the idea was put to me again."

---

[741] Taken from: Q&A: Martin Gore of Depeche Mode, Vanityfair, 7 June 2011. Words: Marc Spitz.

By then, they needed it in around two weeks, and he had to spend his holiday doing it. "Jonathan told me the band would prefer that I did something new, from the era after which I left the band, and I thought it was a good challenge to do that. I hope they like it, they said they do. Martin seemed to be really keen on it, which was nice of him. I think the others like it too; don't know about Fletch - he didn't say anything. I think it is a more dynamic version of what they had."[742]

Some fans speculated whether this remix had been some kind of a "test" to see if Alan suited the current line-up. It's possible, if there really were some considerations about a reunion. But again – it seems that the band and Alan didn't talk to each other about this remix. "Martin seemed to be really keen on it", "I think the others like it too" says all you need to know about their communication. And if you think that Dave and Alan write to each other very often, you are wrong. Dave sometimes says he emails Alan (although there are other interviews in which he says he doesn't like computers and just texts a bit sometimes) but Alan says Dave writes about twice a year. This is not what you could call a "lively conversation."

Unfortunately, things still didn't go well for **Alan**. "Times are tight for everyone these days, and divorce plus lack of any finance for making records means I need to do some belt-tightening."[743]

This even endangered the planned DVD-release of *Selected*. Obviously, the record company wasn't really interested in this release, so most of the project was self-financed.

Alan finally decided to sell parts of his large *DM* collection. The auction was held on **3 September 2011** in Manchester, and was a rather bittersweet event for many fans. And if there ever had been considerations about a reunion, it seems that Alan spoilt things with this auction. According to rumours, the band was upset because he sold keyboards still programmed with original samples.

However, in some ways it seems as if Alan burnt some of his bridges in connection with *DM* and his former life.

---

[742] Taken from: Alan Wilder - collected thoughts, Releasemagazine, 19 August 2011. Words: Fredrik "Schlatta" Svensson.
[743] Taken from: Recoil / Alan Wilder, Reflections Of Darkness, 1 September 2011, Words: János Janurik.

There was a re-launch of his website in **2012** (almost all sections about *DM* are gone now), and in **2013** he even offered his house and his studio for sale. It's exciting to wait and see what will happen next. Maybe there will a reunion some day, maybe he will surprise the fans with something completely different.

Meanwhile **Dave** recovered. "For a while there I almost turned to my manager and said, 'I'm not coming back.' I spent a lot of time with my wife and kids. It was beautiful in New York, the blossom was on the trees, everything seemed a little brighter. It was similar to the feeling of waking up after a week or two in rehab. You notice s***. I was noticing a lot of stuff that I liked in my life and I was afraid to leave it in case I didn't get the chance to come back to it.[744] That lasted a couple of weeks, then I really wanted to get back on the road."[745] He laughed.

He didn't go back on the road directly but got involved in a record project that would have a kind of influence on the 13th album of *DM –Delta Machine*.

---

[744] Taken from: We're dysfunctional. Maybe that's what makes us tick, The Guardian (UK), 28 March 2013. Words: Dorian Lynskey.
[745] Taken from: Depeche Mode on synths, drugs and Basildon, The Times (UK), 21 March 2013. Words: Ed Potton.

2012

*- The final chapter in the contract expires soon
(Secret to the End) -*

In **2011** and **2012** Martin and Dave were busy with some solo projects. The band just recorded the cover version of *So Cruel*, which was released on a tribute album to *U2* in **2011**. Martin was the vocalist of the song *Man Made Machine* by the band *Motor*, and he collaborated with Vince; the project's name was simply *VCMG*. *EP1 Spock* was released on **9 December 2011**, *EP2 Blip* on **27 February 2012**, the album *Ssss* on **13 March**, and finally *EP3 Aftermath* was released on **20 August**. It is an instrumental techno-like record.

The collaboration started when **Vince** thought about making "some kind of a techno album," although he had "never taken an interest in techno music at all but I was just completely blown away by the way the people were using synthesisers."[746]

He thought, "'Well, I never worked with Martin, really,' and I knew he was interested in synths. It felt like a good email to send.[747] After drinking six beers, I composed an email. I think he was genuinely surprised to hear from me."[748]

Martin was surprised, indeed. He didn't even know Vince had his email address. "It's funny because he tweets all the time and everyone thinks he's really, really talkative and really, you know - he's not. And I just got a really short email that said, 'Thinking of making a techno album. Interested in collaborating? Vince.'"

"After 25 years, you know, you expect a little more, but ...," **Dave** chipped in.

"So I felt, I mean, I like techno," **Martin** said. "It might be quite an interesting thing to do. So I said, 'Yes. Martin.'"[749] (Sometimes communication can be so easy ...)

---

[746] Taken from: Interview: VCMG, The Stoolpigenon, 16 February 2012. Words: Tim Burrows.
[747] Taken from: VCMG, 'Ssss': Album Preview, Billboard.com, 17 January 2012. Words: Kerri Mason.
[748] Taken from: Interview: VCMG, The Stoolpigenon, 16 February 2012. Words: Tim Burrows.
[749] Taken from: The Complete SXSW 2013 Interview, NPR, 25 March 2013.

He had some downtime at the time, so he decided to collaborate. They didn't work together physically but worked via the Internet by taking out bits they didn't particularly like, adding new bits and sending the tracks back and forth. There were usually three or four versions of a track before they were both happy.

"One of the reasons I had fun doing this project is that I wanted to make a 'dancy' album," **Martin** explained. "I think the electronic scene is really alive, and today many young people can create dance music on a budget."[750]

They seldom met personally, and if they did, e.g. at *Short Circuit* at the *Roundhouse* in London in **2011**, they didn't talk about the record but about their children.

"I think making *Ssss* together helped Martin. It certainly cleared up a lot of weird old resentments that they had,"[751] **Dave** commented who had the opportunity to meet Vince again, too, and talked to him for the first time after 25 years.

After Dave had recovered from *Touring the Universe* he was asked to collaborate in a project of the band *Soulsavers*. It consists of two people: Rich Machin and Ian Glover. Dave got to know them through bassist Martyn LeNoble, a friend of his, and became friendly with them when *Soulsavers* opened for *DM* during *TOTU*.

"Martyn LeNoble was doing some session work with them in a studio in LA, and I just happened to call him up for a chat on that day, and it happened that he was in the studio with them," **Dave** explained how the *Soulsavers* became an opening act. "Rich was in the background and yelled out, 'You should take us on tour!' I said to Martyn, 'Is he serious? Does he really want to go on the road with *Depeche Mode*?', because, you know, it'd be a little bit difficult opening for *Depeche Mode*. You never know which way it's going to go: whether you're going to get rocks thrown at you, or something else, I don't know. It's a difficult opener, but he was totally into it, and so we took them on tour."[752]

Words: Jason Bentley.
[750] Taken from: Clarke e Gore, L'Uomo Vogue, January 2012. Words: Uncredited.
[751] Taken from: Depeche Mode: Brits wouldn't show our set so we said 'f*** them', The Sun, 22 March 2013. Words: Uncredited.
[752] Taken from: Soulsavers & Dave Gahan: 'We Were On The Same Page

On tour he talked about songwriting with Rich Machin, and Machin asked him whether he could send him some ideas. Dave didn't think anything would come of it, but Machin did indeed send him something.

Dave immediately felt inspired by it. It felt very natural for him to get involved in the project. "*I Can't Stay* was one of the first things I worked on. These songs really kind of wrote themselves. I can't describe it in any better way."[753]

The album *The Light the Dead See* was recorded at studios in London, New York, Los Angeles, Berlin and Sydney and was released on **21 May**. Dave wrote all lyrics and was the leading vocalist.

Probably for the first time, many *DM*-fans bought an album of the *Soulsavers*. It was quite successful, peaked No. 69 of UK album charts, No. 28 of US *Top Heatseekers Albums* Chart and No. 12 in Germany. The latter shows that Germany is still one of the most important markets for *DM*.

The first single taken from the album *Longest Day* was released as digital download on **2 April**. The second single *Take Me Back Home* was released as digital download on **20 August**.

"It was definitely a very new experience for me," **Dave** said. "I know some of the songs will come across as quite dark and moody, but it was the most uplifting experience I've ever had making a record."[754]

It wasn't only a new experience for him, he also became inspired for the songs he wrote for *DM*'s next record. *Delta Machine* and *The Light the Dead See* aren't similar, but there's an influence, nevertheless.

"The title *The Light the Dead See* works so well because sometimes when you're still and not trying to steer things in a certain way is really when the magic can happen," **Dave** explained.

The project also had an influence on his way of singing. "I think some of that stuff comes from the way I used my voice. I go to a very visual place when I'm singing. It's very

---

Very Quickly', Features, DIY, 23 July 2012. Words: Huw Oliver.
[753] Taken from: Depeche Mode frontman Dave Gahan gets spiritual, Special to CNN, 8 June 2012. Words: Abbey Goodman.
[754] Taken from: Dave Gahan Discusses Soulsavers & New DM, The Quitus, 1 March 2012. Words: Sam Spokony.

cinematic and I get this feeling of space. I love when music does that."⁷⁵⁵

His way of singing, that had changed from *Playing the Angel* to *SOTU*, caused a lot of discussion among the fans. Some people didn't like that he almost over-emphasised the syllables, and tried to vary his voice a lot. On *The Light the Dead See* he sang differently again, and he carried this style over to *Delta Machine*.

Because of the new *DM* album Dave didn't tour with the *Soulsavers*. However, the band played an invitation-only "secret show" at *Capitol Studios* in Los Angeles on **21 July.**

"We have begun to record the album [*Delta Machine*]," **Dave** said in **May**, when *The Light the Dead See* was released and he focused on *DM* again. "I have written 6-7 songs," - he was working with Kurt Uenala -, "Martin has 13 or 14, we play into all, and we'll see what we include on the album. I think three or four of my songs going with, so it gets the more than before. The album seems to have a strong sense of the blues. Not as *Violator* and *Songs of Faith and Devotion*, but definitely more blues, and more direct. We will take good care not to overproduce this time. Too many sounds are not necessary. If the melodies are good, they do not need more.⁷⁵⁶ I push all the time, much to the annoyance of the other guys sometimes, to keep things as raw as possible. They get a little bit afraid of that, in case we're all gonna get judged. Yes, you are going to get judged, but I'd rather get really s*** reviews than mediocre reviews. I'd rather hear people saying 'what the f***'s going on with the band?' than just 'yeah, hmmm, it's an okay record'."⁷⁵⁷

But exactly this would happen when *Delta Machine* was released. Many fans liked the album a lot, saying it's the best since *SOFAD* (or since *Ultra*), many said it's an okay record, and only a few asked what the f*** is going on with the band. It is noticeable that many of the critical fans had lost interest long before the release, and didn't say any-

---

[755] Taken from: Depeche Mode frontman Dave Gahan gets spiritual, Special to CNN, 8 June 2012. Words: Abbey Goodman.
[756] Taken from: Sanger på tro og ære, dagsavisen.no, May 2012. Words: Geir Rakvaag.
[757] Taken from: Depeche Mode Album Update, Clash Music, 25 July 2012. Words: Mat Smith.

thing at all about *Delta Machine*. Sometimes this says a lot. It seems that the band lost some fans along the way, but it hasn't done them any harm. *Delta Machine* and the tickets for the upcoming tour sold well.

The band met in **January 2012** to listen to demos, and started recording *Delta Machine* in **March** in Santa Barbara. This time they only worked in Santa Barbara and New York, but they worked with Ben Hillier again.

Some things were different compared to previous albums. So Martin reworked Dave's demos before starting the recording session probably to give all the demos a sense of consistency in terms of sound and direction. It was really difficult to guess who had written which song.

With Christoffer Berg from Sweden they had a second producer. The band liked to work with him because he wasn't afraid to bring in ideas. He makes his own music and he's a lot younger than the band so he brought in some new energy.

The band members don't spend much time with each other when they are not in the studio or on tour together – or at least Dave doesn't meet Martin and Fletch very often – so it always takes a while to get on with each other after a break.

"Coming into the studio with *Depeche* for the first time in a while is just a different process.[758] We're probably not finished til the end of the year, and we're talking about touring next year. But right now it's like a science lab here," **Dave** said in **May**. "We're working in two rooms at the moment, just full of electronics and guitars and everybody's getting very creative."[759]

Then it didn't take them until the end of the year, but they completed recording ahead of schedule. This time another problem had to be dealt with. It was the first time in their career that they didn't have a label. It's a complex topic. When *Mute* was signed to *EMI* Daniel Miller retained complete artistic control. Right before *DM* were set to record *Delta Machine*, there were rumours about *EMI* folding, and they didn't want to be stuck in limbo. Miller tried

---

[758] Taken from: Out, demons, out!, The Word magazine, 17 May 2012. Words: Uncredited.
[759] Taken from: Depeche Mode Working on 'Punchier' Songs, Eye Tour in 2013, Billboard.com, 29 May 2012. Words: Gary Graff.

to buy *Mute Records* back, but he got outbid. At that point *DM* decided to look for a new label.

"*Sony* came up with the best offer to make sure Daniel is still around for us, and to make sure we were able to gain control of what we're doing," **Dave** said. "Most importantly, in **2015**, we'll be able to get control of our entire catalogue. We'll own it. After *Delta Machine*, we'll be in real control."[760]

It meant that they released a record without the famous *Bong* label. This was especially disappointing for collectors, but it seemed to be the best deal for them, because they were still aware of keeping some independence. They took on all the costs for the production themselves, because they didn't want to be tied to a record company. So the deal with *Sony* is obviously a kind of logistic deal rather than a real record deal.

There were plans to collaborate with other musicians, but it didn't work because most musicians Ben Hillier talked to knew electronics, but didn't know really how to use the massive modular hardware systems *DM* used to work with.

So there weren't many other people involved. And, of course, they got on well again, although **Dave** admitted that he wasn't patient enough. "Making a record with *Depeche Mode* is not a simple process. It's quite complicated and long. We have the luxury of time. I'm not sure that's such a good thing when you're being creative. I kind of like that process of working a little faster in the studio. It gets boring for me. They are in their laboratory surrounded by all these twiddly things with all these things that make bleeps and noises and I sit there, like, 'Can I sing now? Can I sing now? Can I sing now?'[761] We're not a band band. We're not *The Rolling Stones*, jamming together in the studio. Things are very constructed between Martin and me. Fletch has ideas and input; he's the one who'll say, 'What are you doing? You've been working on this for three days, it's rubbish!' But he's not conceptual. He's the mediator. He's the luke-warm water between fire and ice."

---

[760] Taken from: Through That Darkness You'll Find the Light, Electronic Beats Magazine, 12 March 2013. Words: A.J. Samuels.
[761] Taken from: Delta Force: A Q&A with Depeche Mode's Dave Gahan, Time Entertainment, 4 April 2013. Words: Melissa Locker.

He laughed. "He'll do his crossword, and as long as he gets to lunch by one o'clock, he's fine."[762]

"I think this album was one of the easiest to make,"[763] **Martin** commented.

You remember the last time he said that a record was easy to make, in fact it was very difficult, but I don't think that this time we will hear unpleasant stories afterwards.

When it came to the mixing process, an old acquaintance appeared.

"It was good on this record to kind of have Flood back on board and have Flood mixing the record," **Dave** said. "That technology was good there, because Martin and I would get on *Skype* with him and he'd be in London mixing while we were in New York still recording. That's the only way we'd communicated with him! We did not spend any time in the studio with him. I think this record as well is the end of a trilogy of records that we're doing with Ben Hillier."[764]

As has been previously referred to – fans tend to attach too much importance to the role of the (former co-)producers, especially to the role of Flood. Hearing that he was to mix the record, some people had very high expectations. But mixing a record doesn't mean producing a record, and producing a record doesn't automatically mean having a huge musical influence.

---

[762] Taken from: Interview with Dave Gahan, Mojo, 22 March 2013. Words: Martin Aston.
[763] Taken from: Survival Mode, Irish Times, 22 March 2013. Words: Uncredited.
[764] Taken from: Depeche Mode Q&A: Dave Gahan Talks 'Delta Machine,' Massive Tour Plans, Billboard.com, New York, 8 March 2013. Words: Jason Lipshutz.

2013 H 2014

- Love is all I want (Should Be Higher) -

The first single of *Delta Machine* was *Heaven / All That's Mine*. It was the 50th single of the band. It was released digitally in most territories on **31 January**, and physically the following day. In the UK it was released digitally on **17 March**, and physically the following day. The video for *Heaven* was directed by Timothy Saccenti and filmed at *The Marigny Opera House*, a former Catholic church in New Orleans, in **November 2012**.

Heaven (© Ingo Bittrich)

The chart performance was low in the average, but it was No. 1 of the US *Hot Dance Club Songs* and in Hungary and No. 2 in Germany. *Heaven* was a courageous choice because it is a quite slow and moody song, nothing you could call a hit-single.

"It flopped a bit because of the sound," **Fletch** admitted. "We're old timers. We thought radio might play a slower track. Turns out, they won't."[765]

"Funnily enough, *Heaven*, the lead single, is not very representative for the rest of the sound," **Martin** said. "So for a lot of" the songs on the album "I would start off with

---

[765] Taken from: Andy Fletcher interview, News, 3 April 2013. Words: Uncredited.

like, you know, like a bass line and then create some drums and some effects with the modulars and start from there, really, and then just start singing along. That's what I do. I'm sorry. And when I sing along, I don't sing along like, you know, little pretend words. When I sing, then sort of words just come out. It starts with words. A lot of people do that, you know, like, singing, you know, strange languages or whatever. But I always just start singing."[766]

At first, they thought that *Angel* was the better first single, but Martin and Dave liked *Heaven* so much that they decided to release it as the first one.

"It's not like we felt it was going to be a big hit or something, but that doesn't really drive us to make music," **Dave** said. "We all like to have hits, it's nice to have hits, of course, but after making 13 records together, it's not what drives you. What drives you is to make a great record."[767]

On **22 March** the album *Delta Machine* was released. It was labelled to *Columbia Records* and *Mute Records* in the U.S. and to *Sony Music* in the rest of the world.

The album debuted at No. 2 on the UK Albums Chart, selling 28,450 copies in its first week. In the U.S. the album entered the *Billboard 200* at No. 6 with 52,000 copies sold in its opening week. And it debuted at No. 1 on the German Albums Chart with first-week sales of 142,000 units.

"Delta" stands for the blues elements and "Machine" stands for the electronic elements of the album. The title immediately caused some irritations in the messageboards because some people started to use the acronym "*DM*" for "*Delta Machine*". Unfortunately, this has been the acronym for "*Depeche Mode*" for 30 years.

"We had a few permutations of the title, like 'something' *Machine* and *Delta* 'something' before Martin said, '*Delta Machine*?' But I wouldn't dare say this is a blues record as Fletch has said a couple of times. That's insulting, to blues musicians, on so many levels. Well, OK, we have influences coming from the blues. And *Depeche Mode* is

---

[766] Taken from: The Complete SXSW 2013 Interview, NPR, 25 March 2013. Words: Jason Bentley.
[767] Taken from: Delta Force: A Q&A with Depeche Mode's Dave Gahan, Time Entertainment, 4 April 2013. Words: Melissa Locker.

fundamentally us whining, searching for something, moaning our way through life." **Dave** laughed.

As usually they didn't tell much about the single songs of the album.

"*Broken* is up-tempo, but lyrically it's dark,"[768] **Dave** offered. "The lyrics of *Broken* are probably based on a friend who's been struggling for a while with his own demons. I see myself in him."[769]

"Funnily enough, I think that out of all of my songs on the album, that's the one that changed dramatically," **Martin** said about *My Little Universe*. "You know, for ages we were thinking that it wasn't going to go on the album because it somehow didn't quite fit. It was too fiddly. There were, you know, chord changes in it that it didn't need. So, you know, we stripped it right back. And I think our programmer, Christoffer Berg, should take a lot of credit for that. You know, he was the one who kind of started stripping it back and started it on that path."[770]

About *Should be Higher* **Dave** explained that, "it's reflecting on my interest quite often initially in something that is not necessarily real." He laughed. "And can quite often get me in trouble. But I'm still quite often attracted to this, the other side of things I think influence the optimistic side of my head. But sometimes I do find that the line is basically, saying initially how you might, something seems more exciting that could be quite dangerous for you. But the truth takes longer to achieve. But it ultimately is more rewarding. Cause the line that follows that line is: *you should be higher. I'll take you higher.* And I'm referring to something that I feel quite often in life, which is life itself – which is just a beautiful thing. But you have to work a little harder to be part of it. And I also follow those lines with the line: *Love is all I want.*"[771]

A little surprise was the song *Slow*.

"That, believe it or not, was a song that was written for *Songs of Faith and Devotion* and for some bizarre reason

---

[768] Taken from: Interview with Dave Gahan, Mojo, 22 March 2013. Words: Martin Aston.
[769] Taken from Depeche Mode: Brits wouldn't show our set so we said 'f*** them', The Sun, 22 March 2013. Words: Uncredited.
[770] Taken from: The Complete SXSW 2013 Interview, NPR, 25 March 2013. Words: Jason Bentley.
[771] Taken from: Dave Gahan Talks About Depeche Mode's Delta Machine, staticmultimedia, 12 April 2013. Words: Uncredited.

never got recorded," **Fletch** explained. "Martin was going through his demos and came across it and said, 'Actually, this is quite good,' so he did a new demo and it's a great song."⁷⁷²

"As soon as I heard it, I said to Martin, 'That's an old song'," **Dave** recalled. "And he said, 'Yeah, I needed to reinterpret it.' He'd kind of reworked it. When Martin was demoing before, I seem to remember sitting in a meeting when we listened to the demos, and Alan kind of not getting it, just kind of … well, out of songs that we were going to record it just wasn't chosen at that particular time. So I guess Martin put it away, and it fits really well with everything we're doing now."⁷⁷³

Slow caused a little discussion among the fans. One group thought it would have suited *SOFAD* well, the other group thought that there must have been a good reason why it wasn't chosen at that time.

"Alan kind of not getting it" is probably a diplomatic way to say that he didn't like it, that he saw it as too "lightweight" (one of his favourite descriptions to say that he doesn't like something), as too simple. And well, if you look at the lyrics of most *SOFAD*-songs and at the lyrics of *Slow*, which are quite simply about having sex in a slow, intensive way, you might get an idea why it was turned down. Lines like *I don't need a race in my bed when speed's in my heart and speed's in my head instead* or *Slow, slow, slow as you can go that's how I like it* (from *Slow*) cannot really compete with ambivalent lines like *oh girl, lead me into your darkness when this world is trying its hardest to leave me unimpressed* (from *One Caress*) or thoughtful lines like *Is simplicity best or simply the easiest? The narrowest path is always the holiest* (from *Judas*.) Nevertheless, a song like this can fit into a different context, which the band thought they had found with *Delta Machine*.

During the promotion for *Delta Machine* **Martin** said in an interview – being asked for his opinion about the general music business - that "somebody should shoot Simon Cowell", (an English A&R executive, television producer,

---

⁷⁷² Taken from: Revealing the Depeche Mode Plan, Exclaim, 26 March 2013. Words: Vincent Pollard.
⁷⁷³ Taken from: Dave Gahan Talks About Depeche Mode's Delta Machine, staticmultimedia, 12 April 2013. Words: Uncredited.

entrepreneur, and television personality. He is known for his role as a talent judge on TV shows such as *Pop Idol*, *The X Factor*, *Britain's Got Talent* and *American Idol*), something that caused some trouble, at least when **Cowell** Twittered, "A ton of people have got shot this year, and people like weirdo Gore encourage this."

"That was great," **Martin** laughed. He didn't think that "a little flippant comment" would get such a response. "I think the majority of the world agreed with me." He grinned.[774]

To be honest it was almost the only funny bit that I was able to find. The band members hadn't lost their sense of humour, but most interviews showed them as being serious and more mature. Also, almost all journalists brought up the same old stories again - at least Dave's overdose in **1996** was mentioned in almost every article. It's 17 years ago now, they should be over it. But you still find this angle – Dave almost died in **1996**, then he suffered from cancer during *TOTU* and now he has written a song like *Broken*, so the lyrics MUST have a connection to all these experiences. When you are being asked about the bad things in your life all over again, it's definitely difficult to be anything but serious. I personally think you could have a funny chat with Dave (and nevertheless get something serious about the new album) if you just leave out the subjects of drugs and cancer.

The second single release was *Soothe My Soul*. It was physically released as CD single and CD maxi single in Germany, Austria and Switzerland on **10 May**, worldwide on **13 May**, in the U.S. on **14 May**, and as 12" single worldwide on **10 June**, in the U.S. on **11 June**. The music video directed by Warren Fu was premiered on **28 March**.

Of course, they toured the album, and as usual they had their difficulties to find a setlist (and as usual it turned out not being that different to the previous tours, except that they played some more songs from the new album this time.)

"Our last album, *Sounds of the Universe*, I don't think many of the songs really translated live that well," **Fletch** admitted, "but this album seems to be completely the op-

---

[774] Taken from: Depeche Mode on synths, drugs and Basildon, The Times (UK), 21 March 2013. Words: Ed Potton.

posite, it's quite a minimal but powerful album and a lot of the tracks are sounding very good like *Soft Touch/Raw Nerve*. *Angel* is sounding really, really powerful, and *Should Be Higher*. We can't play, unfortunately, too many songs from the new album because we have fans that go back such a long way, it'd be a bit selfish, I think, just playing a lot of songs off the new album and disregarding tracks from our career."[775]

"Naturally you have to throw things in the fans want to hear," **Dave** said. "With us it's a constant debate: 'Should we do *Just Can't Get Enough?*' – 'I don't know, should we?' You've got to look at it as a song that means a lot to a lot of hardcore fans, but when you do something from thirty years ago, it can be like putting on a pair of pants from thirty years ago: they don't quite fit anymore, you know? You might really, really like them, but they might not, uh, work."[776]

The hardcore fans probably don't need songs like *Just Can't Get Enough*, *Enjoy the Silence* and *Personal Jesus* anymore because they have heard them too often but of course, fans who don't go to many gigs will enjoy them.

Speaking of fans, the band was asked again why they thought they were so popular and had such a strong, faithful following.

"I think people do see us as their little secret," **Martin** guessed. "Even though it's not that much of a secret - if you go into Europe about every third person has got one of our records somewhere."

"A lot of people know the name *Depeche Mode* but can't point to the individuals in the band," **Fletch** added.[777]

"There are certain places where people seem have more of an affiliation with us; generally Europe as a whole - even Holland's starting to get on board a little bit more than it used to," **Martin** said. "But the UK is the one place where we probably do least well. In Europe and especially when you get to places like Germany and anywhere eastwards, it seems to be more than just about the music, it's

---

[775] Taken from: Interview with Andy Fletcher, Canadian Press, 24 March 2013. Words: Michael Oliveira.
[776] Taken from: Through That Darkness You'll Find the Light, Electronic Beats Magazine, 12 March 2013. Words: A.J. Samuels.
[777] Taken from: Depeche Mode on synths, drugs and Basildon, The Times (UK), 21 March 2013. Words: Ed Potton.

like a lifestyle for them. They follow us, they wear uniforms of black - we call them the *black swarm* - we seem to be really really important to them."

"I think it's also because we come from a real place emotionally," **Dave** guessed. "I mean there's an image which has developed over the years and we're quite comfortable with that as well: we'd much rather be with the misfits than be with the norm. That's always been the case, we were ridiculed for it in the beginning and now we're praised for it."[778]

Welcome to my world ... (© Ingo Bittrich)

It seems that they have learned a lot about their followers over the course of time. So they were very critical of the film *The Posters Came from the Walls* by Jeremy Deller which tries to depict the fan culture. It was released in **2008** originally, but went online in **2013**, that's why **Dave** was asked about it.

On the whole he thought it was a good film, "but what I felt about the film was, and I can't speak for Martin and

---

[778] Taken from: Depeche Mode: 'We were ridiculed and now we're praised', Musicweek, 19 November 2012. Words: Rhian Jones.

Fletch, the whole thing was just too sycophantic, almost to a point of being comedic. And not in a good way. It didn't show the diversity of our fans and focused in one area. The whole drum corps and the Russian girl with the drawings of us, and of course the German family ... it wasn't objective enough for me. Even if it was well done. And the timing was weird, much too focused on what was and not what is today."[779]

Well, the fan culture was born in the **1980s**, so it might be no surprise that the film focused on the past. Of course, the film shows mainly real fanatics, not the "normal" fans, but the "normal" fans mostly came a long way with the band too. The average *DM* fan is between 30 and 50 years old, and got to know the band and its music in the **1980s**, or at least in the early **1990s**. There are some younger fans as well, but they are definitely in the minority. (And sometimes these younger fans came to the band through their parents.) The survey of *depechemodebiographie.de* shows a ratio of 70% to 30%. 70% of respondents became fans before *Ultra* (**1997.**) So the fan culture is almost as old as the band itself, and maybe this is one of the reasons why the fans are so faithful, and sometimes weird.

On the tour the band members were confronted with them again, but obviously they weren't bothered.

The tour started on **7 May** in Tel Aviv with the European leg. Before that there had been some short promotion gigs, and a warm up concert in Nice on **4 May.**

At this tour the band, especially Dave, showed up in a very good shape and mood. This is the complete opposite to the picture the media and the general public obviously still have about them. As I've said above, it was difficult to find something funny and up-lifting these days although the band maybe has never been in a better mood. It became obvious now that Dave had really been ill during *TOTU*. At *Delta Machine*-Tour he was full of energy and very present, and his voice was much better than on previous tours.

I asked a fan if I may tell an anecdote which happened during this first leg of the tour. As I've said above the

---

[779] Taken from: Through That Darkness You'll Find the Light, Electronic Beats Magazine, 12 March 2013. Words: A.J. Samuels.

hardcore fan as such doesn't need songs like *Personal Jesus* or *Just Can't Get Enough* anymore. Nevertheless, the band decided to play *Just Can't Get Enough* again. Now, this fan thought that there are many other old songs they could play instead. He noticed that the starting beat of the live version of *Just Can't Get Enough* is similar to the beat of *Boys Say Go!* So he initiated a little campaign with shouting *Boys Say Go!*, whenever *Just Can't Get Enough* was played. More and more people got involved shouting, "*Boys Say Go! Boys Say Go! Boys Say Go!*" during *Just Can't Get Enough* at each gig on this leg.

At the show in Dusseldorf on **5 July**, one *Boys Say Go!*-group was loud enough to be noticed by **Dave**. "And now, *Boys Say Go*," he said. Nevertheless, they played *Just Can't Get Enough*. "Yeah, this is *Boys Say Go*," he said in the middle of the song and was quite amused. The group enjoyed themselves and didn't notice it at all, learned about it later.

And almost every time, when Martin was singing *But Not Tonight* (*Oh God it's raining*) it started to rain. Two or three times it even happened that it just rained during this song. Martin's face when getting aware that he could make it rain tells more about him than any interview.

The North American leg started on **22 August** in Detroit and ended on **11 October** in Austin, Texas. The third leg, another European one, started on **7 November** in Belfast. The tour DVD *Live in Berlin* was released on **14 November 2014**.

Before the last leg had started, the band was the headliner at the *Yasalam After Race Concert*, after the Formula One Grand Prix in Abu Dhabi on **3 November**. This was another thing they have never done before. Not all their fans were really enthusiastic about it. Their band is going increasingly mainstream, and there were critical voices talking about "a complete sell-out," and that the band members are apparently trying to make as much money as possible while they are still on the road.

2015, 2016 H 2017

- We are not there yet (Going Backwards) -

After the end of the *Delta Machine* Tour, both Dave and Martin worked solo. Martin released an instrumental record titled *MG* on **24 April 2015**, Dave worked with the band *Soulsavers* together again and released the album *Angels & Ghosts* on **23 October 2015**.

"When I was writing for the *Delta Machine* project I had about four or five instrumentals written which we didn't use," **Martin** said about *MG*. "I had all these instrumentals without a home and that gave me the idea to continue in that vein and complete a whole instrumental album. I just thought that was a good concept, and something new for me, something I've never done."[780]

"We never really stopped writing after the first *Soulsavers* album," **Dave** explained about *Angels & Ghosts*. "Even when I was on tour with Depeche, ideas would pop into my head. At the end of that Depeche tour I spent a bit of time staring at the walls, as you do, but this time it seemed more severe. I felt a tremendous sense of loss. "It's over." It hit me pretty hard. So I sat around moping for a bit, and when Rich from *Soulsavers* started sending me music over, I started to find working on it quite therapeutic. I started to write myself out of the hole I'd fallen into."[781]

The „transformation" from the solo project to the new DM record was an easy one. "When I finished my *MG* solo project in **2015**, I just kept writing," **Martin** said. "When I felt as if I had enough songs like *Going Backwards* together, and Dave - who had finished his solo - had enough songs together, we met up. We talked about changing producers as we did the last three with the same man, found James Ford, and we were off."[782]

The production of *Spirit* was a fast one.

---

[780] Taken from: Europa Hymn, Martin Gore interviewed, Clashmusic, 01 April 2015. Words: Mat Smith
[781] Taken from: Dave Gahan: "People would throw bags of drugs on stage", The Guardian, 8 October 2015. Words: Peter Robins
[782] Taken from: A conversation with Depeche Mode's Martin Gore, Magnet Magazine, 2017. Words: A.D. Amorosi.

"We have a different producer this time, James Ford," **Fletch** explained, "and we worked at a much faster pace than we normally do. We actually finished early, which is unbelievable. It normally is four sessions, plus mixing. This was done in three sessions. Normally, we finish the album just before Christmas, then we go out, have a couple of weeks off before we go into promotion mode. But this time, we actually had some more time off."[783]

"We called the album *Spirit*, because it's like, 'Where's the spirit gone?' or 'Where's the spirit in humanity?'" **Dave** explained. "We considered calling it *Maelstrom* – that was a bit too heavy metal."[784] Would have been an interesting title, though.

Spirit was a lot more political than any other album before.

"I really felt during the writing process for *Spirit* that the world was in a complete mess," **Martin** said. "Humanity had lost its way. By pointing that out, maybe you could somehow get some sort of values back. Now, I may just be imparting too much importance to music and what it can do - I don't know if it can change the world - but even if one person is affected, then maybe I've achieved something."[785]

Dave saw the line *Where's the revolution? Come on people you're letting me down* as "a linchpin on the album. We're really asking that question of ourselves and of the world. What's happening? What's happening? We're all feeling it and none of us seems to have the answer. I would say that this album definitely reflects what's going on outside more than what's going on inside. And the outside world is becoming too much."[786]

Where's The Revolution was not directly influenced by current events.

"Martin wrote the song a couple of years ago," **Fletch** said. "We didn't jump on the bandwagon because it was literally a couple of years ago."

---

[783] Taken from: Depeche Mode Thinks We've Lost Our Spirit, Track Record, 03 March 2017. Words: Jessie Peterson.
[784] Taken from: Depeche Mode's Dave Gahan on Urgent New Spirit LP, David Bowie influence, Rolling Stone, 02 February 2017. Words: Kory Grow.
[785] Taken from: A conversation with Depeche Mode's Martin Gore, Magnet Magazine, 2017. Words: A.D. Amorosi.
[786] Taken from: Depeche Mode, interview: Maybe it would be the death of us if we suddenly started being recognised, Standard, 14 October 2016. Words: David Smyth.

But they have become experts on American elections because their first year of recording is almost always a year when the election takes place.

"Normally, we write songs about the world we live in and life in general," **Fletch** said, "you know about relationships and problems people have in their lives. Martin felt there were so many things going astray, that he felt that he should write about it."[787]

And **Martin** explained: "It's quite coincidental that the album has come out right now. I can't claim that the songs were all written for Trump. It just seems like such perfect timing, because the world is in such a mess. But the majority of these songs were written in 2015-2016, so the world was in a mess then too. It's just gotten a little worse."

He was shocked about how many people had elected "that idiot," but nevertheless, alt-right leader Richard Spencer called them "the official band of the Alt-Right."

"We were quite shocked, I have to say," **Fletch** said. "We're the opposite of that if anything."

"He says he's a big fan," **Martin** added, "but he obviously hasn't completely listened to our lyrics. I just think he's not all there. I think people always kind of know where we stand politically — everyone in the world except Richard Spencer."[788]

Dave thought that one could listen to the songs quite differently as well. "Some on the songs have a political content lyrically, but I don't listen to music like that. Music informs me. So it informs you to do something or to raise a question or to check your own position about how you feel about something, great. But at the same time, it's music and it's there to entertain you."[789]

But **Martin** also wrote a few personal songs. "There's dark, humorous lyrics in *Eternal*, which was written for my daughter. I had to slip in a vision of a black mushroom cloud rising and the radiation falling."[790] Well, I have to

---

[787] Taken from: Depeche Mode Thinks We've Lost Our Spirit, Track Record, 03 March 2017. Words: Jessie Peterson.
[788] Taken from: 'I Can't Claim That The Songs Were All Written for Trump', Yahoo Music, 17 March 2017. Words: Chuck Arnold.
[789] Taken from: The Landscape Is Changing: Depeche Mode Singer Dave Gahan on the Band's World-Weary, Pissed-Off New Album 'Spirit', Billboard, 14 March 2017. Words: Andrew Unterberger.
[790] Taken from: A conversation with Depeche Mode's Martin Gore, Magnet Magazine, 2017. Words: A.D. Amorosi.

admit that the vision of radiation falling is kind of strange when you think about your baby girl …

As usually, they claimed that the atmosphere and the communication had been great, just to find an example that showed that they still don't understand each other completely.

"It's about the beauty of communication, of wanting to be understood and loved," **Dave** said about *Cover Me*. "I've spent most of my life trying to get that. But sometimes when I get it, I don't know what to do with it. When I feel that side of me that is yearning for connection, I try to get it – and then it goes away again."

He showed the lines to Martin who didn't understand the metaphor, which drove Dave crazy. "What the f*** do you know? I never question *your* songs, Martin, I just sing them!"[791]

The train is coming (© Ingo Bittrich)

Spirit was released on **17 March 2017** by Columbia Records and Mute Records. Before, on **3 February 2017**, the single *Where Is The Revolution* was released, followed by *Going Backwards* on **23 June 2017** and *Cover Me* on **6 October 2017**.

---

[791] Taken from: Depeche Mode's Dave Gahan: why I don't understand my own band, newstatesman, 01 June 2017. Words: Kate Mossman

Dave contributed four songs to the album, *You Move* (co-written with Martin), *No More* (assisted by Kurt Uenala) *Cover Me* and *Poison Heart* (both assisted by Christian Eigner and Peter Gordeno.) He took care of the lead vocals, except of *Eternal* and *Fail*, which were sung by Martin. There were no instrumental tracks.

And of course, they were planning to tour the album, especially as **Dave** is still a restless guy. "I try desperately to do nothing – it seems like a good idea at the time. But I get into a weird place if I'm not doing things. My wife will indulge that for a while, then she'll tell me to go and do something."[792] That will probably be the main reason for going on tour. Not so much the money, as some people suspect.

"The stage is the only place where I don't feel my age," he explained. On the other hand: "It horrifies me to think that I might be on stage at 70 years old. It really horrifies me. I've got the idea of me walking on some remote beach somewhere, hopefully still with Jennifer, and a couple of dogs, and a beard that's down to here. I feel like I'm getting close to the point where I will actually have to stop doing this."[793]

Well, not for now. After some pre-tour performances in different cities between **1 March** and **3 May**, the *Global Spirit Tour* kicked off on **5 May** in Stockholm and saw a European leg with 33 gigs until **23 July**. The second leg started on **23 August**, took place in North America and saw 30 gigs until 27 October. The third leg was a European one again and started on **15 November**. There is a fourth leg planned in South America and an fifth leg in Europe again in **summer 2018**, which will probably end on **25 July** in Berlin. (The edits and additions to this second edition were done in winter 2017/2018.)

The tour saw a tribute to David Bowie by singing the song *Heroes*, which was the one - as every *DM* fan knows - that brought **Dave** to *DM*. "I had seen the news but it wasn't until my wife told me he had died that I just broke down in tears. My daughter came out and they were both

---

[792] Taken from: Dave Gahan: "People would throw bags of drugs on stage", The Guardian, 08 October 2015. Words: Peter Robins.
[793] Taken from: Depeche Mode's Dave Gahan: why I don't undestand my own band, newstatesman, 01 June 2017. Words: Kate Mossman.

hugging me. It really affected me. I felt a huge gap.[794] Bowie, since I was in my early teens, had an extraordinary effect on me. He represented something that was a little different and he didn't feel comfortable going along with what was considered to be the norm. That really appealed to me and somehow comforted me, certainly as a teenager. His music has been with me throughout anything I've ever done. And I've seen him time and time again over the years. My daughter and his daughter went to the same school for a couple years, so I'd see him at these school functions. One thing I regret — of course when he passed away — is never telling him how much his music had meant to me all these years. I always thought it was kind of weird to do that, especially when we were at school together, just two dads with their kids, but it was shocking to me when he passed away. He was too young."[795]

While *depechemodebiographie.de* itself can be updated any day, it was necessary to find an end for this print edition. It isn't easy to sum up the whole story in a few sentences. But maybe you can say that *DM* is the story of three (formerly four) quite normal English men who are sometimes a bit weird, and make "pop music with an edge" that touches a special group of people, big enough to make the band famous, without being really well-known to the masses. The band dressed up strangely, then got undressed, went to hell and back, lost a member and some of their specific sound, but never gave up, never really failed, and never lost their sense of humour. They lost some of the critical fans on the way, nevertheless they can still build on a large and faithful fanbase worldwide. And sometimes they even reached the masses that at least know one or two hit-singles.
Martin said once: "We kinda subtly corrupt the world. Basically if you call yourself a pop band you can get away with anything."[796]

---

[794] Taken from: Depeche Mode's Dave Gahan on Urgent New Spirit LP, David Bowie influence, Rolling Stone, 02 February 2017. Words: Kory Grow.
[795] Taken from: 'We're the most opposite' of an alt-right band / on David Bowie's death: 'I broke down', USA Today, 13 March 2017. Words: Patrick Ryan.
[796] Taken from: If You Call Yourself a Pop Band You Can Get Away With Anything, Record Mirror, 23 August 1986. Words: Andy Strickland.

Maybe this sentence sums it all up. We don't know what the future will bring. Maybe *DM* really will turn out like *The Rolling Stones,* and have a world tour in **2030**. Maybe they will quit after the *Global Spirit* tour, but they will probably go on as long as the fire burns.

SOURCES

The sources that are mentioned in the footnotes aren't the only ones that were used. Over the course of time I read, watched or listened to thousands of sources. They can't be all counted.

The attentive reader will have noticed that there are often remarks like, "other sources say that ..." Maybe these sources weren't worth quoting but they were necessary to put together a story that is as accurate as possible.

The reasons are simple: Not all articles are accurate, the band members were not always quoted correctly, sometimes the band members don't remember a special event later, but had mentioned it before in a different way, and sometimes journalists tend to "style" an article in their own way. You can't rely on information given only once. When a record is released, several interviews are given to several journalists. Mostly the band members say pretty much the same thing in every interview. You have to piece the stuff together, and also have to compare and try to find out what is correct, and what might be a distortion of the truth.

To write this biography several websites were used. The main sources were:
- depechemodeblog.com
- depechemode.com (official website)
- depeche-mode.com (Home)
- depechemode.tv depmod.com
- dmtvarchives.com mute.com
- recoil.co.uk
- sacredDM.net
- setlist.fm/setlists/depeche-mode tuug.fi

And, of course, several other websites (like erasure.de and vinceclarke-music.com), fansites, collector's sites, blogs and message-boards – for dates, setlists, releases, articles and opinions. Some of these websites aren't online anymore.

As far as it was possible, I listened to every radio interview, and watched every video interview. I didn't transcribe every one. It would have been too much work, and it has to be said that many of these interviews weren't really informative. But, of course, a radio or video interview is a good source, because the band members didn't have to rely on being quoted correctly. They are good for being sure that quotations taken from articles are correct.

Of course, I also read the existing (and commercial) biographies. They weren't used as sources to avoid legal conflicts. But it has to be noted that they mostly used the same sources, and don't offer many of their own individual sources.

There are also some TV formats, but they are mostly inaccurate.

There are also some official sources, like official interview CDs, or the short films that were released with the re-releases of all the albums in **2007**. Sometimes these sources were used, but especially in the case of the short films that were released with the re-releases, it has to be mentioned that I sometimes couldn't avoid the impression that some stories had been brightened up or related in a way the band WOULD LIKE them to have happened, while other sources tell a different version. (Don't get me wrong – they didn't lie in these films, but tended to make things work in their way.)

Further on, I read many more articles and interviews than the ones that were finally used for quotations. If possible I avoided using articles in languages other than English. The danger that quotes had been distorted in translation is too great, but sometimes there weren't any native speaker interviews on a certain topic. Nevertheless, ALL the articles I've read are a source in their way – to compare, and to take information from.

These sources won't all be listed here, simply because there are too many. We are talking about 2,000 websites, radio/video interviews, books, films and articles in different magazines and newspapers. The articles from which small quotes or information were taken can be found in the footnotes and on the website.

Printed in Great Britain
by Amazon